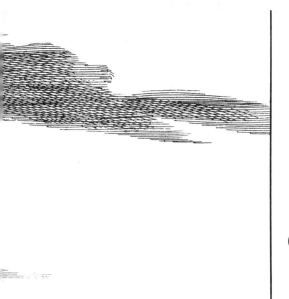

SEVENTEENTH CENTURY NORTH AMERICA

Carl O. Sauer

1980

TURTLE ISLAND : BERKELEY

Seventeenth Century North America is published by Turtle Island Foundation for
the Netzahualcoyotl Historical Society, a non-profit educational foundation
engaged in the multi-cultural study of American Literature and Cultural
History. Address all inquiries to: The Netzahualcoyotl Historical Society,
2845 Buena Vista Way, Berkeley, CA 94708.

LCCN 77-82309
ISBN 0-913666-22-X (paper)
ISBN 0-913666-23-8 (hardbound)

TABLE OF CONTENTS

LIST OF FIGURES

Foreword

CHART OF MY COURSE

Geography, well established at European universities, came late to academic attention in the United States, geologists mainly fathering its introduction. At the University of Chicago R. D. Salisbury, Professor of Geographic Geology, formed a Department of Geography, independent but closely associated with Geology. Physiography, which now would be called geomorphology, was Salisbury's special field, a field in which all of his students were instructed in the processes that have shaped the earth's surface. We learned to recognize land forms as to their origin within the larger context of Earth history. Learning about the nature of the terrain led to inquiry into patterns of vegetation and human response, as it then was called. Regional studies were proposed, of the natural environment and its utilization by man. To this end Salisbury secured support by the Illinois State Geological Survey for a series of field studies.

After a year of graduate study at the University of Chicago I was sent in 1910 to study the Upper Illinois Valley. When I asked Professor Salisbury about the range of observations required, his reply was that this was left to me to determine and defend. The result, published in *Geography of the Upper Illinois Valley and History of Development*,[1] was in the main physical geography, with some addition to knowledge of Ice Age land forms. The prairie plains of the area were the start of my interest in the origin of grasslands and led to reading what pioneer histories told of their nature. The record of local history began with the French and Fort St. Louis, built in 1683 on top of Starved Rock. This landmark, newly made a state park, its sandstone cliffs and miniature canyons a scenic attraction, had my detailed notice as to physical origin and historical significance, but I paid little attention then to the Indian history of the valley. As to human geography this first study was an attempt to apply the orientation then prevailing of human adaptation to physical environment, with some early doubts that this direction was adequate or proper.

The Geography of the Ozark Highland of Missouri was my doctoral thesis, the subject area a compromise cutting off the large natural region at the Missouri-Arkansas border.[2] The component lesser natural regions were outlined by belts of rocks encircling the granite Ozark dome, escarpments of beds resistant to weathering. The limitations of such classification were apparent: not all the soils were derived from the weathering of the underlying rock; vegetation paralleled only in part the stratigraphy; kinds of people and their habits did not sort out by physical environment. It was important to know the different terrains, but it was apparent that these only helped to understand the different ways of life. The people at the north and east were early German immigrants; at the southwest, a settlement of anti-slavery New Englanders; in the interior, hill folk from Tennessee and Kentucky; and each of these communities carried on the usages of their

1. Carl O. Sauer, *Geography of the Upper Illinois Valley*, Illinois State Geological Survey, Bulletin no. 27 (Urbana, 1916).

2. Carl O. Sauer, *The Geography of the Ozark Highlands of Missouri*, Geographical Society of Chicago, Bulletin no. 7 (Chicago, 1920).

own very distinct and different traditions. Cultural geography, it had become evident, was more than "response to natural environment"!

Geography of the Pennyroyal,[3] the field work done while at the University of Michigan, had as subtitle *A Study of the Influence of Geology and Physiography upon the Industry, Commerce and Life of the People*, a definition chosen by its sponsor, the Kentucky Geological Survey. In the Preface I wrote: "The dominant theme is the expression of the individuality of the region as the site of a particular group of people and of their works," the marks of this tenure being the cultural forms inscribed on the land. One chapter treated the problems of conserving land resources, in particular soil erosion, shown by maps of type localities. Man was recognized as a major agent of physical change.

The move to California in 1923 opened larger horizons of place and time. Field studies began in Lower California and continued in Sonora and Arizona. South of the border the land was little known except to naturalists. Villages had been Jesuit missions, in part still had an Indian population, and grew crops of native origin in the native manner. A centuries-old past still survived only partly modified by European ideas and skills. The northwest of New Spain had been a Jesuit mission province comparable to Paraguay, and of similar age, from the late sixteenth to the Jesuit expulsion in the eighteenth century. In their best tradition Jesuit missionaries wrote large and perceptive accounts of the land and its diverse natives, in fact a series of geographies ranging through two centuries. These were manuals that helped to introduce us to a larger and different perspective of cultural persistence and change, allowing us to review the attitudes of native peoples to land and life.

From arid north Mexico we went on to the tropical lands of the Pacific coast, using Spanish accounts of their condition in the past. By chance we came upon a forgotten area of high Mesoamerican culture well preceding the Spanish conquest. For almost half a century geographers have continued to go from the University of California into Mexico, Central America, and South America to compare past and present conditions and inquire into the activities of man in whatever ways and times human societies have intervened to alter the physical and biotic environments.

After retiring from academic service I had leisure time enough to write *The Early Spanish Main*,[4] the land about the Caribbean as the Spanish found it at its discovery by Columbus and what they did to it in the first quarter century. I made use of what I had seen during a field season in the Dominican Republic, in travels about Cuba, Jamaica, Puerto Rico, and the Lesser Antilles, and in visits to the mainland coast. With this background of observation in mind I then studied the early reports as to places, plants, animals, and people, items peripheral to the interest of historians of the Spanish Indies. It was possible to trace the routes taken by the Spanish and to identify what they found, beginning with the Greater Antilles of Arawak population and continuing to the Isthmus of Panama, Chibchan in culture. The records give extensive information on the various native economies and societies. Starting with Columbus, prosperous and

3. Carl O. Sauer, *Geography of the Pennyroyal*, Kentucky Geological Survey, Series 6, Geological Reports, XXV (Frankfort, Kentyucky, 1927).

4. Carl O. Sauer, *The Early Spanish Main* (Berkeley, 1966).

well balanced native ways of life were broken down in a few years, and a population of millions reduced to the point of extinction, all of this competently documented by Spanish sources.

Northern Mists took its title from Fridtjof Nansen's classic study of sea faring into the North Atlantic before the time of Columbus.[5] The global shape of the earth, known from classical times, was applied by the Portuguese in the fifteenth century in seeking a western passage from the Azores to the Orient. There was information from fishing ships in the fifteenth century that crossed the North Atlantic to western lands. The Norse settlement of Greenland, begun at the end of the tenth, lasted into the fifteenth century, the abandonment according to Nansen not due to adverse change of climate. Climatic change was rejected also by Vilhjalmur Stefansson.

Vinland was placed in southern New England by early, well informed students. Later, others located it in northern Newfoundland, inferring either a climate much milder than at present or that *vin* did not signify grapes. Reviewing what the sages said of plants, animals, and people, I found additional evidence in support of Vinland as having been in southern New England, the climate as at present.

Norse sagas told of a Great Ireland beyond Vinland. Irish monks with their households were the first settlers of Iceland, which they left after the coming of Vikings. They did not return to Britain, but the way west was open and inviting. There is unnoticed evidence of their having been in Greenland, whence the route to Newfoundland, later used by the Norse, was available. I have suggested that Irish monks settled on shores of the Gulf of St. Lawrence in the tenth century or earlier.

Sixteenth Century North America has the sub-title *The Land and the People as Seen by Europeans.*[6] European explorations made known the Atlantic coast from the Gulf of Mexico to Davis Strait, the interior to Tennessee, Arkansas, and Kansas, and at the west the coast of California. Coronado and De Soto went in search of treasure and mines, Verrazzano, Cartier, Frobisher, and Davis to seek the western passage to the Orient. Spanish, French, and English attempts were made to found colonies in Florida, Canada, and Virginia. These earliest accounts give good descriptions of vegetation and animals: of oak and nut trees differing from those of Europe, of kinds of wild grapes, of herds of strange wild cattle on great grasslands, and of great flocks of water fowl including white cranes that shouted in unison like an army of men. The native peoples of the Eastern Woodlands were good farmers, cultivating a kind of tobacco, sunflowers, and a *Chenopodium* in addition to Indian corn, beans, and squash. Some had orchards of plum trees and vineyards. In some parts the coming of white men was followed by great sickness then death among the native population, an affliction unknown among these cultures on anything like the same scale before. The historical geography of the first century of European presence was assembled, therefore, from observations by participants, and from my own knowledge of terrain and biota.

The view presented here of seventeenth century North America as it was known to the French and Spanish has drawn me back to the experiences of my early years, going back to 1910, when I was beginning to learn geographical observation in the Illinois

5. Carl O. Sauer, *Northern Mists* (Berkeley, 1968); paperback edition from Turtle Island Foundation (Berkeley, 1973).

6. Carl O. Sauer, *Sixteenth Century North America* (Berkeley, 1971).

Valley. I have known the Mississippi Valley, the Great Lakes, and the Southwest widely and, I think, well enough to recognize the geography as it was before the changes brought by civilization.

Land and life are depicted by selected excerpts, given in my own translations. The Spanish reports for the most part are terse, of distances, places, native numbers, hardships, and frictions, the bare bones of geography and history. The empire Spain had acquired in the sixteenth century, greater than the world had known, was too much for its declining strength. The Viceroyalty of New Spain, charged with the support of New Mexico and Florida, had more pressing problems than those of these remote and profitless lands.

France began settlement in Acadia and Canada in the first decade of the seventeenth century. The profitable fur trade, supplied by Indian purveyors, gave access to the Great Lakes. In the course of the century habitants settled the lowland St. Lawrence Valley, Jesuit missions served the upper Great Lakes, and the Mississippi Valley was explored to the Gulf of Mexico.

The publication of French observations began with Champlain's *Des Sauvages* in 1603 and continued through the century in volume after volume, a lively and widely read literature of the time, some of which was translated into other languages. More memoirs and documents were found in the nineteenth century, in particular the series published by the French archivist Pierre Margry. From time to time historians have continued to add more records of early Canada, Acadia, and Louisiana.

I offer this study, then, as an introduction to the condition of land, nature, and Indian life as seen and influenced by French and Spanish participants.

The work has been eased and made enjoyable by the cordial participation of Adrienne Morgan who has designed the maps, Marijean Eichel who has assisted me in numerous ways without requiring direction, and Margaret Riddall who has done the bibliography and checked the text.

Carl O. Sauer

Publisher's Note:

Shortly after completing this manuscript, and arranging for its publication with *Turtle Island*, Carl O. Sauer died in his home in Berkeley on July 18, 1975.

Seventeenth Century North America: French and Spanish Accounts is offered here according to Carl Sauer's sense of chapter arrangement and overall anthological design: "I am quite aware that the chapters could be arranged differently," Dr. Sauer said, "and the itemized and quoted material summarized and/or eliminated from the body of the text. But that is simply not the point of this book. For one thing these accounts have become rare, and historians should pay more attention to these obscure sources than they have. I have sought only to create an anthology of these rare writings, and supplied a relatively light narrative to provide general perspective." (Early in his career Carl Sauer had mastered the art of understatement.)

"As for chapter arrangement, the book works as my mind works, and the arrangement follows the order of my thought. It's too late to change that now, and I don't think I'd change that even if I could." (Like all the fine historical geographers who preceeded him, Carl Sauer recognized the high art which stands behind all good story telling forms.)

Since Dr. Sauer's death my friend Kenneth Irby has gone over this manuscript for bibliographic reference; and in accord with Dr. Sauer's specific instructions and wishes both Irby and I have recast certain fugitive sentence structures where we felt the weight of detail required additional clarity. In addition Irby has also provided an index for the text. A special debt of thanks is therefore due to Ken, and to all the others who have helped to make this publication possible. I feel, finally, that in this text Carl Sauer has once again provided us with an original & unique body of insights into our own natural & cultural heritage. It was a rare honor to have known and worked with this very great man.

Bob Callahan
Berkeley
Late Summer, 1978

Seventeenth Century North America

I.

Legacy of the Sixteenth Century

SPAIN AND THE SPANISH INDIES

Columbus sailed to find the western seaway to the Indies and continued in that belief to the end of his life. His obsession with gold, which he imagined the islands to have in fabulous amount, began the grievous exploitation of the native population of Haiti. Gold, provided as tribute by the natives, slaves, and dyewood were to be the sources of great wealth. One by one the Greater Antilles were depopulated. Ponce de León, finding the Bahama Islands stripped of inhabitants, went on in 1513 to raid Florida. *The Early Spanish Main* presents the tragic course of the first twenty-five years of the Spanish Indies.

New Spain was added to the Spanish realm by Cortés, acting without authority. The troops repeatedly sent against him took their course west along the north coast of the Gulf of Mexico, the last attempt made by Narváez, his expedition leaving Cuba in February 1528 and ending in disaster on the Texas coast in November. By official designation Florida then included the mainland north of the Gulf of Mexico and extended well beyond the mouth of the Río Grande. Thus early Spanish political geography gave a vague foreshadowing of the boundary between the United States and Mexico.

The New Spain that Cortés took was the land of the high native cultures of Mesoamerica from central Mexico south to Honduras. This land yielded vast treasure in gold and silver. Placer gold deposits were exploited, expecially south of the central belt of volcanoes as far as Honduras, and silver mines worked by natives in Michoacan and in other parts of southern mountain ranges were also put into Spanish operation.

Tales that the far north was another Mexico, rich in treasure, led Antonio de Mendoza, first Viceroy of New Spain, to interview the four survivors of the Narváez expedition who had found their way overland from Texas to Mexico. Mendoza then sent Fray Marcos north by the route the refugees had taken, the friar bringing back a fabulous account of the soon to be legendary Seven Cities of Cíbola. The resulting Coronado expedition of 1540-1542 discovered the land of the Pueblo Indians, the Grand Canyon, and the Staked Plains, and moved north as far as the woodland and prairies of Kansas. Finding no treasure, the Spanish then lost interest in the north for about half a century.

In 1542 Mendoza sent Cabrillo by sea to explore the coast of California. The survey was made as far as the California-Oregon border; but again there was no follow-up to the survey. The vacant grant of Florida, without limit inland, was given to De Soto by the crown in 1537. He landed in Tampa Bay in 1539 with a formidable host to begin the four years' march that left a trail of injury to the inhabitants as far as northeast Arkansas. No riches were discovered. The grant lapsed with the death of De Soto.

17

By mid-century silver mines, newly discovered in the north of New Spain and richer than any known in the Old World, were producing bullion in large amounts from as far north as Zacatecas. The silver was loaded on ships at Vera Cruz and taken to Spain by way of the Straits of Florida.

Treasure ships were caught by storms and wrecked on the Florida east coast; others were captured east of Florida by French corsairs. Luís de Velasco the Elder, successor to Mendoza as Viceroy of New Spain, was instructed in 1557 to establish a port and colony in Florida for the protection of east bound ships, Florida to be thereafter a dependency of New Spain. Santa Elena, located on what is now Port Royal Sound of the Sea Islands of South Carolina, was properly chosen at the point where the ships left the coast to cross the Atlantic.

Velasco thought to amend the instructions by beginning with a settlement on Pensacola Bay on the northeast coast of the Gulf of Mexico. From this safe harbor he would then build a road across the base of the Florida Peninsula to Santa Elena. The large and well equipped party of colonists included families of Tlaxcalan Indians, free farmers who were to provide the agricultural support for the community. Shortly after their arrival in 1559 a hurricane swept Pensacola Bay, destroying ships and supplies. The enterprise was wrecked at its start and was abandoned in 1561. No road or port was built on the Atlantic coast.

Observing the Spanish failure at Pensacola, the French, having been expelled from Brazil in 1560 by the Portuguese, now turned their attentions to Florida. The French occupation began in 1562 with a fort built in the Sea Islands on the great sound they named Port Royal, the Spanish Santa Elena. The main fort and settlement was made in 1564 on the St. Johns River, below Jacksonville. Menéndez de Avilés led the Spanish counterattack of 1565, taking advantage of a great storm to destroy the French colonists.

The camp on the small inlet that served Menéndez in the emergency was maintained as the fort of St. Augustine. Another settlement was made at Santa Elena, for a number of years the more important place and a center of the missions. Florida was now a remote appendage of New Spain, a charge only by strategic necessity, St. Augustine being the only surviving Spanish settlement remaining within the limits of the United States.

BEGINNINGS OF NEW FRANCE

Verrazzano was sent in 1524 by France to explore the western shores in search of a sea passage to the Orient. He sailed north from South Carolina to Nova Scotia, giving a favorable account of the nature of natives and land, thereafter called New France.

Ten years later Cartier and a Breton crew explored the Gulf of St. Lawrence looking for the western passage. In the second voyage (1535-1536) he went up the St. Lawrence River to the rapids at Montreal, spent the winter at Quebec, and returned to France in May. Despite the long hard winter and the suffering from scurvy, Cartier reported favorably and in detail on the fertility of the valley he called Canada, its friendly natives, and the expectation of mineral riches. North of the valley he heard of a kingdom of Saguenay (the Laurentian Highland) as having great wealth of metals. Colonists were brought in 1541 to settle, provided with tools, seed, and livestock, but they abandoned the attempt after a winter of scurvy. A second lot, in the summer of 1542, fared as badly

18

as the first and returned to France in 1543, ending for the rest of the century French attempts to occupy Canada. After the failure of colonial ventures in Brazil and Florida, French activities overseas were limited to raids by corsairs on Spanish shipping and to fishing and trading furs in and about the Gulf of St. Lawrence.

ENGLISH INTERESTS

Elizabethan England turned quickly and strongly to navigation and discovery, and to confrontation with Spain. John Hawkins started the contraband slave trade from Africa to the West Indies in 1562, soon joined by his kinsman Francis Drake. In 1568 they ran into a fight with Spanish ships at Vera Cruz. Drake raided Nombre de Dios in 1572, and in 1577 started his three years' voyage around the world, sacking Spanish ships and ports on the previously untroubled Pacific coast. In 1585 Drake sacked Santo Domingo and Cartagena and burned St. Augustine, before the outbreak of war between England and Spain.

The English search for the northwest passage to the Far East began with Frobisher in 1576, who made a brief try at settlement on Baffin Island. Sir Humphrey Gilbert was given a patent to discover and found a colony, which he undertook to do in 1583, sailing to Newfoundland and then turning south, losing his life without getting beyond waters already familiar to European fishing ships. His stepbrother, Sir Walter Raleigh, with a patent from the Queen to select a coast for settlement, sent a party out on reconnaissance in 1584. It brought a favorable report on the land and natives about Cape Hatteras. Raleigh's colony of Virginia began on Roanoke Island in 1585 and was last heard of in 1587.

During the century the Atlantic shore was explored from the Gulf of Mexico north to Davis Strait, the Pacific coast to northern California, and the interior of New Mexico, the plains of Kansas, and the Appalachians of Tennessee. Numerous participants wrote of the land and its inhabitants, giving the first descriptions of its physical, plant, animal, and human geographies, the theme of my *Sixteenth Century North America*.

Fig. 1. Northern Florida portions of 1703 Delisle map of Mexico and Florida. *Delisle Atlas.*

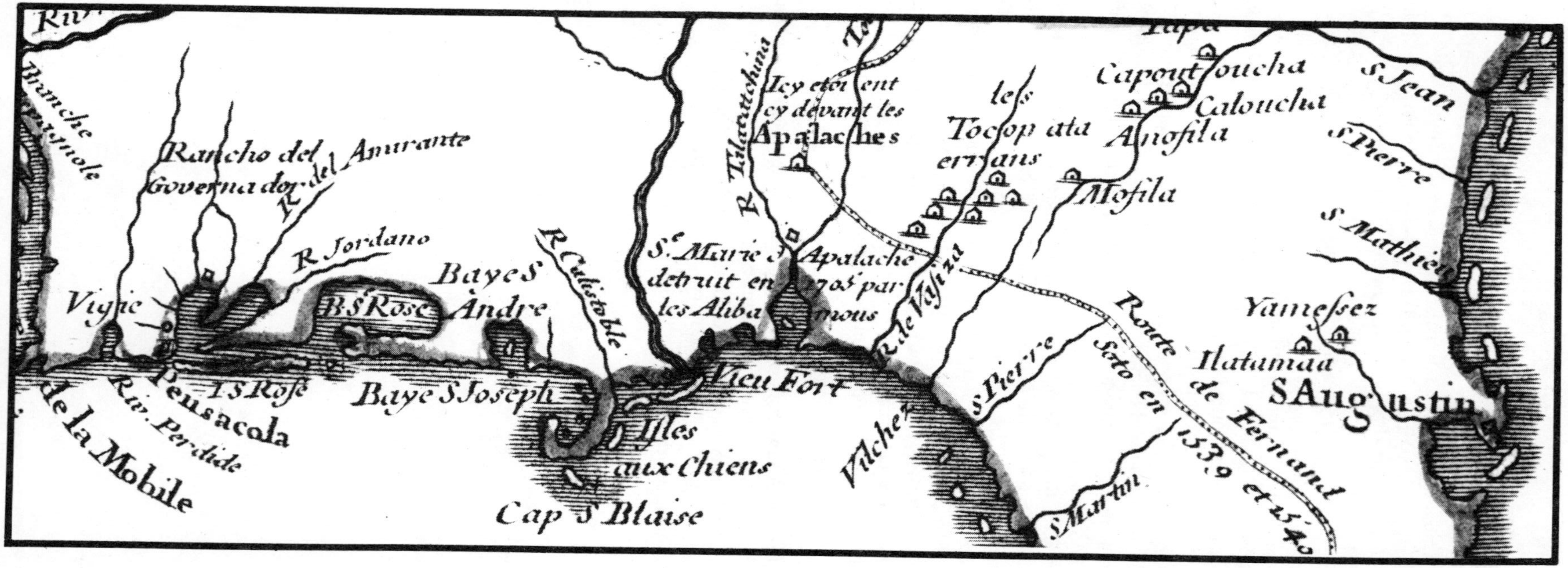

II.

Florida, Northeastern Borderland of New Spain

FLORIDA A LIABILITY

Carrying the wealth of New Spain and Peru to Spain the life line of the Indies passed through the Florida Straits and the Bahama Channel. Assembled at the secure naval base of Havana cargo ships were convoyed through this channel hence eliminating the danger of an attack. Shipping was thus properly protected without the need of a fortified port such as the one located at Santa Elena (the present U.S. Marine Corps base on Port Royal Sound [Fig. 1]). The Spanish post and settlement at Santa Elena was therefore withdrawn in 1589. St. Augustine, built by Menéndez in 1565 in his counterattack on the French, alone remained as a Spanish settlement in 1600, a settlement of minor significance in terms of guarding the sea route.

St. Augustine Inlet, then, was a tidal channel across the strand of the Florida east coast, shallow and narrow, and led to a lowland of sand and swamp, of palms and palmettos. The small post located there, meagerly supported, served mainly to support the Franciscan missions established to work with the Indian peoples of the interior. The population of St. Augustine changed but little during the century:

> 1604—190 effective troops and about 30 negroes.
> 1607—300 to 500 persons in and about St. Augustine.
> 1621—250 on the rolls, including 35 priests, 18 sailors, 20 pensioners, and 36 negroes.
> 1662—180 soldiers.
> 1669—200 effective troops at the time of British attack.
> 1676—300 Indians brought in as laborers, these being from the west and the north.
> 1681—100 families living in St. Augustine.[1]

NOTES ON FLORIDA BY ANTONIO VÁZQUEZ DE ESPINOSA

The Carmelite friar Vázquez de Espinosa spent ten years, from 1612 to 1622, travelling about in the early Spanish Main, collecting material for his *Compendium and Description of the West Indies*.[2] Espinosa's section dealing with Florida is reported at

1. John R. Dunkle, "Population Change as an Element in the Historical Geography of St. Augustine," *Florida Historical Quarterly*, XXXVII (1958), 5-6.

2. First published in English translation by Charles Upson Clark, Smithsonian Miscellaneous Collections, CII (Washington, D.C., 1942). The Spanish version, *Compendio y descripción de las Indias Occidentales*, is CVIII of that series (Washington, D.C., 1948).

second hand and includes information that he obtained at Havanna (in 1622?). Espinosa learned that St. Augustine had more than 300 Spanish residents, mostly married soldiers, the town well built of stone (a first reference to the use of coquina), a good church, convent, hospital, and fort, and about 30 friars engaged in instructing Indians in their villages. Spanish fruits and vegetables grew very well, quinces, pomegranates, pears, and melons being named. (Figs, grapes, and citrus fruits, staples of Franciscan horticulture in mild climates, are not mentioned.) The Bishop of Cuba did not dare to visit Florida "because of the dangers and risks from enemy pirates, who commonly go robbing and infesting these coasts and the sea and are a part of the other thievery based in Bermuda, where they have two forts" (an early reference to the English occupation of ermuda in 1615, held to be a base from which they preyed on Spanish ships). Espinosa's account concerning the interior appears to have been taken from reports of the De Soto expedition. On the coasts and islands of Florida there were pearl-bearing oysters and much ambergris, very fine and more than in other parts, awaiting exploitation, (oysters especially on mangroves and on banks in the Gulf of Mexico; ambergris from sperm whales stranded on the east coast).

BARCIA'S CHRONOLOGIC ESSAY

González de Barcia, founding member of the Spanish Academy and a distinguished author, wrote a history of Florida in the form of a chronology, recording the notable events year by year, from 1512 to 1722.[3] These items being few and occasional, he expanded his collection to include European activities north as far as Hudson Bay and west beyond the Mississippi Valley. In addition to the published literature Barcia made good use of Spanish sources in part otherwise not of record. In its breadth and competence the volume is a comparative history of eastern North America in process of penetration by Europeans. A good example of the use of chronology to chart connections of time and place.

Spanish Florida was a very minor part of Barcia's chronology because very little was happening there. Many years are without any entry of events in Florida. Those which do appear are as follows:

> 1600—A year of famine.
> 1602—A new lot of Franciscans came to resume the missionary work interrupted by Indian revolts.
> 1612—Florida was made the Franciscan mission Province of Santa Elena, with its main convent at Havana.
> 1613—8 Franciscans went to join the 23 in Florida.
> 1615—12 more came; 20 convents were served. The Indians on the mainland more civil (culto) than those on the coast.
> 1628—Piet Heyn, in command of a Dutch fleet, captured a convoy of Spanish ships laden with treasure. Storm-driven, he put into Florida harbors for repairs. The Dutch captured galleons with eight millions of treasure in silver and gold.

3. Andrés González de Barcia Carballido y Zuñiga, *Ensayo cronológico para la historia general de la Florida* (Madrid, 1723). An English translation, *Chronological History of the Continent of Florida*, was made by Anthony Kerrigan for the St. Augustine Historical Society (Gainesville, 1951).

1630—The Franciscans, being in great need, were to be supplied with food and clothes from Mexico.

1634—A storm caught a Spanish convoy in the Bahama Channel, a number of ships wrecked on the coast of Florida. "Notices of Florida in those years were too confused to be understood by reason of the lack of reports and papers."

1638—Apalachee Indians attacked St. Augustine and were repulsed. (The Apalachees lived two hundred miles to the west, north of Apalachee Bay.)

1639—The holy fervor of the Franciscans had marvelous success at conversion.

1640—Indians living about St. Augustine were made to work at its fortification.

1647—Fifty Franciscans were based at the convent of St. Augustine.

1655—Cromwell's forces operated in the West Indies. The appointment of an abbot was requested for Florida; no action taken.

1656—A January storm caught a convoy of galleons bound for Spain.

1668—"The Apalachee Indians felt the hardship of forced labor in St. Augustine."

1670 & 1676—More Franciscans to Florida.

1679—The Governor of Florida sent a party to reconnoiter the land of the Cacique Carlos. (This was Florida south of Lake Okeechobee, the country of the Calusa Indians, where Menéndez had established a garrison and mission a century earlier, soon abandoned. The hereditary head chief of the Calusas controlled the southwest of the peninsula, the Spaniards changing the name from Calusa to Carlos. That there was still a Cacique Carlos at this later time indicates that the old Indian order still existed.) Because of the multitude of Indians on the Gulf coast, Barcia added, the missionaries prepared to go there, "assured by the fort that had been built in the Province of Apalache." (This new fort appeared on Delisle's map of Louisiana as *St. Marie d'Apalache détruit en 1705 par les Alibamous.*)

1680—The governor visited the fort "in the Province of Apalachee and all its villages."

1681—The mission province of Santa Elena in the Sea Islands was visited by the Bishop of Cuba, who died there.

1686-1687—Concern about La Salle's Lousiana resulted in a Spanish reconnaissance from Vera Cruz to Apalachee Bay, finding no French but evidence that they had been there. Troops sent from St. Augustine restored the Apalachee Indians to obedience. The mission Indians of the north were in rebellion because those on the mainland were to be moved to the Sea Islands. Some fled to the English settlements in Carolina, the chief of the Yamassees taking his tribe, which had lived in Guale (the lower Savannah River), to the new English territory. English traders came as far south as the Apalachicola River in 1685-1686.

1691—There was serious discussion of removing the presidio from St. Augustine to the harbor of Pensacola.

1698—Calusa Indians of south Florida engaged in trade with Havana, going by
dugout canoes from the Florida Keys to Havana in 24 HOURS. Cardinal birds were in demand at Havana, bringing a price of six to ten pesos.
(These would have been taken as nestlings and raised in cages.)

The short and simple annals were of an outpost barely maintained, to which soldiers
and friars were sent on tours of duty. The Indians were Muskogean tribes, Creeks to the
north, Timucuas about St. Augustine, Calusas in the south of the peninsula,
Apalachees to the west. Indians were taken to St. Augustine for forced labor resulting
in revolts that were suppressed by force of arms. At the north the Yamasees escaped
from Spanish control by removing to English Carolina. There was little record of
nature or Indian life. The abandonment of St. Augustine was now under consideration.

RENEWED ATTENTION TO PENSACOLA BAY

Spain became worried about French designs on the Gulf coast. La Salle's project of
Louisiana claimed possession of the Mississippi River to its mouth and also aimed at the
seizure of the silver mines of northern Mexico. La Salle's death did not end the threat,
which the government of New Spain was now moved to counter.

Pensacola Bay, where Viceroy Velasco had started the ill-starred colony in 1559, was
indicated as the base for a fort and settlement to block French expansion. An expedition
was sent from Vera Cruz in 1686 to reconnoiter the north coast of the Gulf as far as
Apalachee Bay, and this expedition visited Pensacola Bay, where it reported "fine
grapes, fields [*milpas*] of maize, beans, squashes, tomatoes, chiles, etc. and very many
fish."[4] (Tomatoes and chile peppers were unknown to Indian farmers of the Eastern
Woodlands and are therefore inferred as having been introduced about Pensacola Bay
by the Tlaxcalan Indians in 1559, and after their withdrawal continuing to be grown by
the local Indians, apparently not passing into Indian cultivation farther inland.)

REPORT BY SIGÜENZA Y GÓNGORA

The party sent to select a site for settlement sailed from Vera Cruz in March 1693,
Carlos de Sigüenza y Góngora in charge of the survey. Sigüenza, professor of
mathematics at the University of Mexico, was known as a cartographer, geographer,
and orator, and was considered the local savant of the time. The Barcia version and the
documents published by Leonard differ only in minor details.

Pensacola Bay was entered April 8, at the height of the spring season. Sigüenza
named it Santa Maria de Galve, Santa Maria the name of the former colony and Galve
that of the current viceroy. The observations by Sigüenza are the most detailed of the
century for that part of the Gulf coast.

On landing they found tracks of buffalos (*cíbo*), very fine pine trees and many bay
trees (*laureles*), the latter in bloom that perfumed the air. There were woods of
deciduous and live oaks and pines, growing in very open stands. Coming to a hastily

4. Carlos de Sigüenza y Góngora, *Documentos in*éditos de Carlos de Sigüenza y Góngora, ed. Irving A.
Leonard (México, 1963), 52.

abandoned Indian camp they helped themselves to excellent buffalo meat and to fish. Maize and squash seeds were found stored in baskets of cane *(otate)*. There were mussel shells, pouches made of buffalo skins, and, tied to trees, feathers of turkeys, cardinals, and other birds. A roasted buffalo still had the head attached. Pottery, not ill made, included *ollas*. There were spoons of buffalo horn and also of calabash rind. They found a dozen dressed buffalo hides and skins of marten, fox, and beaver, and many undressed deer skins. Baskets were noted, filled with roots resembling those of lilies and ginger, some sweet tasting and staining the hands the color of rose then to blue. There was a good store of buffalo wool, both coarse and fine. Other items were mint-like herbs, combs, a kind of shoe, and (of European origin) a worn iron pick and part of an adze. The huts were covered with slabs of pine bark. There were two sturdy dugout boats, also arrows fitted with bone points. A mute dog was in process of giving birth. The Spanish named this site El Baratillo, "the junk store."

Continuing up the bay the Spanish next came to a river they named Jordan (East Bay River), its banks lined with great trees, one kind having leaves larger than those of laurel and loaded with white flowers of delicate scent, the flowers of six petals about a conspicuous pistil (*Magnolia grandiflora*). Sigüenza thought it like the *yolosuchitl* of Mexico *(Talauma*, a near relative of our southern Magnolia). The pines along this river were tall enough to provide masts for ships of six hundred tons. There were very many oaks bearing large acorns, judging by their cups littering the ground (*Quercus prinus*, the swamp chestnut oak). The land was fertile, as indicated by its herbage.

These things were seen on the first day ashore, and were so noted by Sigüenza, whose principal assignment was to make a chart of the harbor. The next day they found more laurels and stout grape vines in good flower as well as good sized green grapes, also in bloom. They continued on to higher ground, of pine woods and deciduous and live oaks, growing in open stands. After a night of storm they continued through woods in which there were mulberries, nut trees, *sabinas* and *cipreses* (according to Mexican usage *sabina* was *Taxodium* [bald cypress] and *cipres*, *Juniperus* [red cedar], the former on wet, the latter on dry land), and other kinds for which names were given which appear to be inaccurate.

On the fourth day (April 13), looking for Indians, they found a rectangular hut, built on four posts with a roof of palm thatch. Inside was a deerskin, a well woven sash of buffalo wool, and a long piece of blue cloth of Spanish make. Baskets hung from posts, containing shells of nacre, fish and other bones, and heavy locks of human hair. At the foot of a large pine a chest of cane held a worm-eaten human body. There were many foot prints of children and women. At a distance two men were seen.

Two more weeks were spent sounding the bay, exploring the land, and loading wood and water. At the mouth of one river the growth was so dense "as to seem that since the creation of the world no living being had visited it, for we saw neither birds nor animals but only some *caimanes* [alligators] crossing the river, frightened by the strangeness of our felucca." (A river large enough to be entered by sail . . . the dark solitude of a cypress swamp? The Perdido or Escambia River?)[5] The exploring party feasted on fish

5. On April 17 Barcia changed from the Sigüenza account to one by a Juan Pedro Matamoros, of later date, which added a reference to an acorn-like nut recognizable as pecan. This account is not limited to Pensacola Bay and I think does not negate the statements by the De Soto expedition that no pecans were seen until they had crossed west of the Mississippi River.

taken by hook and line, on palmetto cabbages, and on *zarzamoras* (dewberries in April?).

Pensacola Bay was left April 27, a look taken at Mobile Bay, and on May 1, the Spanish arrived at the delta of the Mississippi, called Río de la Palizada by Sigüenza, without explanation of what was meant by palisade. Here they found marshy open land (*muy rasa*), with cranes wading about the shallow water. "An immense number of gulls, pelicans, and other water fowl by their clamor made sleep impossible." There were large and small mud banks, great beds of oysters, and masses of tree trunks stranded by the river at time of flood. (Spring is a stage of low water in the Mississippi River delta.)

The journal of Sigüenza took note of trifles that told a good deal about native life. The Spanish met no inhabitants, the Indians fleeing at the approach of the visitors, indicating that they now had reason to fear strangers who came by ship. Hastily abandoned huts and their contents were investigated, also food materials, containers, and oddments, a rare inventory. At the time this was territory of Choctaw or an affiliated people.

Sigüenza had been given thirteen questions to answer. He was unable to report on Indian settlements other than the vacated houses. The bay was well suited for defense. Good materials were at hand for building a fort. The surrounding country was well adapted to *haciendas de labor y ganado*, farms and stock ranches, having extensive *campinas* (open country) adjacent to woods. Stores of maize, squashes, and edible roots were found. There were *nopales* bearing *tunas* (fig-like fruits of flat-stemmed *Opuntia* cacti). Fifteen kinds of marine food, fish and turtles were listed. "On land there are buffalos, deer, rabbits, partridges, beaver, otter, ducks, plovers."

The wild cattle of North America were called by the Spanish *vacas* or *cíbolas*, by the French *bœfs*, and by the English *buffs*, *bufflers*, and then *buffalos*. These animals attracted attention wherever seen. They were not mentioned east of the Mississippi by the Spanish of the sixteenth century, the De Soto party first reporting seeing them in northeastern Arkansas. By the end of the seventeenth century they had spread to the coast of Florida, in sufficient numbers to be taken for meat, hides, horn, and wool by the natives, as described by Sigüenza. The dispersal was, I infer, mainly south from prairies north of the Ohio River, and, perhaps also east across the lower Mississippi River.[6]

FLORIDA AT THE END OF THE CENTURY

Arriola was sent from Vera Cruz in 1696 to found the Spanish post of Pensacola as a defense against French encroachment on the Mississippi River. At the end of the century Spanish Florida, under the government of New Spain, had a garrisoned town at St. Augustine, another at Pensacola, and, halfway between, a small temporary post at the head of Apalachee Bay. In rough outline Spanish Florida had shrunk to about the limits of the present state of Florida.

---

6. Erhard Rostlund, "The Geographic Range of the Historic Bison in the Southeast," Association of American Geographers, *Annals*, L (1960), 395-407.

III.

California, Entry-Way from the Orient to New Spain

WEST TO THE ORIENT AND RETURN TO NEW SPAIN

Magellan's voyage across the Pacific found that the continental barrier of the New World extended south into high southern latitudes. Cortés sought a shorter and easier route by sending an expedition to the Spice Islands from the Pacific coast of New Spain. In 1542 Viceroy Mendoza sent a fleet from Navidad on the coast of Jalisco across the Pacific. These and later voyages followed the Northeast Trade Winds to the Malay islands, those going to the Philippines making a stop at Guam.

The outbound route was soon well established, the return difficult and uncertain until Urdaneta charted in 1565 the route northeast from the Philippines into mid-latitudes where westerly winds prevail. Except for infrequent contact with the Bonin Islands, no land was sighted until the California coast was reached. The Hawaiian Islands remained unknown to Spanish navigation in its clockwise course between Mexico and the East Indies (Fig. 2).

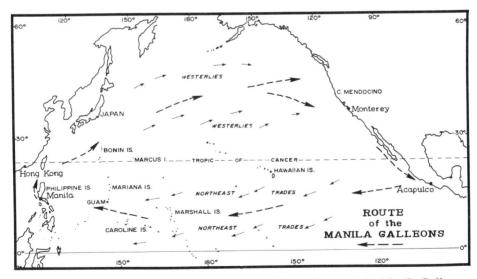

Fig. 2. Route of the Manila Galleons.

THE PHILIPPINE ISLANDS UNDER THE VICEROYALTY OF NEW SPAIN

The city of Manila, founded in 1571 on the South China Sea, was the Spanish commercial center of the Far East. Chinese merchants came with junks bearing spices, scents, silk, porcelain, lacquer, and other luxury wares to trade, chiefly for Mexican silver. Shortly thereafter, cargo and passenger ships known as the Manila galleons began to make yearly voyages between Acapulco and Manila.

Spain controlled the most direct and least costly route to the Orient. The voyage between Manila and Acapulco, a third of the circumference of the Earth, had the benefit of following wind and sea currents in both directions, and of the southward current along the coast of California. A constructed road connected Acapulco and Vera Cruz, passing through a populous and productive country that supplied provisions, pack animals, and workmen, and had in the City of Mexico a good market for wares from the Orient.[1] At Vera Cruz the products of the Orient were loaded on cargo ships and taken under naval convoy to Cádiz and Sevilla, a transport across two oceans with a portage across Mexico. The Philippines were a part of the Kingdom of New Spain, giving access to the Orient for trade and Christian missions. The sailings between Acapulco and Manila and their routes continued to be under the charge of the government at the City of Mexico.

SPANISH CONCERN ABOUT THE SECURITY OF THE PACIFIC OCEAN

In contrast to the harassment of Spanish shipping and ports on the Atlantic, the Pacific was untroubled by raids until 1579, when Drake entered by the Strait of Magellan and took ships and ports along the coast of Peru and southern New Spain. In 1587 Thomas Cavendish, following the route taken by Drake, captured the richly laden Manila galleon Santa Ana, off Cape San Lucas in Lower California.[2] In 1600 the Dutch corsair Olivier Van Noort repeated the incursion north along the coast of Peru and New Spain, making the fourth circumnavigation of the world. The circuitous and difficult access to the Pacific was too rarely used to warrant the maintenance of a Spanish naval force.

Search for a sea passage from Europe west to the Orient continued through the sixteenth century and later. Such a route would expose the Manila galleons to attack from the north. Tales circulated of finding such a passage, a passage already named the Strait of Anian. A Captain Lorenzo Ferrer Maldonado addressed a memorial to the Spanish king, claiming that he had gone through this strait in 1588, entering it from the Atlantic, going beyond the Arctic Circle before turning south, and coming out upon a

1. Vázquez de Espinosa described the tamarind, planted in the hot lands of southern New Spain, as brought from the Philippines to Acapulco (§727), and many different kinds of oranges "imported from Great China, small yellow ones with skins as thin as paper" (§788). The diversity of citrus fruits in rural Mexico needs study. Thin-skinned globose limes, some growing wild in western Jalisco, are known as limón, from the Malay name for citrus fruits, limau. Our lemons are of late and limited commercial introduction. The pomelo or shaddock (Citrus grandis) is known as toronja, a name now also given to the grapefruit, lately planted commercially. The present variety of citrus fruits and their notice in early accounts are not accounted for by introduction from Spain.

2. W. Michael Mathes, ed. and tr., The Capture of the Santa Ana (Los Angeles, 1969).

great plains covered with shrubs and then to a land of great trees, some bearing fruit like the apples, pears, and plums of Spain, the dry fruits still hanging on the trees in spring. On this land there were many wild pigs and some cattle and, in the sea, crabs about a yard wide. At the western end of the strait a ship of eight hundred tons was met, coming from the south, its crew looking like Arabs but in fact Lutherans from a city subject to the Great Khan.[3]

A fictitious voyage by a Greek named Juan de Fuca was published by Richard Hakluyt as a story originating in Venice. The Greek had been on the Manila galleon captured by Cavendish in 1587, lost a fortune in the capture, found his way to New Spain, and was appointed by the Viceroy to fortify the Strait of Anian, without explanation as to how he knew the location of that strait. The voyage failed because of a mutiny, but Fuca started out again in 1592, sailing north along the coast of California to 47 degrees or more, where he entered the Strait of Anian, found much gold and silver, and passed east through to the Atlantic in twenty days. Spain failing to reward him for his discovery he went to Italy where he told the fiction to an Englishman, who passed it on to Hakluyt. Two centuries later a strait at 48° N. Latitude that Fuca never saw or heard of was given his name.

REPORTS OF EASTBOUND MANILA GALLEONS

The course of voyages east across the Pacific was determined by shifts of air masses, in particular of cold fronts. Accounts of the voyages were sent to the Viceroy in Mexico and their content of new information communicated to Spain.[4]

Moya de Contreras, Archibishop of Mexico and interim Viceroy, wrote King Philip II in 1585 of a Portuguese captain who had gone to Japan, his ship thereafter storm driven at sea to two islands of friendly white inhabitants. The captain remained for a month in a large city, procuring silver. (This is an early version of the mythical islands Rica de Plata and Rica de Oro in the North Pacific Ocean.) Moya also reported that a Manila galleon had landed in the winter of 1584-1585 at 37°50′ N. Latitude (the latitude of San Francisco) and found bays, coves, seals, rivers, abundant growth of trees, and no snow. (The description may apply to the coast of central California.) Moya proposed further reconnaissance, to find a port of rest for the Manila galleons and discover the Strait of Anian.[5]

In 1587 Pedro de Unamuno, starting from the Chinese port of Macao, took a northeasterly course in search of the Rica de Plata and Rica de Oro islands and made a landfall on the American mainland at about 37° in a large bay filled with kelp beds, many fish, a beach with fresh water, sand dunes, and pine covered hills, the trees also suitable for masts (Monterey Bay?). Continuing south they came to a vacated Indian rancheria of seventeen partly subterranean houses, some large enough for a dozen persons, with ridges inland against the eastern horizon (Santa Barbara coast?). Farther

3. *Colección de documentos inéditos relativos al descubrimiento, conquista, y organización de las antiguas posesiones españolas de America y Oceánia . . .* (Madrid, 1864-1884), V, 420-437. (Hereafter cited as *CDI.*)

4. W. Michael Mathes, *Vizcaíno and Spanish Exploration into the Pacific Ocean 1580-1630* (San Francisco, 1968), is the latest and best informed monograph, which I am following as to the sequence of events.

5. Mathes, *Vizcaíno,* 12-14.

on at a rancheria of twenty houses they had an encounter with Indians who tried to steal their water jugs. Sailing at night along the coast of Lower California they escaped meeting the English ship of Cavendish.[6]

Viceroy Velasco the Younger was ordered in 1593 to have the coast of California explored for a safe harbor which the Manila galleons might use. The assignment was given to Rodríguez Cermeño, who had been pilot of the Santa Ana galleon at the time of its capture by Cavendish. Cermeño reported landfall at 42° (the boundary line between California and Oregon) and followed the coast south, entering a bay facing southwest. (This has been taken to be Drake's Bay and was confirmed a few years ago by items found there.) The expedition spent a month there being well entertained by the natives (as Drake had also been). The Indians used canoes made of bundles of *tules* (rushes) and had houses built partly undergound. A storm sank the Spanish ship, forcing the Spanish to take to the longboat, living by fishing and supplies given them by natives along the way. The Cermeño voyage ended in January 1596 at a Spanish settlement on mainland New Spain.

During the reign of Philip II (1556-1598) the Philippines, named in his honor, were occupied, a profitable commerce with China developed, and a missionary base was established to convert the Chinese of the mainland to the Catholic faith. Spain and Portugal at the time were united and thus had common interest in the Orient. The Portuguese route around Africa was supported by way stations. The route from Acapulco to Manila made use of supplies at Guam. The route of return enjoyed harbors on the coast of California that served for shelter and supplies. Stories of the Strait of Anian and of the two islands of silver and gold were now to be seriously investigated.

VIZCAÍNO'S SURVEY OF THE COAST OF CALIFORNIA

Sebástian Vizcaíno entered into the affairs of the Pacific as a merchant voyaging to Manila in 1586. In 1593 a group of partners, Vizcaíno being one, was given exclusive rights to the pearl fishery Cortés had begun at the lower end of the peninsula of California, with additional privileges and duties. The only result was a voyage by Vizcaíno in 1596 north along the gulf coast of the peninsula. His proposal for the exploitation of the resources and the conversion of the natives of California was approved by the Viceroy and the Council of the Indies in 1598, and Vizcaíno was named to head this new program.

When Vizcaíno took charge, however, it was not to govern Lower California but to prepare the survey of the Pacific coast of California, the need of which had been stressed by Van Noort's raid of 1600. Officers and crew were assembled during the year 1601, Gerónimo Martín Palacios to serve as cosmographer, responsible for making the charts of the coast.

The final instructions by the Viceroy to Vizcaíno were given in March 1602. The ships were to sail from Acapulco directly to Cape San Lucas, then to sail north, as close to land as possible as far north as to Cape Mendocino, enter all bays, take soundings, and determine latitude. The harbors were to be given saints' names, established names to be retained. Having reached Cape Mendocino, conditions permitting, they should

6. Mathes, *Vizcaíno*, 14-16.

go on to Cape Blanco or beyond, not to exceed a hundred leagues.[7] The capes named in the instructions were thus known to pilots of the Manila galleons, as were their approximate latitudes as far north as Cape Blanco (in southern Oregon). The main purpose of the expedition was to locate harbors suitable for shelter and provision (Figs. 3 and 4). Vizcaíno left Acapulco with three ships May 5, 1602, taking two months to get to Cape San Lucas and three more (November 10) to the harbor he named San Diego. This was charted and found to be a suitable port, with a supply of fresh water, wood, fish, and game, and friendly Indians. During the next three weeks the Channel Islands were mapped and given saints' names as directed. The Indians about Santa Barbara Channel were many, and quite adept at handling their plank canoes. They invited the visitors to stay.

It was early December and time to speed up the survey. Vizcaíno sailed along the foot of a mountain ridge on December 13, the day of Santa Lucia, and gave her name to that part of the Coastal Range. In mid-December the ships anchored in a fine bay that Vizcaíno named Monterrey in honor of the Viceroy. It had fresh water, pines suitable for masts, oak trees, water fowl, and land game, from quail to bears. A ship was sent back with the sick and a letter describing the advantages of the bay for ships from Manila. On a reconnaissance inland they came to a river which was named *Carmelo* (Carmel). New Year's Day was very cold, a spring found frozen.

Continuing north, Point Año Nuevo was named January 4 and Cape Mendocino was reached on January 12. A storm carried them north beyond Cape Blanco, both capes well known to voyagers from Manila. The ships were back at Monterrey Bay January 25, 1603. North to this bay the survey followed the instructions to map the coast line. Beyond, a storm intervened, land was sighted only occasionally, and the voyage was unable to enter any harbor, thus failing to discover San Francisco Bay.

The return was rapid: Cape Mendocino January 20, Monterrey Bay January 25, Cedros Island February 6, Cape San Lucas February 11, Mazatlán February 18, where the scurvy-ridden crew found relief in the acid fruits of a plant (*Bromelia pinguin?*).

The Viceroy wrote the King of the success of the survey which had found two fine ports, San Diego and Monterrey, the latter especially well suited for the needs of ships of Manila. Vizcaíno recommended that a settlement be made on Monterrey Bay.

LOSS OF INTEREST IN A CALIFORNIA WAY STATION

At the end of his term as Viceroy the Count of Monterrey appointed Vizcaíno General in charge of the Manila galleons and of continuing the coastal exploration (November 1603). His successor, the Marquis of Montesclaros, revoked the appointment and sent Vizcaíno to be alcalde of Tehuantepec and to build a road across the Isthmus of Tehuantepec, a short and low-altitude crossing from sea to sea. Ordered in 1606 to develop a California port, preferably on Monterrey Bay, and to put Vizcaíno in charge, Montesclaros objected that Vizcaíno was engaged in other services, that when Manila galleons got that far they were at less than a month's sail from Acapulco, and that the indicated bay was exposed to enemy attack.[8]

7. Mathes, *Vizcaíno*, 54-59.

8. Mathes, *Vizcaíno*, 108-154, has documented the events under Montesclaros and later viceroys.

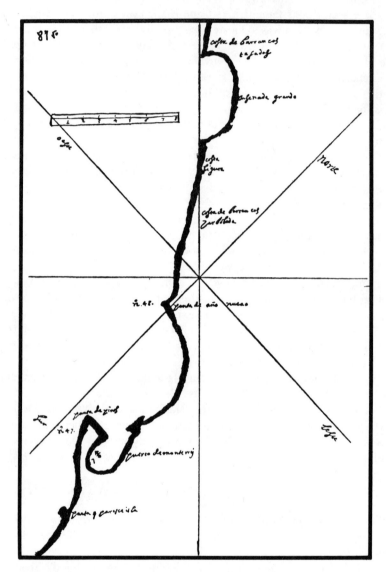

Fig. 3. Chart of Monterey Bay.

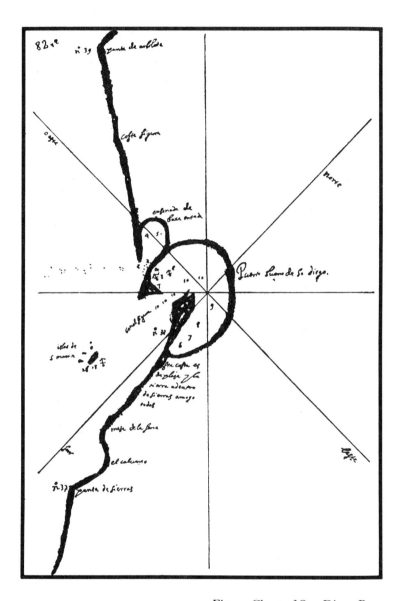

Fig. 4. Chart of San Diego Bay.

Viceroy Velasco the Younger was interested in relations with Japan, the reports of the Rica de Plata and Rica de Oro islands, and the Strait of Anian. When he was returned to a second appointment in 1607 he brought Vizcaíno back into maritime service.

A Japanese embassy to Spain, returning by way of Mexico, embarked at Acapulco in the spring of 1611, Vizcaíno in charge of the sailing. Vizcaíno remained in Japan to the fall of 1613, searching meanwhile for the two fabled islands yet finding no sign that they ever even existed. Vizcaíno's experiences in Japan and later services guarding the Pacific coast of Mexico are an important and neglected story, well reconstructed by Mathes. The futile search for the two rich islands in the North Pacific Ocean ended the interest in a midway station between Manila and Acapulco. The Manila galleons continued to sail south along the coast of California without benefit of a Spanish way station.

CALIFORNIA AS AN ISLAND

The representation of California as an island on maps of the seventeenth century has been newly restudied by John Leighly, my friend and colleague of half a century.[9] The fabrication began with a Carmelite friar, Antonio de la Ascensión, who was on Vizcaíno's California survey in 1602-1603, which he claimed to have accompained as assistant cosmographer. The friar's yarn was first published in Torquemada's *Monarquía Indiana* in 1613 and in revised form in his own *Relación Breve* in 1620. San Diego, he wrote, was a place where gold colored flowers grew, indicating the presence there of gold; also there was word of white men in the interior, Dutch or English, who must have come by the Strait of Anian. A pilot named Morena, he said, had been put ashore at the strait by Drake and walked from there to the mining town of Sombrerete (in Zacatecas), having seen Muscovites on horseback on the way. The Gulf of California extended north to the Strait of Anian, separating California from New Mexico. This nonsense was repeated and elaborated by the friar in testimony given in 1629 and 1632.[10]

Vázquez de Espinosa heard of a voyage north from Acapulco and of another that had originated from the lower Colorado River, proving that California was "an island and not continental as it is represented to be on the maps by the cosmographers." Vázquez apparently picked up these stories in Mexico at some time between 1614 and 1622.

The appendix to Leighly's essay lists 182 maps that show California as an island, the first published at Amsterdam in 1622. The majority of the maps were printed in Amsterdam, London, and Paris, the major centers of cartography. None are listed from Spain or Portugal.

The tale of the great island of California does not, however, appear to have been accepted officially in Spain or New Spain. The Vizcaíno survey and its charts were

9. John Leighly, *California as an Island* (San Francisco, 1972).

10. Mathes, *Vizcaíno*, 160-164, and Leighly, 24-26. The text of Ascensión's *Relación breve* is in *CDI*, VIII, 539-574, and is translated in Herbert E. Bolton, ed., *Spanish Exploration in the Southwest, 1542-1706* (New York, 1916), 105-134. The account is summarized in Juan de Torquemada, *Monarchía indiana*, ed. Antonio González de Barcia y Zuñiga, 2nd ed. (Madrid, 1723), I, 693-725, and II, 337. The story of Morena as recounted by Salmerón is given in *Documentos para servir a la historia de Nuevo México, 1538-1774* (Madrid, 1962), 197-198.

transmitted to the Council of the Indies and utilized in later communications concerning navigation of the Pacific. Governor Oñate reported his ride in 1604 from New Mexico to the Indian villages on the lower Colorado River. The accounts of the Coronado expedition of the 1540's were filed, in part were published, and included Alarcón's voyage up the Gulf of California into the lower Colorado River and also Melchor Díaz's ride across the desert of southern Arizona and the Colorado River into the desert to the west. The record by sea and land was known and clear: California was part of the mainland.

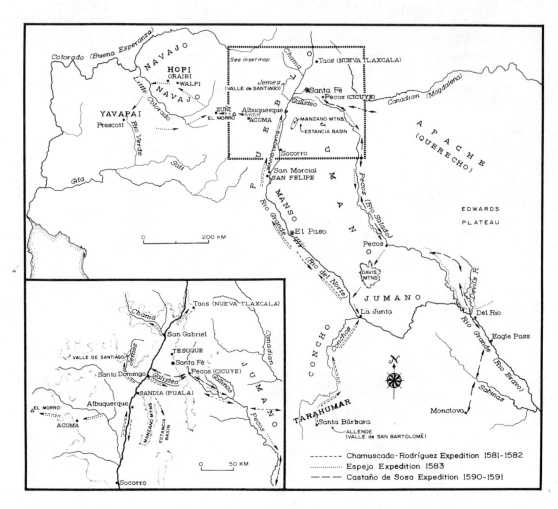

Fig. 5. Expeditions to New Mexico, 1581–1591.

36

IV.

New Mexico Reentered

APPROACH TO NEW MEXICO FROM THE INTERIOR SOUTH

Cabeza de Vaca and his companions wandered west from Galveston Bay across southern New Mexico without seeing any part of the Pueblo Country. Coronado's troop came north by southwestern approach through Sinaloa and Sonora, climbed the Colorado Plateau from the Gila River in southeastern Arizona, and began entry of the Pueblo country at Zuñi. They returned by the same western route, having found neither the promised Indian treasure of another Mexico nor having discovered any new mines.

By mid-sixteenth century fabulously rich silver mines were being discovered north of the former Aztec and Tarascan states, along the mountain margins of the interior plateau, known as the Meseta Central. The mining camps brought stock-raising estancias and mission establishments. The most northern of these was in the upper reaches of the Conchos drainage, the present Parral mining district of southern Chihuahua.[1] The earliest mines were at Santa Bárbara, with a Franciscan mission serving the Tarahumar Indians. Adjacent to it the fertile and well watered Valle de San Bartolomé (now Allende) grew fine crops of wheat, maize, and fruits, some under mission, some in private Spanish cultivation.

THE CHAMUSCADO-RODRÍGUEZ EXPEDITION (1581-1582)

Santa Bárbara, San Bartolomé, and Río Conchos were the places of departure of the next exploration north. Franciscans sought new missionary fields, miners hoped to discover new mines. An expedition, led by the soldier Sánchez Chamuscado and the Franciscan friar Agustín Rodríguez, left Santa Bárbara June 6, 1581, with a dozen Spaniards, Indian servants, and a remuda of riding and pack animals. Its notary, Hernán Gallegos, kept a faithful record (Fig. 5).[2]

---

1. Robert C. West, *The Mining Community in Northern New Spain: The Parral Mining District*, Ibero-Americana 30 (Berkeley, 1949).

2. Testimony given at México condensed in *CDI*, XV, 80-93. The full report by Hernán Gallegos to the Viceroy was used by J. Lloyd Mecham, "The Second Spanish Expedition to New Mexico," *New Mexico Historical Review*, I (1926), 266-291; and was translated by George Hammond and Agapito Rey from a copy in the Newberry Library, "The Gallegos Relation of the Rodríguez Expedition," *New Mexico Historical Review*, II (1927), 249-268 and 334-362.

The party followed the Conchos River to its mouth and then turned north up the Río Grande (called Río del Norte). About the junction (thereafter known as La Junta) were numerous Indian villages of large, rectangular houses of wattle daubed with mud, with cribs of wattle for storing maize and mesquite pods. Going up the great river they heard of people far upstream who dwelt in towns, saw ornaments of turquoise, and heard of the passage years before of men like themselves, whom Gallegos surmised to have been the party of Cabeza de Vaca. They passed an abandoned settlement which they named Carneros because of the numerous horns found there of marvelous size and weight, ram horns greater than those of cattle. (Presumably mountain sheep, then native to the mountains of western Texas and Chihuahua.) They went from tribe to tribe along the river and passed a marshy stretch of eight leagues (below El Paso). In a leisurely journey of two months they found numerous villages and rancherias of several tribes. Beyond El Paso they continued up river for fifteen days without seeing people or houses.

On August 21 they entered the Pueblo country. The first town appeared to have been long abandoned, its adobe walls partly fallen. A few miles beyond was an occupied pueblo of forty-five houses of three and four stories, amid fields of maize, beans, squash *(calabasas)*, and cotton. The houses were well built, white-washed, and decorated with frescoes. There was a lot of painted pottery, including *ollas, tinajas*, and *comales*, as in New Spain but of better quality. Turkeys were kept in pens and there were many small, shaggy dogs, unlike the Spanish ones. The inhabitants fled but returned when assured of the peaceful intentions of the strangers and soon were joined by others, Gallegos estimating that more than twelve thousand assembled. The nation to which they had come had some twenty pueblos they were told, some smaller, one twice as large as this one, which they named San Felipe. (They were beginning their acquaintance with Pueblo life among the Piros, most southerly of the Pueblo peoples. San Felipe was thirty miles or so south of present Socorro, near the head of Elephant Butte Reservoir.) Thus far they had explored a route previously unknown to white men. The headlong flight of the people of San Felipe told that these people had reason to fear white strangers, having met such before. The party had come to territory that had been rudely used by the Coronado forays forty years earlier.

They continued up the valley of the Río Grande (called Guadalquivir) from pueblo to pueblo. The farther they went the larger were the pueblos and the higher the houses, ladders being used to enter the upper stories. The people were very industrious, starting to work at daybreak. Men did the field labor and carried the loads. Women did the work in the household, and ground cornmeal on stone slabs that were set in stands, unlike the portable ones of New Spain. Women made the pots, of better quality than in Portugal (home of the scribe), and they spun and wove cotton cloth in colored patterns, worn in full length skirts. The people were clean and bathed often, the baths like those in New Spain *(temescal*, steam bath*)*.

In late September they turned east from the Río Grande to look for ore bodies and wild cattle (by way of the Galisteo Valley southwest of Santa Fé). The party rode for days beyond the pine covered mountains without seeing buffalos or Indians, crossing a river bordered by trees (the Pecos River) to find the first buffalo herds on October 8, and continuing east on the plains to October 19. A month was spent visiting pueblos of the Río Grande (below and about Albuquerque), a second month to go to the buffalo plains, thereafter visiting more pueblos in the upper Río Grande Valley and west thereof, the pueblo of Puaray (Sandía) serving as base. The return began at the end of·January 1582, over the same route by which they had come.

Gallegos told of meeting two kinds of Indians on the plains, one painted in stripes (Jumanos, not as yet thus named), the other were buffalo hunters (Apaches of the Great Plains). The latter were said to be enemies of the Pueblo Indians, whom they visited, however, to trade buffalo and deer hides and meat for maize and cotton cloth. Beyond the Pecos River they came to an Apache camp *(rancheria)* of fifty skin tents, like army tents, and several hundred bowmen dressed in skins. They had dogs carrying packs, in harness of maguey fiber. The reception was cordial and they were given a guide who led them to watering places on the plains, about which herds of buffalo were gathered. At times they saw herds of several thousand bulls, at that season segregated from cows. Forty were killed, the meat found delicious and the hides and wool excellent. The animals ran well, with a lumbering gait like that of pigs, and they were easy to kill because they came to a stop when wounded.

Returning from the buffalo plains there was trouble. At a pueblo of three hundred houses, all built of stone (in the Galisteo Valley), the people refused to supply corn meal until forced to do so. The threat sufficed and at subsequent pueblos they were awaited by a contribution of cornmeal and turkeys. At one pueblo three horses were killed by the natives, their flesh later found in their houses. One of the three Franciscans who had remained behind during the trip to the buffalo plains had been killed. The Indians were plotting against them, Gallegos wrote, but the Spanish, numbering eight men at arms, decided not to punish the criminals, after those who had stolen the horses were identified. Gallegos continued his narrative with a description of Pueblo ceremonials, of the rain dances that began in December, with rituals using prayer sticks and rattlesnakes, also of marriage rites.

The Gallegos *Relación*, a clear account of where they went and what they saw of country and people, ended with a summary list of the pueblos that had been visited, each given a Spanish name or a Nahua name if it was thought to resemble an Indian town of central Mexico. Thus the great pueblo of Taos was called Nueva Tlaxcala. The list began with the ten Piro pueblos first visited (on the Río Grande from San Marcial to Sevilleta), totalling 357 houses of two or more stories. Thirty-two pueblos (perhaps all Tigua speaking) were named on the upper Río Grande and lower Chama valleys. These totalled about 3,500 houses of three to four stories, Taos, the largest, having five hundred houses, some of seven stories. Cold and snow prevented further discovery to the north, a dozen more being reported but not visited.

East of the valley of the Río Grande pueblos of 300, 140, 100 and 40 houses were visited (Galisteo Valley). A party went to the salines (Estancia Basin east of the Manzano Mountains) where five pueblos were visited, totalling 625 houses, with word of three more.

The enumeration continued west of the Río Grande Valley. In the Valle de Santiago (Jémez) a pueblo of a hundred houses was inspected, heavy snow blocking the way beyond, thirteen pueblos reported as being farther up the valley. A party went west, passing the great stronghold of Ácoma pueblo to the Zuñi basin, where pueblos of 75,

100, 42, 125, and 43 houses were counted, each of eight or more rooms, plastered and painted, the houses of stone, and the fields so carefully tended that not a grain of corn was lost. Farther on there were other pueblos (Hopi), it was said, beyond range of the visit.

Gallegos listed sixty-one pueblos as visited, named, located, and estimated as to number of houses. These totalled about 5,400, ranging from two to five stories, with Taos having some of seven stories. This manner of living in apartment houses holding numerous families impressed the visitors as novel. Distance and winter cold prevented visits to more than a score of pueblos to the north, east, and west.

Rodríguez and the other Franciscan remained at Puaray to convert natives. Chamuscado died on the way back to Santa Bárbara. The notary Gallegos, accompanied by two soldiers, went on to Mexico to report to the Viceroy in May 1582, Gallegos filing his *Relación* there in July.[3] The account and samples of ore roused renewed interest in the north.

Another report was made at Mexico by two companions.[4] This told that they had passed through 61 pueblos which they estimated held more than 130,000 souls. Also that they had gone to the plains of the humped cattle, which were not very wild, were larger than domestic cattle, and of better meat. They had found eleven prospects of silver mines and brought back samples from three, which the Viceroy had assayed and found to be rich. Also they discovered a great *salina* of very good granular salt.

THE EXPEDITION OF ESPEJO IN 1583

Antonio de Espejo, a rich resident of Mexico City, was licensed to continue exploration of New Mexico at his own expense. He left Santa Bárbara November 10, 1582, with fourteen soldiers, 115 horses and mules, and one Franciscan friar. The party followed the route taken the year before by Rodríguez and Chamuscado, moving somewhat more slowly, and got to the first Pueblo town February 1, 1583. Diego Pérez de Luxán wrote the main account.[5]

Luxán had been beyond La Junta previously in a party from the mining real of Indé (in Durango) that had gone to capture Indians. A number of Indian tribes were named on the way up the Río Grande, some as of wandering habit, others as living in flat-roofed houses, partly subterranean, grouped in villages. They were well received by Jumano villagers (thus named) who offered maize, beans, squashes, gourd vessels, and buffalo hides, these taken at a distance of thirty leagues. At the largest village they were told of the passage of white men whom Luxán also thought to have been the Cabeza de Vaca party. Arriving at the marshes (below El Paso) where ducks, geese, and cranes abounded, they found Indians engaged in taking fish in pools by small dragnets. Above the marshes they met no people but saw many human traces, and smoke in the mountains.

3. *CDI*, XV, 80-93.

4. Moya de Contreras, Archbishop of Mexico and interim Viceroy, had it abstracted in 1583 (*CDI*, XV, 146-159).

5. *CDI*, XV, 101-181, mainly deposition by Espejo. George Hammond and Agapito Rey made an annotated translation of the journal of Diego Pérez de Luxán, *Expedition into New Mexico* (Los Angeles, 1929), from a manuscript at the Heye Foundation in New York. It is the account of the itinerary here used.

The Pueblo country was entered February 1, 1583, at the abandoned pueblo near San Marcial, as the previous expedition had done. Luxán's description enlarged on the prior account. The people were like Otomis (small and slight), wore their hair in braids, were clothed in small blankets, some in deerskin jackets and mantles of turkey feathers, and wore shoes of buffalo hide and deerskin boots. The first pueblo had fifty houses, its walls half a yard thick, the doors T-shaped.

The route as outlined in the Luxán journal again was north through Piro pueblos to the cluster of thirteen Tigua pueblos (the valley above Albuquerque densely settled, as it had been in the time of Coronado when it was called Tiguez). Puala (Puaray, the later Sandía) had four hundred houses of two stories above the ground floor. Its people fled to the mountains but soon returned with offerings of food. Continuing north they came to the Queresan (Keresan) pueblos, one having a thousand houses and four thousand men. (Luxán, and Espejo even more so, were given to exaggeration of numbers.)

Having spent February visiting pueblos in the Río Grande Valley they turned west to Ácoma (March 4), a pueblo built on a high rock, reached by steps cut in the rock and supplied with water stored in cisterns. Taking the Indian road to Zuñi they passed a pond at the foot of a great rock *(estanque del peñol)*, now El Morro National Monument. The first of six Zuñi pueblos was reached March 10, the people noted as being Mexican in their habit of walking, voice, even in their dwellings, but neater than Mexican Indians. They spun cotton, brought from Mohose (Hopi), and another fibre (of agave or a related plant) so well prepared that it resembled flax. Fields were irrigated by canals. The Hopi pueblos were visited during the latter half of April and gave the visitors more food than could be used. At Walpi, which was built on a high rock, they were showered with corn meal, so as to make them look like clowns. Water was provided from deep wells. Hundreds of cotton mantas, large and small, white and colored were given as presents. Luxán gave a good description of the Hopi country and people, overestimating as usual the actual native population.

A quick excursion was made southwest in search of mines. On May 1st they came to a river crossing (Little Colorado), beyond which they rode through forests of pine and aspen, and then descended from the plateau into warmer country, where there were grapevines and parrots, and where they found a rustic people, living in rancherias and attending at the time to planting maize. A copper ore body was found and considered poor. (The Indians are thought to have been Yavapais on the upper Río Verde, in modern times a major copper mining district.)

The return east was by way of Zuñi and Ácoma (the latter passed on June 4) and so back to the Tigua pueblos, where they had a fight at Puala (Puaray) and executed a number of Indians, the charge being that Franciscans of the prior expedition who had chosen to remain there had been killed at that place. On July 1, the party took its way east (up the Galisteo Valley). No longer welcome guests, they were denied entry to the multi-story houses, the inhabitants raising the ladders out of reach. The divide was crossed through forests of pine to the pueblo of Cicuye (Pecos) in the headwaters of the Pecos River, gateway to the Great Plains through which Coronado had gone on the long ride to Quivira.

Espejo's party followed the Pecos, "River of the Cows" as they called it, downstream, finding lots of buffalo tracks, dung, and bones but "as God willed, we saw no cattle" (Luxán). They went down river for about a month, meeting three Jumanos on August

41

7, the first people noted on the Pecos. These were the same sort of people as the villagers who had given them a cordial send-off at the start of the journey from La Junta. The new guides told that the river discharged into the great river far below La Junta and offered to take them there by a direct and convenient route, which they did.[6] The Pecos was left in the vicinity of the present city of Pecos, Texas, other Jumanos along the river being found gathering mesquite pods or fishing, in particular catfish which were very plentiful. On August 10 they turned south up a small stream that had its source in mountains (the Davis Mountains) and soon came to a cool and pleasant land of oak groves, grape vines, and *capulines* with ripe fruit (*Prunus serotina*, wild black cherry). Occasionally Jumano rancherias and patches of cultivated land were passed. Having crossed the Davis Mountains they reached the Río Grande on August 21, 1583, at a permanent Jumano village, two days' journey above La Junta. Back in familiar country, they rested to enjoy the green corn, beans, and squash, were served with fish fresh from the river, and then they went down stream to La Junta, up the Conchos River, and so to journey's end at Santa Bárbara.

Espejo wrote Philip II of his successful journey of more than four hundred leagues, having found eleven provinces, with notice of many more. Many thousand souls awaited salvation from idolatry, a good plea to present to the son of Charles and grandson of Isabela, who still took the obligation of Catholic King as his duty. Espejo asked that twenty-four Franciscans accompany his return, at the expense of the King. He would undertake himself to take four hundred men, a hundred of them married, and their wives and children, to be assembled at the mines of Zacatecas and then go to the mines of Santa Bárbara and the valley of San Bartolomé, the farthest place pacified. They would be divided into four companies, one traveling by cart. They would take a thousand mares, eight hundred stallions, four thousand cows and bulls, and five thousand sheep, taking care not to damage the native plantings. The hundred married men were to make a settlement at Ácoma. In addition a port on the Atlantic would be needed. He had spent sixty thousand ducats and with his partners would guarantee a greater amount to be spent in a new manner of settling a province.[7] Nothing came of the proposal.

MORE DESIGNS ON THE NORTH

The silver mines of the north produced a newly rich class that was accepted into the high society of New Spain. One of the richest of the newly rich, Juan Batista de Lomas Colmenares, asked to be given the government of New Mexico, to have jurisdiction over all the land beyond Santa Bárbara, beginning with the Río Ebro (Conchos), to conquer, settle, and pacify. His petition of 1589 asked for supreme civil and military authority, perpetual entail, control of mines, the building of hospitals, churches, and monasteries. Also he would find a northern seaport where he would build ships to enter both oceans, at the west to the Philippines and Peru, and at the east by the North Sea to Spain. (An enlarged version of the current notion of a Strait of Anian.) He had made no discoveries but he would use his wealth to found a New Mexico without limits other

6. J. Charles Kelley tracked the route in detail in "Historical Materials Related to the West Texas Route of Antonio de Espejo," *Sul Ross State Teachers College Bulletin*, XVIII (1937), 7-25 (West Texas Historical and Scientific Society, Publications no. 7).

7. *CDI*, XV, 152-159.

than those of the oceans. No one since Columbus had asked for or been granted such rights. The Viceroy approved the request and recommended it to the Crown, which was the last heard of that project.[8]

Mines had been opened also along the eastern margin of the North Mexican Plateau, known as the Sierra Madre Oriental. With the miners came stock raisers. The north-eastern outpost, like that of Santa Bárbara at the west, was the frontier province of Nuevo León, then including the eastern part of the present state of Coahuila. Its Captain General, Gaspar Castaño de Sosa, decided that he too would explore north-ward and find another way to New Mexico.[9] He assembled a train of ox-drawn, high wheeled carts (carretas) and ample riding stock at Monclova, northernmost Spanish settlement in Nuevo León. The expedition started July 27, 1590, on a leisurely course in which they prospected for mines, following an easy route north, still used by railroad and highway. Crossing and naming the Río de las Sabinas, after the bald cypress trees growing along it, they noted many nut trees (pecans) in the river bottoms. Coming to the Río Bravo (Río Grande about Eagle Pass) they continued up that river for about nine days to a large pool (charca), perhaps at the mouth of Devil's River above Del Rio.

The next leg of the journey turned north, away from the big river and avoiding the difficult canyon of the lower Pecos River, known to them as Río Salado, by inference named thus by earlier Spanish acquaintance. The going was slow and hard as they climbed the margin of Edwards Plateau, perhaps along the divide between Devil's and Pecos rivers. Horses lost shoes on the rough terrain and goats strayed in search of water. The carts got through, there being no mention of loss. On October 26 they reached the river (Pecos) above the canyon and thereafter had easier travel. That Castaño de Sosa was able to take ox carts through to the Pueblo country suggests that he followed a well travelled Indian road.

On the Pecos a band of Tepehuán Indians was met, who gave the explorers buffalo hides, buckskins, shoes made after Indian fashion, and much meat. These were encountered far north of the Tepehuán country and well to the south of the range of buffalo. The identification may be valid. The Tepehuán of Durango were one of the best known people of northern Mexico and were on friendly and familiar terms with Spaniards. That village Indians from Durango would have gone on distant hunts into Texas at the season when buffalo and deer were in good flesh is inferred. At that time Texas was open, according to accounts, to diverse bands hunting and collecting, as it had been in the time of Cabeza de Vaca. Territorial boundaries and conflict over trespass do not seem to have applied until later.

Four days after they came to the Río Salado (Pecos River) and met the Tepehuán Indians, they found an abandoned camp (rancherias viejas), a large dry lake of white salt (salina), and four Indians with many dogs carrying packs, "a thing new to us, never before seen," the harness described. These were Apaches well to the south of their usual range. Three days later (November 2) unidentified Indians showed up in number and stole some oxen, for which offense one Indian was hanged.

The itinerary continued up the Pecos River into December: November 5, an abandoned large rancheria. November 7, very large sand dunes. November 8, good savan-

8. *CDI*, XV, 54ff.

9. *CDI*, IV, 283-354, and XV, 191-261.

nas in a large plain of much mesquite. November 10, many fish. November 11, a savannah in which wolves killed some of the goats. November 13, tracks of wild cattle. November 14, very good fishing. November 17, lots of mesquite and fish. November 20, having passed the dunes, they were in a good savannah of mesquite and good fishing. November 23, a large corral in which Indians had enclosed cattle (?). November 24, the largest catfish of the trip. November 26, the first spring of fresh water seen since leaving the Río Bravo. November 28, a grove of very large willows. November 29, camped in a large grove where were found a jar *(olla)* and freshly shelled corn cobs. November 30, a large rancheria from which the people had fled.

On December 23, at a time of great cold and snow, they came to the first pueblo, which was of flatroofed houses, and were given a quantity of maize. On December 31 they forced entry to a large pueblo (Cicuye/Pecos?) of four and five stories, each house of numerous apartments and entered by ladders. There were five plazas. It was thought that thirty thousand fanegas or more of maize were in storage, some two and three years old, of very good quality and of many colors. Corn meal was dry ground, not prepared as *nixtamal* (the Mexican manner of soaking and wet grinding) and was used for *atoles* and *tamales*. There was abundance of beans of many colors, of squashes and *quelites* (grain amaranth, the first reference that I know of this important Pueblo crop). There was a lot of pottery of different shapes, some red, some black, some painted in colors, some of the ware glazed. Firewood was stored in quantity. The cold was so strong that the streams were frozen in the headwaters of the Río Salado (Pecos).

On January 6, 1591, they set out to cross the watershed (into the Galisteo Valley) and continued from pueblo to pueblo in the valley of the Río Grande. The fields were irrigated by ditches of an excellence that had to be seen to be believed. One large pueblo was of four quarters about a plaza in which there was a round house, half subterranean, which they judged to be a mosque. There were many idols here. At another pueblo there were many *chalchihuites* (turquoise), some made into a fine bracelet.

The return began January 24 with a guide who took them through pine woods to the carts they had left on the Pecos. They took time to repair these, and in late February took the route south by which they had come. This is a factual and detailed account that includes observations not found elsewhere. It has had the least attention of all the New Mexico journeys.

INDIANS OF THE SOUTHWEST
AS KNOWN IN THE LATE SIXTEENTH CENTURY

The public as well as officials in Mexico were informed of the kinds of people living in the north, that the summers were hot and the winters cold, that plants and animals were similar to those in New Spain, except for great grasslands on which there were huge herds of wild cattle hunted by wandering people who traded with the industrious farmers of the pueblos who lived in many houses of several stories. The first expedition north from the mines of Santa Bárbara went to look for mines and for Indians to convert. The second hoped to be awarded the government of a large addition to New Spain and to locate mines. The third set out from Nuevo León, the Spanish frontier to the east, curious to see what it could see. The Gallegos report of the first party is remarkable for its systematic record and relevant detail. The second, the Espejo party,

44

gave a less reliable account of population but added knowledge of peoples round about. Castaño de Sosa, taking a different route, outlined the length of the Pecos River and took note of significant things unseen or unrecorded by others. Nature and natives of a major part of the Southwest were pretty well known before the end of the century, including the location and names of most of the pueblos.

The Town Dwellers of the north were recognized as having a common and distinctive way of life, differing in languages, grouped in clusters each called a province. Unlike the Spanish experience elsewhere, these people were not ruled by chiefs or caciques, a term introduced from the Arawak islands and found applicable in other areas of New Spain. Pueblo society was not based on class but on independent self-governing communities in amicable contact, having common spiritual as well as material bonds. This society henceforth was known as Pueblo.

In New Spain pueblo meant a permanent and compact Indian community, the native parallel of the rural village of Spain. The north had pueblos resembling those of central Mexico in houses built wall to wall, of stone and clay, plastered, divided into rooms, and having flat roofs. However, the houses of pueblos of the north were commonly of three or four stories, ranging to seven in Taos, and each occupied by a number of families, condominiums of related families. Ladders gave and denied access to the houses. Pueblos ranged from less than a score of houses to several hundred. Commonly there was an open space or plaza in the interior, several in the larger pueblos. Subterranean council chambers *(kivas)* puzzled the Spaniards as to their function and were called *estufas* (stove-heated rooms).

The first expedition made an enumeration of pueblos visited, about sixty, the location and number of houses estimated for each, adding up to about fifty-four hundred. Gallegos said that thirteen additional pueblos were reported in the upper Río Grande watershed, unseen because of cold weather, and about ten more at other margins of the Pueblo country. It appears to have been as good an estimate as time permitted. The Viceroy had word from two soldiers that by their estimate the Pueblo population was of more than a hundred and thirty thousand, which was in agreement with Gallegos' number of pueblos. The expedition included pueblos east of the Río Grande basin and west as far as Zuñi, and was soberly reported by Gallegos as to location and size. The second expedition, by Espejo, added the cluster of Hopi pueblos at the west, exaggerating their size. The visit by Castaño de Sosa did not get west of those located on the Río Grande nor go above present-day Albuquerque, but added important details, in particular as to farming.

All the pueblos grew maize, beans, and squash as staple crops. Castaño de Sosa alone mentioned *quelites*, grain amaranth. Later known as an important crop as far west as the Hopi, it is inferred that it was overlooked by the others, as has been the case largely in accounts of Indian farming in central Mexico. Cotton was a major crop in the valley of the Río Grande and also among the Hopi, the latter growing it successfully in a land of extremely short growing season. Espejo mentioned *piciete* (tobacco) without location. There is no reference to chile peppers, now ubiquitous among the Pueblos.

Men planted and took care of the fields, both as *temporales* depending on summer rains and as irrigated fields. Irrigation was by admirably constructed ditches, using streams, reservoirs, and among the Hopis, wells. Maize and beans were stored in quantity and supplied the Spanish abundantly. Castaño de Sosa wrote that some of the store was of two or three seasons past. Storage made in good seasons carried the people over the not infrequent seasons of shortage or failure. The visitors neither knew or cared what happened to the native supply after they had helped themselves. Turkeys were kept in goodly numbers and were freely supplied to the expeditions. The information does not say whether these were raised from wild turkeys native to the Southwest or were of the Mexican domestic stock, as were the crop plants.

Household arts, such as cooking with dry ground corn meal, spinning and weaving, making superior pottery, including glazed ware, were described with appreciation. The Pueblo natives were held to be of better skills, industry, habits, and of greater cleanliness than the Mexican Indians. (The Mexicans had already been under a half century of submission and cultural loss.)

There was fear of the strange visitors, memories of the time of Coronado. At the farthest pueblos, those of the Hopis, the newcomers were showered with confetti of corn meal and given great numbers of decorated mantas; but, Luxán added, twelve thousand Indians trembled before ten Spaniards.

From the time of Coronado another people of plains and mountains were known. The Pueblo called these people Querechos (the name Apache was not used until later). The Querechos came to trade with the Pueblos, bringing buffalo hides, dressed buckskins, meat of buffalo, deer, and probably of antelope, also salt, in exchange for cotton goods and items made by the Pueblos. Gallegos told of meeting such people as friendly buffalo hunters living on the Great Plains and coming to trade at the pueblos. In Pueblo usage both southern Athapascan groups, Apaches and Navahos of related language, stock, and habit, were recognized as one people. They were always of particular interest to the Spaniards and for a long time were friendly.

Espejo, riding from the Hopi pueblo of Oraibi down the rim of the Colorado Plateau in search of mines, found a different, rustic people, planting corn in warm valleys. By the description these were Yavapais, a Yuma tribe, later of minor Spanish interest.

THE JUMANO PROBLEM

On the eastern plains Coronado had met a people who were called Rayados, from their practice of painting or tattooing face and body with stripes.

Gallegos described sedentary farming Indians, named Cabris and Amotomancos, living along the Río Grande above La Junta, as striped, handsome, tall, clean, and merry people, having Turkish (compound) bows and buffalo hide shields, good houses and granaries, and chiefs *(caciques)*. Up river there were more people of the same language, who said that their nation extended more than a hundred leagues.

Espejo, passing by the same villages above La Junta, first used the name Jumanos, also Patarabueyes (Spanish for buffalo trackers?). On the return as the Spanish came down the Pecos River more Jumanos were met. These Jumanos served as guides on the short route across the Davis Mountains to the Río Grande, where the party was welcomed back at the same villages through which it had set out. Espejo described them as tall, and well built. Luxán added that they ranged thirty leagues from the Río Grande on buffalo hunts and used reinforced bows of Turkish type.[10]

10. France V. Scholes and H. P. Mera, "Some Aspects of the Jumano Problem," *Contributions to American Anthropology*, VI, no. 34, Carnegie Institution of Washington, Publication 523, 265-299 (Washington, D.C., 1940). J. Charles Kelley, "Juan Sabeata and Diffusion in Aboriginal Texas," *American Anthropologist*, LVII (1955), 981-996. W. W. Newcomb, Jr., *The Indians of Texas* (Austin, 1961), Chapter 9.

The three expeditions made known an important Indian people, called Jumanos by the Espejo party. On the Río Grande above La Junta they lived in villages, with houses and storage cribs built of wattle and daub, cultivated fields on the valley floor, fished in the river, and hunted with a powerful kind of bow, new to the Spanish. They made salt from salines and engaged in distant trade by which they were supplied with cotton mantillas. These mantles were patterned in blue and white and were procured from the west, the Spanish were told, indicating trade with the Opatas of Sonora. Later the Jumanos were known as traders from the Río Grande to northeast Texas. The Spanish took note that their villages were ruled by chiefs.

North of the Río Grande, Jumanos lived in valleys and mountains of southwest Texas in temporary camps, collecting, fishing, hunting, and cultivating small pieces of ground. They also ranged onto the buffalo plains to hunt. They appear to have been in friendly contact with their neighbors on all sides, from the Conchos at the south to the Pueblos and Apaches in the North.

Shortly the direct and easy route was opened to the Pueblo country from Santa Bárbara across the plains of Chihuahua, to the west of the territory of the Jumanos. For some decades little was heard of the Jumanos, except at the pueblos of the salines. When they came to later attention it was mainly in northeastern Texas, where they played an important and neglected role.[11]

11. My *Distribution of Aboriginal Tribes and Languages in Northwestern Mexico*, Ibero-Americana 5 (Berkeley, 1934), proposed their classification in the Uto-Aztecan linguistic family. Frederick W. Hodge, *Handbook of American Indians North of Mexico*, Smithsonian Institution, Bureau of American Ethnology, Bulletin 30 (Washington, D.C., 1907-1910), I, 636, thought them probably the southwesternmost Caddoan people, which I think is correct. The chapters on the French in the Southwest will present evidence that the Jumanos were in contact with and related to the Caddos of northeast Texas. A Caddoan extent of territory is thus inferred from the Pawnees of Nebraska and the Wichitas of Kansas, the Caddos and Texas of Texas, to the Jumanos on the Río Grande.

47

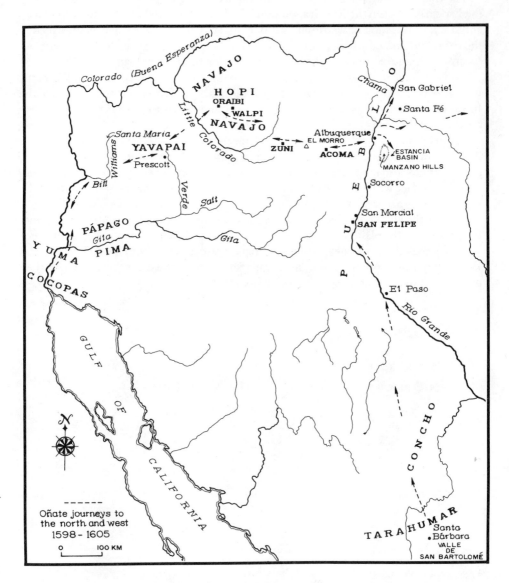

Fig. 6. Oñate's Journeys to the North and West, 1598-1605.

48

V.

The First Decade of Spanish Rule in New Mexico (1598-1608)

GOVERNMENT OF OÑATE BEGUN IN 1598

The Oñate family had a major part in the founding of Nueva Galicia and Nueva Vizcaya, northern frontiers of New Spain, and had become very rich, largely from silver mines. When Juan de Oñate asked to be made governor of the unoccupied north, he offered to pay the costs, and was thus appointed.[1] New Mexico was to be of unlimited extent, its core the land of the Pueblos, familiar by prior visits and description. The buffalo plains to the east had been explored repeatedly. To the southwest the rim of the Colorado Plateau had been crossed into the hot and dry lowlands of Arizona. A large geography of the northern interior as to nature and peoples was common knowledge. Oñate would undertake to organize a Spanish government, hope to discover mines, and explore farther.

The start began in January 1598 from the Valle de San Bartolomé, still the northern frontier of Spanish settlement. He brought with him a large body of soldiers, settlers with their families, and Franciscan friars. The party travelled in large wheeled carretas and on horseback, and was accompanied by herds of livestock. Instead of following the Conchos River to the Río Grande and then going up the latter, the direct and easy route was taken north over the plains of Chihuahua, crossing the Río Grande at the place since known as El Paso. The mining districts of the north were linked to the city of Mexico by a wagon road over which carts hauled supplies and metal. Oñate extended the track north along the present line of railroad and highway to El Paso and thence up the valley of the Río Grande to the Pueblo country, a road passable by high-wheeled carts (Fig. 6).[2]

During the summer of 1598, pueblos, unrecorded as to number or name, were allotted by Oñate to the care of the Franciscans. One, well up the Río Grande, at the mouth of the Chama River, was seized by him as his headquarters and named San Gabriel. This was the only Spanish settlement until Santa Fé was founded in 1609, and was in violation of the Laws of the Indies, which required that Spanish towns and residences be located on sites apart from Indian settlements.

The first fall and winter were given to reconnoitering the country. A nephew, Vicente de Zaldívar, was sent east in mid-September to report on the buffalo plains.

1. George Hammond and Agapito Rey, ed. and tr., *Don Juan de Oñate* (Albuquerque, 1953), two volumes of a translation of documents, with a large and competent introduction. The documents are in chronological sequence.

2. The major documents on Oñate's New Mexico are in *CDI*, XVI.

Oñate also crossed the mountains east of the Río Grande (Manzano Mountains) to take a look at the great salines and their pueblos (Estancia Basin), then went west from the Río Grande over the ancient Indian road that Coronado and Espejo had travelled, past Ácoma to the Zuñi pueblos and on to the Hopi towns. Another nephew, Juan de Zaldívar, his *maese de campo*, followed him with a body of troops. Thinking it an apt diversion to rush Ácoma atop its great rock, Zaldívar was killed along with a dozen of his soldiers. In January 1599, Oñate returned to take terrible revenge on the people of Ácoma, meanwhile sending Farfán de los Godos from the Hopi country to follow up Espejo's search for mines below the Colorado Plateau.[3]

The regime began by driving the inhabitants of one pueblo from house and home and by making a warning example of the pueblo of Ácoma.

THE PROSPECT AS OUTLINED BY OÑATE

In March 1599, Oñate wrote Viceroy Monterrey of his successes, trials, and plans.[4] The letter is the main account by Oñate of what he had learned of the country and of what he expected to do. It gave his version of the affair at Ácoma, a pueblo of about "three thousand *indios*, that he destroyed," and listed the Pueblo "provinces" as extending from two in the west (Zuñi and Hopi), the farther one he thought rich in mines, to two at the east beyond the mountains (the Pecos and Salinas pueblos). "There are seventy thousand Indios living according to our manner, house by house, and having quadrate plazas; they do not have streets, but live in pueblos of many plazas and quarters, going from one to another by narrow alleys, the houses of two or three stories, some of four to seven. Their clothes are very good, mantas of cotton, white, black and in colors, some woven of another fiber. Others dress in buffalo skins, of which there is great abundance, the wool very fine." The fruits grown included watermelons, melons, and plums.[5]

The letter continued about other nations such as "the Querechos who live in tents of dressed hides among the cattle of Cíbola; there is an infinite number of Apaches of whom we have also seen some and although I was told that these live in rancherias, shortly I have been assured that they live in pueblos," including one of vast size. (Oñate's Querechos also were Apaches. He had only a vague notion of peoples and parties unseen.) There were new worlds to pacify, greater than the one Cortés had given to His Majesty: 1) rich mines, the discovery of which he had begun; 2) certainty of the nearby South Sea, to be used for future trade with Peru, New Spain, and China; 3) new vassals and tribute; 4) greater riches of salines and rock sulphur than anywhere else, the natives "eating and sucking salt as we do sugar"; 5) also there were great herds of wild cattle; and finally 6) the mission to preach the Holy Gospel.

---

3. The Vicente Zaldívar and Farfán reconnaissance are noted below.

4. *CDI*, XVI, 302-315.

5. Melons were known earlier by the Espejo party as cultivated in the La Junta area. Melons, in particular watermelons, were found in Indian cultivation in many areas at the first arrival of Europeans, their rapid dissemination giving rise to the notion that they were of pre-Columbian introduction. Prior and some later accounts agreed that the Pueblos had no fruit trees. Oñate also said that at the west there were bees that produced quite white honey, a curious and unsupported statement.

The rich mines had not been found, nor would they be. The Pacific Ocean was remote. The vassals to be were poor Indian farmers. Salines existed, but were far from the mines to the South in which salt was used to reduce ores. He promised a new state to the crown, to which he would bring Spanish settlers, including those of noble birth.

THE ZALDÍVAR AND FARFÁN EXPEDITIONS OF 1598-1599

The two major expeditions of the first year are known by Bolton's translation of the manuscripts.[6] Vicente Zaldívar was sent east over the Indian route taken by earlier Spanish parties through the Pecos gateway to the Great Plains.

The first Vaqueros (meaning Apaches) were met on a river that carried little water, but had lots of fish, five hundred catfish being hooked in a short time (Gallinas River near Las Vegas, New Mexico). Six leagues farther across hilly plains they came to the first (Apache) encampment, where they were well received and well fed (upper drainage of the Canadian River). Seven leagues farther east they saw the first bull and soon were among herds of several hundreds, feeding about pools of water. As they followed down the valley (of the Canadian River, about to the Texas-New Mexico state line), the herds increased to a thousand and more. At that season many Vaqueros were returning home from trade at the Taos and Picuries pueblos of the Río Grande, where they exchanged hides, meat, tallow, and salt for cotton mantas, maize, pottery, and turquoise. At the farthest camp, there were fifty hide tents, bell shaped, bright red and white in color, the hides so well dressed that they were waterproof and remained soft in the heaviest rain. One tent was acquired by trade to show its quality. Dog travois and mode of harness were described. Impressed by the quality of the wild cattle and their gentleness it was thought that they could be raised as livestock. An attempt was made to round up a herd in a corral and failed, whereupon calves were captured but they soon broke loose and escaped. The Spanish visitors were impressed by the bounty of the buffalo plains and the good life of the Indian hunters.

Farfán was sent southwest from the Hopi country in search of mines, retracing the route Espejo had taken and reported as being of little interest because only copper was found. In winter cold the party traversed a land of tall pines (Pinus ponderosa) and descended from the southern rim of the Colorado Plateau into a valley where there was no snow, where cottonwoods grew along the watercourses, and where nearby desert vegetation, with cactus and maguey (agave) could also be found. There were numerous small rancherias and fields used for growing maize. (Espejo had gone in May. Farfán went in midwinter over the same route into the headwaters of the Río Verde, cut into the escarpment of the Colorado.) The Indians of the rancherias were painted with mineral colors and therefore were called Jumanos in error. (This was Yavapai country well into the nineteenth century and it is inferred that both expeditions met with Yavapais.) The Farfán party took time to go prospecting and found a shaft of a depth of three estados (the height of a man) and a dump of blue ore. (There are prehistoric diggings in the Verde district.) In the belief that a valuable ore body had been found, more than a score of mining claims were staked out, the earliest such possessions in the territory of the United States. (In the late nineteenth century the high grade ores of the

6. Bolton, *Spanish Exploration*, 223-249.

upper Verde Valley were to produce great fortunes during the "Era of the Copper Kings.")

ACTION EASTWARD

At Christmas 1600, a numerous reenforcement of soldiers and friars arrived at San Gabriel and activity turned east of the Río Grande. The pueblos about the margins of the salt pans of the Estancia Basin had been of earlier interest to Oñate, who thought their salines would bring great revenue. This was the eastern cluster of Piro Pueblos, the Jumanos also living at one or more of these pueblos at the time. The Salinas pueblos were said by Oñate to have been insolent, not giving the tribute demanded, and were punished, Abo in particular, with the taking of numerous captives. The events are obscurely recorded for the winter 1600-1601.[7]

Oñate set out again from San Gabriel in June 1601, to follow up Zaldívar's visit to the buffalo plains. A good account of this expedition was written by the Franciscan Francisco de Velasco.[8] The party consisted of seven hundred men, a like number of horses and mules, and six mule and two ox carts. A road for wheeled traffic was opened from Río Grande east across the mountains. On the plains beyond travel was possible by cart and on horse as far as desired. The friar wrote with appreciation of the pleasant country, its vegetation, game, and its Indians.

At the beginning of July Oñate crossed a tree lined river (Pecos), of clear water and teeming with fish, to come in a day to the river of catfish (Gallinas), and in three more days to the Río Magdalena (Canadian), which they followed down stream for days, finding "it green and delightful, bordered everywhere by vines and fruit trees . . . one of the best rivers that we had seen anywhere in the Indies." (They were retracing the route taken by Zaldívar [Fig. 7].) Shortly they were met by welcoming Indians (Apaches) who brought black and yellow fruits of the size of small tomatoes (unidentified). In early August (still following the Canadian River across the Texas Panhandle) they began to see the monstrous *cíbola* cattle in herds, which became larger as they went on. In a single day there might be seen as many as all the cattle on the greatest estancias of New Spain. These wild cattle were quiet and did not run away, "did not become angry like ours and were never dangerous." They were described at length, with comment on the superior quality of the meat.

The river (Canadian) abounded in fish. In a hundred and fifty leagues there was hardly a day when they failed to find groves with plum trees in variety and with grapevines, and with springs flowing through the groves. Here and there were rancherias of friendly Indians. There were herds of deer as big as horses, in bands of two to five hundred (the American elk, largest of the genus *Cervus* in the New World). Following the Canadian River east they descended from the High Plains to about two thousand feet above sea level at the Oklahoma-Texas line.

Having come to sand hills (Antelope Hills, Oklahoma), they left the river and turned north across a great prairie plain traversed by eastward flowing streams. This plain, over which the carts had easy going, was pastured by innumerable wild cattle. There

7. In the report of Luis Gasco de Velasco, in Hammond and Rey, *Oñate*, II, 608-618.

8. Translated by Bolton, *Spanish Exploration*, 250-267, and again by Hammond and Rey, *Oñate*, II, 746-760, the two versions differing in minor details.

was great diversity of flowers in midsummer, Velasco observing that wherever there were many flowers there were also many cattle. (The prairie grasses, mature and less palatable at that season, were less nutritious than the legumes and the other herbs then in bloom.) The rivers were noted as lined by groves of oaks and walnuts, and as being rich in fish. It was a land of many cattle, turkeys, deer, and other game. (They were traveling northeast into Kansas toward the Arkansas River, somewhere northwest of Wichita.)

Seven leagues before reaching the river (Arkansas) they came to a great rancheria of six hundred hide-covered huts formed in a large circle. The people of the rancheria numbered more than five thousand, both men and women using bow and arrow, hunters without cultivated fields. Their name was heard as Escanjaques. The Spaniards were well entertained and guided to the river (Arkansas) through grass tall enough to hide a horse (a proper remark concerning the tall grass prairies, the big bluestem grass [*Andropogon*] in full growth in late summer). In the valley they enjoyed a fruit of fine flavor, like a small pear or the sweet chicozapote of Mexico, which suggests that they found ripe papaws *(Asimina)*, then ripe in the woods, northern kin of the tropical custard apples. There were mulberries ripe in the valley and many fish in river pools.

The Escanjaques are thought by Newcomb to have been eastern Apaches. Hammond is inclined to consider them as a Siouan people either Osages or Kansas, which seems correct, their enmity with the neighboring Caddoan Wichitas weighing against Caddoan kinship. A map of Oñate's route Bolton found in the Archive of the Indies, shows 600 *ranchos de Scanjaques*. The unlimited bounty of the buffalo plains was shared by tribes from all sides.

Oñate got as far as the land of the Wichitas on the Arkansas River in Kansas, the Quivira that Coronado had reached sixty years earlier. A village on the far side of the

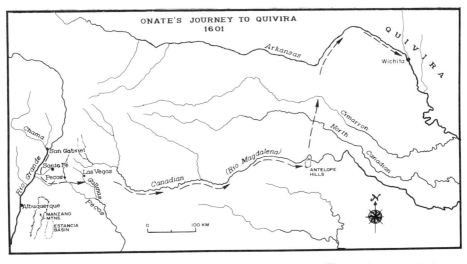

Fig. 7. Oñate to Quivera.

53

river was of 1200 circular and domed houses, built of a frame of poles covered with thatch, each house with an extended entry. (The Caddoan tribes of Kansas and Nebraska still built thus at the time of American settlement.) The visitors were given great round loaves of corn bread, big as a shield and three to four fingers thick. The village was surrounded by fields in which a second planting of corn was six inches tall, the only cultivation done by pulling weeds. There were many beans and squashes, also plum trees in the planted fields. Having gone several leagues through a very fertile and populous land, the party started back late in September over the route by which it had come, having a fight at the previously friendly rancheria of the Escanjaques. San Gabriel on the Río Grande was reached November 24, 1601, five months after the departure.

THE DETERIORATING SITUATION

Oñate came back to San Gabriel to find that the majority of the settlers and some of the friars had left for Santa Bárbara and its ease and security. Complaints reached the Viceroy in Mexico of misconduct by Oñate and Zaldívar. The most specific charges were by Captain Gasco de Velasco, sent before the return of Oñate.[9] The supplies of the party that had entered to take possession in 1598 ran short fifty leagues before they came to the first pueblos, the Governor therefore sending eighty pack animals ahead to bring relief, to the great grief of those pueblos. "Getting to the pueblos we had to support ourselves, taking as much as we could from each one. Because of these and other annoyances the Indians fear us so much that, on seeing us approach from afar, they flee to the mountains." In the three years of trying to find something of value there had been no success. To feed more than five hundred persons men were sent in various directions to bring maize. Each house was required to tribute a blanket or dressed skin annually, sometimes taken by force. Horses were let loose in the corn fields. The Indians had decreased notably in number. Ácoma was taken because its people refused to supply blankets. Hundreds were killed and more after they surrendered. Hundreds were taken prisoner at Ácoma and the feet of twenty-four cut off. Vicente Zaldívar attacked the Jumano Pueblo, killed more than 900, burned the pueblo, and took more than 200 captives, who escaped shortly. No attention had been paid to the good conduct ordered by the Viceroy, and so on.

Viceroy Monterrey ordered an investigation in July 1601.[10] The friars, it was reported, had succeeded in making only a few converts and there had been great violence used against some pueblos. Four witnesses added assorted information.

The first witness described Indian ways, such as raising turkeys for their feathers, neither flesh nor eggs being eaten, the underground community centers (kivas), and the absence of trade except for the exchange of maize and blankets with the buffalo hunting Vaqueros. The Governor had settled his party in an Indian pueblo of more than four hundred houses. There might be fifty to sixty thousand Indians in the tributary pueblos, giving two thousand cotton blankets, five to six thousand fanegas of maize and beans and a small number of turkeys. Six friars remained, who had baptized only a hundred Indians, mostly at the Spanish settlement.

9. Hammond and Rey, *Oñate*, II, 608-618.

10. Hammond and Rey, *Oñate*, II, 623-667.

The second witness added melons and watermelons as Indian crops. There were wild sheep, with horns heavier than those of a bull. Oñate had introduced five hundred brood mares, eight hundred horses, six hundred cows, four hundred oxen, three thousand five hundred sheep and goats, and seven hundred mules. Of Spanish crops a harvest of at least three thousand fanegas of wheat and a little barley was expected that very year. The Pueblo population was estimated as twenty-two to twenty-four thousand men and women.

The third witness deposed that the Governor had gone to a pueblo named Jumanos, hanged several people, and burned their houses. Livestock numbered about a thousand sheep, five hundred horses, and four hundred head of cattle. He estimated the Indian numbers as twelve thousand, not counting women or children, all told about thirty thousand. The complaints he thought were mainly by late comers who expected too much, such as having to bring firewood from a distance of a half dozen leagues, the fire of cottonwood so smoky that women and children were in tears night and day. In summer they slept outdoors to escape the unbearable plague of bedbugs. Mice ate up the chiles but not the cheese. (Bedbugs, chile, mice, and cheese: all Spanish introductions?)

The fourth witness told of trade with the Vaqueros and of bighorn sheep. About 630 cows and steers had been brought, half of which had been eaten, and only a few remained. The Pueblo numbers were twelve to thirteen thousand, not counting women and children.

The Franciscan commissary, Juan de Escalona, wrote his superior on October 1, 1601, (before the return of Oñate), that most of the people had left San Gabriel because of privations resulting from the hard usage of the Indians who were dying of starvation, the Governor and his captains having plundered the pueblos and taken the corn that had been saved for years past, leaving the natives with hardly a kernel. Escalona had given permission to four friars at San Gabriel to leave and await developments at Santa Bárbara.[11]

Adherents of the Governor on the other hand laid the blame for events at Ácoma and the Pueblo of the Jumanos on the Indians, who had always been the aggressors.[12]

By the summer of 1602, the Council of the Indies in Spain was concerned about New Mexico, having read the charges of Gasco de Velasco and of Fray Juan de Escalona of excessive cruelties and tyrannies by Oñate, Vicente Zaldívar, and others. It ordered the Viceroy to continue the inquiries and to put a stop to outrages. In 1602, the Governor reported good results of his Quivira expedition and sent his brother to Spain to appeal in his interest. The Audiencia of Mexico meanwhile considered whether it was worthwhile to continue the occupation of New Mexico. Discussions went on to the end of Monterrey's term as Viceroy in 1603, without decision, but with Oñate under continuing criticism.[13]

ACTION TAKEN AGAINST OÑATE

The new Viceroy Montesclaros was ordered by the King in January 1604 to take whatever steps he deemed proper concerning New Mexico. Montesclaros reported in

11. Hammond and Rey, *Oñate*, II, 698-700.
12. Hammond and Rey, *Oñate*, II, 701-739.
13. Hammond and Rey, *Oñate*, II, 770-795.

March 1605 that by his information its people were rustic, wretched in clothes and spirit, and that there was neither silver or gold, the samples Oñate sent assaying only copper. Backers of Oñate sought royal support, "whereupon this worthless land, the object of such ill-advised expenditures, would be transformed into an object of greed . . . I feel quite sure that both the time and expenditure put into it will be wasted or that at best it is a fable." The charges against Oñate at the time were insufficient to justify sentencing but did warrant withdrawing his appointment. On October 28, 1605, Montesclaros wrote the King of Escobar's report (see below) of the expedition to the mouth of the Colorado River: "From his signed report and from four witnesses who returned with the friar I cannot help but inform Your Majesty that this conquest is becoming a fairy tale" concerning naked people (Yumas), a handful of inferior coral, and some pebbles, these (garnets and turquoise) being forwarded to the King. "There is no end to this business because they keep expanding it by passing from one undertaking to another."[14]

The Council of the Indies decreed the recall of Oñate January 22, 1606, and ordered that "there be appointed in his place a prudent and Christian man." In June 1606, the King ordered Montesclaros to halt discovery in New Mexico, recall Oñate, and keep him confined in Mexico.[15]

SEARCH FOR THE SOUTH SEA

The promise Oñate made that he would be another Cortés came to nothing. He was in trouble, but still had the notion that the north adjoined the South Sea, the great ocean by which one could sail to China or Peru. Perhaps he could save the situation by proving his geography correct. He set out October 7, 1605, with thirty men on his last expedition, the only one in which he explored an unknown land. Friar Francisco Escobar's diary provides the account of the journey and was addressed to Viceroy Montesclaros who used it, as cited above, against Oñate.[16]

The friar began his report by telling of the poor condition of the Río Grande pueblos, because of yearly tribute demanded beyond their means, for which reason many abandoned their homes when tribute was collected. Four Zuñi pueblos were inhabited, but were largely in ruins. The Hopi pueblos were about half in ruin, with at most five hundred occupied houses.

The route beyond the Hopi country can be reconstructed from the streams crossed or followed. At ten leagues they reached a river flanked by trees (Little Colorado). Nearby were great forests of pines. The next river was seventeen leagues farther west (Verde River), flowing from north to south, between mountains, carrying more water, and with good fishing, the climate more temperate. The third river was five leagues farther, at the base of a high range, where Espejo had found copper, and where there were friendly and simple Indians, whom they called Cruzados (Yavapai), also many deer and wild sheep. (The branches of the Verde River which they crossed were in Yavapai County, Prescott the county seat. In addition to the great mines of the Río Verde of the

14. Hammond and Rey, *Oñate*, II, 1009-1010.
15. Hammond and Rey, *Oñate*, II, 1035-1037.
16. Hammond and Rey, *Oñate*, II, 1012-1031.

present century numerous mines were worked east and west of Prescott in the nineteenth century in the mineralized margin of the Colorado Plateau.)

Leaving the mineral country they took a westerly course across the desert, the mountains mostly of bare rock, the stream bed dry, except for short distances where water rose to the surface. There were signs of occasional high flood. In this climate there was no snow in midwinter. At the end of a hundred miles, following a dry stream bed of occasional pools, they came to its junction with a river as great as the Duero in Spain. (The only such channel across the desert is that of Bill Williams River, in its upper part called the Santa Maria River.) This great river, named Búena Esperanza by them, is the Colorado.

Along the Colorado they found tribes that grew crops without irrigation on the rich flood plain, especially below the place where the river issued from a narrow passage enclosed by mountains (Chocolate Mountains) and was joined by another river from the east (Gila). The latter was well populated by farmers growing maize, beans, and squashes. Hearing a few words of their speech Escobar thought that these might be Tepehuán, such as he had known in New Spain. He came close; the Gila Indians were Pápago Pimas, whose language is closely related to Tepehuán.

The great lower flood plain, extending twenty leagues from the mouth of the Gila to the head ot the Gulf of California, had many people living in good sized rancherias, clusters of huts of wood and straw. The friar noted their names and size (all being Yuman). The tribe farthest downstream, extending as far as salt water, were Cocopas (still so called), listing nine rancherias and an estimated total of five to six thousand persons. East of the Colorado River he thought the native population to be more than thirty thousand. The people were well fed, somewhat lazy he thought because they did not cultivate all the alluvial land available. In addition to maize, beans, and squash, they grew a grass for its seeds (a domesticated *Bromus* known only here and among the Indians of northwest mainland Mexico). Cotton also was correctly reported as grown in the area.

The people of the valley were noted as tall and well built and as generous hosts. Twenty horses had been left in care of one rancheria and when the party started back up the river it found that thirteen had been eaten, apparently by misunderstanding. The Spanish asked about silver by showing some pieces and were told, they thought, that they would find much a few days' travel west or northwest, also a yellow metal. By sign language they learned wondrous things of strange people, some sleeping under water, others always in trees, some who lived on the odor of food, some who lacked an anus, and some with monstrous genitals.

The return was briefly noted, through the land of the Cruzados (Yavapai) and of the Moqui (Hopi), where they saw small stones of garnet red and emerald green (garnets and turquoise). They stopped at Inscription Rock (El Morro National Monument) to carve the date of their passage, and reached San Gabriel April 25, 1605.

END OF THE OÑATE REGIME

The recall of Oñate, ordered in 1606, was not carried out until a new governor was appointed in 1608. Oñate's *residencia*, the official inquiry into conduct at the end of a term, was long delayed, perhaps because of family status. The belated action made the disgrace of his government of New Mexico a matter of public record.

Oñate was sentenced to perpetual exile from New Mexico, to a ban of four years from the City of Mexico, and to a fine of 6,000 ducats. His nephew and second in command, Vicente de Zaldívar, was found guilty of mistreatment of soldiers, of the killing of Indians at Ácoma and of other innocents, of killing a captain, of misconduct with women, and of other derelictions. A half dozen subordinates were also sentenced for crimes committed. The sentence was least severe on Oñate, but it marked the end of his public career and an end of the worst abuses of the Pueblo peoples, who had come to regard all the Spaniards as evil.

VI.

Pueblo Decline and Revolt

REORGANIZATION OF SPANISH ADMINISTRATION

Oñate presented himself as another empire builder like Cortés. New Mexico would yield wealth of silver such as had made his father rich, but no new mines were to be discovered. Oñate would find a port from which to cross the ocean but reached only the head of the Gulf of California, which had already been known for two generations. He and his nephews were belated predators, rather of the stripe of the Pizarros, doing grave and willful injuries to the natives, causing a serious decline of condition and numbers. The Oñate regime was an anachronism, in conflict with the spirit of the New Laws of the Indies.

New Mexico gave little promise of material returns to Crown or individuals, nor did it have the strategic importance of Florida or California. There remained the responsibility of the Spanish Crown as Christian Kings to extend the true faith to all their realm, an obligation acknowledged since the time of Queen Isabela. The Council of the Indies decided that New Mexico should be maintained as a Christian mission.

The Viceroy of New Spain was charged with providing funds to support the missionaries and the civil government. The friars needed but little financial help, and a small number of soldiers and civilian personnel would suffice to keep order. In 1609, Viceroy Velasco the Younger appointed the new governor and sent a new lot of Franciscans, soldiers, artisans, and families to New Mexico.

The Franciscans made their headquarters at the Keresan Pueblo of Santo Domingo, in good location among the cluster of pueblos of the most fertile part of the Río Grande Valley and, being at the mouth of the Galisteo River, also on the road east to the Estancia Basin and the Pecos drainage.

To replace Oñate's San Gabriel the Spanish villa was located, as prescribed in the Laws of the Indies, apart from any Indian settlement, its name Santa Fé declaring that New Mexico would be governed for the salvation of the natives. The site was well suited to Spanish needs and preference. At an elevation of seven thousand feet it had good pasture for livestock and land suited to grow wheat. At the foot of the Sangre de Cristo Mountains it had mountain streams, wood for fuel, and timber and stone for building. Tesuque Pueblo was a few miles to the north, and to the south pueblos were strung along the Indian road from the Río Grande to the Pecos. Its first inhabitants (1610) were the governor's household, staff, and about fifty married soldiers. A Franciscan church and convent served the Spaniards and their servants. Santa Fé remained the only Spanish settlement in New Mexico to 1680 when it was abandoned during the Pueblo revolt.

The planned reform was that the Franciscans would take charge of the pueblos while the lay authority would take charge of security and communications. Trouble began at once. The new governor removed the Indians from the pueblos to labor in the building of Santa Fé. The Franciscans objected and, at one point in the dispute, locked up the new governor. The quarrels, usually about Indian rights, went on year after year, at times verging on civil war.[1] When the friars withdrew from Santa Fé, its town council *(cabildo)* filed complaint indicating that the friars had exceeded their rights by refusing sacrament and by applying excommunication.[2]

The second governor was charged with the impropriety of establishing estancias on which he raised cattle and sheep *(ganado mayor y menor)*, and of also giving the Spanish the land near the pueblos, to the damage of the villages.[3]

Viceroy Marqués de Guadalcazar in 1620 ordered an end to illegal and injurious usage of Indians: they should not be made to serve as *tamemes* (burden bearers), nor should they be taken from their planting or other needed work, as was being done, sometimes by the hundreds and without pay. Labor was to be only at proper times and places, with pay, and to be restricted to pueblos that could furnish field labor and herdsmen without hardship.

A common complaint by the friars was that the land was taken by the officials for their own use. The treasury of New Spain spent very little on New Mexico. Officials of New Mexico added to their meager salaries by stock ranches they established, without title but without interference by higher authority. Soldiers, in lieu of pay, were assigned individual pueblos by the governor, from which they collected tribute, determined as to kind and amount. These so-called encomiendas, illegal, were a burden on the pueblos, the beneficiary tending to exact as much as he could get, and were strongly protested by the friars.

The Viceroy, charged with the support of the missions, sent an occasional supply train, once a year or less often.[4] The friars built convents, churches, and hospitals with the labor of pueblos under their charge. They extended irrigation and added cultivation of European plants, especially of winter wheat. At some missions herds of livestock were established. The missions were managed for the benefit of the pueblos, and the missionaries opposed their exploitation by Spanish officials and soldiers, which at times included raids on mission livestock.[5]

---

1. France V. Scholes, "Church and State in New Mexico, 1610-1650," five articles in the *New Mexico Historical Review*, XI (1936), 9-76; 145-178; 283-294; 297-349; and XII (1937), 78-106.

2. Charles W. Hackett summarized the antagonisms in *Historical Documents Relating to New Mexico, Neuva Vizcaya, and Approaches Thereto, to 1773, Collected by Adolph F. A. Bandelier and Fanny R. Bandelier*, Carnegie Institution of Washington, Publication 330 (Washington, D.C., 1923-1937), III, 3-17.

3. Lansing B. Bloom, "A Glimpse of New Mexico in 1620," *New Mexico Historical Review*, III (1928), 371-380.

4. France V. Scholes, "The Supply Service of the New Mexico Missions in the Seventeenth Century," *New Mexico Historical Review*, V (1930), 93-115; 186-210; and 386-404, includes an invoice of items and quantities of a shipment of supply for three years, needs for religious services, medicines, tools for building and farming, and small items of comfort.

5. France V. Scholes, "Troublous Times in New Mexico, 1659-1670," *New Mexico Historical Review*, XIII (1938), 66-67.

THE BENAVIDES MEMORIAL

The first and most important review of the condition of New Mexico after Oñate is the Benavides *Memorial*. Fray Alonso de Benavides came to New Mexico in 1625 as commissary in charge of the missions. On his return to Spain he presented his report to the Franciscan Commissary General of the Indies, who sent it to Philip IV in the year 1630. It was given to the Pope in revised form in 1634. The first version is here used.[6]

Benavides arranged his material by "nations," more or less in geographic order. The first nation, the Mansos, was encountered at El Paso, a hundred leagues before coming to the Pueblo country. Their name Mansos, by which they identified themselves to Oñate as friends, was in common Spanish use. They were known also as Gorretas because they trimmed their hair to resemble a skull cap. They were well built, naked except for scant clothes of the women, and lived in huts made of branches. They did not plant crops but lived on fish and rodents *(ratones)*. Benavides thought their wish to have a friar living with them should be carried out, and that they would provide a halfway station to New Mexico for the supply train of the missions (an early note of the significant location of the river crossing at El Paso).

His party traveled thirty leagues north through and beyond the Manso nation and came to a part of the great Apache nation, here called Perrillos. (They were taking the tedious Jornada del Muerto between Rincon and San Marcial, east of the Río Grande.) The Apaches were described as warlike but trustworthy. (This may be the first indentification of Apaches as occupying the mountain country on both sides of the middle Río Grande.)

The province and nation of the Piros marked the beginning of the Pueblo country, noted as a nation of many pueblos of houses of adobe and of plazas entered by corridors. "They are great cultivators of their own crops as well as those that we have brought," and had good hunting and fishing and abundance of piñon nuts. Although this was the first Pueblo nation known it was one of the last to be converted. Benavides took credit to himself for founding three convents, one in their largest pueblo Pilado, dedicated to the Virgin of Socorro, one at Senecú to San Antonio de Padua, and one at Sevilleta to San Luis Obispo. Sevilleta, he said, had been depopulated by wars(?), and was reestablished by himself, by bringing in people from other places. Each of the three convents served other pueblos, fourteen in all, to a distance of fifteen leagues on both sides of the river. In all there were six thousand souls, all baptized. A cerro near Socorro had rich mines awaiting exploitation.

In the valley above the Piro province was that of the Teoas (the Tiguez of Coronado, now spelled Tiwa or Tigua), seven thousand more souls, all baptized, in fifteen or sixteen pueblos, with the convents of San Francisco de Sandía and San Antonio de la Isleta. Four leagues beyond it the Queres (Keres) nation held ten leagues of very fertile land, beginning with the Pueblo of San Felipe, with seven pueblos and four thousand souls in all.

Having gone up the Río Grande to the mouth of the Galisteo River Benavides shifted attention east across the mountains to the pueblos in the basin of the great salines, the

6. Printed in Madrid in 1630. I have used *The Memorial of Fray Alonso de Benavides*, tr. Mrs. Edward E. Ayers, annotated by F. W. Hodge and C. F. Lummis, with a facsimile of the original (Chicago, 1916).

61

Tompiro nation (the eastern Piros, in some accounts called Salineros). Here there was less crop land and poorer yields because of the great winter cold and scant water. From Chilili at the west the province extended for more than fifteen leagues, fourteen or fifteen pueblos of more than ten thousand souls, served by six convents, one being the large pueblo of the Jumanos.

Turning north to the nation of the Tanos, five pueblos were under one convent, with more than four thousand baptized. (These, now extinct, occupied the Galisteo Valley.) To the northeast, the pueblo of Pecos was of the Jémez nation, living well apart from their kindred west of the Río Grande. The pueblo of Pecos (Cicuye in earlier accounts) was of more than two thousand souls, growing enough maize for their needs in a very cold and not very fertile country.

The Villa of Santa Fé, northwest of Pecos and northeast of the Tanos, had about a thousand persons, Spanish, mestizos, and Indians, about seven hundred servants and fifty soldiers. The soldiers were not paid, the governor giving them encomiendas of pueblos, from which they collected yearly tribute of a cotton manta and a fanega of maize from each household. The vicinity, although cold, was the most fertile in all New Mexico.

And so back to the Río Grande, beginning above the mouth of the Galisteo. These Teoas (now called Tewas in distinction from the Tiguas, and of different language) had eight pueblos of six thousand souls, San Ildefonso being the most important.

The main Jémez nation lived west of the river (in the Jémez watershed). When Benavides came they were scattered far and wide, their land almost depopulated. He settled them at two pueblos, one, San Joseph (now pueblo of Jémez), not as yet finished. More than half of the nation had died, but more than three thousand had been reassembled.

The upper Río Grande, mountain girt, belonged to the Picuries nation, still in process of being baptized. At the pueblo of Picuri two thousand had been baptized of a formerly indomitable people. They had a fertile land, fine trout streams, and unworked mines of fine garnets. Seven leagues farther north was Taos, with two thousand five hundred baptized, in a very cold country, but with abundant food and livestock.

The Peñol de Ácoma, twelve Leagues west of the Río Grande, was reduced to peace in 1629 (the late date suggesting that it had been slow to recover from the destruction by Oñate). Beyond it to the west the Zuñi nation had about a dozen pueblos and more than ten thousand converts. Farthest west the Moquis (Hopi) had another ten thousand souls in process of being baptized. Benavides did not get to the Zuñis or Hopis and was poorly informed of the western pueblos.

"These are the populations that we have converted and baptized . . . which together will have nearly eighty thousand souls." Among the pueblos the women worked at building the churches, the men spun and wove, hunted and fought. Everybody went dressed in mantas of cotton or skins, ornamented according to their manner, the women using colored and patterned mantas. They had turquoise mines and made necklaces and earrings. (The distinctive dress of the Pueblo people always had attention.)

As to the fertility of the country he gave a list of cultivated and other useful plants. As had been true of earlier Spanish he was impressed by the piñon pines of the southwest, differing from those of Spain and bearing large, soft-shelled nuts. In the list of Spanish introductions watermelons and very good apricots and peaches were named, and wheat

62

yielding as much as a hundred and twenty fanegas for one fanega sown. By that time there were goodly numbers of European livestock.[7]

The pueblos were surrounded on all sides by the great Apache nation, of a different language and habit. Their conversion had begun, while that of the nearby Pueblos lacked completion only among the Hopis. The remaining challenge would be the gentile Indians who came to the pueblos for purposes of trade. Benavides was attracted to these "noble savages" of proud and grave demeanor, had begun their conversion, and projected its success.

Benavides' first reference to Apaches was by the name Perrillos, located on the Río Grande below the Piro pueblos. Later, when he was preaching at Senecú to the Piros, an Apache chief came often to hear him, a chief of Xila Apaches living in the mountains to the southwest. (The name Gila thus appears for mountain Apaches of southwestern New Mexico before the Gila River was known.)

Conversion of the Navajo Apaches also had begun. They lived north of the Pueblo country and were very good farmers, the name Navajo meaning tiller of the soil. Navajos were accustomed to come to trade at the Tewa Pueblo of Santa Clara on the upper Río Grande. Navajos were the most bellicose of all Apaches and lived in mountains where stone used for dyeing cloth was found(?). Benavides founded a convent and church for them at Santa Clara. He related the elaborate ceremony at length, with dancing and passing the peace pipe of tobacco between the great chief, subchiefs, and missionaries. This Apache province extended along the northern frontier of the Pueblos for more than fifty leagues and west for a great and unknown distance, according to Spaniards who had made forays into it, a land of more than two hundred thousand souls(!).

At the east were the Apaches Vaqueros, who hunted the cattle of Cíbola. The wild cattle were the sustenance of all the Vaquero Apaches, had better meat and fat than Spanish cattle, grunted like pigs, and had curly hair like fine fleece, which was used to make good cloth and hats like those of vicuña wool. These cattle alone would suffice to make a prince powerful. Except at time of mating, bulls and cows were kept apart. The Spanish had learned to take newborn calves and raise them with goats. The cattle shed their coats in summer, the wool strewn about the plains and in trees and ravines in such amounts that it could be a source of wealth. When the hides were dressed with the hair left on they were like velvet and served as clothing for Indians and Spaniards. When Apaches came to trade they brought their women and children, also tents on the backs of dogs lined up in a train one behind another.

Conversion of the Jumanos also was proceeding. This nation lived east of Santa Fé, for a distance of more than a hundred leagues south of the Apache country. Some years earlier a missionary engaged in the conversion of Tampiros and Salineros (pueblos of Estancia Basin) had been asked by the Jumanos of that vicinity to come and live with them. A missionary was sent in 1629 and the conversion was proceeding wonderfully well.

Word of the mission to the Jumanos also had reached the Quiviras (Wichitas) and other distant nations who sent an embassy to ask for priests.[8] It was known that the

7. The remark was added that Indians joined to drive different kinds of game by encircling them.

8. Another suggestion that the Jumanos like the Wichitas and the intervening Teyas or Texas were Caddoan tribes.

63

Quiviras had much gold, and that it was traded to the Dutch and English on the east coast. By their conversion a direct road would be opened to the bay of Espíritu Santo (on the Texas coast of the Gulf of Mexico). (Quivira-Wichita, first visited by Coronado, again by Espejo and by Oñate, was proposed by Benavides as a missionary field, the Jumanos of the Salinas [Estancia Basin] the connecting link. His projected route between Quivira and Espíritu Santo Bay anticipated by half a century La Salle's establishment on Matagorda Bay and the French contact with the Caddos in northeast Texas. The correct geography of the plains was learned by Benavides, I infer, from the Jumanos of the Salinas.)

The concluding part of the *Memorial* departs widely from Benavides' own experiences. The Coronado expedition was described by place names that it had used, without recognizing that they had since been replaced by still other names. In the final section Quivira was given an extension along the Pacific coast from the Sea of California to the Strait of Anian. The *Memorial* was written in Spain, and the concluding part drew on the misinformation of maps current in Europe. The summation is out of character with the body of the *Memorial*. Presented as a plea to the King by the Franciscan Commissary General of the Indies to expand the missions of New Mexico, I suspect that it may have been written by a different author.

Benavides was attracted by the Apaches, whom he held in high regard and whose conversion he said that he had begun. He made early contact with the mountain people of the southwest, his Gila Apaches. To the north of the Pueblos was the land of the Navajo Apaches whom he identified correctly as being Apache. These were farmers, their territory extending west beyond the limits of Spanish knowledge. They came to trade at pueblos of the upper Río Grande, where he founded a convent for them at Santa Clara. A third Apache tribe of the eastern plains, known as Apaches Vaqueros, were the Querechos of Coronado's time. These buffalo hunters came to pueblos of the east to trade skins, meat, and wool for grain and cotton cloth, bringing their wives and children, skin tents, and dog trains. His observations of the different Apache tribes were made during their visits at pueblos, a symbiosis of contrasting cultures which he recorded as an eye witness. Except for the Hopi and Zuñi, Benavides' descriptions of the Pueblos were also eye witness accounts. The missions were grouped as provinces; and provinces, pueblos and convents were all given their exact geographic location. The pueblos were noted as to their construction, size, and productivity, including notes on the fertility of soil, water supply, climate, and other resources. Native crops, manner of cultivation, yield, and storage were given, however, much less attention than in the early accounts. Wheat growing had become important as had livestock at a number of missions. European vegetables and fruit trees had been introduced successfully. The mission economy was presented as doing well except for official interference. A muted criticism may be inferred from statements such as: the Governor did not pay wages to the soldiers but gave them instead the tribute of pueblos as encomiendas; more than half the population of the Jémez pueblos had died and the rest had scattered throughout the country until Benavides resettled them; Ácoma was not reduced to peace until 1629.

Benavides has been a guide to modern ethnologists on Pueblo culture except for his estimates of population which have been considered exaggerated, not because of evidence to the contrary but because opinion of scholars has been that Indian numbers were small, except in the high cultures of Mexico and the Andes. Later revision of

Indian demography has been little concerned with the Southwest and the early Spanish records. These are in good agreement as to the continuing large decline of Pueblo population from the time of the Chamuscado-Rodríguez entry in 1582. Pueblo demography needs restudy.

THE FRANCISCAN COMMISSARY GENERAL'S REPORT

Juan de Prada, Commissary General of the Franciscans in New Spain, reported on the condition of New Mexico in 1638.[9] The Crown asked whether the time had come to change from missionary to secular clergy and thus to collect tithes and tribute, the friars having performed their services of preparing the Pueblos for integration into the civil administration of New Spain. The Commissary General argued against the proposal.

Prada outlined briefly the extent of the Pueblo country, along the Río Grande from Senecú to Taos, from the eastern pueblos of the Salinas to those of Moqui (Hopi) at the west, in all forty thousand persons or less. Although more than sixty thousand must have been baptized, "today the conversions are diminished on account of the very active prevalence during these last years of smallpox and the sickness which the Mexicans call cocolixtli." The Indians were poor, raising a little cotton made into mantas to trade for buffalo and deer skins with the unconverted Indians adjacent, with whom they lived in insecure peace. The Spanish administration was maintained only by the industry and management of the friars, of whom there were no more than fifty in the thirty convents and numerous visitas. Idolatry had been banished, only the true God was now being worshipped.

Santa Fé, the sole Spanish settlement, had about fifty vecinos (citizens), about two hundred persons being occupied in bearing arms. As to the prospects of the country, the winters were very rigorous and the summers intolerably hot, yet the land was fertile. The rivers abounded in fish, and there was unlimited game in the mountains. The land was well suited to cattle and sheep. Mines were available but thus far none had been worked.

The pueblos were already burdened with tribute. The soldiers in New Mexico received no pay from the Crown nor any salary other than their income from the encomiendas (given them by the Governor), each household paying its encomendero a fanega of maize and a piece of cotton cloth annually. Prada estimated that there were more than eight thousand households thus contributing, each household consisting of a related group (extended families). It was neither right nor possible to expect more payment. As to establishing a bishopric and exacting tithes, these could be paid only in wheat and livestock, both in small supply. A bishopric would offer no advantages.

FRICTION AND REVOLT

The Pueblo had experienced merciless violence from Coronado's party, mainly in the communities of the Río Grande Valley later know as Río Abajo (downriver from Santa Fé). When Oñate came a half century later, Ácoma was given exemplary punishment; a pueblo to the east, called Jumanos, was burned and a great part of its population killed;

9. In Hackett, *Historical Documents*, III, 106-115.

and pueblos in the Río Grande Valley were plundered of their store of food and reduced to starvation.

The new order introduced with the founding of Santa Fé in 1610 began with friction between the religious and the civil authority, and it continued or was renewed in succeeding administrations to the injury of the third party, the Indians of the pueblos.[10]

The record is dismal and became more so. Disease and crop failures due to droughts added to the distress, the native provision of storage against adverse seasons having been eliminated by the tributes imposed. Spanish estancias of livestock hemmed in Pueblo lands. The seventeenth century was one of continued disruption of Pueblo livelihood and of declining native population.

For the thirties, there is record of a Zuñi revolt and also Prada's report of the ravages of smallpox and another epidemic. Under Governor Lopez (1659-1661) it was reported "this land does not have more than about one hundred citizens [vecinos], and among this number are mulattoes, mestizos, and all who have any Spanish blood." The Governor engaged in trade with Plains tribes, buying captives the Apaches got from other tribes to sell south to mines and ranches. Missionaries were suppressing Indian ways, marriage customs, ceremonies, and beliefs, and resorted occasionally to physical punishment. In one extreme case, a Hopi who had hidden an idol was whipped to death. In 1670 both Spaniards and Indians were reduced to eating hides and straps boiled with herbs and roots. In 1671 there was great pestilence among people and cattle. In 1672 Apaches looted the country, especially of cattle and sheep, of which it had been previously very productive.

Scholes, writing of the pueblos of the Salinas, including Jumanos, noted profanation of churches by Apaches from 1652 on, their raids becoming frequent after 1665. The year 1666 brought drought and crop failures. In 1669 it was reported that there had been no harvest for three years and that nine hundred fifty persons died of hunger in the pueblo of Jumanos. In 1670 Apaches attacked this pueblo. In 1671 there was a severe pestilence. By 1679, five of the Salinas pueblos had been abandoned, five hundred families being moved to the Piros pueblos on the Río Grande or to lately founded missions below El Paso. The Salinas district lacked running streams and depended on *pozos*, artificial ponds and dug wells. Its people, originally Piros, had been joined by Jumanos, whose name was given to one of the pueblos.[11] By the third quarter of the century Apaches were raiding west of the Pecos to steal cattle and sheep, initially from Spanish holdings but soon also from the missions. By the late seventies the situation had deteriorated to the abandonment of a number of missions, wide raiding by Apaches, want, distress, and resentment in general.

The Pueblo Revolt broke out suddenly and fiercely in the summer of 1680.[12] The immediate cause was repression of native religion. Missionaries, aware that converts

10. See the articles by France V. Scholes on "Church and State in New Mexico, 1610-1670," cited above, and also the full series by Scholes on "Troublous Times in New Mexico, 1650-1670," *New Mexico Historical Review*, XII (1937), 134-174; 380-452; XIII (1938), 63-84; XV (1940-, 249-268; 369-417; XVI (1941), 15-40; 184-205; and 313-327.

11. It is thought to be the ruin now named Gran Quivira National Monument. There is no connection with the Quivira of Kansas.

12. Charles W. Hackett collected the documents, with a comprehensive introduction, in the two volumes of *Revolt of the Pueblo Indians of New Mexico and Otermin's Attempted Reconquest 1680-1682* (Albuquerque, 1942).

continued heathen practices and beliefs, had moved sharply against their religious leaders, priests, shamans, or medicine men, who constituted the underground resistance. In 1675, forty-seven such were captured, three hanged, the others subjected to punishment, in part severe. Two of these are thought to have organized the revolt by long and carefully hidden preparation with Apache aid.

Taos and Picuries, mountain pueblos of the north, were headquarters of the conspiracy. The signal to attack was sent out in August by cord message. With the help of Apaches the Spanish stock ranches of the upper Río Grande were destroyed and their occupants killed. The Tewa pueblos to the south, on both sides of the Río Grande, joined the action, Tesuque, nearest to Santa Fé, attacking the Spanish town, which was promptly isolated. The Tano pueblos of the Galisteo Valley and the Pecos pueblos closed the ring about Santa Fé. The pueblos of the Jémez Valley and the Keresan pueblos, Santo Domingo, San Felipe, Santa Ana, Zía, Cochiti in the Río Grande Valley, also Acoma to the west, took part, as did the Tiguas of Río Abajo, about and above the later site of Albuquerque. The slaughter was greatest about Sandía, where seventeen estancias were destroyed. All aliens were killed in the Zuñi basin as were the missionaries among the Hopi. From Taos to Isleta all Spanish estates were destroyed and their people driven out or killed, as were most of the missionaries.

The refugees gathered at Isleta among the Piros who had remained peaceful. It was estimated that there were about fifteen hundred refugees, a hundred twenty people capable of bearing arms, four hundred had been killed. The flight continued south to El Paso, where a mission among the Manso had been founded in 1659. Those besieged in Santa Fé were told to get out and be granted their lives, or to remain and be killed, according to Sigüenza y Góngora (of whom more below). By his account eighty did so, were helped on their way by Indians of Isleta, and joined the other refugees at El Paso. Sigüenza wrote that the churches were profaned and that hatred of the Spanish extended to destroying the poultry, sheep, the Castilian fruit trees, and even uprooting the wheat.

By Hackett's resume there were at that time about sixteen thousand Christian Indians in New Mexico and about two thousand eight hundred of Spanish and mixed blood, most of these on stock ranches and farms.

Attempts were made to retake the country, setting out from El Paso and getting beyond the Keresan pueblos as far as the ruined mission of San Buenaventura de Cochiti before being stopped 'by Indian treason' and forced to return to El Paso. The Piros not having joined the revolt were evacuated from Isleta and Senecú to resettle in missions below El Paso. Two more missions of refugees from the north were added, one at the Manso mission and one at the monastery of Guadelupe del Paso. For the duration of the revolt the vicinity of El Paso was the northern outpost of Spanish control.

The reconquest of New Mexico was celebrated by Sigüenza y Góngora under the title of *Mercurio Volante*, written and printed in 1693, under commission from the Viceroy Conde de Galve.[13] It told of a succession of Spanish captains who made expeditions from El Paso up the Río Grande, one in 1689 getting up the Jémez Valley as far as Zía, which was destroyed, six hundred rebels dying, many being burned in their houses. In the summer and fall of 1692 Governor Diego de Vargas marched out of El

13. Carlos de Sigüenza y Góngora, *Mercurio volante con la noticia de la recuperación de las provincias de Nuevo México . . .* (Antwerp, 1693).

Paso to begin the reconquest of New Mexico. Sigüenza told of the course of the expedition through the Río Grande pueblos, the fields in standing corn, the people fleeing to the hills, and on to Santa Fé, its walls crowded with Indians who surrendered without a fight, their water supply having been cut off. From there a company went across the mountains to the Pueblo of Pecos whose two thousand families fled but soon offered their obedience. The pueblos of the upper Río Grande were entered as far as Picuries, all submitting without a fight. In November 1692 troops moved west to Ácoma and Zuñi, the latter found reduced from five pueblos to one by Apache hostility, and so to Moqui (Hopi), entering to the farthest pueblo of Oraibi. The conquest was made, Sigüenza said, without using an ounce of powder or drawing a sword; seventy-four mestizo captives were freed and two thousand two hundred fourteen infants were baptized.

Vargas returned in October 1692 with a party of a hundred soldiers, seventy families, eighteen friars, numerous Indian allies, two thousand horses, a thousand mules, and nine hundred head of livestock.[14] Santa Fé was taken with the loss of only one soldier. Seventy of the principal Indians were executed. The final campaign was in the summer of 1694, after the spring floods of the Río Grande had ended. A raid was made on Taos to collect a store of maize, its people fleeing to the mountains. The rebuilding of missions began, only Picuries, Taos, Ácoma, Zuñi and Moqui (Hopi) remaining uncontrolled. Another Pueblo revolt broke out in 1696 and was sharply put down by Vargas. Lasting peace under Spanish rule was attained in 1697.

The recovery of the north by Vargas also had the objective of mineral discovery.[15] Vargas had been in charge of the supply of quicksilver for the mines of New Spain, needed in the amalgamation of ores by the patio process. The demand was large and was supplied by imports. A Captain de la Huerta addressed a memorial to King Charles II in 1689, offering to restore New Mexico at his own expense if he were given the profit of mines he claimed to have discovered there in a range called Sierra Azul, a range rich in silver. Another locality between Zuñi and Moqui, he wrote, would supply all the quicksilver needed for the mines of New Spain. The Viceroy was asked to investigate the matter as of serious interest to the Crown. The government's concern for a promised new source of quicksilver provided all the incentive needed to send Vargas, appointed Governor the year before, on a new and well equipped expedition. No mines were discovered, however, but a blue mountain remained for years an imaginary mineral treasure of the Colorado Plateau.

The century was a series of disasters for the Pueblos, with a great loss of population. They survived by giving in to mission control yet maintained their languages and much of their cultural identity. The dozen years of freedom during the revolt gave sufficient leeway to recover the strength to retain their identity when New Mexico was retaken. Apaches, including Navajos, took part in the revolt, learned the benefits of predation on the herds of livestock, thrived on the disordered times, and emerged, especially to the east and south, as the increasingly feared enemy of the Spanish. Jumanos, who had not taken part in the revolt, gradually were absorbed into the Apaches, as were other tribes, to form in the eighteenth century a powerful pressure against the north of New Spain.

14. J. Manuel Espinosa, ed. and tr., *First Expedition of Vargas into New Mexico, 1692* (Albuquerque, 1940).
15. Irving A. Leonard, introduction to his translation of *The Mercurio Volante of Don Carlos Sigüenza y Góngora* (Los Angeles, 1932), 31-36.

VII.

Seas and Shores About and Beyond Newfoundland

THE NEW FOUND LANDS

Western Europe of the fifteenth century knew tales of legendary islands to the west, of the Seven Cities of Brasil and Antilia. Portuguese ships searched for the Western Passage to the Orient, English ships followed fishing grounds over seas north and west. The North Atlantic was crossed before and after Columbus sailed on his voyage of discovery, its farther shores thought to be of Asia. By 1500 northern newly found lands west of the ocean began to appear on maps, the one by Juan de la Cosa in 1500 showing a mainland, subsequent ones usually a great island. In 1596 an English company was formed of Adventurers to the New Found Lands.[1]

The attraction was not the new land but the seas, the cod, whales, walrus, and the hope of a passage to the Orient. In the course of the sixteenth century the mainland shores became familiar, from Labrador to Maine, about the great bay that cartographers named Gulf of St. Lawrence, and the large island that has retained the name Newfoundland. Beyond reach and sight of the tides the land remained little known.

GREATEST OF THE ATLANTIC FISHING GROUNDS

The fishing grounds about the northeast headland of North America are a product of the Ice Age. The continental ice deposited its debris widely and deeply. As the ice mass melted the sea level rose hundreds of feet and submerged the lowlands. The present greatly irregular coastline of islands and headlands and reentrants took form about the Gulf of St. Lawrence. Morainic ridges deposited at the front of the ice cap formed submarine banks from the Grand Banks of Newfoundland to George's Bank off Cape Cod (Fig. 8).

The cold Labrador Current on passing the Grand Banks meets the northward flow of warm waters of the Gulf Stream. The Gulf of St. Lawrence receives the fresh water discharge of a large interior, rich in mineral and organic nutrients, part of it carried into the open Atlantic through its two straits. The mingled waters in a diversely modeled basin are one of the world's greatest aquariums.

Shoals along shore and banks at sea are the greater western counterpart of the fishing grounds off northwestern Europe. Ships came to fish the new found western waters late in the fifteenth century. In the course of the sixteenth century these voyages increased

1. Sauer, *Northern Mists*, Chapters 1-4.

Fig. 8. Gulf of St. Lawrence and Environs.

GULF OF ST. LAWRENCE and ENVIRONS

200 KM

C. BONAVISTA
St. John's
Ferryland (Farillon)
C. RACE (C. RAZ)
Placentia Bay
NEWFOUNDLAND
Miquelon Is. (San Pedro)
St. Pierre
Blanc Sablon
Antigosti (Île Assumption)
Bird Rock (I. of Penguins)
Brion I. (Brians)
St. Georges Bay
Magdalen Is. (Ramea)
CABOT STRAIT
ST. LAWRENCE RIVER
GULF OF ST. LAWRENCE
Gaspé Bay
GASPÉ PENINSULA
Île Percée
Chaleur Bay
NOVA SCOTIA
C. BRETON
Canso
C. SABLE
Sable I.
SABLE I. BANK
Saguenay
Tadoussac
Île d'Orleans
Quebec
Trois Rivières
Montreal
St. John
Kennebec
Penobscot
Bay of Fundy (French Bay)

50°
60°
70°

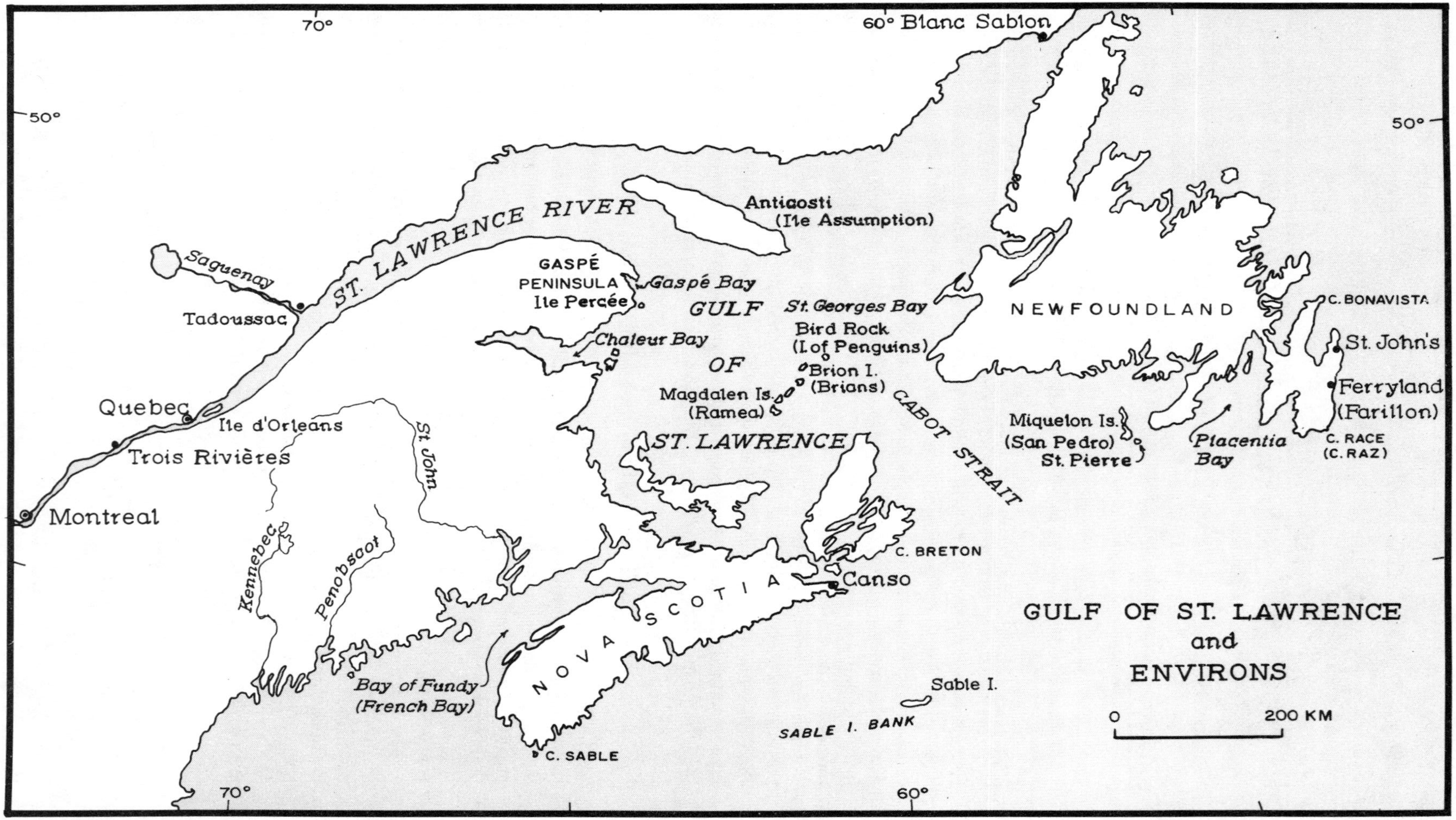

to hundreds of ships and many thousands of men each year, Portuguese from North Portugal and the Azores, Basques from Spanish and French ports of the Bay of Biscay, Bretons from Brittany, French from Normandy, Saintonge, and La Rochelle, and English and Welsh from Bristol Channel. They left their home ports each spring, fished overseas during the summer, and returned home in fall.

The fishery was private enterprise. Merchants of the home ports provided ship and supplies, townsmen made up the crew that did the sailing, fishing, and preparation of the catch. By ancient tradition the seas were free to all to fish, ships of different nationalities usually sharing amicably the harvest of the sea.

The harbor of St. John's on the ocean coast of Newfoundland was a major meeting place of ships of various nations, busy during summer, deserted the rest of the year. Other frequented harbors on the Atlantic were Placentia Bay in Newfoundland and Canso in Nova Scotia. In the Gulf of St. Lawrence ships gathered at St. George's Bay in Newfoundland, at Blanc Sablon at the northern entry to the gulf, and at Île Percée at the tip of Gaspé Peninsula. Numerous place names on the Atlantic, from Labrador, to Cape Bonavista, Cape Race and the Bay of Fundy record that Portuguese were early visitors.

The shoals and banks were the breeding and feeding grounds of prodigious numbers of codfish, prized above herring and mackerel in the trade of Europe. The exploitation began in coastal waters, and is known as dry fishery because the catch was cured to low moisture content, a process that was carried out on land. The fishermen located a suitable cove or beach and set up camp at which the fish were dressed and slowly dried by exposure to air and by smoking.

The ocean coast of Newfoundland, washed by the Labrador Current, is subject to great summer fogs and therefore difficult for dry fishery. To the south the Atlantic coast from Nova Scotia to Maine, sheltered from Arctic waters and open from May through fall, provided good cod fishing and convenient stations on land for curing the catch, also good provision of shellfish, berries, and game.

The Gulf of St. Lawrence, especially its shoal southwestern side, was exploited by dry fishery. Its codfish were reputed to be of better quality and larger size than those of the banks, indicating abundant nutrients brought by streams from the adjacent highlands and the St. Lawrence River. Here the fishermen had the advantage of sunny summers, plenty of wood, sandy strands, and large provision of plant and animal food. Its southern strait (now called Cabot Strait, though neither Cabot is known to have entered it) was open from spring to the end of the fishing season and led to excellent fishing grounds.

The wet fishery developed somewhat later. Larger ships, larger crews, and different equipment were needed to fish the banks at sea. The fishermen lived on shipboard, where the fish were dressed and stored wet packed in salt. Contact with land was occasional and brief, to fill water casks, get wood, raid bird rookeries, or make repairs. The fishers of the Grand Banks made use of harbors on Newfoundland, in particular St. John's, those of Sable Island Bank used Canso and other Atlantic harbors of Nova Scotia.

EXPLOITATION OF MARINE MAMMALS

Basques learned the business of whaling in the Bay of Biscay, where right whales came to overwinter. These were hunted commercially for their blubber which was rendered into train oil for lamps and lubricants, and for their whalebone, the horny plates of baleen through which they strained the plankton on which they fed. Basques followed the right whales north into their Arctic summer waters, developed a whaling ship called the balinger, and learned of their great numbers in the waters about Newfoundland, thus entering also into the Gulf of St. Lawrence. Small whales, porpoises and belugas, also yielded train oil, as did seals and walruses.

Walrus tusks brought a higher price than elephant ivory; their hides were sought for exceptional durability and strength. Like seals they could be surprised ashore and dispatched by clubs, and soon came to be grievously hunted by codders as well as by whalers.

HAKLUYT'S ACCOUNTS OF THE GULF OF ST. LAWRENCE (1591-1597)

Richard Hakluyt published *The Principal Navigations* to promote English trade and colonization and to that end collected letters written by English seamen of their experiences in the Gulf of St. Lawrence.[2]

Thomas James of Bristol told (1591) of taking a St. Malo ship carrying forty tons of walrus train oil, these animals coming by thousands in April, May, and June to the island of Ramea (the Magdalen Islands in the Gulf of St. Lawrence). These 'fish' were very big, had two great teeth, and a hide like *buffe* (buffalo) used as hogsheads to hold the train oil, "which train is very sweet, which if it will make soap the king of Spain may burn some of his Olive trees" (castile soap, made from olive oil). Size and strength of the hides were noted and the tusks as being a foot and more long; these in turn were sold in England to comb and knife makers at twice the price of the best ivory, and were also reputed to be as good as unicorn's horn against poison.

In June 1593, the ship Marigold left Falmouth in Cornwall bound for the island the Bretons called Ramea, carrying two butchers to skin the *morsses* or sea oxen (walrus) that gathered there from April to June, one thousand five hundred having been killed there by one small bark in 1591. They arrived too late at the islands, the Bretons of St. Malo and Basques of St. Jean de Luz having preceded them. They "found a ship of St. Malo three parts freighted with these fishes." The Bretons fled, abandoning a score of men and three shallops, which were taken as prizes. The English, unacquainted with the waters, wandered about between Newfoundland and Cape Breton. Landing on that cape they found ponds and weirs made by natives, with whom there was a brief encounter (an early mention of the Micmac Indians). There were goodly oaks, firs of great height, lots of berries, aromatic herbs good for scurvy, also very rank grass. They saw a number of ships sailing to southwest of Cape Breton and judged them to be Christians trading in that direction. Cod were taken and hung to dry in the air; "they also lay them upon rafts and hurdles and make a smoke under them." The voyage continued southwest (along the Atlantic coast), seeing "exceeding great store of seals, and abundance of porpoises," also whales and cod.

2. Richard Hakluyt, *The Principal Navigations* (London, 1927-1928), VI, 91-115; and IX, 368-373.

Hakluyt commented that these two accounts and the two following "are the first, for aught that hitherto is come to my knowledge, of our own Nation, that have conducted English ships so far within this gulf of St. Lawrence, and have brought us true relation of the manifold gain which the French, Bretons, Basques and Biscaynes [Castilians of Asturias] do yearly return from said parts; while we this long time have stood still and have been idle lookers on." (English ships had long engaged in the banks fisheries but were only beginning to learn about the gulf.)

The next report was by Rice Jones in 1594 and concerned the voyage of the Grace of Bristol. The course was by way of San Pedro (St. Pierre and Miquélon Islands) where they found two ships of Sibiburo (Basques) fishing for cod and stopped to do the same. Continuing west through the strait into the gulf to Bay St. George (southwest Newfoundland) they "found wrecks of two great Biscayne [Basque] ships, which had been cast away three years before: where we had some seven or eight hundred whale fins" (plates of baleen), the train oil having leaked out of the casks. "Here we found the houses of the Savages, made of fir trees bound together in the top and set round like a dovehouse and covered with bark," also a dish of sewn bark, a wooden spoon, etc., and numerous tracks of men, women, and children. (This first notice of Micmacs in Newfoundland will be referred to later.) "Then being informed, that the whales which are deadly wounded in the Grand Bay, and yet escape the fisher for a time are wont usually to shoot themselves on shore on the Isle of Assumption [Anticosti], which lies in the very mouth of the great river that runs up to Canada," they went there, found no whales but "wonderful fair and great codfish, exceeding fair great woods of tall fir trees and heard and saw store of land and sea fowls." They turned back by way of the Island of Penguin (Bird Rocks off the Magdalen Islands) and passed through the southern strait to the Bay of Placentia (southeast Newfoundland). Here there were threescore Basque codfishing ships "of whom we were very well used." being given two pinnaces and a ship's boat. Arriving at Farillon (Ferryland) on the Atlantic coast of Newfoundland they met with twenty-two English sails and made up their cargo of cod.

Charles Leigh of London made a voyage into the Gulf of St. Lawrence in 1597. On June 4 "a great island of ice" was passed south of Cape Raz (Cape Race) and on June 12 the ship anchored north of Cape Breton where cod, "larger and better fish" than those off Newfoundland were caught as fast as they could be hauled aboard. On June 14 they came to the two bird islands (Bird Rocks) "where there were such abundance of birds as is almost incredible to report . . . great stores of morses or sea oxen, which were asleep upon the rocks, but when we approached near unto them with our boat they cast themselves into the sea and pursued us with such fury as that we were glad to flee from them." Another passage has "the birds sit there as thick as stones lie in a paved street." At Brians (Brion) Island there was great fishing. At Ramea (Magdalen) they found two ships from St. Malo and two Basque ships. A hassle ensued, starting with a demand on the Basques to prove that they were not subject to be taken as fair prizes. The quarrel between English on one side, French, Basques, and Indians on the other, continued about Cape Breton and beyond. Near Canso (Nova Scotia) Leigh noted "the greatest multitude of lobsters that we ever heard of, for we caught at one haul with a little draw net above a hundred and forty."

Hakluyt published the letters to show that the Gulf of St. Lawrence was rich in resources that were turned to profit by other nations. A few English ships had begun to venture there and brought back accounts that he hoped would result in English participation or control. Bretons and Basques knew the proper places to take codfish and walrus, the latter strange to English eyes and mistaken as to habits. Basque ships of great size hunted whales in the gulf, rendering train oil and taking baleen, thereby identified as right whales. These letters fill a gap in information about the gulf in the last decade of the sixteenth century and also give one of the first English notices of Cape Breton and the Atlantic coast of Nova Scotia. There is no mention of furs or of trade with Indians.

FISHING SHIPS ENGAGE IN THE FUR TRADE

The dry cod fishery was carried on all about the shores of the Gulf of St. Lawrence and on the Atlantic coast from Nova Scotia to Maine, the ships accustomed to return season after season to the same landing places and camps. Natives visited the fishing camps and learned that the visitors had things unknown and desirable, items of metal, cloth, brandy, and that all these items could be had in exchange for dressed pelts. Fishermen added furs as a side line; Indians, awaiting the return of ships the next year, took and dressed additional pelts in winter for trade in the summer ahead.

Indian participation in European commerce developed rapidly. A Basque trading ship is of record in the Bay of Fundy as of about 1522. Verrazzano in 1524 found Indians of the coast of Maine prepared to trade. In 1534 Cartier exploring Chaleur Bay in the west of the Gulf of St. Lawrence as a possible passage to China, was greeted by Indians offering pelts for trade.[3]

The suppliers of pelts were Algonquian tribes, inhabitants of a land of long, cold winters and of many streams and lakes, prime habitat of beaver, otter, marten, fisher, and mink. The natives were experts at trapping and dressing pelts and increased their take of fur-bearing animals to meet the growing demand by Europeans. Micmacs, known to the French as Souriquois, inhabited Nova Scotia and were in familiar relations with ships from French ports. Late in the century they expanded to occupy southern Newfoundland.[4]

The northern home ports of the dry cod fishery, Norman, Breton, and Rochellais, became depositories of furs that found their largest market in Paris, by then already a principal center of high life and fashion.

FREE COMMERCE OR COLONY

States are territorial bodies defined by the land and the waters they enclose. European nations laid claim to lands in the New World by formal acts of possession ashore. They began with Columbus in the West Indies and were followed on the north coasts by John Cabot in English service and the Portuguese brothers Corte-Real. Maps of the early sixteenth century recognized such claims by planting national flags along the shores. The open seas were not the property of states but remained free to peaceful

3. Sauer, *Sixteenth Century North America*, 50, 61, 80.

4. As shown by the description of Hakluyt above. Hakluyt did not name them or know who the "savages" told of by Rice Jones were. These also stole boats of the Englishmen and aided French and Basques against the English, by further account of Hakluyt. They have since continued to live on both sides of Cabot Strait.

commerce and fishing; in the northern part of the Atlantic Ocean they were made use of by private shipping of diverse nationalities.

The wet cod fishery of the banks was carried on mainly by English, Portuguese, and Spanish ships, Basque ships engaging mainly in whaling.[5] The dry cod fishery of the Gulf of St. Lawrence was for the most part conducted by ships from France, Basque whalers also entering the gulf. The Atlantic coast from Nova Scotia south to Maine was used by dry cod fishers of France and visited by Basque whaling ships.

The crews left home in spring, took a month or so to cross the sea, had four months or more to fish, and were back home by winter. They did so year after year, generation after generation, earning a livelihood that gave support to family and townsfolk and experience of distant localities and strange people. It was an accustomed and satisfying way of life, carried on by communities according to their own manner and counsel.

The French Crown desired possessions in the New World that would bring profit and prestige such as Spain and Portugal already enjoyed. Francis I laid claim to prior rights of discovery by Bretons before Columbus. (Breton fishermen gave name to Cape Breton early, the date unknown.) Verrazzano and Cartier were sent on voyages of exploration by Francis, followed by the unsuccessful attempts in 1541-1543 to found a colony at Quebec, its failure due to the long hard winters.

The next French colonies were attempted in warm lands, at Rio de Janeiro (1555-1560), driven out by the Portuguese, and in Florida (1562-1565), destroyed by the Spanish.

Interest in a northern colony revived during the reign of Henry III (1574-1589). At the time Humphrey Gilbert, Martin Frobisher, Sir Walter Raleigh, and John Davis were engaged in English exploration and colonization from Davis Strait to Newfoundland and Virginia. In 1577 and 1588 the French Crown gave monopoly rights to individuals to colonize in and about "the New Lands and Canada," including mines and the fur trade. Merchants of St. Malo and the Estates of Brittany protested, asserting their traditional rights to freedom of trade and commerce. "The problem of rivalry between crown and merchants was clearly posed . . . In this first conflict the partisans of free trade won . . . Either freedom of commerce for all and no colony, or exclusive monopoly and colonization." The colonial grants were not put into effect.[6]

In 1598 Henry IV appointed the Marquis de la Roche Lieutenant General of New France, including Canada (the lower St. Lawrence Valley), Hochelaga (the upper valley), Terres-neuves (the lands about the Gulf of St. Lawrence), the river of Grand Baye (the salt sound of St. Lawrence River), Norumbega (New England), and lands adjacent not inhabited by subjects of a Christian prince. La Roche was to grant estates under feudal tenure, the holders to defend the colony. The insignificant result was the landing of fifty men on Sable Island, from which eleven survivors were brought back to France in 1603.

At the end of the sixteenth century New France was a nominal title. The French dry cod fishers continued to make summer camp on the beaches and to trade with the natives for furs.

5. Anthony Parkhurst reporting to Hakluyt in 1578. Cited in Sauer, *Sixteenth Century North America*, 240-241.

6. Marcel Trudel, *Histoire de la Nouvelle France* (Montreal, 1963-1966), I, Chapters 5 and 6.

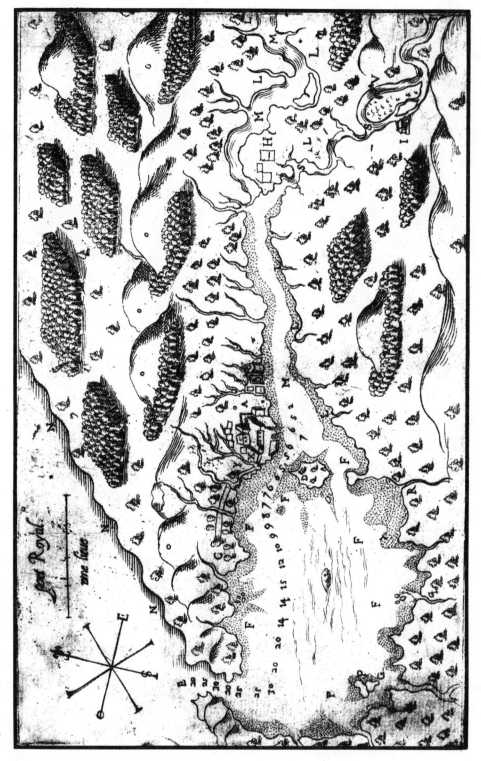

Fig. 9. Map of Port Royal.

VIII.

France Seeks a Location for a Colony

DE MONTS' CONCESSION OF ACADIA

In 1603 the French Crown appointed the Sieur de Monts Lieutenant-General of L'Acadie, with authority over all the lands situated from the forty-sixth to the fortieth parallels, which would mean from Cape Breton to Long Island, with monopoly of trade with the Indians. The concession did not affect the sea fishing rights, which continued as they had been, free to all.[1]

The name Acadie (Acadia) has been attributed to Verrazzano. Sailing north along our middle Atlantic coast in the spring of 1524, he praised the green land and its simple and happy inhabitants as another Arcadia, map makers then applying the name to the coast north of Florida. By another interpretation Algonquian place names ending in 'acadie' (such as Passamaquoddy) assonant with Arcadie, gave rise to the official name. The Levasseur map of 1601 showed a *Coste de Cadie*.[2]

CHAMPLAIN HEARS OF MINES ON THE COAST OF ACADIA

In 1603 Samuel de Champlain took passage on a ship trading to Tadoussac, his purpose to know the land of which he had read in the *Cosmographie* of Jean Alphonse, pilot of the attempted settlement of Canada sixty years earlier.[3] The result of the summer's experience was *Des Sauvages*, published at the end of the year, first of the accounts of New France Champlain wrote during the thirty years following.[4]

From Tadoussac, a summer-time trading port, Champlain made an excursion. He went up the St. Lawrence River and later visited Gaspé Bay and adjacent Île Percée, a rendez-vous of fishing and trading ships.

At Île Percée he met a trader from St. Malo, named Prévert, who told of having been taken by Indians to a mine located several score leagues to the south:

> It is a very high mountain, jutting out somewhat into the sea, and glitters brightly in the sunlight; it contains a large quantity of verdigris which issues out of the said copper mine. He said that at the foot of this mountain at low water there were quantities of pieces of copper, such as he showed us, which fall from the top of the mountain. Some three or four leagues farther along the coast of Arcadia [*sic*], there is another mine, and a small river which

1. Trudel, II, especially 9-15.

2. Trudel, I, 62-63; and II, 20. Andrew H. Clark, *Acadia. The Geography of Nova Scotia to 1760* (Madison, 1968), 71n.

3. Sauer, *Sixteenth Century North America*, 97-104.

4. *The Works of Samuel de Champlain*, ed. H. P. Biggar, Publications of the Champlain Society (Toronto, 1922-1936), I, 83-192 (ed. and tr. H. H. Langton).

extends some little way inland, towards the south, where there is a mountain of black pigment, with which the savages paint themselves.

Prévert's story told of other metals, one of which Champlain thought might be silver. Mines, it said, extended along this coast of Arcadia (*sic*) for a hundred leagues and more, into a country of hostile savages. Champlain recorded Prévert's detailed description of the southern land and coast, and judged that the proper approach to the ore bodies would be by sailing from France to Cape Breton and then south along the Atlantic coast.[5]

DE MONTS' VOYAGE IN SEARCH OF THE REPUTED MINES (1604)

De Monts' concession gave him the choice of a large coast on which to locate his colony. Champlain's report of Prévert's story resulted in De Monts' exploration of the Atlantic coast south of the Gulf of St. Lawrence. In the spring of 1604 De Monts sailed from France with two ships, bearing sundry gentry, two master miners, and Champlain to make charts and keep a journal (which he published as *Les Voyages* . . . in 1613).[6]

The first landfall was at Canso harbor, where four Basque ships and a French ship were seized for trespass on territory of the concession. Champlain was sent ahead by pinnace to survey the coast for suitable ports, taking one of the miners along to look for ore.

Champlain followed the coast to Cape Sable and turned into French Bay (Bay of Fundy) as far as St. Mary's Bay, which was named by him. Notes were taken of shorelines, channel, anchorage, and tides, the latter increasing as they went farther into the bay. Water fowl were present in great numbers. At one stop a barrel of cormorant eggs was gathered, at another they supplied themselves with gannets, clubbed on their nests. A score of different water and shore birds were identified as in an abundance "that no one would believe possible unless he had seen it." In an embayment north of Cape Sable there was excellent fishing of cod and in the high tidal range of St. Mary's Bay the great abundance of mussels and clams was noted. On land there were fine hardwood trees, with occasional pines and firs, the soil appearing suitable for cultivation. The miner reported finding a silver mine and nearby an iron mine (on St. Mary's Bay). This was the first sketch of the physical geography of Nova Scotia and its biota, good observations except for the miner's findings.

Hearing the good report by Champlain De Monts followed, getting to St. Mary's Bay in the latter part of June, and from there on Champlain wrote, "to one of the finest Harbors I had seen on all these coasts, where some thousands of vessels could lie in safety . . . which I named Port Royal [Annapolis Royal]." He made a chart (Fig. 9) and described the harbor "as most suitable and pleasant for a settlement."

Following Prévert's report that the sea was at the foot of the mountain of ore, "we left to go farther into French Bay to see whether we could find the copper that had been discovered the year before." They found that the inner bay was divided into two arms but located no mountain of ore. Crossing to the far side of the bay they came "to the

5. Champlain, *Works*, I, 180-185.

6. Champlain, *Works*, 204-469 (ed. and tr. W. F. Ganong); and II (tr. J. Squair). Volume II reproduces sixteen of his charts with parallel modern charts showing the competence of Champlain's surveys. Vegetation, animals, and Indians were added according to the engraver's taste.

mouth of one of the largest and deepest rivers we had yet seen, which we named the river Saint John," arriving there on the day of that saint (June 24). The St. John River, it was learned, served as a canoe route by which natives went north to the St. Lawrence and along it, they told, were prairies and woods of oaks, beech, nut trees, and grape vines, the first notice of the nature of the land of New Brunswick.

Passing by a number of islands they continued their course southwest to the mouth of the river of the Etchemins, as the natives called themselves. (This Algonquian tribe was known to the French thereafter by that name. When the English came to Maine and New Brunswick they called them Malecites.) De Monts named the river and an island in its mouth Ste. Croix (now St. Croix, marking the boundary between Maine and New Brunswick).

FIRST SETTLEMENT, MORE EXPLORATION, AND A HARD WINTER

The island appeared to be well suited for settlement. "This place we considered the best we had seen, both on account of its situation, the fine country, and the communication we expected to have with the savages of these coasts and the interior." Fish entered the river in such numbers that ships might load them for return cargoes. Gardens were cleared and planted and a mill was built to grind the wheat they expected to harvest the following year. Living quarters were constructed "though mosquitoes (which are little flies) gave us great annoyance," some of the workmen bitten so badly that they could hardly see.

Champlain was sent back to explore the bay for the reputed copper mine, and brought back samples that the miner thought might be profitable ore.

At the beginning of September Champlain was sent on to examine the coast ahead. He named a large island, its mountains topped with bare rock, Mount Desert Island. Farther on Indians, fishing and hunting in canoes, guided the party to their homes on the river Peimtegouet (in later French spelling, Pentagouet, the English Penobscot). Champlain thought it might be "the one several pilots and historians called Norumbega." He described bay and river in attentive detail and found the land attractive, having stands of oaks that appeared as though planted for pleasure (park-like open growth). The natives came to visit this coast in summer to fish and hunt. Their cabins were covered with bark and built like those of the Souriquois (Micmacs of Nova Scotia). The French party was welcomed with singing, dancing, and leaping and by exchange of pledges of friendship. The voyage continued almost to the river Quinnibequy (Kennebec), still the land of the Etchemins. Bad weather caused the return to Ste. Croix after a month, Champlain offering observations, "which are not the marvels reported by some."

At Ste. Croix "winter surprised us sooner than we had expected." The first snow fell on October 6. Ice drifted down river early in December. The cold was greater than in France, was continuous, and lasted into April, with snow-drifts three to four feet deep. All beverages were frozen solid, except the fortified Spanish wine; cider was served by the pound. "We ate only salt meat and legumes during the winter, which engendered bad blood."[7] In March Indians brought fresh meat, Champlain mentioning that it

7. The Jesuit Pierre Biard, who came to Acadia in 1611, had another version: "Of all Sieur de Monts' people who wintered first at Ste. Croix, only eleven remained well. These were a jolly company of hunters, who preferred rabbit hunting to the air of the fireside; skating on the ponds to turning over lazily in bed; making snowballs to bring down game to sitting around the fire talking about Paris and its good cooks." (Champlain, *Works*, II, 305n.)

bettered the sickness. When snow was deep the Indians had good hunting on snow-shoes, in particular of moose, at other times they too might lack food. Later Champlain learned that the winter sickness was scurvy.

De Monts was about to send for help to take the survivors back to France when ships arrived in June 1605, bringing plentiful supplies, enabling the search to go on for mines, and allowing them additional time to find a place to settle.

SEARCH TO THE SOUTH FOR A PLACE TO SETTLE

"The Sieur de Monts decided to go in search of a more suitable site for a settlement and one where the climate was milder," and left Ste. Croix June 18, 1605, in a pinnace of fifteen tons and about thirty persons, including an Indian couple, Champlain recording the six weeks' reconnaissance of the coast of New England.

An unknown coast was entered at the Kennebec River, the land there noted as of little promise, of small oak trees and covered with stones (glacial boulders), the waters offering good fishing. Indians in canoes were engaged in taking water fowl, in moult at the time and unable to fly (swans and Canada geese).

At the next bay and river, called Chouacouet (Saco) they came to a better land and another people. "The Sieur de Monts visited an island, very beautiful in what it has, with fine oaks and nut trees, cleared land, and many vines that bear good grapes in season, the first we had seen on all these coasts since Cap le Have [southern Nova Scotia]. We named it the isle of Baccus." (Identified as Richmond Island in a footnote by Ganong.) As they landed on the mainland they were met by a large number of dancing Indians, Almouchiquois, differing in speech from those known before (another Algonquian tribe). "They work and cultivate the land, which we had not seen previously. Instead of plows, they have an instrument of very hard wood, made in the shape of a spade." A visit to their fields in the valley followed:

> We saw their grain, which is Indian corn. This they grow in gardens, sowing three or four grains in one spot, afterwards heaping a quantity of earth with a *signoc* [carapace of horseshoe crab]. Then at a distance of three feet they do the same, and thus go on. Among the corn in each mound they plant three or four beans of Brazil, that come in different colors. As they grow they wind about the corn that grows to a height of five to six feet; and they keep the field very clean of weeds. We saw there a lot of squashes, pumpkins, and tobacco [*citrouilles, courges, petum*], likewise cultivated. The Indian corn we saw there was two feet high at the time. The beans were beginning to bloom as were the squashes and pumpkins. They sow their corn in May and harvest it in September.

This is the earliest account of Indian farming in New England. Except for the use of crab carapaces to mound the earth it would apply as well to other Indians of the eastern woodlands. The corn of moderate height and short season suggests flint corn. The beans of different colors and climbing habit were *Phaseolus vulgaris*, perhaps navy beans, recognized as being like those known from Brazil and as cultivated in France. The name *petum* (petun) for tobacco had been learned by the French from the Tupi Indians of Brazil, and was the usual French term for tobacco wherever they found it cultivated in North America. This was *Nicotiana rustica*, of South American origin, strong in nicotine and potent, smoked in the ceremonial peace pipe. The two names for cucurbits suggest different kinds of fruits, probably varieties of *Cucurbita pepo*, squashes and pumpkins in common cultivation by the Indian farmers of the eastern woodlands.

At Saco they found permanent homes, cultivated fields, and fine oak, beech, and elm trees of very open growth.

> The Indians live permanently here, and have a large cabin surrounded by palisades made of rather large trees ranged one by another to which they retire when their enemies come to make war against them. They cover their cabins with oak bark. This place is very pleasant and as agreeable as one may see anywhere.

They had come to a land of sedentary farmers, living in palisaded villages, surrounded by cultivated fields and park lands.

They sailed on south July 12, along a largely sandy coast with bushes of red currants, redwinged blackbirds, and countless pigeons, of which they took a good number. As they neared the Cape of Islands (Cape Ann) Indians approached in a canoe, then turned to a beach where they started to dance, which they did with more vigor after they were given presents.

> After I had drawn for them with charcoal the bay and the island cape where we were, they drew for me with the same crayon another bay which they represented as quite large. On it they placed six pebbles at equal intervals, giving me to understand that each indicated a chief and tribe. They then drew on that bay a river we had passed, quite long and with shoals [Merrimac].

As far as Cape Ann the canoes had been made of birch bark. Beyond they were dugouts, which Champlain thought laborious to make and likely to capsize, adding a description of the manner of charring and scraping them to the desired shape. All along the coast they saw much land sown to Indian corn. The features the Indians had drawn on the map were recognized as they coasted along the bay (Massachusetts Bay), continuing to be met by Indians in number coming in canoes from islands and mainland. Smoke signals invited them to land, which they did at a cape (north of Plymouth) and were greeted by about fifteen canoes, some filled with natives, exhibiting great signs of joy.

> Those we sent to them brought us little squashes, fist sized, which we ate as salad like cucumbers, and are very good, also *pourpié* [purslane] that grows abundantly among the Indian corn, and of which they take no more account than of weeds. We saw there a great many small huts, situated in the fields of their Indian corn.

Several canoes were fishing for cod and other fish, plentiful there and taken by hooks made of a piece of wood to which a bone shaped like a harpoon was attached, the whole forming a small crook and tied to a line made of tree bark.

The pinnace then crossed the bay to double a cape they called White Cape on account of its sand dunes (Cape Cod), the cape forming a southward bending hook. As seen from the ocean side the coast had conspicuous sand banks. They found a harbor with shoal and narrow entry but commodious within, huts round about it. They named it Malebarre because of the bad bar (Nauset Harbor). Fields were planted to corn in the manner previously described. Some corn was in flower and stood five and a half feet tall. Again there were beans of Brazil, squashes of various sizes, and petun tobacco. Roots having the taste of artichoke were cultivated, Champlain thus adding the tuberous sunflower (*Helianthus tuberosus*) to the list of field crops. (It was commonly grown in Indian farming of the Eastern Woodlands and was known to the English as Jerusalem artichoke.)

There were also some fields not in cultivation while they were being left to rest. The woods are full of oaks, nut-trees, and very fine cypresses, which are of reddish color and have a very pleasant smell [red cedar, *Juniperus virginiana*]. When they wish to plant they set fire to the herbage and then work the ground with their wooden spades. Their cabins are round, covered with heavy thatch made of reeds, and on top there is a hole in the middle, of about a foot and a half, through which the smoke of their fire comes out.

Looking for a place to settle where the winters were less severe, the French heard that the harbor never froze and that snow fell to no more than a depth of a foot.[8]

In review Champlain summarized the condition of the natives south of Cape Ann. They wore no skins or furs, except rarely, painted their faces red, black, and yellow, and used spears, clubs, bows and arrows. They were great thieves and if they were unable to use their hands to steal did so with their feet, yet he thought that if they had things to barter they would not resort to thievery. Corn was crushed in wooden mortars, baked into cakes, or boiled in earthen pots. The horseshoe crab, the point of its tail used to tip arrows, was described. Champlain ended with a comparison of the local wild turkey with the domestic bird called *coq d'inde* in France (introduced from Mexico, smaller and lacking the bronze color).

The Indians on all these coasts where we were, say that other birds come when their corn is ripe, which are very big; and they imitated their cry for us like that of the coq d'Inde. They showed us their feathers at several places, with which they feather their arrows and which they put on their heads for show. Also a kind of hair the birds have under the throat, as do ours in France, and they say that a red crest falls over their beak. They represented them to be as large as a bustard, which is a kind of goose [Canada goose], having the tail longer and twice as wide as our turkeys . . . They are good to eat. The savages say that they come in flocks in summer and at the beginning of winter leave for warmer places. [A good description except for the last remark. The turkeys left the Indian fields for the woods after the corn was harvested.]

The return voyage from Malebarre began July 25. They were back at Ste. Croix August 3, 1605, making a stop at Saco and again at the mouth of the Kennebec, where they traded for a few furs and were told that men of a fishing ship had killed five natives under cover of friendship, the description indicating Englishmen.

This was a remarkable six weeks' reconnaissance extending the whole length of the east coast of New England. The report is earlier than English accounts and preceded the pestilence that shortly wasted the Indian population about Massachusetts Bay. The Indians were friendly and from Saco south were sedentary, agricultural, and numerous. The vegetation and the crops promised shorter and milder winters. At Malebarre they were told that the harbor remained open year round. The question was opened whether settlement of Acadia should not begin somewhere to the south.

SETTLEMENT AT PORT ROYAL

De Monts decided to move for the coming winter from Ste. Croix across the Bay of Fundy to the better location at Port Royal, where there was a superior harbor, diversity of resources, and a most amiable chief and tribe. Port Royal would suit as well in the search for mines, still a major objective. The buildings at Ste. Croix were taken down,

---

8. The only casualty happened here. A sailor had gone to fetch water in an iron kettle and was robbed of it and killed in the ensuing scuffle. The local people blamed outsiders and the French accepted the explanation.

the lumber ferried across the bay to build a rectangular compound of living quarters, warehouse, kitchen and forge. Champlain was one of forty Frenchmen who stayed, built quarters, and made gardens. He added that he built a pleasure garden and a fish pond for himself.

De Monts returned to France in the fall of 1605 to report to the King and the shareholders on the prospects of the grant. He took along as exhibits a bark canoe colored red, a live moose calf, a caribou (first mention of that name?), the horns of a moose of extraordinary size, a muskrat, three horseshoe crabs, a live hummingbird, heads and feathers of birds, Indian artifacts, and drawings of natives and of birds.[9]

Again there was scurvy during the winter, but less severe than in the previous one, the winter being mild and fresh meat in good supply by Indian neighbors. In the spring of 1606 two ineffective attempts were made to renew exploration to the south. De Monts' promise to send a ship from France not fulfilled, the Frenchmen started home late in July. As they rounded Cape Sable they met the relief ship with supplies and new personnel and all went back to Port Royal.[10]

END OF INTEREST IN THE SOUTH

The last voyage south set out from Port Royal September 5, 1606, Poutrincourt in charge, Champlain again reporting and continuing to draw charts. At the abandoned site of Ste. Croix they found that wheat and pot herbs sown the year before had survived the winter. At Saco (September 21) the corn harvest was completed and they were provided with corn, squashes, and beans. At the Cape of Islands (Cape Ann) Champlain remembered that on the prior voyage he had seen from afar and sketched a harbor (Gloucester Harbor). It was entered, mapped in careful detail, and named Beau-port, in appreciation of its beauty.

> We saw some very fine grapes which were ripe, peas of Brazil, pumpkins, squashes, and some good roots with a flavor like that of *cardes* which the Indians cultivate. They gave us a number of these in exchange for small trifles. They had already completed their harvest. We saw two hundred Indians in this place, which is very agreeable, and here there are many nut trees, cypress, sassafras, oak, ash, and beech, very fine.

The peas of Brazil perhaps were the small navy beans that later were a staple of New England cooking. *Cardes* were the Jerusalem artichoke he had noted before on Cape Cod. Sassafras, here near its northern limit, was known to European medicine from the time of French Florida.

> Some of the land is cleared, and they were constantly clearing more, in the following fashion. They cut down the trees at a height of three feet from the ground; then they burn the branches on the trunk and sow their corn among the cut timber, and in the course of time remove the roots. There are also good prairies on which cattle in number can be supported.

From the beautiful port of Gloucester they sailed on the first of October to leeward of White Cape (Cape Cod) and anchored at a port (Wellfleet) of many oysters, shellfish they had not encountered before. After doubling the cape they came to the former

9. Trudel, II, 50.

10. De Monts granted Port Royal to the Sieur de Poutrincourt in 1604 as seigneurie. The latter returned to take charge, De Monts remaining in France.

landing (Nauset) to be welcomed by a host of natives, singing and dancing. Continuing south into new waters, where there were many shoals (Nantucket Sound), they located a shallow harbor on the mainland with a settlement of Indians 'much given to agriculture'.

> They make holes in the sand on the side of hills, more or less six feet deep, and take their corn and other seed, placed in large grass sacks, which they drop into the holes, and cover them with about three or four feet of sand, to use at their need. It keeps thus as well as it would in our granaries. [Years later the Pilgrims observed the same manner of pit storage.]

These people were good fishermen and tillers of the soil rather than hunters.

> Their lodgings are separated one from another according to the land each can occupy; they are large, circular, covered with matting of grass or leaves of Indian corn, furnished only with a bed or two, raised a foot above the floor, made of small branches laid one against another, on which is a thick mat of reeds, and on this they sleep. They have many fleas in summer.

More than a week was spent looking over the country about Nantucket Sound to determine whether this was the place to lay 'the foundations of a state'. The country appeared attractive, with a scattering of many huts, abundance of fish, shellfish, and game, the drawback being the shoals.

They stayed over-long as they roamed about inland. The natives became alarmed, took down their huts, and moved families and belongings into the woods. An attack followed, a new experience to the French. Snow was beginning to fall, provisions were running short, and they turned back from their farthest landing, which they called Misfortune Port, to reach Port Royal in mid-November.

Champlain had little more to add. Search continued for mines about the head of the Bay of Fundy, at present called Minas Basin. Champlain finished charting the coast from Cape Breton to Nantucket Sound, and wrote its geography, physical and cultural. The book was published in 1613 after he had founded Quebec.

LESCARBOT'S HISTORY OF NEW FRANCE

The newcomers of 1606 included Marc Lescarbot, lawyer and man of letters, who wanted "to know the land with his own eyes and flee a corrupt world." He lived at Port Royal until it was evacuated in 1607 and got beyond it only as far as Ste. Croix across the bay. His *History of New France* was first printed in 1609.[11] Of its six books, Book IV deals with the voyages of De Monts and Poutrincourt, that is with Acadia, Book VI with the life of Indians as compared with that of Ancient times in Europe.[12] Lescarbot's text was an exercise in belles-lettres, attentive observation, and innovating colonization.

New France was a land of promise. Its wood cleared and the land put under cultivation; the land would grow all the crops of France, as had already been demonstrated by his experience. The poor people of France would find there a place to live in comfort. Naval stores, metals, and furs awaited commercial exploitation.[13]

11. Marc Lescarbot, *Histoire de la Nouvelle France* (Paris, 1609).

12. The references cited herein are to the three volume reprint, *History of New France*, tr. W. L. Grant, with reprint of 3rd. French edition, Paris, 1618, Publications of the Champlain Society, I, VII, XI (Toronto, 1907-1914). The second volume of this edition contains Book IV of the original; the third volume, Book VI.

13. Trudel, II, 78-79.

The voyage to Acadia is described beginning with the departure from New Rochelle on May 13, 1606.[14] On June 18 "we found for the space of three days the water of the sea quite warm, and our wine in the hold was the same, though the air was no warmer than before" (crossing the Gulf Stream). On June 21 they were "surrounded with cold fog, and the sea water extremely cold." (They had passed into the cold Labrador current.) On July 7 they sighted a high coast (Nova Scotia); a heavy fog coming on that lasted for a week delayed their landing at the bay of Canso. On July 15 he noted "two long boats coming straight towards us with sails all set, one manned by savages, who had a moose painted on their sail, the other by Frenchmen from St. Malo." (At Canso, long a meeting place of cod fishers, Indians had adopted European use of sails.) The French fishermen made complaint that "Basques, contrary to the King's prohibition, had bartered with the savages and carried off more than six thousand beaver pelts." Beyond Canso they made stops along the coast, Lescarbot noting plants including calamus (sweet flag) and angelica. Port Royal was reached July 27.

While Poutrincourt and Champlain were on southern exploration, Lescarbot told of life at Port Royal, of the planting of gardens, and the daily assignment of someone to provide game, such as water fowl. The daily ration of a pint and a half of wine per person was reduced to a pint. An Etchemin chief from the river St. John came to visit, and also a Souriquois chief from La Have (south coast of Nova Scotia). "They had much merchandise, which they came to sell—to wit, kettles, large, medium, and small, hatchets, knives, dresses, capes, red jackets, peas, beans, biscuits, etc." (Indian chiefs had gone into business as merchants of French goods, procured apparently from illicit trading ships.)

The winter of 1606-1607 brought only minor affliction of scurvy, which occurred in February and March. Social activity included a fortnightly dining club, the *Ordre de bon temps*, for which the steward of the occasion provided the fare, "no meat so tender as moose or so delicate as beavers' tail, at times a half dozen sturgeons."

LESCARBOT ON INDIAN WAYS AND FRENCH CONTACTS

The final book VI considered Indian ways and the results of their contact with the French.[15] His best information was of the Souriquois (Micmacs) who lived about Port Royal. The Etchemins, across the Bay of Fundy, came occasionally to visit. The Almouchiquois, farther south, he knew only by reports.

The Almouchiquois were good farmers. They manured their plantings with shells (shellfish and fish?). Because the green corn was much liked by wild animals they kept watch in fields during its growth. The ripe corn was stored in pits.[16] They cultivated a very good root, which "when planted multiplies as it were out of spite. We brought some to France, which have increased so much that all gardens are full of them. I have a grudge against those who have induced the criers of Paris to call them *Topinambours*."[17]

14. Lescarbot, II, 296-313.

15. Lescarbot, III.

16. Lescarbot, III, 249-250. Perhaps references to Indian farming as seen from Saco to Nantucket Sound.

17. Lescarbot, III, 254. The tuberous sunflower is still called topinambour in French, a Brazilian Indian name by unexplained error, the plant not being in South America. Digging may cause it to become a pest in gardens, but hardly at the rate he claimed. The introduction to France must have been earlier, perhaps from Florida, where it was grown by Indians, and where there had been a French colony.

The Indians to the south brayed their maize in wooden mortars and baked it into cakes and parched corn at the fire. "The men make earthen post in the shape of a nightcap. Our Souriquois formerly did the same and tilled the ground, but since the French bring kettles, beans, and biscuit they have become slothful", no longer planting or making pottery.

Smelt were the first fish to enter the streams in spring, followed by sardines (alewives), sturgeon, and salmon, "ascending in such numbers as to carry away the nets we have set for them." Indians took fish by weir, sturgeon and salmon also by spear. "They also eat eggs, which they gather along the shore and laden their canoes with them when the geese and bustards [Canada geese] have done laying in the springtime, and they use all [eggs], old as well as new." All animals were eaten except wolves. Moose was the most appreciated and plentiful game, hunted in winter on snowshoes. Bear and racoon were good meat. In winter the Indians moved inland to the shores of lakes in order to take beaver. No salt was used in their cooking.

The Indian freedom from scurvy was aided by their use of sweat baths. They wore shoes called *mekezen*. Those in the south used only buckskin for their clothes. Their bodies were greased with oil for protection from flies, which were very troublesome from mid-June to early September.

In spring women stripped the bark of trees to make canoes and to cover the houses. Women were skillful at making rush mats in colors and square patterns, also baskets, dishes of bark, and purses of skin. "Our savages have the art both of painting and carving, and make beasts, birds, and men in stone and also in wood, as prettily as good workmen in these parts," tobacco pipes being an example. Except for their ignorance of the true religion, the natives enjoyed "the life of the ancient golden age."

Native ways had been changed by European trade, Lescarbot observed, in the decline or loss of planting crops, replaced by trade for biscuit and dry peas from France. Metal pots and cutting tools had taken the place of earthen pots and stone implements. The shell wampum of traditional importance in ceremony and trade had been supplanted by porcelain imitation. The fur trade also had changed. Beaver pelts, held in no esteem at the time of Cartier, had become the staple because a tall, cylindrical hat made of beaver had become a requirement of male fashion. Rats had come with the ships and moved into the Indian settlements. "Savages had no knowledge of these animals before our coming, but in our time they have been beset by them." Acculturation, it appears, was well under way.

WITHDRAWAL

In May 1607, while the men at Port Royal were planting gardens, orders came from Sieur de Monts directing that all return to France. A last trip was made across the bay to the St. John and Ste. Croix rivers to trade furs. Poutrincourt went to the head of the bay to make a final search for the copper mine. Three longboats left Port Royal in July, carrying most of the party to meet the ship waiting at Canso to take them to France. Poutrincourt followed in a shallop taking time for Champlain to finish mapping the coast.[18] The buildings at Port Royal and the gardens were left in care of their friendly Indian neighbors, the French expecting to return before long.

18. Six leagues west of Canso Champlain mapped a harbor, named Savalet for the Basque captain of a ship from St. Jean de Luz who was fishing there and told them that this was his forty-second voyage to those parts and that his eighty-ton ship could load a hundred thousand dry fish (Lescarbot, II, 362).

De Monts had stayed in France in order to preserve his monopoly and had failed. The merchants of the fishing ports who had provided the capital complained that it had been diverted into an unneeded costly establishment at Port Royal, to fruitless search for mines, and to long excursions south to contact Indians who had neither furs nor other trade. Furs in small amount were being procured from about the Bay of Fundy but no trading posts had been established nor had the trade been organized. Attention had been directed to the south, none given to the Gulf of St. Lawrence. The occasional confiscation of a fishing ship trading with Indians in violation of the monopoly had failed to stop the illicit trade, which had become much more profitable with the great rise in price of beaver pelts.

De Monts retained the title of Lieutenant Governor of New France. Neither he nor Champlain returned to Port Royal or to the Atlantic coast which they had learned to know so well. Their later interest was directed north to the St. Lawrence River, its valley beginning to be known as Canada.

IX.

Conflicting Interests in Acadia
Decline of Indian Population

FRENCH RETURN TO ACADIA (1610-1613)

Poutrincourt brought a group of settlers to reoccupy Port Royal in 1610. They were met by the local Souriquois (Micmac) chief who showed them that the buildings, furnishings, and grounds had been well taken care of during the three years' absence of the French. The Indian friends Lescarbot had praised at the earlier settlement greeted their return.

A second contingent from France came in the spring of 1611, with two Jesuits to begin missionary work among the Indians. In 1613 a third lot of settlers was sent to establish a plantation and trading station on Mount Desert Island, the two Jesuits going along to the new location, named St. Sauveur.

In July 1613, while the settlers at St. Sauveur were living in tents, clearing land, and planting crops, an English party from Virginia under Captain Argall seized the place. Fifteen Frenchmen were released to find their way back north to fishing ships. The rest, including the Jesuit priests, were taken to Virginia, thence to England, and finally back to France.

Argall set up a marker of possession at St. Sauveur, did the same at the abandoned site of Ste. Croix, and went on to loot and burn Port Royal.[1] The London Company's charter of Virginia extended from 34° to 45° N. Lat. Argall was sent with orders to take possession to the northern limit of the charter and did so on the claim that the French were trespassers.

FATHER PIERRE BIARD'S RELATION

On his return to France the Jesuit Father Pierre Biard wrote of his experiences in Acadia, an intimate account of Indian life a half dozen years after Champlain and Lescarbot.[2] The observations were of Souriquois (Micmacs) about Port Royal and Etchemins (Malecites) of Mount Desert Island, Algonquian tribes of similar habit and habitat.

Biard composed a calendar of Indian food provision:

January: seal hunting.

---

1. Trudel, II, 130-146.

2. The Biard Relation is in Reuben Gold Thwaites, ed., *The Jesuit Relations* (Cleveland, 1896-1901), III, 21-28[3]; and IV, 7-167.

February and March: the great hunting season of beaver, otter, moose, bear, and caribou, weather permitting.

March: at midmonth fish began to run up the rivers to spawn, smelt being the earliest.

April: in late April the run of herring (shad, alewives?), sturgeon, and salmon was under way. Bustards (Canada geese) arrived from the south and began nesting; time to collect eggs.

May to September: the season when the natives lived free of all anxiety. Cod, other fish, and shellfish abounded in the coastal waters. Ships came to traffic that began with *tabagies* (ceremonial festivals).

September: at the end of the month the natives left the coast to move up the rivers, taking eels, then at their best.

October and November: a second hunting season of beaver and moose.

December: by wonderful act of Providence, *panamo* (tomcod) came to spawn under the ice.[3]

The native population had declined greatly:

They complain that since the French mingle with and carry on trade with them they are dying fast, and the population is thinning out. For they assert that before this association and intercourse all their countries were very populous, and they tell how one by one different coasts, according as they traffic with us, have been reduced more by disease.[4]

Biard estimated that from Newfoundland to Saco there were no more than nine to ten thousand inhabitants, a third of them Souriquois (Micmac), most of the rest Etchemins (Malecites). (Hakluyt, cited above, had described unnamed Indians in southern Newfoundland who must have been Micmacs. Biard was the first to my knowledge to actually identify them by name.) Ships brought brandy and wine to trade for furs and thereby the natives had become addicted to drinking. Autumn, Biard noted further, was the season of dysentery; also, women bore children at two year intervals at most and often continued nursing them for three years.

A HALF CENTURY OF SHIFTING FRENCH AND ENGLISH CONTROL

The illegal and usually unreported trade by ships went on summer after summer. There were small legitimate French trading posts, as at Cape Sable and perhaps on the St. John and Penobscot rivers. Yet, by 1627, no more than a score of French residents lived in the area throughout the year.[5]

In 1621 James I gave Sir William Alexander charter to Nova Scotia, roughly Acadia. The bringing of a Scots colony to Port Royal was delayed, probably to 1629, and then maintained to 1632, when New France was restored to France.[6] A few French traders remained during the British occupation, carrying on commerce well with Indians.

In September 1632 several hundred French settlers, including a number of wives,

3. Thwaites, III, 105.

4. Thwaites, III, 111.

5. Trudel, II, 437.

6. Clark, 83-84.

were landed at La Have, a harbor frequented both by dry and wet cod fishers, the latter fishing on La Have Bank a day's sail to the south. The *habitants* came in time to build cabins and sow fields to wheat before winter set in. The local glacial drift provided cultivable soil, useful timber, and pasturage.

The settlement spread across the peninsula to reoccupy the superior land about Port Royal, and engaged in draining tidal marshes for wheat, hay, and pasture. Andrew Clark estimated forty-five to fifty households in the two settlements in 1650, and sixty single men.[7]

English control took over again in 1654 and continued about to 1670. It put some constraint on French trading and fishing but did little to disturb the life of the habitants. A French census taken in 1671 estimated 400 persons, of whom all but about 50 lived in Port Royal and vicinity, cultivating about 400 arpents and having about 650 cattle and 430 sheep.[8]

NICOLAS DENYS' FORTY YEARS IN THE AFFAIRS OF ACADIA

Nicolas Denys came in 1632 with the party that settled at La Have and engaged there for a time in lumbering and fishing. In 1645 he moved north and built a trading post on Miscou Island at the entry to Chaleur Bay. Ousted by a French claimant, Denys built another trading fort in 1650 at St. Peters at the southern end of Cape Breton Island, was thrown out again, tried again at Nepisiquit in Chaleur Bay, lost, went back to St. Peters, and was carried off to Port Royal and imprisoned by his French rivals.

The fortunes of Denys changed in 1654 when the English captured Port Royal. Freed by the English, Denys left for France where he secured from the Company of New France a grant for the coast and islands of the Gulf of St. Lawrence from the cape of Gaspé to that of Canso, including Cape Breton Island. He was also appointed Governor and Lieutenant-General, with privilege to form a company for sedentary fishery along the coasts of Acadia as far as the limits of Virginia.

A curious state of affairs existed during the English interregnum. The English controlled the Atlantic coast south of Cape Breton Island. Denys was allowed to trade on the Gulf of St. Lawrence, from Cape Breton Island to Gaspé Peninsula, which he did, at times from his southern base at St. Peters, at other times from Nepisiquit in Chaleur Bay.

For the years from 1632 to 1670 Denys is therefore the main informant on the condition of Acadia. In 1672, after retiring to France, he published in Paris the two volumes entitled *Description Géographique et historique des costes de l'Amérique septentrionale, avec l'histoire naturelle du pais*.[9] The title is excessive, the content being limited to what Denys knew of the country from Gaspé Peninsula to Maine.

DENYS' GEOGRAPHICAL DESCRIPTION

The Geographical Description begins at the south with Penobscot Bay. Thence to Canso Denys outlined the coast of which Champlain had given a detailed account at the beginning of the century.

7. Clark, 100.

8. Clark, 121-124.

9. The edition used here is *The Description and Natural History of the Coasts of North America (Acadia)*, ed. and tr. W. F. Ganong, with reprint of original, Publications of the Champlain Society, II (Toronto, 1908).

Cape Breton Island was given its first adequate description. Denys' fort at St. Peters was at the southern end of the saltwater arm that divides the island in two. (The strait between them, then called Labrador, of unexplained meaning, is now corrupted to Bras d'Or.) The eastern island had a secure and commodious harbor at Havre l'Anglais (now Louisburg) formerly frequented by fishermen from La Rochelle. These fishermen spent the winter there in order to be the first to fish on the banks, to take the first cargoes of cod to France, and thus to get the best price. To the north of the harbor wave-cut cliffs exposed beds of very good coal at several places. (Ganong identified one as the modern coal mining town of Sydney.) At the northern inlet of Labrador (Great Bras d'Or) there was good fishing of salmon and mackerel in the harbor of Ste. Anne (St. Ann's Bay). Having rounded Cape North the circuit of the western island was outlined as far as the Strait of Canso.

Chapter VIII described the shores of the Gulf of St. Lawrence from the Strait of Canso to Chaleur Bay. About Pictou Harbor there were many ponds with an astonishing abundance of game, fine hardwoods, conifers, grapevines, fertile land, and in the coves, oysters of fine quality and great size. Beyond Cape Tormentine (earliest record of the name?) he gave the name Cocagne to one place:

> because I found there so much with which to make good cheer during the eight days that bad weather obliged me to stay there. All my people were so surfeited with game and fish that they wished no more, whether wild geese, duck, teal, plover, snipes large and small, pigeons, hares, partridges and young partridges, salmon, trout, mackerel, smelt, oysters, and other fish. All I can tell you of it is that our dogs lay beside the meat and fish, so much satiated were they. The country there is as pleasing as the good cheer.

Île St. Jean (Prince Edward Island) was briefly noted as covered with woods of firs mingled with birch and beech, having caribou, no moose, yet good feeding and nesting grounds of waterfowl, such as cranes and white and gray geese. Its Gulf coast had the disadvantage of shoal water; some Basque ships managed entry to a harbor by unloading, careening the ships, and towing them in by rowboats.

Cod fishing was excellent about the Magdalen Islands, seals also being taken. At the Bird Rocks fishing vessels were accustomed to send boats ashore to collect eggs and fowls. (Walrus, of major importance in the sixteenth century, are not mentioned.)

Denys was well acquainted with Chaleur Bay from his habitation on Miscou Island and later at Nepisiquit River. Quaking bogs on Miscou were nesting grounds of bustards. At Nepisiquit there was an incredible abundance of geese, brant, and ducks, of shellfish, lobster, flounder, mackerel, salmon, and sturgeon.

The Geographical Description ends (Chapter IX) with Gaspé Peninsula, the northern limit of his concession. Coves on its high and wave beaten coast were frequented by cod fishers because of the good fishing and for refuge during storms. Its familiar landmark was Île Percée, a rock eaten out by the sea so that boats could pass under its open arch. Adjacent to it Baye des Molues (codfish bay, now corrupted to Mal Baie), long known as a good drying place to codfishers, had gardens of cabbages, peas, beans, and greens, grown during their long stays ashore.

DENYS' NATURAL HISTORY AND INDIANS

The second volume deals with natural history, beginning with a comparison of the climates of France and New France. From the classical doctrine that climate was determined by latitude it followed that New France should have the same seasons as the same latitudes of France. The much greater and longer winters of New France therefore were attributed to the forest cover. As these could be cleared and the ground opened to warming by the sun, as in France, the contrast would disappear and the same husbandry could be followed. In so stating, Denys expressed a commonly held view of the time.

The famous fifteen chapters on cod fishing follow, the fullest account of the dry cod (*merluche*) fishery of its time. The daily routine of the summer camps ashore is given in intimate detail as to preparation and storage of the product, including the extraction of cod-liver oil. Attempts had been made by him to replace the seasonal codfishers by a sedentary population, but without success. (This was a privilege he had asked for and had been given in his appointment as Governor.)

Chapter XVII treated of other 'sea fish', beginning with seals, prized by the Indians and taken by Europeans for their train oil. The sea shores had great abundance and diversity of food, including shellfish such as oysters and lobsters. There was large store of big and excellent halibut, of swordfish that grew to the size of a cow, of squids and other kinds. Indians speared sturgeons as these entered the river mouths, fishing from canoes at night by torchlight. Notes on the preparation of different kinds of sea food concluded the chapter.

Chapter XVIII described 'fresh water fish of four feet', muskrat, otter, and beaver. Muskrats, properly prepared, were good food, and the skins taken in season were good fur. Beaver tails were best eaten boiled or fried, the thighs and shoulders best roasted. The flesh of beaver resembled mutton in taste but was somewhat different, "otherwise it would not be fish." Beaver pelts were dark brown, occasionally black or even white and were in less demand than formerly when beaver hats had been the fashion. Beavers built dams as though by plan and supervision. Denys thought that the greater part of the ponds and lakes had been made by beavers.

Chapter XIX recounted the birds of water, marsh, and strand; bustards (Canada geese), brant, mallard, teal and other ducks, plover, sandpiper, heron, and the like, with notes on their qualities as food.

In Chapter XX Denys verified by a long trip Indian reports that the woods in the interior were of greater growth and more open stand, making it possible to hunt moose on horseback. Prairies and ponds were found in all parts. Hardwoods were of diverse kinds, beech, black birch, paper birch, oak, elm, ash, and maple. Maples were tapped for their sweet liquid at the time when the sap was running. This drink of the Indians was also liked by the French. Pine, spruce, and fir provided lumber and pitch. The impression given is of the predominance of mixed hardwoods.

Chapter XXI treats of land animals, beginning with moose and black bear, followed by descriptions of lynx, porcupine, fox usually red but occasionally black, wolverine, and pine marten. Flying squirrels fed on beechnuts which they stored for the winter. Rabbits were taken in winter by snares set in their runways. The list of land birds begins with the bald eagle. The black partridge (Canada grouse) had flesh that tasted of juniper berries, the silly birds letting themselves be shot one after another as they perched in a tree. Robins were acceptable eating. Unsuccessful attempts had been made to rear red throated hummingbirds.

In Chapter XXII Denys reports that, of the native fruits, raspberries were of better quality than those of France. They grew

in all places deprived of their woods and also in our clearings. If one of the latter is left for a year without cultivation, all of it is filled with raspberry bushes . . . It is troublesome to rid the land of them. If, after having removed them, the land is left without being cultivated or sown it produces hazelnut bushes, the nuts of which are good. Remove the hazel bushes and again if the land is not cultivated it grows up to woods as before. [A correct observation of secondary ecologic succession.]

DENYS ON CHANGES IN INDIAN WAYS

Early in the century Father Biard had found Indians living in small numbers on the coasts of Acadia and reported that they claimed to have been very many before European traders mingled with them and introduced alcoholic beverages and other evils. Independently Denys came to a like conclusion.

In the final chapters (XXIII to XXVII) the changes in Indian ways are set forth. When Denys came in 1632 the natives were already using iron kettles, axes, knives, and arrowheads, but few had firearms. Since then kettles had replaced the hollowed out tree trunks in which they had formerly boiled their unsalted food by dropping in hot stones. Possessing kettles the Indians were free to move anywhere and became more mobile, changing their habitations often.

This led him to a discourse on the division of labor. Women did the work of carrying belongings to the new camp and of building the wigwams, which were circular if of one fireplace, oblong if of more. Women were the artisans of birch bark with which they covered their habitations, so well sewed that no water could enter. Women made the birch bark containers and dishes. Women dressed the skins, carried home the game, and fetched the wood and water. Women joined the men at paddling canoes, prepared the gum of fir with which the canoes were waterproofed (to the chewing of which Denys attributed their sound white teeth), and women made the cords of snowshoes.

Men hunted and fished, made the bows and arrows, spears, snowshoes, canoes and paddles, and they fashioned the tobacco pipes. Moose were speared in winter by hunters on snowshoes, at other times were stalked with bow and arrow, usually requiring three shots to be brought down. In the rutting season moose were attracted by imitating the call of the cow moose. In summer beaver were taken by breaking their dams, in winter by spearing through holes cut in the ice. Hibernating bears were detected by the vapor of their breath. Fish were speared by torchlight, as were geese and ducks. Fish traps were set on streams, nets also being used.

Roast dog was a special mark of friendship, some Frenchmen having come to prefer it to mutton. Puppies might be suckled by Indian women.

In the old days the people did to one another as they wished done to themselves. Families lacking food were supplied by neighbors. Wives were faithful. "They were not subject to disease and knew nothing of fevers" or of gout, gravel, or rheumatism. The sweat house was in general use, a small tight hut in which water was poured on heated stones, the bathers thus continuing for an hour or longer, singing and telling stories, after which they ran out to dash into a stream or the sea. The French had learned its use to the benefit of their health. Medicine men were held in high repute and lived at ease on the offerings of patients.

The ancient customs had changed greatly. The old manner of burial was retained but they no longer placed objects with the body, which formerly had been buried with their rarest and finest possessions. The devotion to the *manito* had become less, the natives abandoning traditional offerings. In former times they had hunted and fished only as they had need of food.

The altered condition was set forth in Chapter XXVII: Iron arrow points replaced those of stone, swords were affixed to spears, and now harpoons were made of metal. During his time the musket had come into use for hunting birds as well as beasts.

> With an arrow they killed only one bustard, but with one shot of a gun they kill five or six of them. With the arrow it was necessary to approach an animal closely; with the gun they kill it from a distance with one ball or two. The axes, kettles, knives, and everything supplied to them are much more convenient and portable than what they had in former times, when they were obliged to camp near their gigantic kettles [hollowed out logs], in place of which they are free to go camping wherever they wish. One may say that in those times the immovable kettles were the chief regulators of their lives, since they could live only where these were.

Denys had remarked on excessive hunting in his Geographical Description. Moose, formerly in great numbers on Cape Breton Island, had been exterminated by Indians hunting with muskets. There were no longer any moose on Prince Edward Island and the caribou were in reduced number. (The supply of muskets became common during his time, Denys stated. Metal implements and kettles it is implied had been distributed since earlier times.)

Alcohol, however, was the major cause of the Indian decline:

> Since they have taken to drinking wine and brandy they are subject to fighting. Their quarreling comes ordinarily from their condition; for, being drunk, they say they are all great chiefs, which engenders quarrels between them. At first it needed little wine or brandy to make them drunk. But at present, and since they have frequented the fishing vessels, they drink in quite another fashion. They no longer have any regard for wine, and wish nothing but brandy. They do not call it drinking, unless they become drunk, and do not think that they have been drinking unless they fight and are hurt. However, when they set about drinking, their wives remove their guns, axes, mounted swords, bows, arrows, and knives.

The fishermen were ruining the Indians wholly. At the trading posts there was some restriction of drinking but ship captains and crews plied the natives without limit as long as these had something to trade. The start of trade was primed by drinks, ended in lawlessness, and led to the debauching of their women. Indians who were taken to France came back to add vices they had learned in the Old World. To stop the ruin of the country it would be necessary to end the uncontrolled commerce in liquor by settling fishermen to live in villages on the coasts.

END OF THE CENTURY

At the end of the century the French population numbered about fifteen hundred, a third in the Port Royal settlement and a like number in the Minas Basin, both by that time having drained and put under cultivation much fertile marshland. Perhaps half of the remainder may have been at Beaubassin at the head of the long arm of Chignecto Bay, with like attraction of marshes. There were small settlements on the south coast at La Have and near Cape Sable and across the Bay of Fundy at St. John, and here and there along the coast were some traders, perhaps in métis menage.[10] The relations with the Indians were friendly and the backwoods were safe, the larger coast settlements occasionally subject to raids by ships.

Dry cod fishermen continued to use their accustomed staging grounds on western shores of the Gulf of St. Lawrence and to trade liquor and other things for Indian furs. At times, Recollect friars came from Quebec to minister to French and Indians. The last report of the century was by one such, Father Chretien Le Clercq, *Nouvelle Relation de la Gaspesie* (1691).[11] Indian customs had been corrupted and the people reduced to misery by the fishermen who plied them with brandy. One such fisherman boasted that he could do more with a bottle of brandy than the missionary could with a bottle of holy water. The traders claimed that if they failed to provide the Indians with brandy these would turn to the English and Hollanders, and Acadia would be lost to France. Shortly Acadia was lost to France; its habitants remained, however, and multiplied.

10. Clark has examined the data in his fifth chapter.

11. The edition cited herein is *New Relation of Gaspesia, with the Customs of the Gaspesian Indians*, ed. and tr. W. F. Ganong, with reprint of original, Publications of the Champlain Society, V (Toronto, 1910).

X.

Canada in the Time of Champlain

NAMES FROM THE TIME OF CARTIER

Cartier's second voyage (1535-1536) brought the first written knowledge of land west of shores already visited by European cod fishermen. Cartier had left the main gulf known as Grande Baie by a strait at the northwest now called Jacques Cartier Passage, to enter unrecorded waters of the long salt arm of the gulf that he called a river. "This river begins above the island of Assumption [Anticosti]." This strange term is still used to this day; the name St. Lawrence River applied both to its fresh water course and the salt water sound as far as Anticosti Island.

Continuing up the great salt sound Cartier named and entered the Saguenay River, came to lowland at Île aux Coudres, so named for its growth of hazel, and on the next day to "the beginning of the country and province of Canada." The exploration of the freshwater river and its lowland was continued by boat as far as rapids, beyond which they could not pass, at the Indian town of Hochelaga, adjacent to the mountain named Mont Real.

The name St. Lawrence was given by Cartier only to a small bay (Pillage Bay?) where the Breton crew celebrated the day of that favorite saint of Brittany (August 10) as they set out to discover what is now known as the Jacques Cartier Passage. Cartographers at midcentury, Mercator's world map of 1569 in particular, extended the name St. Lawrence to the river and sound and to the gulf the French called Grande Baie. French usage continued to designate the gulf as Grande Baie and the river and valley as Canada.[1]

THE FRENCH RETURN TO CANADA

In 1600 Chauvin de Tonnetuit, a French nobleman of distinguished services, was granted a hundred leagues along the River of Canada, on which he was to settle French colonists and to build a fort at Tadoussac at the mouth of Saguenay River. Being of modest means Chauvin secured financial backing from the merchants of Rouen, which served to set Norman against Breton interests. The latter protested that they were accustomed to voyage to the River of Canada, were known to its natives as friends and that Cartier, who was from their own city of St. Malo, had explored the land about Tadoussac and found it unsuited for colonization. They spoke in support of the summer fisheries and for free trade with the natives as against a colony and monopoly. Tadoussac was in good location for taking walrus, seals, and dolphins, in particular belugas, as well as for the cod fishery. It was also a place where Montagnais Indians lived and were in the habit of bringing pelts to trade, as did other tribes from south of the salt St.

1. Sauer, *Sixteenth Century North America,* Chapter 5.

Lawrence. The monopoly of Chauvin would ruin the Breton trade and, it was argued with reason, would not be a suitable location for a French colony.

Chauvin sailed from the Norman port of Honfleur in 1600, built a post at Tadoussac, left sixteen men with supplies, and returned to France. The winter brought scurvy, hunger, and death. The survivors scattered to find refuge in Indian camps. There was no further attempt to colonize. Ships continued to come in summer from Rouen to trade at Tadoussac, where the buildings Chauvin had constructed were maintained but occupied only in summer.[2]

Pont-Gravé had gone to Tadoussac with Chauvin in 1600 and after the latter's death in 1603 was sent to report on what should be done about colonization. He was accompanied by young Samuel de Champlain, making his first visit to northern America, to exercise his bent at drawing charts, and to write about a strange land and its people.

CHAMPLAIN'S *DES SAUVAGES* (1603)

The scouting for a location of the colony took three months, from May to August 1603, and was presented by Champlain in *Des Sauvages*, the first description of land and people since the time of Cartier.[3]

The ship entered the Great Bay of Canada by the ice free southern strait (now Cabot Strait) and landed at Tadoussac on May 26, 1603. Tadoussac, being in a land for the most part rock and sand and hemmed in by mountains, was reported as unsuited for settlement.

The party was welcomed at the lodge of the sagamore by a *tabagie*, a ceremonial that began with a speech by an Indian whom they brought back with them from France. He told of his reception by the French King, who wished to settle in their land and to either make peace with their enemies or to subdue them. The sagamore then passed the peace pipe and expressed his satisfaction that the King would be their great friend, settle in their country, and make war on their enemies. A feast followed in which different meats were served, dished from iron kettles onto bark plates. Days of dancing followed in which the local Montagnais were joined by their Etchemin and Algonquin allies, during which a hundred Iroquios scalps were displayed and the Algonquins staged a dance in the nude by their women.

This is the first identification of three Algonquian tribes and their location, Montagnais of the north shore, Etchemins (Abnakis) from south of the salt sound, and Algonquins from the interior of the St. Lawrence Valley. The three tribes were allied against the Iroquois and proposed that the French join them against the common enemy. Thus unexpectedly the French were confronted with a deadly enmity between Indian tribes, its cause unknown to them, and they were asked to take part in a war against a new people, the Iroquois, a people they had not yet met and a people they did not yet know.

From Tadoussac Champlain made an excursion up the Saguenay fiord, finding the land mountainous and of bare rock, noting no animal life other than small birds. He was told that canoes used this route, passing falls, rapids, and lakes, to come in ten days to

2. Trudel, I, especially 235-242.

3. Champlain, *Works*, I.

another Indian tribe (Asitibis?) that traded pelts of marten and beaver to the Montagnais in exchange for French merchandise, and that these people knew a salt sea beyond their land. This was the first notice of a canoe route between Tadoussac and James Bay.

On June 18 Pont-Gravé and Champlain left Tadoussac to explore the River of Canada. Above Quebec, the name meaning river narrows, Champlain described the valley as fertile, free of stones, with fine woods, grape vines, and berry bushes, also a plant with nut-like roots that had the taste of truffles (*Apios tuberosa*, the groundnut of the eastern woodlands).

Trois Rivières, where a river from the north and another from the south joined the great river, he thought would be a suitable site for French settlement, having open woods and good land about it. Passing through a lake (St. Pierre) they came to the mouth of the river of the Iroquois (Richelieu River) flowing out of the south and found there an Indian party preparing to invade the Iroquois country. The excursion up the main river ended at a great rapids by the side of a large island, (Cartier's Montreal). The woods about the island were very open (the formerly cultivated fields of Hochelaga?). Champlain had his Indian companions draw a map of canoe routes west beyond the rapids and thus learned of a river to the west (Ottawa River, the home of the Algonquin nation) that led to three great lakes.

On the way back to Tadoussac Champlain acquired more information from Algonquins traveling on the river. One of the interviews was at Île aux Lièvres, a short distance above Tadoussac, where he was told of a southern great lake (Ontario), at the head of which was a waterfall a league wide (Niagara), and to the south the country of the Iroquois, where much corn and other crops were grown. Inquiry about mines brought information about a 'nation of good Iroquois' (Hurons), who lived west of the Algonquins (on Lake Huron) and were provided with French goods by the Algonquins. Champlain was shown copper bracelets that the 'good Iroquois' had traded and which came to them from a distant northern mine of pure copper (native copper of Lake Superior).

The three weeks' reconnaissance of the St. Lawrence gave the first outline of the great drainage system of the St. Lawrence and Great Lakes. Champlain began here the practice of having Indians draw maps of waters they traveled by canoe. His informants seemingly were of the Algonquin tribe, engaged in trading between Tadoussac and the tribes of the interior. Trade from tribe to tribe was carried on apparently as far as Lake Superior. Except for the Hurons, 'the good Iroquois', who were western neighbors of the Algonquins, all were of Algonquian speech and custom, this bond as yet unrecognized.

The French party was back at Tadoussac on July 11 and sailed promptly to chart the south shore of the salt St. Lawrence. At Gaspé Bay, Baie de Molues (now Mal Baie), and Île Percée they found the usual summer assembly of fishermen preparing dry cod. Crossing to chart the north shore of the salt sound they came to a locality frequented by Basque whalers (who may have been rendering train oil of marine mammals other than whales). Place names recorded at the time for both shores of the sound are still used, and were thus known to traders before 1603.

On the return to Tadoussac they found a Montagnais war party celebrating another victorious raid against the Iroquois. Ten canoes had gone more than three hundred miles to the river of the Iroquois (Richelieu), ascended it to the first lake of the Iroquois

(Lake Champlain), and attacked the Iroquois in their homeland. This was the third account in three months of invading Iroquois territory.

The ship left Tadoussac August 16 for France. A week was spent at Île Percée where they chanced to meet the Sieur Prévert of St. Malo and heard his story that led to the reconnaissance of Acadia.

THE LOST IROQUOIS SETTLEMENT OF THE ST. LAWRENCE VALLEY

In 1535 Cartier found the St. Lawrence Valley occupied by Iroquois, from Île d'Orleans above the head of salt water to the palisaded town of Hochelaga on the island of Montreal. He encountered Iroquois peaceably fishing at Gaspé Bay in Etchemin territory and Iroquois canoemen hunting sea mammals along the Montagnais coast north of the Gulf of St. Lawrence.

In 1603 Champlain found three Algonquian tribes making raids against the Iroquois living well to the south of the St. Lawrence Valley. The Iroquois who had occupied the valley in Cartier's time were gone, their cultivated fields and settlements repossessed by wild vegetation, the size and nature of the regrowth suggesting that the Iroquois had abandoned the valley just shortly after the departure of Cartier.

To this day the disappearance of the Iroquois remains a mystery. The viewpoint of A. G. Bailey, cited by Trudel, that the Iroquois were driven from this valley by an Algonquin alliance armed with European weapons supplied by neighboring trading ships seems unsatisfactory. For one thing the valley was abandoned shortly after the departure of Cartier; and yet, as Cartier himself reports, the Iroquois in this area were still living at peace with their neighbors at the time of his departure. It seems unlikely, though possible, that an alliance could have been founded, European arms obtained, and the total destruction of the Iroquois accomplished in such a short period of time. But more importantly: during his stay Cartier had built quarters for the winter near the Iroquois village of Stadacona (Quebec), and during that winter a great sickness broke out among the Indians, who were confined by the cold to the close quarters of their long houses and thus exposed to contagion, which it may be inferred was communicated by their new French neighbors. Epidemics commonly followed contact with Europeans, especially where the natives were closely congregated, as were these village-dwelling Iroquois. The Iroquois of this valley, it is therefore suggested, were reduced and weakened by the newly introduced diseases, and left shortly after to join their kin in upper New York State.

Along the way, it is true, they were harassed by roving Algonquin bands. At his arrival Champlain found three Algonquian nations by then leagued in deadly enmity against distant Iroquois nations south of Lake Champlain, in a war that was to grow in ferocity, involve more Indian nations, and eventually dictate events that shaped the history of Canada and the United States.

ACADIAN INTERLUDE

The 1603 expedition made a competent reconnaissance of the St. Lawrence River, both salt and fresh water, from Cape Gaspé to Montreal. The valley had land well suited to French settlement, with woods of vigorous growth of trees like those of

France. Champlain heard from Indians of waterways traveled by canoe and had them draw maps of the route west to the Great Lakes. He was shown copper said to come from a distant source. There were good prospects in the interior but with Prévert's story of rich mines on the sea coast to the south in mind, the next inquiry shifted to Acadian shores.

The attempts from 1604 to 1607 to settle Acadia are outlined in the previous chapter. No mines were found, there was no return to the investors, and the Acadian venture was suspended in 1607.

QUEBEC FOUNDED IN 1608

In 1608 Champlain was sent to occupy Canada and manage its affairs, which he did to 1634, writing its history, drawing its charts, and discussing its potential strengths and weaknesses.

Champlain returned to Tadoussac in the spring of 1608, took another and longer look at the fiord of Saguenay, and again found the land barren, 'nothing but disagreeable mountains'. He heard again that, having passed rapids and falls, one came to a lake that took three days to cross (Lake St. John), about which lived Indians who took pelts of good quality to Tadoussac.

The site he had in mind was at Quebec, a high point of rock projecting into the St. Lawrence River, with land suited to cultivation above, below, and across the river. (This had been the location of the Iroquois village of Stadacona and the short-lived colony of Cartier and Roberval). Quebec had tillable land and meadows, controlled entry to the St. Lawrence Valley, and would be the port of transatlantic shipping. Construction began in July, the felling of trees and the sawing of planks of green lumber, the digging of cellars and ditches, and the clearing of the land to plant gardens. Three two-story buildings formed a compound, placed so as to overlook the river (walnut was noted as the preferred lumber; the white walnut or butternut, here at the polar limit of its range).

Fall was a time of ease and plenty. Indians came to camp by the river and took eels returning to the sea. In November two Frenchmen and a number of Indians died of what Champlain called a dysentery, caused he thought by eating improperly cooked eels.

At the onset of winter beaver were in prime condition and provided staple food of the Indians. When the snow cover thickened Indians hunted moose on snowshoes, 'a kind of large racket attached to their feet, by means of which they walked over the snow'. As winter wore on the natives, lacking the skill to grow crops, Champlain wrote, suffered times of great hunger. By February half starved Indians (Montagnais) hung about the French quarters to be given handouts and to scavenge among the garbage.

Among the French "the sickness of the country began very late, lasting from February to April." Champlain had experienced two winters of scurvy in Acadia and thought it in part due to vapors from the wintry ground, in part to dependence on salt meat. The winter sickness affected the French but not the Indians. An Indian who lived with the French also "was attacked by this malady because he changed his diet to salt meat, and died of it." When the ship from France arrived in early June 1609 with supplies and men, eight of the twenty-eight French who had founded Quebec were alive, four of them in poor health.

RAIDS AGAINST THE IROQUOIS (1609-1610)

The important event of the summer of 1609 was the great raid into Iroquois country, Champlain with a dozen Frenchmen accompanying a horde of Montagnais, who were joined from the west by Algonquins and by their neighbors the Hurons, 'the good Iroquois', who here made their first appearance in the alliance against the Five Nations of New York. The adventure that Champlain entered into lightheartedly was to cost the French dearly in later years.

The fleet of canoes paddled up the St. Lawrence through Lake St. Pierre to the mouth of the river of the Iroquois (Richelieu River).[4] Here they came to country 'no Christian had ever penetrated', the no man's land between the St. Lawrence and the Iroquois land south of Lake Champlain, which thus received its name from Champlain's role in the raid. Islands in the lake had been inhabited formerly (by Iroquois) but were abandoned because of the wars. There were fine grape vines on the banks of the lake and chestnut trees, not seen previously. At the southern end of the lake they came upon a party of two hundred Iroquois, Champlain signalling the attack by firing his arquebus at one of the chiefs, killing him, also a second, and mortally wounding a third. The Iroquois, surprised by the strange weapon and the loss of their leaders, fled to the woods. Some were killed, a number captured, and a store of Indian corn and meal taken. The victory was celebrated by putting one of the prisoners to exquisite tortures that continued until Champlain put him out of his agony.

The Hurons and Algonquins left for home with their prisoners and the promise of alliance from Champlain. Montagnais and Frenchmen made a rapid canoe trip down the St. Lawrence to Tadoussac, where the victory was celebrated by a scalp dance. Champlain was given a scalp to take as a present to the King of France. He and Pont-Gravé were back in France in October 1609.

Champlain arranged to meet with Montagnais, Algonquins, and Hurons in the spring of 1610 at Trois Rivières for another campaign against the Iroquois. Now the Iroquois were found barricaded on the Richelieu River, their defenses breached by arquebus fire, and the defenders killed except for fifteen taken prisoner. These were "preserved to be put to death at the hands of the wives and daughters, who in this matter show themselves no less inhuman than the men." The Hurons arrived to aid after the victory was won.[5]

THE SO-CALLED THIRD VOYAGE (1611)

The St. Lawrence River highway of Canada was traveled by birchbark canoes, and at times by small sailboats. In winter it served for transport on ice. Champlain made another examination of it in 1611, to find a site for a second French settlement.[6]

The island of Montreal, with rapids at its base, appeared suitable. There were prairies (former Indian fields), woods of trees like those of France, and fish and game in abundance. Champlain made a trial of its fertility by planting two gardens, one in the woods, another in a prairie, both yielding well.

4. Champlain, *Works*, II, 65-106, describes the raid.

5. Champlain, *Works*, II, 122-142.

6. Champlain, *Works*, II, 155-221.

A party of two hundred Hurons came to visit, bringing word that a larger number of Algonquins were on their way. Champlain learned about the nature of the Huron country and of parts farther west, again using the device of having the informants draw maps. The Algonquin party came late, having been delayed and reduced by the outbreak of a fever that took a chief and many of the tribe (an introduced epidemic?). The long conference of speeches and exchange of gifts concluded with pledges of friendship and of joint action against the Five Nation Iroquois.

Champlain returned to France to present his report, taking two maps that outlined the interior as far as the Great Lakes based on Indian information.

VISIT TO ALGONQUIN LAND (1613)

In the spring of 1613 Champlain made his first tour beyond the rapids at Montreal to visit the Algonquins in their homeland. The trip up the river, later called the Ottawa, went about to the present site of Pembroke.[7] The narrative told of alternating long stretches of paddling and weary portages over rough terrain, plagued by mosquitoes as the party carried heavy loads. After five days' journey up river they came to a lake in a sandy region covered with pines, most of which had been burned by Indians. Among the stumps grew red 'cypresses', the first seen in those parts (*Juniperus virginiana*, red cedar following fires). The next lake had an Algonquin settlement among new plantings of maize. When the Indians wished to plant sandy ground they first set fire to the trees, which was done readily since these were resinous pines. The burned ground was then stirred about and the maize planted grain by grain. Eight leagues farther on (on Lower Allumette Lake) they came to a burying ground of tombs made of carved and painted wood, furnished with grave goods according to the rank of the deceased. A tabagie was held at the lodge of the chief, the feast a stew of maize ground between two stones and cooked with bits of meat and fish without salt. A time of silent pipe smoking by the elders followed. Champlain added, "To pass the rest of the day I took a walk through their gardens, which consisted of squashes, beans, and some of our peas, which they are beginning to cultivate."[8] (This is the earliest mention of the Old World yellow field pea, still a mainstay of French Canadian cooking.) The Algonquins lived by fishing and hunting on this fringe of the Laurentian Highland and also by cultivating patches of sandy land (deposited by the ice sheet and its melt waters).

After promising the chief to return again the next year and to jointly war upon the Iroquois, Champlain left for Quebec, the party increased to eighty canoes carrying a lot of peltry to Quebec.

ENTRY TO HURONIA (1615)

Champlain spent the year 1614 in France. There was concern that nothing had been done to bring the Christian faith to the numerous and friendly nations of Canada, whereas Jesuits had been laboring for several years in Acadia. In the spring of 1615 he returned with four Recollect priests, two to build a chapel at Quebec and minister to the

7. Champlain, *Works*, II, 239-309.

8. Champlain, *Works*, II, 287.

French and Indians there, one to go the great rapids (Montreal), and the fourth, Father Joseph Le Caron, to continue on to the Huron land, where he would learn the language, different from the speech common to all the Algonquians.[9]

Father Joseph went ahead, Champlain following in July, taking the route of the Ottawa River to the Algonquin village at the cemetery visited two years earlier. The next thirty-five leagues up the river were "through an ill-favored region full of pines, birches, and a few oaks, very rocky, and in parts rather hilly." At that season there was great abundance of blueberries and raspberries which the natives were drying for winter use.

Leaving the river and turning west, portaging from lake to lake, they came to the Lake of the Nipissings, a people of seven to eight hundred souls (also an Algonquian tribe). The natives there paid little attention to cultivating the soil, being occupied at the time in taking and drying fish. Their land was described as of attractive waters, woods, and meadows and well stocked with beasts, birds, and fish.

The river (French River) by which Lake Nipissing discharges took them west through an area with scarcely any arable land until they neared the great lake (Huron) where they came to fields of corn and squashes and met a people of strange appearance, called *Cheveux Relevées* because of their roached hairdress. The bodies of these new people were tattooed, faces painted different colors, nostrils pierced, and the ears hung with beads. They carried bows and arrows and round bucklers made of hide like that of the *buffle* (buffalo). Champlain again used the device of having a map drawn with charcoal on a piece of bark. This was the first French introduction to the Algonquian tribe later known as Ottawas, whose homeland was neither the Ottawa River nor any of the places in the United States now of that name.

As they turned south along the shore (Georgian Bay of Lake Huron), they found the country greatly improved, of excellent soil and largely cleared. (They were on the fertile lake plain, the floor of Pleistocene Lake Algonquin, the northern part of Huronia.)

Passing from one Huron village to another they found Father Le Caron living at the fifth village, which was surrounded by a triple palisade, thirty feet high.[10] The visitors arrived in August when the corn was almost full grown. They were well received at each village and were served with corn bread, fish, and squash, meat at that season being in short supply.

From the village of Father Le Caron, which was near the bay, they turned inland to visit five more large villages, each palisaded, and so came after fourteen leagues to the principal village, Cahiague (at the north end of Lake Simcoe). Champlain described the twenty to thirty leagues of Huronia he saw as well cleared and planted, of "much Indian corn which does very well, as do also squashes and sunflowers, from the seeds of which they make oil with which to dress their hair." There were several kinds of wild fruits, one by its description the may apple (*Podophyllum*). The people, who were very numerous, dressed in skins of beaver and deer, which they traded from the Algonquins and Nipissings in exchange for corn and cornmeal.[11]

9. Champlain, *Works*, III, 1-230, is his account of the years 1615-1618.

10. Palisaded villages were found at intervals from here south at least to Panama, features of woodland farming societies. The custom, or lack of it, is not explained merely as a defensive measure.

11. Champlain, *Works*, III, 50-53. He also noted that at the outlet of Lake Simcoe fish were taken in great numbers in weirs that almost closed the outlet (56-57).

HURON CAMPAIGN AGAINST THE IROQUOIS (1615)

The Hurons awaited Champlain's arrival at Cahiague to begin the campaign against the Iroquois. The party of five hundred warriors started from the north end of the lake (Simcoe) the first of September on an easterly course, paddling their canoes through a series of (morainic) lakes with long portages between. They passed through a fine country that Champlain said formerly had been inhabited but had been abandoned because of fear of enemies. The travel was by short stages, stopping for deer drives, to hunt bear, and to take water fowl, cranes as white as swans being noted (whooping cranes).

Having reached the shores of the lake of the Onondagas (Lake Ontario) in the vicinity of five islands (Quinté, Picton), they crossed the lake, paddling fourteen leagues to the opposite shore (Sackett's Harbor, N. Y.), where they hid the canoes. After four days of travel afoot they reached a beautiful smaller lake (Oneida) with a fortified Iroquois town on its far side. Champlain said that he planned the attack, but that after some skirmishing the warriors, Algonquins and Hurons, rushed the palisades, were thrown back, and could not be rallied. The invasion was abandoned, the wounded, including Champlain, carried in panniers to the place where the canoes had been left.

Crossing to the north shore of Lake Ontario at the end of October, the party made its leisurely return, fishing, hunting swans, cranes, bustards, and ducks, and organizing elaborate deer drives, in one of which a hundred twenty were killed, their hides and fat taken home. On a solitary hunt Champlain followed a strange game bird, the first description for Canada of the wild turkey, here at the northeastern limit of its range. By December the waters were frozen, enabling them to transport their loads on wooden sleds (tobaggans made of bark?). At Christmas Eve they were back at Cahiague, having gone about three hundred miles on a futile raid.

CHAMPLAIN'S SUMMARY OF HURONIA AND LANDS BEYOND

In February 1616 Champlain went with Father Le Caron to visit the Petun Nation to the south of Georgian Bay. (Petun was the French name for tobacco, learned at their shortlived colony in Brazil.) These neighbors and near relatives of the Hurons had cultivated fields, villages, and customs like those of the Hurons. The party continued northwest to get acquainted with the homeland of the Cheveux Relevées (the Ottawas of Bruce Peninsula). This nation was very numerous, each chief ruling his own district. They were good warriors and farmers and traded to a distance of hundreds of leagues with other peoples. His first meeting with Ottawas found them living about Georgian Bay and ranging as traders far about the Great Lakes.

Champlain outlined the geographic pattern he had learned, the cluster of Great Lakes at the west draining through the St. Lawrence River to the ocean, a highland border (Laurentians) along the north, "covered in some places with great rocks . . . and inhabited by savages who live wandering about the land without tilling the soils." To the south the country was very well populated, the land fertile, the climate more temperate, with more kinds of trees and fruits, and game of different kinds, one such being *buffles* (buffalo).[12]

12. Champlain, *Works*, III, 117-121.

Huronia, largely cleared land, was estimated as having eighteen villages, two thousand warriors, and thirty thousand souls. At intervals of ten to thirty years, he wrote, a village might be relocated at a new site a league or more distant. Houses were arched like bowers, twenty-five to thirty fathoms in length and a half dozen wide, with a passage running from end to end, in the middle a storage space for corn kept in bark casks. A cabin might have as many as twelve fireplaces and twenty-four households, the smoke escaping through the roof, for which reason there was much eye trouble.

The staple food was corn and beans, which were crushed in wooden mortars, boiled, and baked in loaves, or steamed in wrappings of corn husks. A common dish was *mingan*, a thin porridge of cornmeal with bits of fish or meat (pemmican), another was dry corn, toasted and pounded into meal, which the natives carried on journeys and which Champlain found tasty. Ears of corn were also kept in mud under water until judged properly putrid and then boiled. Dog meat was a delicacy at feasts, especially in winter. Bears were kept to be fattened for such occasions.[13]

Random recollections followed. Sweat baths were also of major importance, to sit, sing, and steam out whatever rage they had. Ritual masks were worn at ceremonial dances. Villages went to masquerade one another, as the French did at Mardi Gras. Women did the work of spinning and cooking. Men made the nets for catching fish. In winter, fish were caught under the ice by seine or line. Land was cleared by stripping the trees of bark, piling the waste at the base of the tree, and setting it afire. Grains of corn were planted in the cleared ground, several together at intervals of a pace, enough being planted to provide against the mishap of poor seasons.[14]

Champlain left the Huron country in May 1616, accompanied by his hosts as far as the rapids at Montreal, by then called the rapids of St. Louis. It was his last and greatest exploration. Huronia remained in his mind as the gateway to the interior and the key to the future of New France.

PROSPECTUS AND PROPOSAL BY CHAMPLAIN

It was time to go again to France to report to King and Council on the state of New France, of the friendship he had cultivated with Indian nations, and of what should be done to make it a successful colony. Champlain wrote the third volume of his *Voyages*, which he presented to the King, giving account of how he had joined the savage nations as far as the great freshwater sea into an alliance with France. He drew up also two memoirs, one to the King and his Council, the other to the Chamber of Commerce, outlining the steps that should be taken and the financial returns that would result.[15]

The proposal to the King began with the establishment of the Christian faith among an infinite number of souls, to which the Recollect friars bore witness. The King would thus become master of almost eighteen hundred leagues of country, watered by the fairest rivers and greatest lakes, abounding in fish, the land being of vast prairies, champaigns, and forests that included walnut trees and grape vines bearing grapes as large as in the vineyards of France. Champlain would undertake to discover by way of river and lakes the passage of the South Sea to China and to the Indies, a passage

13. Champlain, *Works*, III, 125-130.

14. Champlain, *Works*, III, 157-168.

15. Champlain, *Works*, III, 326-345.

assumed after visiting towns palisaded in the manner of Muscovy. In addition to the profit of the merchandise of New France there would be great returns from China and India, the northern passage shortening the time by a year and a half without risk of pirates or perils of the sea.

He would undertake to build a goodly town at Quebec with strong forts on opposite sides of the river narrows. Another fort would be built at Tadoussac, where the greater ships anchored. Fifteen Recollect friars were needed as missionaries and three hundred French families, supplied with live stock. Unless the land was thus maintained by settlers the English and Flemish, neighbors to the south, would take possession as had happened in Acadia. Loss of the country would make an end also of the cod and whale fisheries in which more than a thousand ships were engaged.

The memoir to the Chamber of Commerce gave optimistic estimate of future profits by diverse enterprises, the fur trade being a minor part of anticipated gains.

The cod fishery, carried on by permanent residents, would require local salt making and earn 1,000,000 livres annually. Salmon fishing in harbors and rivers would add 100,000; sturgeon and sea trout for German and other continental markets 100,000; eel, sardines, herring, etc. 100,000; train oil 200,000; whalebone, walrus tusks, and seals 500,000. (The Gulf of St. Lawrence thus was expected to yield two million livres a year.)

Another million was estimated from forest products. Good ships could be built of native trees, including masts, beams, joists, and planking, using oak, elm, beech, walnut, plane, maple, birch, and other woods. Staves, window frames, and other interior trim of dressed lumber would have a value of 400,000 livres. Potash made of useless wood would produce 400,000 livres; pitch, tar, and resin from pines and firs 100,000 livres.

More than a million livres a year were to be expected from the exploitation of wild and cultivated native plants. Wild hemp, not inferior to the cultivated hemp of France, would yield 300,000 livres, made into sailcloth and rigging it would produce an additional 400,000 livres. A wild root, the dye of which resembled cochineal (blood root, *Sanguinaria*?) would be of good profit under cultivation.

Mines of silver, iron, lead, and copper awaited exploitation, to yield 1,000,000 livres, to which the profit from marble and other valuable stone was to be added. The traffic in furs was not to be scorned, marten, beaver, fox, lynx, and also the dressed skins of deer, moose, and buffalo adding up to the value of more than 400,000 livres.

Noted as of major promise but not estimated as to value of return were the cultivation of native grapes, the raising of cattle such as had brought wealth to Peru, and the opening of the short route to China.

THE SECOND DECADE

Quebec remained the sole French settlement, as yet not a colony but a small post of a few soldiers and officials and a number of traders, some resident, others lodging there occasionally. Louis Hébert moved from Acadia to Quebec in 1617 with his family, the first and for some years the only household. Hébert was perhaps the first grantee (1623) of a parcel of land, on which he grew plants of European origin, and is considered therefore the first Frenchman to have farmed in Canada.

In the winter 1620-1621 sixty French are on record at Quebec, two as living among Indians, in 1627-1628 seventy-two at Quebec and six in Indian country. From 1620 to 1627 ten deaths and six births of French were recorded.[16] At the time when the English and Dutch settlements to the south were growing greatly by immigration and reproduction Quebec had a few score of Frenchmen, in part transient residents and mostly without families.

The first priests came in 1615, Recollects, dividing their ministry between Quebec and Huronia. They were well received by the Hurons and met with continuing success in the Huron villages.

FATHER SAGARD'S LONG JOURNEY ACCOUNT

In the mid-twenties Father Gabriel Sagard came to work among the Hurons and wrote his *Grand Voyage du Pays des Hurons,* an important addition to the earlier observations of Champlain.[17] Sagard, open-eyed newcomer to America, wrote in intimate detail of homely items such as how fire was made by revolving a drill of hard wood between the hands, of mush made of corn meal called *sagamité* (an Algonquin name) which he found unappetizing, of ears of corn saved for seed strung like tapestry in the interiors of the long houses.

The Hurons, he noted, grew more corn than they needed, storing the surplus against a bad season and to trade to other tribes. A field belonged to its cultivator as long as he worked it; other land was held in common. The Hurons had adequate land to support them with crops, fish, and game. They chose the sites for their villages with care, as to defense, running water, and wood. When the wood within convenient distance was used up or the sandy land no longer yielded good crops the Hurons relocated to another site, which might be after ten to thirty years. Sagard knew twenty-five towns and villages, a number of them elaborately palisaded. The warriors numbered two to three thousand, the total population twenty to thirty thousand.

Sagard also dealt with the fauna of Huronia, beginning with the hummingbird. There were many eagles, nesting in tall trees and on cliffs along streams. There were wild turkeys in some parts. Doves (passenger pigeons) were in immense flocks, feeding in particular on acorns, which they swallowed whole. Cranes, geese, and crows took heavy toll of standing corn. Some Recollect fathers had seen skins of buffalos (suggesting that these did not range into Huronia). Wolves were rare, as were moose. Black foxes brought the highest price of all peltry because of their rarity. Beaver had been taken in such numbers that he thought they were close to extermination. Bear cubs were captured and fattened to be eaten at feasts. Dogs also were prized meat at festivals. These were prickeared like foxes, and howled but did not bark. Their fleas were a great annoyance, more so than the lice of the Indians. The large game fish were pike and sturgeon, smaller kinds being taken by seine. The list of fauna ended with a description of bullfrogs that could be heard at evening for more than a quarter league.

In summer Hurons engaged in raids against the Iroquois. Five hundred or more

16. Trudel collated all records of the decade: II, 428, 492, 499, 504, and 505.

17. It was first published in Paris in 1632 and reissued in 1636 as *Histoire du Canada*. The edition used here is *The Long Journey to the Country of the Hurons,* ed. G. M. Wrong, tr. H. H. Langton, with a reprint of the 1632 edition, Publications of the Champlain Society, XXV (Toronto, 1939).

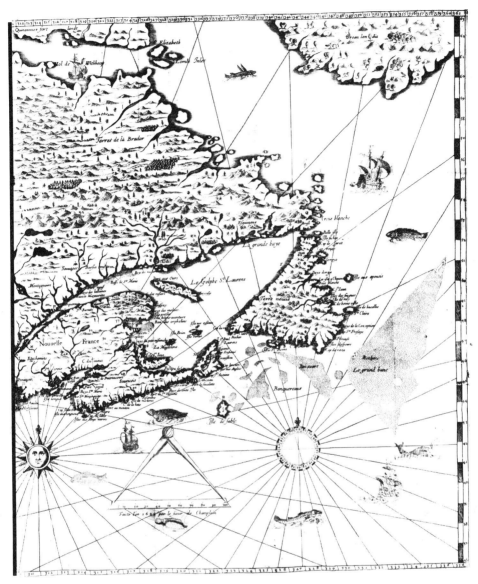

Fig. 10. Nouvelle France, 1632, in the *Portfolio* to accompany *The Works of Samuel de Champlain, III,* edited by H. P. Biggar, Toronto, 1922.

young warriors would start out from Huronia, split into smaller bands to kill and seize prisoners. Iroquois captives were well fed, the better to endure torture. Women and children usually were spared, the children brought up as Hurons to go to war against their own kind. The purpose of the raids was not to gain territory but to take revenge for some past wrong or disagreement.

Father Sagard gave the first account of the Neutral Nation, thus called because it lived at peace with both Hurons and Iroquois, much more numerous than either. The Hurons had been about to attack the Neutrals but were persuaded by the Recollect fathers not to break the peace.

He included in his *Histoire* a letter written in 1627 after his return to France by a young Recollect missionary, La Roche d'Aillon. Aillon left his post in Huronia in 1626 to begin missionary work among the Neutrals, whose country he wrote was incomparably greater, more beautiful and better than that of the Hurons. (The lacustrine plains and ground moraines north of Lake Erie are the most fertile part of the Province of Ontario.) The Neutrals were superior farmers and grew mostly Indian corn, squash, beans, and sunflowers. They provided themselves with deer by organized drives. Winter in their land was so mild that geese, cranes, and turkeys remained through the year. Also the land of the Neutrals was more accessible than that of the Hurons because it could be reached by going up the St. Lawrence River into Lake Iroquois (Lake Ontario).

Sagard continued that the Hurons, aware their advantage would be lost if the Neutrals became attached to France, gave Aillon a bad name and made attempts on his life that caused him to leave. The proposed new route by way of Lake Ontario would require peace with the Iroquois. French policy was to have peace between the Indian nations but, Sagard was told, if the Neutrals replaced the Hurons, the Indian trade would be diverted from Quebec to the Dutch on the Hudson River, the Dutch being trading partners of the Iroquois. It was better to leave matters as they were, retain the Huron friendship and leave the Neutrals alone. (The waterways of the interior had become a matter of geopolitics.)

INTERRUPTION (1629-1632)

A British party led by the Kirkes, father and sons, raiding on their own initiative, seized Quebec by surprise in 1629. Pelts to the value of three hundred thousand livres were taken and whatever else of value was found. Champlain and the French, including the Recollects and Jesuits, were evicted. (The first Jesuits had come to Quebec in 1625.) Fishing and trading about the Gulf of St. Lawrence continued to be carried on by ships of various nationalities, a Basque ship reported as meeting a Turkish ship in the Gulf, its flag bearing three crescent moons.[18]

Champlain spent the years from 1629 to 1632 in France, writing the sixth and last book of his *Voyages* and drawing his last map, *Carte de la Nouvelle France* (both published in 1632). The large map (Fig. 10) was accompanied by a gazetteer of noteworthy places, Indian tribes, and their territories.[19]

The Hurons were listed as good farmers living in seventeen well palisaded villages. Their neighbors the Petuns (Tobacco Nation) grew a lot of tobacco to traffic with other nations, also grew corn and lived in palisaded villages. The Cheveux Relevées (Ottawas) were great fishers, hunters, and voyagers, who grew corn and dried blueberries and raspberries in exchange for peltry, wampum, nets, and other items. The powerful Neutral Nation had forty large villages and lived at peace with all but one people (the

18. Champlain, *Works*, VI, 198-220.
19. Champlain, *Works*, VI, 221-252.

Potawatomies about Detroit). Champlain visited the Abnakis, seven days south of the St. Lawrence on the canoe route to Kennebec; they also grew corn. A fine country (northeast of Lake Ontario), formerly cleared and cultivated, had been deserted on account of wars and was only visited by several nations for winter provision of fish and game.

By hearsay and the maps that Indians drew for him Champlain was able to draw the great falls (Niagara) at the head of Lake St. Louis (Ontario), the river of the Puans (the Winnebagoes of Green Bay), whence the pieces of native copper were said to come, and the rapids of Gaston (Sault Ste. Marie), beyond which was another great lake, thirty days distant by canoe (Superior). Champlain charted the coast by his own observations from Nantucket Sound and Cape Cod north through the Gulf of St. Lawrence, and the inland waters as far as Georgian Bay. His final map was the summary of the geography he had learned in thirty years, first as volunteer observer, later as captain in charge of the land of New France, from which he had been driven by the English and to which he hoped to return.

XI.

Return of the French: Destruction of Indian Nations by Feud and Disease (1632-1663)

RESTORATION OF NEW FRANCE

The seizure of Quebec and Nova Scotia by British irregular forces was revoked by the Treaty of St. Germain-en-Laye in 1632 restoring Canada and Acadia to France. The Company of New France, also called the Company of One Hundred Associates, was in control to the time of revocation of its charter in 1663. Champlain was returned to govern, serving to his death in 1635.

The Company had the monopoly of trade and was charged with bringing settlers to Canada at a rate of two to three hundred a year, which it failed to do. The establishment of the seigneurial system required the grantee to bring settlers. Beginning with the first seignory (1634) at Beaupré, below Quebec, the Company granted about seventy seigneuries, extending upriver to Montreal, some grants being of hundreds of square miles. For the most part they remained unpeopled wilderness, except for small holdings adjacent to the French communities. At the end of the Company tenure in 1663 there were only about two thousand French in Canada, mostly officials, merchants, priests, and their employees.[1]

Quebec was the civil and ecclesiastic seat. Champlain returned with Jesuits to take up work they had begun shortly before the French eviction of 1629. Jesuits replaced the Recollects, who had been the earlier missionaries and were excluded after the restoration. The Jesuits built a residence at Quebec and a school for Montagnais children nearby at Sillery. Two orders of nuns founded convents at Quebec in 1639, the Hospitalers to nurse the sick, the Ursulines to teach children. In 1659 François Xavier de Laval-Montmorency was named first Bishop of Quebec, to put his lasting stamp on French Canada. Trois Rivières, convenient to canoe traffic and midway between Quebec and Montreal, became a Jesuit station in 1634 and shortly a settlement of traders. Montreal, founded in 1642, had a Jesuit establishment and convents of nursing and teaching nuns. The three settlements held almost the entire French population.

---

1. Richard C Harris, *The Seigneurial System in Early Canada* (Madison, 1966), with the front end paper a map of the seigneuries in 1663.

REENTRY TO HURONIA

A fleet of Huron canoes came to Quebec in 1652 to welcome the return of Champlain and the Jesuit fathers. For the next thirty years the affairs of Canada are of record mainly by Jesuit accounts.[2] The Huron nation had responded well to missionaries and awaited their return. The harvest of souls, interrupted by the English intervention, was resumed.

Father Jean de Brebeuf took up residence in Huronia in 1634, "the Hurons gradually being won over to the Faith, though at first they were more eager for the advantages they might derive from the French than for religion."[3] Brebeuf described Huronia as a compact area, at its widest traversed in three to four days, of productive though sandy soil (moraines and outwash plains) that supported not only the Hurons but also many Algonquins, a neighboring people who planted but little. Huronia had twenty villages of about twenty thousand souls, all speaking the same tongue.[4] Father Peron elaborated the scene, each village being a compact cluster of long houses in which numerous families lived, one for example being of eighty houses, another of forty, each house having five fireplaces, each hearth serving two families.[5] The examples may have been somewhat overdrawn; the multifamily long house was characteristic of all the Iroquoian nations. Du Creux was informed that all the houses were of the same long form, with roofs arched like pergolas, roof and sides covered with bark, also that residence was matrilocal, and that inheritance was matrilineal, and that the office of the chief passed by female lineage.[6]

PESTILENCE

Brebeuf's letter of 1635 told of a great epidemic that came to Huronia from the east.[7] The greater part of the Indians about Trois Rivières fell sick and many died. Hurons returning home from Trois Rivières brought the contagion, which spread through their villages. A large number died, fishing and harvest of crops were greatly reduced. He described the sickness as beginning with a violent fever, followed by a skin eruption like that of measles or smallpox causing temporary blindness or dimness of vision, and ending with violent diarrhea. The mortality was continuing at the time of his writing. (The French knew the symptoms of smallpox but they did not know that measles were lethal to people exposed to them for the first time.)

Du Creux construed the pestilence as an attempt by Satan to wreck the Faith newly brought to the Hurons. The Jesuits were denied visiting the sick. One village sought to protect itself by discarding their French kettles:

2. Thwaites, *The Jesuit Relations*, seventy-three volumes in all.

3. François Du Creux, *The History of Canada or New France 1625-1658*, ed. James B. Conacher, tr. Percy J. Robinson, Publications of the Champlain Society, XXX and XXXI (Toronto, 1951-1952), I, 185, 200. Du Creux collected letters sent to France by members of his order and from them composed in Latin a history of Canada.

4. Brebeuf's letter of 1635, in Thwaites, VIII.

5. Peron, in Thwaites, XV.

6. Du Creux, I, 98 and 108.

7. Thwaites, VIII.

The belief was general among the Hurons that the Fathers had imported the pestilence which was working such deadly destruction . . . The whole tribe met in council; everywhere there was funereal gloom and everywhere death . . . Most of them enumerated their kin whom the pestilence had carried off. [An elder ascribed the disease to magic by the Jesuits, continuing:] You know that I never speak in council, except in regard to war, but here in this meeting I see that I must speak out, for death has taken all the other chiefs. Before I too follow them to the grave I will utter what is in my heart, and perhaps what I will say will help our perishing country, since the cruel sickness rages more fiercely every day. The plague has entered every lodge in the village, and has so reduced my family that today there are but two of us left, and who can say whether we two will survive? There have been other pestilences, but the evil has spent its strength in one or two moons; health returned and in a few years all was restored and the common calamity forgotten. Already it is now a year since the pestilence began, and as yet there is no sign which would give hope of a limit.[8]

The epidemic continued through the fall of 1636. Jesuits also fell sick but recovered and ministered to the natives as much as they were permitted to do.[9]

Another epidemic, apparently smallpox, broke out in 1639, first at Quebec where Hospitaler nuns had in their care "victims of an outbreak of smallpox supposed to have originated among the English in Virginia."[10] (The attribution to an English source is gratuitous.) Algonquins living on an island in the Ottawa River also "brought a disease with them in which there was great danger of death in consequence of the foul pustules."[11] Du Creux continued:

A party of Hurons on their way back from Quebec met some of the Algonquins who were suffering from the epidemic we have mentioned. They mingled with them without precaution and thus invited the contagion. There was nothing to prevent the spread of the pestilence in all directions; the Hurons are so negligent that no disease, however contagious, will hinder their usual intercourse. The result was that everywhere there was death and universal mourning and the blame again was placed on the French.[12]

The water route between Quebec and Huronia was the common highway for goods, Frenchmen, Indians, and communication of disease. Algonquian bands, mobile and small, were little affected by contagion unless they gathered at a trading station, such as Trois Riviéres. Hurons, living congregated in the crowded quarters of their long houses, were greatly exposed to whatever pathogen was introduced. Brebeuf estimated the Huron population at thirty thousand or more prior to the first pestilence. By 1640 it was reduced by about two-thirds.

The Fathers found solace in the great mortality because of the baptized infants "whose happy lot it was after rebirth to pass at once to Heaven," of the children "removed from this mortal scene before their fifteenth year," and of the adults who had given up their superstitious ways and died saved.[13]

Du Creux, looking back on the course of events, concluded that much of the Indian mortality was due to alcohol and their intemperance:

8. Du Creux, I, 244-246.

9. Thwaites, XIII.

10. Du Creux, I, 274.

11. De Creux, I, 282.

12. Du Creux, I, 300-301.

13. Du Creux, I, 305.

It is the frequent and daily complaint of the Indians that from the time of their first contact with foreigners mortality among them has greatly increased. It has long been a firm conviction among them that they are deprived of their lives by the most unholy charms and poisons, and they say—and there is no more deadly deception by the foul fiend—that they are ruined in this way by the holy water of baptism. At last, however, they have learned that the source and origin of all their trouble is intoxication [French, English and Dutch traded them alcohol for furs] . . . They gorge themselves for several days at a time each year on the arrival of ships from France; they have no restraint in what they eat or drink, and in the absence of self control, why seek for any further explanation of the prevailing Mortality?[14]

MORTAL ENMITY BETWEEN TRIBES OF THE NORTHEAST

The French found tribes of Algonquian speech and related ways inhabiting the Gulf of St. Lawrence and the Atlantic coast, in the Laurentian Highlands, and on the western lakes and rivers. Algonquian tribes wholly surrounded a cluster of Iroquoian tribes. The Iroquois called themselves 'the people of the long house', lived in villages that usually were palisaded, were good farmers, and had a similar social organization. Those of the Five Nations (Mohawk, Oneida, Onondaga, Cayuga, and Seneca) lived south and east of Lake Ontario, the Erie or Cat Nation south of Lake Erie, the Neutral Nation north of Lake Erie, and the Huron and Tobacco (Petun) south of Georgian Bay. At the time of Cartier the St. Lawrence Valley also was inhabited by Iroquois.

Cartier found the Indians, Algonquian and Iroquois, of gulf and river, living at peace. Champlain in 1603 found three Algonquian tribes at Tadoussac celebrating a scalp raid against Iroquois. The participating tribes were local Montagnais, Abnakis from south of the sound of the St. Lawrence, and Algonquins from the distant Ottawa River. Champlain in 1609 joined a war party that attacked the Mohawks in their homeland at the head of Lake Champlain, the aggressors being Montagnais, Algonquins, and Hurons, the latter an Iroquois nation thereafter known as 'the good Iroquois'. On his first visit to Huronia in 1615 Champlain went with a Huron war party on the long raid around the east end of Lake Ontario against the Oneidas. An enmity of unknown origin and ferocity allied Hurons with Montagnais and Algonquins against the Five Nations, the Hurons shortly taking the lead in the attacks on their kinsmen.

The strange and extreme enmity between kinsmen continued after the restoration of New France. In 1634 the Hurons "engaged in dangerous war." Five hundred Hurons who had formed a war party to ravage the lands of the Iroquois were defeated and lost many killed and captured.[15] In 1638 a victorious Huron raid brought back a hundred Iroquois prisoners, "who were distributed among the villages and reserved for butchery with cruel torture and of course in the end, the usual slow fire." Jesuit fathers comforted the doomed captives and administered the last rites.[16]

The earlier record is of aggression by Hurons and of cruelties committed by Hurons. Captives were not sacrificed by solemn ceremonies as in Mexico nor as in the ritual cannibalism of the Caribs, but were put to exquisite torture, insult, and degradation. The raids were not to gain territory or booty other than prisoners and scalps. They

14. Du Cruex, I, 88-90.

15. Du Creux, I, 180.

16. Du Creux, I, 258. Volumes XVI and XVII of Thwaites deal at length with the treatment of prisoners.

began, according to the Jesuit Relations of 1659-1660, prior to the seventeenth century by Algonquian attacks on the Mohawks, easternmost of the Five Nations, Hurons leading the hostilities against the Five Nations from the second through the fourth decade. And it was in the fourth decade that the Hurons suffered great losses from epidemics.

QUIET INTERVAL

Succeeding Champlain, Governor Montmagny undertook to bring peace throughout Canada. The year 1645 was quiet and prosperous promising, according to Du Cruex, "a better crop of Indian corn, a more abundant harvest of fish from the lakes and streams, a more profitable trade, and less violent assaults from disease."[17] The Algonquins and Montagnais agreeing, Montmagny sent an invitation to the Mohawks to meet at Trois Rivières with himself, Algonquins, Montagnais, and Hurons. The conclave continued through the summer, with good will speeches and the exchange of strings of wampum. The Mohawks presented seventeen belts of wampum, each accompanied by a declaration of good will. The eleventh belt was an invitation to the French to come to their land:

> We have much fish and game; our woods are full of deer and moose and beaver; say goodbye to these foul swine that run about your streets; they live on filth; you will dine on choicer food in our country; the trail is open; have no fear.[18]

The next year a French mission, headed by Jesuits, went to the Mohawks, Oneidas also attending.[19]

DESTRUCTION OF THE HURON NATION

The peace was short lived. A Jesuit was killed in Mohawk country in 1647, and the Mohawks raided Algonquins at Trois Rivières.

In 1648 the Senecas, westernmost and strongest of the Five Nations, took to the offensive. A Huron hunting party of three hundred men and women had gone to hunt in the plain north of Lake Ontario. The women went along "to carry the meat of some wild cows killed in the hunt." The Hurons were ambushed by a party of Senecas and many Hurons were killed or captured.[20]

The Huron Mission of St. Joseph was attacked during early mass on July 4, 1648. "About seven hundred were killed or captured, and of these the majority were women and children," the rest fleeing to the Jesuit residence of Ste. Marie (near Midland on Georgian Bay), where there was a small fort and garrison.[21]

Huronia including the land of the Tobacco Nation was laid waste in 1649. "On March 16 about a thousand Iroquois, perhaps more than had ever taken part in any other expedition, arrived unobserved in the territories of the Hurons." The first village

17. Du Creux, II, 415-416.

18. De Creux, II, 410.

19. Du Creux, II, 405ff.

20. Du Creux, II, 505.

21. Du Creux, II, 509.

was taken before its people were aroused, about four hundred killed or captured. The women and children fled, the men and the two Jesuit fathers remained to be taken, Du Creux describing in detail the serenity of the fathers as they suffered martyrdom.[22] Village on village fell, the survivors taking refuge on an island in Georgian Bay (Christian Island), where a village was built in haste and the land cleared and planted. The island providing only temporary safety, the Jesuits and Hurons discussed where they might go to be out of reach of the Iroquois. One of the places considered was the Swedish colony on the Delaware River. The decision was to go to Quebec, taking the canoe route by way of Lake Nipissing down the St. Lawrence River. Finding that the Nipissings "had just been massacred on the shores of their own lake," the exodus took place in 1650, and made passage to Quebec without incident. The refugees were cared for in Quebec until they "were removed to Île d'Orléans where they began to till the land in their own way."[23] This large fertile island below Quebec provided a safe home for the Huron refugees, as did Sillery above Quebec for Nipissings. Other Hurons dispersed to the western Great Lakes. Huronia was at an end in 1650.

DESTRUCTION OF THE NEUTRAL AND ERIE NATIONS

The Hurons for years had been aggressors against the Five Nation Iroquois, inviting the retaliation by which they were destroyed. The Iroquoian Neutral Nation was so called because it had taken no part in the feuding. Its territory was southwest of Huronia, including the fertile plains north of Lake Erie, now the best agricultural land of the Province of Ontario. Its population was larger than that of the Five Nations or that of the Hurons, before these were reduced by epidemics.

In 1650, having destroyed Huronia the Iroquois attacked the Neutral Nation, with whom there had been no previous friction. Du Creux offered two explanations: that the Neutrals gave harbor to Huron refugees and that the Five Nations maintained their numbers by taking captives:

> The Hurons who remained in their country experienced a varied fate. Those who had taken refuge with the Nation of the Neutrals did not find the asylum they had expected. They were destroyed, not by the natives, who received them kindly, but by the common enemy. The fierce Iroquois seeing that they had all but finished the Hurons turned their rage and their weapons upon the neighboring nation; and such was their success then in the hidden providence of God that they captured two of the outlying and populous villages. There was a general massacre in which old men and children were the chief victims; the younger women were carried off so that there might be more little Iroquois. The Huron refugees were either carried off or enslaved. Others of the nation made their way southward to New Sweden. The survivors surrendered to one of the nations of the Iroquois [Senecas?], and they are living among them today as peaceably as if there had been no wars and no hostilities.[24]

The Neutral Nation was overrun and eliminated, with scant record of the manner of its destruction.

The remaining northern Iroquoian tribe, the Erie Nation (Chats to the French, Cat Nation), was liquidated by fighting that lasted from 1653 to 1656. They were western

22. Du Creux, II, 517-523.

23. Du Creux, II, 562-566.

24. Du Creux, II, 566-577.

neighbors of the Senecas and inhabited the fertile country south of Lake Erie, were good farmers and perhaps as numerous as the Neutrals or the Hurons had been. An incident during the visit of an Erie embassy to the Senecas for the purpose of renewing a peace treaty is said to have caused the war. The surviving Eries were taken into the Seneca Nation.

It is not known to what extent the wars involved joint action of the Five Nations. The Senecas were principals in the attack on the Hurons, Neutrals, and Eries, as the Mohawks appear to have been against the Algonquins.[25] The Onondagas were the guardians of the council fire of the League of the Five Nations and were thereby its senior members. They are not mentioned as participating in the wars but are reported as living in peaceful intercourse with the Algonquins. A band of Onondagas came to live with the Algonquins in the winter of 1655 and "there was wonderful harmony and concord among them . . . The Algonquins did not hesitate to intermarry with the Iroquois, giving them in marriage their widows and daughters."[26]

The Jesuit Relations of 1660 told that the Iroquois were in control of five hundred leagues of territory, though their numbers were very small, the Mohawks having not more than five hundred warriors, the Onondagas three hundred, the Senecas a thousand, the Cayugas and Oneidas together four hundred; also that for the most part the Five Nations were composed of conquered people that they had absorbed, remnants of the Huron, Tobacco, Neutral, Cat, and Fire nations. (The Fire or Mascouten Indians were an Algonquian tribe living at the southwest end of Lake Ontario. This is an early mention of their expulsion. Later they were well known in their new home, Illinois.) As the Mohawks once had been so reduced by Algonquin attacks as to appear to be on the way to extinction, the Algonquins by 1660 were in that danger.[27]

The Five Nations became lords of the interior as far as the head of Lake Erie and Georgian Bay, which they swept clean of inhabitants in the course of eight years. They did not resettle what they had taken but continued to live in their old seats, occasionally sending parties to hunt and patrol the new wilderness they had made.

DUTCH AND FRENCH RIVALRY?

The Company of New France had the monopoly of trade until its charter was revoked in 1663, its income dependent almost wholly on the fur trade. The Dutch establishments on the Hudson River had the advantage of offering better price and easier access to the Great Lakes. They were in friendly relations with the Mohawks and the other members of the Iroquois confederacy, whereas the French were still burdened by the partisan involvement Champlain had entered into with the Hurons and Algonquin tribes.

Jesuit antipathy to the Dutch stressed their heresy. Father Jerome Lallemont in 1640 wrote Cardinal Richelieu from Huronia that the Dutch of New Netherland, "enemies of God and the State, must be gotten rid of, powerfully supporting the enemies of our allies, among whom we live, and by whose means alone we can advance either south or

25. Du Creux, II, 628, reported that a great chief of the Mohawks was captured by Algonquins and burned at the stake in Trois Rivières in 1651.

26. Du Creux, II, 681-682.

27. Thwaites, XLV, 205-241.

west."[28] Lallemont attributed part of the decline of Huron numbers from thirty to ten thousand to the Dutch, the manner unexplained. The Dutch, however, were not inciting the Five Nations against Hurons, who still held the offensive. Nor did the Jesuit extension of missions westward depend on an alliance of French and Hurons. Indeed, Governor Montmagny at the time was undertaking a general reconciliation.

Du Creux, writing of the destruction of Huronia, said that the Iroquois "were armed with guns (Oh shame and crime!) the Dutch had furnished to the pagans."[29] This is an erroneous imputation of hostile intent to the Dutch. The Iroquois did not destroy Huronia because they had guns and the Hurons lacked them. Guns were freely traded both by French and Dutch, and were prized by the Indians, as Nicolas Denys had described, for hunting and ceremonial show; but these guns were inferior to Indian arms and tactics in warfare.

The enmity between Hurons and Five Nations existed before the coming of French, Dutch, or English. The war was an ancient feud, its origin forgotten. Dutch merchants wanted no clash with the French. The government of New France in turn was trying to bring a general peace.

The surge of Iroquois power is not explained by economic motivation. Their acts of force were not for booty, nor to take and hold territory. They raided and returned home, travelling light and on foot, without the convenience of transport by birchbark canoe. The confederation of the Five Nations was not concerned with profit of furs or other goods but was a body politic established to serve the common weal.

28. Quoted by Percy Robinson in his introduction to Du Creux, I, xix-xxii.
29. Du Creux, II, 517.

XII.

The Great Lakes Explored

CHAMPLAIN'S SEARCH FOR THE GREAT LAKES

During his first summer in New France Champlain learned of the widespread use of the birchbark canoe, and that travelling by canoe the Natives had mastered the pattern of the waterways deep into the interior. More, Champlain also learned that these Indians were able to draw reliable charcoal-birchbark maps of these waterways from memory. In 1615 Champlain obtained an outline of the Great Lakes in this manner from one particular Native cartographer, and in 1616 Champlain provided his King with this first account of the freshwater seas which lay off to the West.

Champlain had also sent young Frenchmen to live with a particular tribe, to learn its language and customs, and to serve as interpreters. Thus Etienne Brûlé went to live among the Hurons and Nipissings, and was perhaps the first white man to voyage on Lake Huron, to explore Lake Ontario, and to get to Lake Superior.

NICOLLET AT GREEN BAY (1634)

Jean Nicollet came from France in 1618 and was sent by Champlain to live with the Algonquins, where he spent two years taking part in their travels. Thereafter Nicollet spent some eight years with the Nipissings, engaged in their fishing, hunting, and trading with a household of his own. During the English occupation of Quebec Nicollet remained in Indian country. After the restoration in 1634 Champlain charged him with an embassy to the People of the Sea (Winnebagos on Green Bay), the purpose being to make a treaty of friendship between them and the Hurons, the latter the outpost of Jesuit missions and French trade.[1]

Father Sagard's *Long Journey* told, in 1626, of nations of the Great Lakes known to the Hurons, among them the Puans, the early French name for Winnebagos.

Nicollet passed through the Straits of Mackinac into Lake Michigan. (The Nicollet Watch Tower in the state park on Mackinac Island bears a tablet inscribed to "John Nicolet who in 1634 passed through the Straits of Mackinac in a birchbark canoe and was the first white man to enter Michigan and the Old Northwest.") Others may have gone before him, but he is first of record.

At Green Bay Nicollet presented himself dressed in a Chinese robe of damask, embroidered with flowers and birds, and wearing pistols which he fired in salute. Several thousand people were gathered for the feast at which a hundred and twenty beavers were served. The ceremonies and pledges concluded, Nicollet returned to Huronia.

---

1. Thwaites, XXIII (covering the years 1642-1643), and XXIX (1646).

The curious episode tells us that the Great Lakes were still thought a possible passage to China and that Nicollet had hoped to meet Chinese dignitaries at Green Bay. Twelve years later (1646) a Jesuit letter told of their expectation to build a fine mission on Green Bay which would now serve as the entry to China.[2] Traders probably continued to visit Green Bay without record; the Jesuits did not arrive until years later.

GROSEILLIERS AND RADISSON

Little is known of the early years of the fur trade on the Great Lakes, who the traders were, where they went, or what they brought back. The trade was carried by birchbark canoe through a maze of waterways formed by Ice Age sculpture and deposit, which extended from the highlands north of the Great Lakes south to the moraines about Lake Michigan. The pelts most in demand were those of animals that lived in and by cold-water streams, lakes, and marshes. Indians of the north woods took, dressed, and brought the pelts to places to which traders came. Indian canoemen took the cargoes to Montreal, Trois Rivières, and Quebec by the Lake Nipissing-Ottawa River route.

The peace agreed to by the Iroquois in 1654 made the route secure. In that year a homeward bound Indian canoe party picked up two Frenchmen at Trois Rivières, one being Médard Chovart, Sieur de Groseilliers. The two Frenchmen were returning home after two years in the West with fifty canoes and a valuable cargo of furs. The Jesuit Relations told of their voyages as having been of more than five hundred leagues and of their visiting many Indian tribes, including 'the Nation of the Sea who were called Puans', Green Bay being known as a good locality at which to meet Indians who brought furs there to trade. Another Jesuit relation told of an earlier assembly there of three thousand Indians who had met to make a compact of peace, probably the visit of Nicollet of twenty years before.[3]

In August 1659 Groseilliers, joined by his brother-in-law Pierre Radisson, left Trois Rivières to accompany a westward bound Indian canoe party. The exploration is known by Radisson's account, *Voyages of Peter Esprit Radisson*, written in English and published in 1669.[4] Radisson claimed to have been the leader of the western expeditions, including a voyage to Green Bay (which Miss Nute has proved a fabrication). The voyage of 1659-1660 was asserted falsely to have been his fourth. With certain lapses of memory and of truth the book nonetheless provides the earliest published account of the Lake Superior country and its native peoples.

In 1659 the party took the usual route by way of Lake Nipissing to Georgian Bay, following the north coast of Lake Huron through North Channel to Sault Ste. Marie. As their Indian companions had promised they found excellent whitefish, bear, beaver, and moose at the rapids. Portaging around the Sault they entered the great lake (Superior) in fine late summer weather and followed its south shore to high rock cliffs on which birds nested and to which Indians came to venerate the Devil (Pictured Rocks near Munising). Paddling on for several days they came to three beautiful islands they

2. Grace Lee Nute, *Caesars of the Wilderness* (New York, 1943), 8.

3. Miss Nute's study, cited above, is the best reconstruction of the documents and routes of western trading voyages at midcentury.

4. Peter Esprit Radisson, *Voyages of Peter Esprit Radisson*, ed. Gideon D. Scull, Publications of the Prince Society (Boston, 1885).

named Trinity (Huron Islands), and then to a deep bay (Keweenaw Bay), about six leagues wide. Beyond it was a plain changed into a bog by the industry of beavers who had cut down the trees to the extent that no wood was available for a fire. At the carrying place they found a well-worn path two leagues long. The portage avoided a very long detour around a point of land that extended far into the great lake (Keweenaw Peninsula, a ship canal now across its base where the portage trail had been). Pieces of native copper were found and the explorers were told of an island of pure copper in the lake (the native copper of Keweenaw Peninsula).

The winter was spent at a village on a lake to the south (Lake Court Oreille), "where there was abundance of boats made of trees they have hollowed, and [others] of rind." The people were Menominees, the "nation of oats, grain that is much in this country."[5] (Lake Court Oreille drains to the Mississippi River, on which dugout canoes were the only kind of craft used, this being the first report of such in the interior.) The name Menominee was understood to mean gatherers of 'wild oats', the French term for wild rice (*Zizania*). (The Menominee country was a land of shallow morainic lakes in which wild rice provided a staple food.)

The winter was one of heavy snow which made it difficult to hunt with snowshoes, and hunger became extreme. At winter's end a ceremony for the dead took place, and it was attended by many nations. (Radisson, writing ten years later, was uncertain about succession of events, excerpted here in the order of the text.) A delegation of Nadonserons (Eastern Sioux) came, their wives laden with wild rice and a little Indian corn. "They wept upon our heads until we were wetted by their tears, and made us smoke in their pipes," which were made of red stone with long stems to which eagle and other feathers were tied, the pipes passed around in silent smoking. The visitors were also called 'the nation of beef' (English translation of *boeuf*). Eighteen nations (Siouxan bands?) set up skin tents that they brought on their backs. "They arrived with incredible pomp," described as to painted bodies, headdress, and clothes ornamented with buffalo horns, bear paws, feathers, and porcupine quills. "Every one has the skin of a crow hanging at their girdles . . . The elders came with great gravity and modesty, covered with buff [buffalo] coats which hung down to the ground." Speeches, chanting, and passing the calumet were followed by feasting, in which wild rice was served:

> We had there a kind of rice, much like oats. It grows in the water 3 or 5 feet deep . . . They have a particular way to gather up that grain. Two take a boat and two sticks, by which they get the ear down and get the corn out of it. Their boat being full, they bring it to a fit place to dry it, and that is their food for most of the winter.

The assembly gave the Frenchmen occasion to make a pact of friendship between the Sioux and other nations, including Christinos (Crees, living north of Lake Superior, not as yet visited).[6]

Radisson wrote his *Voyages* to recommend himself for employment by the English who were organizing the Hudson's Bay fur trade. At the time Crees, inhabiting a long stretch of country north of Lake Superior, had become important suppliers of furs to the French. By his account Radisson left the place of the assembly to get to the Cree country in three days; the assembly, however, was held at a place three days' journey

5. Radisson, 199, 201.

6. The meeting with the Sioux is told in Radisson, 207-217.

south of Lake Superior, whereas the Crees, it is known, lived *north* of the lake. Radisson went on to say that he found more than six hundred men in a fort, who were in turn joined by another thousand. The ceremonies included climbing a greased pole, beating drums of earthen pots filled with water and covered with skins, and dancing to the cadence of gourd rattles. Neither distance nor customs gave, therefore, credence to the purported visit to the Crees, who like other Algonquin tribes of the Laurentian north lived in small bands, in small settlements, and spent their time fishing and hunting.[7]

The final exploration was west into the land of the Sioux, the 'Nation of the Beef', said to have been by seven days' journey:

> Where we wondered to find ourselves in a town where were great cabins, most covered with skins and other close mats. They told us that there were 7,000 men. This we believed . . . There they have no wood, and make provision of moss for their firing. This their place is environed by perches which are a good distance one from another, that they get in the valleys where the Buffs use to repair, upon which they live. They sow corn, but their harvest is small.

The data are in part obscure and in part invented. The people of the wild cattle were Sioux, whom Radisson had identified by Algonquin name at the assembly at the Menominee village. At the time these Sioux lived west of the Menominees in the woodland of central Minnesota. A journey of seven days west would hardly have sufficed to get beyond the woodlands to the woodless prairie plains where buffalo chips served as fuel (Radisson mistook these chips to be dry moss). The skin covered cabins would have been tepees of buffalo hide, those of mats suggest wigwams of Algonquian tribes. The Sioux did not build great cabins, nor did they live in great towns enclosed by palisades. The information is confused and in part once again invented.

After six weeks with the Sioux, Radisson told of returning by way of Sault Ste. Marie. Spring was at hand, the best season to hunt moose, of which he, his brother-in-law, and a 'wildman' (translation of *sauvage*) killed above six hundred, another obvious fiction.

The Jesuit Relations of 1660 fill in and correct the account that Radisson later gave to the English.[8] Groseilliers is identified as the head of the expedition, the canoe party as getting back to Montreal in August 1660. The fleet of canoes was manned by Ottawas, who by that time had a settlement at Sault Ste. Marie, where they engaged in the transport of goods between the Great Lakes and the French settlements of Canada. (An early notice of the relocation of Ottawas to the west of Georgian Bay.) Groseilliers had visited the Ottawas at the Sault the year before. Returning from the Menominees, he was met by them on Lake Superior with a hundred canoes, sixty going on to Montreal with a cargo of furs valued at over two hundred thousand livres. (Ottawas were traders as well as carriers, the ownership of the furs not stated.)

Groseilliers, the Jesuits learned, had visited the Nation of the Cattle (*boeufs*), consisting of four thousand men living in permanent habitations (as was the case of the eastern Sioux). There was no mention of the Crees of Radisson's account. Natives living at the far end of the great lake (Superior) told of a sea to the north, west, and south that gave hope of a sea that might extend to China. One of the Jesuits gave an estimate of latitude and longitude and the distance to Japan.

7. The Cree story is in Radisson, 217-220.

8. Summarized in Nute, 69-73.

Jesuit attention was drawn to the prospects of the west. Algonquian tribes of similar speech and customs, friends of the French and at peace among themselves, lived to the far end of the Great Lakes. Ottawas were the major intermediaries of commerce and were established at Sault Ste. Marie, a crossing place between the lakes. Beyond Lake Superior a different Indian people, the Sioux, had given friendly reception to Groseilliers, indicating a large new mission field awaited entry. Reports of seas beyond also raised hopes of a new passage to China and Japan where the Company of Jesus was already enjoying its greatest endeavor and success.

In 1663 New France became a crown colony with new officials and new directives. Disappointed in their expectations of a privileged part in the fur trade Groseilliers and Radisson left Canada to promote their affairs with the English, first in New England, and, failing to get support there, in London. The country north of Lake Superior produced prime furs that could be exploited from Hudson Bay at less cost than from Quebec. To this end they offered their services to England. The Hudson's Bay Company was chartered in 1670 and the two brothers-in-law entered its service.

Fig. 11. Early French Settlements on the Great Lakes.

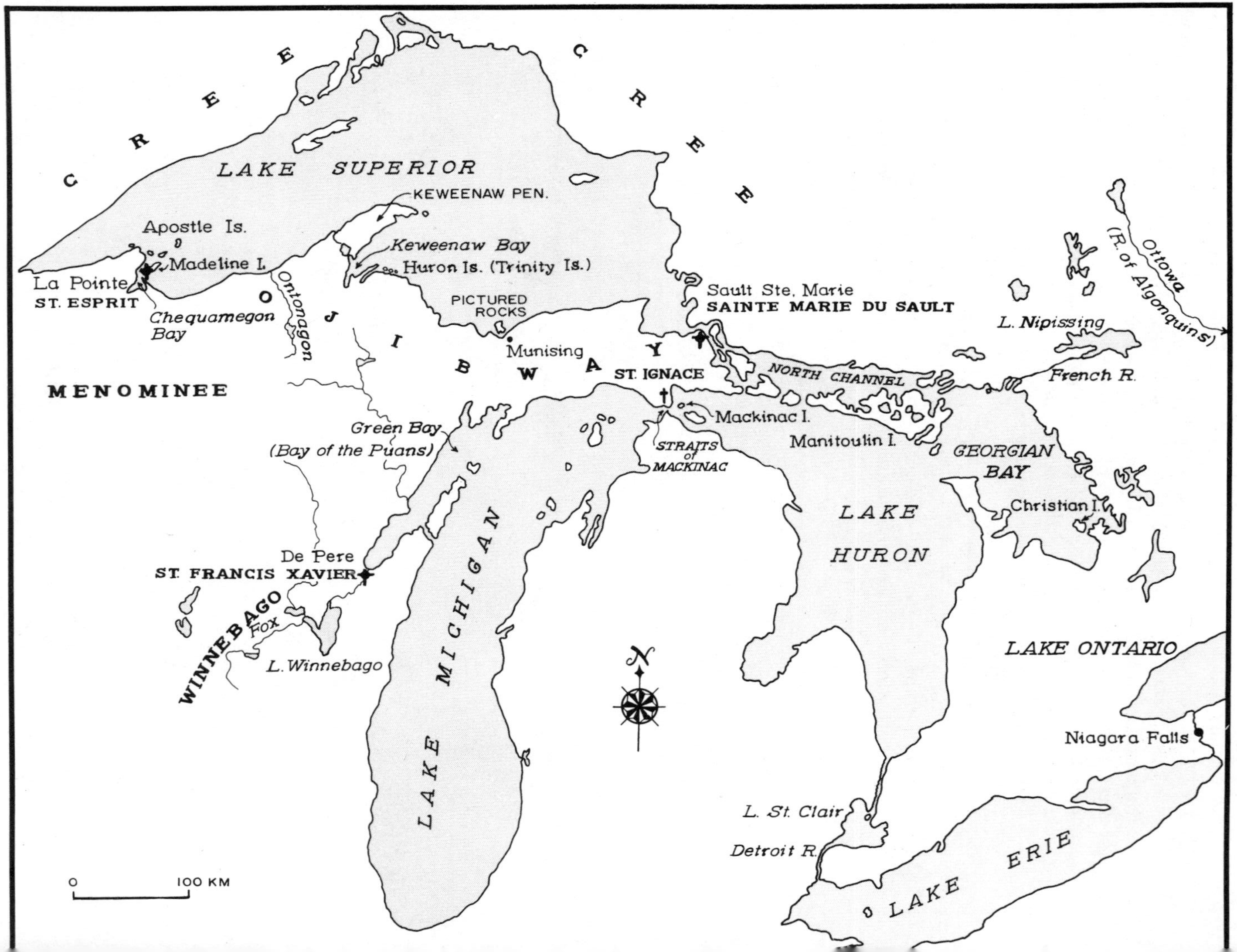

CREE

LAKE SUPERIOR

KEWEENAW PEN.

Keweenaw Bay

Huron Is. (Trinity Is.)

Apostle Is.

Madeline I.

La Pointe
ST. ESPRIT

Chequamegon
Bay

Ontonagon

PICTURED
ROCKS

Munising

Sault Ste. Marie
SAINTE MARIE DU SAULT

NORTH CHANNEL

Mackinac I.

ST. IGNACE

STRAITS
of
MACKINAC

O J I B W A Y

MENOMINEE

Green Bay
(Bay of the Puans)

De Pere
ST. FRANCIS XAVIER

Fox

WINNEBAGO

L. Winnebago

Ottawa
(R. of Algonquins)

L. Nipissing

French R.

GEORGIAN
BAY

Christian I.

Manitoulin I.

LAKE
HURON

LAKE MICHIGAN

L. St. Clair

Detroit R.

LAKE ONTARIO

Niagara Falls

LAKE
ERIE

100 KM

0

XIII.

The Crown Colony / Jesuit Missions on the Great Lakes (1663-1672)

FROM COMPANY TO COLONY

Concerned solely with the fur trade, the Company of New France neglected to bring French settlers, had its charter revoked in 1663, and was replaced by the Crown Colony of New France. Colbert, Minister in charge of the affairs of France overseas, held that New France needed a solid base of French colonists to raise crops, livestock, and offspring, as did the English, Dutch, and Swedes in their colonies to the south. The planting of the stock of the present French-Canadian population began with Jean Talon, Intendant of the Crown Colony from 1665 to 1672.[1]

The census of 1666 recorded a population of 3,215 French, of which one-third was female. About half of the inhabitants lived in and about the town of Quebec, 547 registered as in Quebec, 533 in Côte Beaupré on the north shore below Quebec, and 452 on Île d'Orléans. Montréal and its surroundings counted 625, Trois Rivières 455.

Horses and sheep were introduced in 1665. By 1667 there were 3,107 head of cattle and 11,448 arpents of land under cultivation. In 1671 Talon reported that horses were in sufficient numbers for the needs of the colony and that swine were "as familiar as in Old France, in such number that lard was being exported." Marriageable women were shipped yearly from France, each given fifty livres on finding a husband. At the end of Talon's term the French population numbered 6,705.[2]

During the last months of his tenure Talon granted a large number of seigneuries, sixty at one time, with the obligation to settle and to cultivate land. "If Talon was not wholly the originator, it may be said that he organized the seigneurial institution in Canada." In addition to individual grants seigneuries were given to religious orders. A band of settlement formed along the St. Lawrence River, the houses facing the river, the farms parallel strips running back from the river, as they still do. Mainly the settlement was along the north bank, in part a precaution against Iroquois raids.

Colbert's plan of a French peasantry in Canada was realized without dispossession or subjection of the Indian peoples.

PARTISANS OF KING OR POPE

Louis XIV increased royal and restricted papal authority. Within the Church the division was between the nationalist (called Gallican) clergy and those who held

1. Thomas Chapin, *Jean Talon, Intendant* (Quebec, 1904).

2. Chapin, 158-160, 413-420.

Ultramontaine, papal, authority. In New France the confrontation was marked. François Xavier de Laval-Montmorency was named Vicar Apostolic of New France, came in 1659 to represent Rome, support the Jesuits, and oppose for half a century official and private actions he held contrary to Christian ethics. The antagonism between Laval and the Jesuits on the one hand and public officials and their adherents on the other found early and strong expression in the matter of supplying brandy to the Indians.

Under the new establishment, the Recollect Order was readmitted and the young order of Sulpicians was given entry, both favored by the Crown as counterbalance to the Jesuits. When Talon and then Frontenac sent expeditions into the interior, members of these orders participated, but not the Jesuits.

JESUIT MISSIONS ON THE GREAT LAKES: ST. ESPIRIT ON CHEQUAMEGON BAY

The destruction of Huronia scattered the surviving Hurons and Nipissings. Those taken captive to Iroquois villages were ministered to by Jesuit fathers in the peaceful years of the mid-fifties, when Iroquois conversion was under way. Refugees settled about Quebec under Jesuit care, others dispersed to the safety of the western Great Lakes.

The missions of the western Great Lakes at first were called missions to the Ottawas:

> We called these people the Upper Algonquins, to distinguish them from the Lower Algonquins who are found lower down, around Tadoussac and Quebec. They are commonly given the name Outaouaks because, of more than thirty different nations that are found in these Countries, the first to come down to our French settlements were the Outaouaks, whose name afterward remained with all the others. [Father Dablon].[3]

The Ottawas became known to the French as Cheveux Relevées, living about Georgian Bay. Living astride the great canoe route between the St. Lawrence Valley and the Great Lakes, these Algonquian people served as the middlemen in the fur trade with the Algonquian tribes of the western Great Lakes. When their Huron neighbors were attacked by Iroquois of the Five Nations they abandoned their exposed homes on Georgian Bay. Iroquois raids being made on foot, the Ottawas sought security by moving west across the lakes. Kindred Algonquian tribes lived all about the western Great Lakes and supplied furs to the Ottawas. In part accompanied by Hurons, the Ottawas thus relocated on friendly western shores, as far as Chequamegon Bay of western Lake Superior.

The Indian canoe party, starting back from Montreal in 1660 having delivered Groseilliers and his cargo of pelts, was joined by two Jesuits. The Jesuits were taken to Chequamegon Bay, recommended by Groseilliers' account as a mission prospect. They stayed over winter, using rude quarters left by the French traders, and succumbed to the rigors of the winter cold.

Chequamegon Bay was chosen in 1665 for the first mission of the Great Lakes (Fig. 11). Father Allouez joined French traders there at Madeleine Island, named St. Esprit. The location was at the southern point of the island (the village of La Pointe still thus called), where Ottawas and Hurons, in good part Christian, were settled in number.

3. Thwaites, LIV (1669-1671), 127. The same volume, 126-243, treats of the founding of the Great Lakes missions.

The Jesuit Relations of 1669-1670 told of excellent fishing about the point, of great sturgeon fishing to the east on Ontonagon River, and of the abundance of fish in the rivers and coves of the lake. The fifteen hundred Ottawas living at the point fished a lot, grew Indian corn, and did a little hunting. Conversion of peoples on the mainland began promptly. Thirty villages of Nadouessis (Eastern Sioux) were reported as living at a distance of eight days' journey to the west. Also there were numerous reports of pure copper found about the great lake.

Father Marquette was assigned to St. Esprit in 1669 and there learned of the country of the Illinois, some of whom came to visit at the mission making a journey of thirty days across great prairies. Marquette reported: "The Illinois journey always by land; they raise Indian corn, which they have in great abundance, have squashes as great as those in France, and many roots and fruits." Their country, he was told, had great numbers of wild cattle, deer, turkeys, water fowl, and pigeons. Shawnees also came from afar to visit (an Algonquian people driven out of their eastern homes by the Iroquois). There were other powerful nations in the south. His letter ended with notice from the Sioux and Assiniboines to come to their country and bring the peace that he preached. The conversion of the Illinois became his great commitment, to be realized several years later.[4]

MISSION AT SAULT STE. MARIE

The second mission was founded at Sainte Marie du Sault in 1668, at the foot of the long rapids by which the waters of Lake Superior discharge into Lake Huron. Ottawas lived there, using it as base for the canoe traffic that largely was managed by them. The rapids also were home of a Chippewa tribe, known as Saulteurs.

Numerous bands of other Algonquian tribes came there from near and far, from spring through fall, to take their supply of *poisson blanc*, the salmonid whitefish, most prized of Great Lakes fish. The manner of fishing was described as standing in canoes, thrusting a pole with pocket net at the end into the water, and thus taking half a dozen fish at a time. The supply was great and provided dried fish for the winter. Fur traders visited the rapids to meet Indians gathered from all directions, including some from the highlands to the north.

MISSION ON GREEN BAY

The third mission, St. Francis Xavier on the bay of the Puans (Green Bay), was begun by Father Allouez in December 1669 and was reported by him shortly after his arrival.[5] The first mass was attended by eight French traders, overwintering there. In a nearby village were six hundred souls of four nations, Puans (Winnebagos), who were the native inhabitants, and other newcomers, including Potawatomies and Foxes. (Refugees from the Detroit region, the Foxes had fled their homeland the previous spring.) "These savages withdrew to those regions [Green Bay] to escape the persecution of the Iroquois and settled in an excellent country, the soil of which is black,

4. Thwaites, LIV, 169-195.
5. Thwaites, XIV, 198-243.

yielding them Indian corn in abundance." Allouez named other tribes from the east, Sacs who had built a weir across the (Fox) river to catch sturgeon, and Miamis, at the time absent on a winter hunt. "These people are settled in a very attractive place, where beautiful plains and fields meet the eye as far as one can see. Their river leads by a six days' voyage to the great river, called Messi-sipi." French traders, spending the winter at Green Bay, perhaps told the priest of the distance to the great river and gave its Algonquian name to history.

MISSION ST. IGNACE AT THE STRAITS OF MACKINAC

The next report on the western missions still called them missions to the Ottawas. That of St. Esprit had been troubled by quarrels of Ottawas and Hurons with visiting Nadouessis (Sioux) from the great river called Mississippi. Father Marquette therefore closed the mission and moved to the Straits of Michilimackinac, where he founded in 1670 the Mission of St. Ignace, with an Ottawa village at one side of the peninsula and a Huron village on the other.

THE ATTRACTIONS OF GREEN BAY
ACCORDING TO FATHER ALLOUEZ

Mission St. Francis Xavier served eight nations living about the bay of the Puans, thus called because of the smell of its water (sulphur?). The Puans (Siouan Winnebagos) were the old inhabitants as were the Folles Avoines (Indians of the Wild Oats) who lived along the river where they harvested a lot of the wild grain (Algonquian Menominees, known earlier by their proper name as living in the lake country south of Chequamegon Bay). The lately arrived tribes (all Algonquians), driven out of their homes by Iroquois, were Potawatomies, Sacs, and Fourches about the bay and along the far shores of Lake Michigan. Inland (about Fox River and Lake Winnebago) were Outagamis (Fox), Mascoutens or Fire Nation, and Oumami (Miamis).

South of Green Bay the northern forests were replaced by prairies and groves. "The region of forests and mountains is passed when one arrives here . . . in every direction prairies as far as the eye can see, cut by a river gently winding." On small eminences there were groves at intervals (the so-called oak openings of later American settlers). The prairie country was said to extend for more than three hundred leagues, with *buffles* (buffalo) in herds of four and five hundred. The wild cattle of these rich pastures had superior flesh, their fat mixed with the wild grain making a most delicate dish.

The site chosen by Father Allouez for the mission was at the rapids five miles above the mouth of the Fox River (at the present town of DePere). Indians had built there a great weir across

> the entire river from one bank to the other, making a sort of palisade of stakes, which they plant in the water in a straight line, leaving only spaces enough to allow the water to run between certain hurdles, which stop the large fish. Along this barrier they arrange scaffolds, on which they place themselves in ambush, and await their prey with impatience. When the fish, following up the current, reach the barrier, the fisher plunges a net in the shape of a purse, into which he takes the fish with ease.[6]

6. Thwaites, LVI, 121-123.

In autumn wild rice, growing in the shoal waters of the river, attracted migrating water fowl, and nets were set to entangle both birds and fish. The account continues:

These two kinds of fishing draw to this spot many savages from all directions . . . To all the advantages of this place may be added the fact of its being the only and great thoroughfare for all the surrounding nations, who maintain a constant intercourse, either in visit or trade. Hence it was that we turned our eyes thither, with a view to placing our chapel there in the midst of more than ten different nations, who can furnish us more than fifteen thousand souls to be instructed.

The mission at Green Bay attracted visits by Illinois Indians, who came on foot, as they had thus gone to visit at St. Esprit.[7] Father Allouez wrote of the decorum of the Illinois chief and his party, of "A docility that had nothing to do with the barbarian," of their freedom from superstition and sacrifices. The beautiful country along the Mississippi River that they described, he thought, contributed to their lovable disposition. Also the good life they lived lacked the risks of lake fishing:

As they do not fish, but live on Indian corn, which is easily raised in those fertile lands that they occupy, and on game, which is very plentiful, and of which they are never in want, they have no fear of the perils of the Lakes, where many other Savages perish while fishing.

DISSENSIONS BETWEEN CIVIL AND RELIGIOUS AUTHORITY

Louis XIV and his Minister Colbert considered the loyalties of the Jesuits greater to Rome than to France, Talon being thus warned that the Jesuits exercised improper authority.[8] In a letter to Colbert (October 1667) Talon wrote that he had reproached the Jesuits civilly for not having given enough attention to changing the habits of the Indians and had been promised that this would be done, beginning with instruction in the French language. The newly established order of Sulpicians was opening a school for Indians at Montreal, which he thought promised to bring the desired result.[9]

The Recollects, who had been the first missionaries in Canada and were expelled with the other French when the English occupied Quebec, were not readmitted when the French returned in 1632, the Jesuits having the monopoly of missions for thirty years. Colbert authorized their reentry in 1669, but their functions, they complained, were restricted by Laval as Vicar Apostolic and later as Bishop.[10]

Talon's complaint against the Jesuits, later repeated by Frontenac, was that the Jesuits learned the Indian languages and respected their customs insofar as these were not in conflict with Christian doctrine, and that therefore, not being taught French language and ways, these Indians remained Indians. (The Jesuits in Spanish and Portuguese America were charged with the same failure to integrate the Indians into the national state.)

---

7. Thwaites, LV, (1669-1670).

8. Chapin, 40-41.

9. Pierre Margry, *Découvertes et Établissements des Francais dans le sud de l'Amérique Septentrionale* (1614-1754 (Paris, 1879-1888, I, 79.

10. Recollect Memoirs in Margry, I, 3-33.

Intendant Talon started sending parties in 1669 to explore, take possession, and make report on the nature of the country:

> I have sent resolute men who promise to go farther than has ever been done, some to the west and northwest of Canada, others southwest and south. In all places these adventurers are to keep journals and report on their return on the instructions I have given them in writing; everywhere they are to take possession, place the arms of the king, and write down the minutes that will establish title.[11]

Two such 'resolute men' who thereby entered the pages of North American history and geography were Louis Joliet and Robert Cavelier, Sieur de la Salle.

Joliet left Montreal by the Ottawa River route with instructions to go to Lake Superior and find the copper mine from which pieces of pure copper had been brought, and thereupon to seek an easier route (an all-lakes route) by which to bring the metal to Montreal.[12] La Salle started from Montreal with seven canoes and twenty-one men on July 6, 1669, to go up the St. Lawrence River to its head. Joliet was Canadian born and reared and had experience in canoe travel and Indian trading. La Salle came from France in 1666, acquired property at the side of the rapids at Montreal, soon to be called Lachine, and planned there the discoveries to which he would dedicate his life, seeking to find the passage west to the Orient.

La Salle's party was led by two canoes of Seneca Indians who had come to trade at Montreal, lodged with La Salle, and informed him of interior lands unseen by Europeans. Two Sulpician priests of the seminary at Montreal, Dollier and Gallinée, joined the expedition, hoping to find a virgin field for the conversion of heathen.

The report by Gallinée is the principal source of what is known of La Salle's expedition and of that of Joliet.[13] The young seminarian, wide-eyed observer in a strange world, noted items an experienced traveller might have disregarded. Thus he gave a detailed description of the form and handling of birchbark canoes, which he noted as made only by Indians of Algonquian speech. The Iroquois made their canoes of other bark (elm), heavy and ill shaped, lasting at best a month, whereas the birchbark canoes of the Algonquians, properly cared for, served for five or six years.

The Senecas told La Salle of a river called Ohio which he was determined to discover and descend. Having passed its falls, they said, he would come to a land where wild cattle were as numerous as trees and then come to the river that discharged into the sea. (Ohio is the Iroquois name of the river. They knew the falls of the Ohio at Louisville, the increased number of buffalo downstream, and its course to the Mississippi.) La Salle hoped that the reported sea was the *mer vermeille* (Mar Bermejo, early Spanish name of the Gulf of California) which would therefore open the sea passage to China.

From the head of the St. Lawrence River they followed the south shore of Lake Ontario, well entertained at Iroquois villages, palisaded and located inland from the lake. They were supplied with Indian corn and squash and noted that oil of sunflower seed was used for cooking, as was oil of nuts and bears. Prairies about the villages were

11. Margry, I, 82.

12. Margry, I, 143.

13. Gallinée's "Récit" is in Margry, I, 112-166. It is translated in Louise Phelps Kellogg, ed., *Early Narratives of the Northwest, 1634-1699* (New York, 1917), 167-209.

said to extend east and very far to the west. "Where there are woods, these are of oaks and so open that one can easily ride through them on horseback."

At the Seneca villages near the west end of Lake Ontario they were told that they were a long way from streams that fell into the Ohio but that by going on to Lake Erie they would find a more convenient portage. Instead of doing so directly they continued to the end of Lake Ontario, crossing the mouth of a large and very rapid river, "the discharge of Lake Erie into Lake Ontario" (Niagara River), heard the noise of the falls, which they were told were greater than the height of any pine trees, and so turning north came to a great sand bar, with a small lake behind it (Hamilton, Ontario). They unloaded the canoes to make a stop at a small Seneca village (a late extension of Seneca settlement north of Lake Ontario).

At the village there was an unexpected meeting with Joliet who had left Montreal ahead of time and had gone by way of the Ottawa River to Lake Superior. He had failed to find the source of copper, and had purchased an Iroquois captive from Ottawas, and used the Iroquois as guide to follow the Great Lakes south by a route until then unknown to the French (or at least unrecorded). Joliet gave a description of the new route, of which Gallinée made a chart. Joliet told also of the nation of Potawatomies (about Detroit), who had never been visited by a missionary. This being what the Sulpicians were seeking, they decided to take the way by which Joliet had come.

The party separated at the village early in October 1669. Joliet returned to Montreal by way of Lake Ontario and the St. Lawrence. La Salle was ill and remained at the village, Gallinée not knowing what became of him. The Sulpician party took two weeks to cross overland to the north shore of Lake Erie, which they followed until they came to a place that appeared suitable for spending the winter, which they did in comfort, Gallinée recording it as "the terrestrial Paradise of Canada":

> I call it that for there is surely no finer country in all Canada. The woods there are open, intermingled with very fine prairies, watered by rivers and brooks abounding in fish and beaver, variety of fruits, and what is more, so full of game that we have seen at one time more than 100 *chevreuils* [bucks?] in one band, troops of 50 or 60 *biches* [does?], and bears fatter and of better taste than the most savory pigs of France. Finally, one can say that we passed the winter more comfortably than we would have done in Montreal.[14]

Winter ended, the party took their canoes to the head of Lake Erie, through a river (Detroit River), and a small lake (Lake St. Clair) into Lake Huron, and arriving at Mission Ste. Marie du Sault late in May 1670, noted that Father Marquette and another Jesuit had already been there for a year. The religious services, Gallinée thought, were more for the benefit of the French, of whom there were about a score, than for the Ottawas and other Indians, in whom the Sulpician failed to find that the Jesuits had implanted Christian ways. Gallinée had expected to see a poor station; instead, a large clearing had been made from which a good crop was in prospect. There was a great resource of whitefish by which the Saulteurs could have nourished ten thousand persons. In nearby rivers sturgeon, weighing six to seven pounds, were in great numbers. Meat and pelts were to be had at bargain prices. The Sault was well located to serve the interests of the Jesuits and of French traders.

The relation closed with the fatiguing voyage of twenty-two days by Lake Nipissing and the Ottawa River to Montreal, which was reached June 18, 1670, the final stage slowed by tedious portages, hazardous rapids, and stops to patch damaged canoes.

14. Margry, I, 150.

EXTENSION OF FRENCH CONTROL TO THE INTERIOR

Talon informed Colbert and the King of the explorations he had directed, including a copy of the Sulpician map of the Great Lakes as providing a better route than the one in use. The time had come to establish French possession of the interior to the limits of Spanish Florida and Mexico. The first step should be to secure Lake Ontario and restrain the Iroquois, which would be done by building a post at each end and a ship to patrol the lake (Letter of October 10, 1670).

A month later Talon renewed and enlarged the proposal. French possession of Lake Ontario was necessary to block the English of Boston and the Dutch of Manhattan who were using the Iroquois to gain control of the fur trade. Indians at Tadoussac brought word that two English ships had entered Hudson Bay, conducted there by Groseilliers, formerly a resident of Canada. This (the start of Hudson Bay Company operations) he would counter by inviting the Cree living in the vicinity of the bay to come south to trade their furs.

The grand design of a French continent outlined by Talon's memoirs was initiated by two expeditions. La Salle was exploring to the south, Sieur de Saint-Lusson had been sent northwest to find the copper mine and then to learn whether, by lake or river, there was passage to the South Sea (Pacific Ocean) and to China.[15]

On November 2, 1671, Talon wrote the King that La Salle had not as yet returned from his voyage. (What La Salle did during that long absence is unknown. His later claim to have discovered and ascended the Mississippi River is not supported by evidence.) Saint-Lusson was back at Quebec, having gone almost five hundred leagues, giving expectation that less than three hundred leagues remained to reach the shores of the western ocean. A third expedition, led by the Sieur de Saint-Simon and the Jesuit Albanel, was on its way north, with the commission to take possession of Hudson Bay for France.

Saint-Lusson got to Ste. Marie du Sault, and perhaps farther. He brought back specimens of native copper from Lake Superior and the Ontonagon River. A number of Frenchmen told him of a mass of copper weighing eight hundred pounds, lying in the lake. The Jesuits at the mission had a piece of a hundred pounds. The source of the native metal had not been discovered. Talon speculated that these boulders (*galots*) were rolled down by torrents, as on the Ontonagon River, or that they might have been fused by the heat of the sun.[16] (The rocks bearing native copper, of the Keweenawan system, were determined by geologists in the nineteenth century.)

Saint-Lusson was ordered to go to Ste. Marie du Sault to take possession there for France of lakes Huron and Superior and all lands and waters contiguous and adjacent, from one sea to the other. The formal act was carried out June 14, 1671, the procès-verbal taken and signed by four Jesuit priests and fourteen named French civilians, one being Joliet. Indians of fourteen nations were assembled, Ojibways living there, Crees and Assiniboins from the north, Potawatomies and Miamis from the bay of Puans (Green Bay). The latter were charged to make the act known to their neighbors, the Illinois, Mascoutens, Fox, and others. The attending natives being of Algonquian

15. Margry, I, 76-89.
16. Margry, I, 92-96.

speech, an interpreter translated the proclamation, each part acknowledged with three cries of *Vive le Roi*.[17]

Fur traders and Jesuits were active on the farther Great Lakes, following their own interests. Talon served notice that New France had authority over them wherever they were, proclaiming at the same time the protection of the King to the Indian tribes as subjects under his laws and customs. Other expeditions were sent on their way to extend the limits of New France from Hudson Bay to the Gulf of Mexico (Fig. 11).

THE GEOGRAPHY OUTLINED AS KNOWN TO 1672

In addition to the expeditions of discovery and possession arranged by Talon, Governor Courcelles took a party up the St. Lawrence River to the outlet of Lake Ontario. To prevent the diversion of the fur trade south to the Dutch a fort on Lake Ontario had been proposed, and it was to examine this plan that Courcelles made the reconnaissance.[18]

The anonymous reporter introduced himself as recording only what he had seen. In order that the reader would understand the problems of New France, it was necessary to know the nature of its waters and somewhat of its peoples. The physical pattern was determined by the St. Lawrence, one of the world's great rivers, almost thirty leagues wide at its embouchure a hundred twenty leagues below Quebec (the saltwater embayment). Above Quebec it continued sixty leagues to Montreal and thence for seven hundred leagues, expanding to great lakes, connected by a large river. A brief description of lakes follows, as to size and intervening distance, the first one St. Pierre (above Trois Rivières), the second and third St. Louis and St. François (above Montreal). Beyond Lake Ontario was Lake Erie, from which one entered a lake a dozen leagues in diameter (St. Clair, unnamed); fifteen leagues farther, one came to the Lake of the Hurons, and so finally to Lake Superior, a hundred fifty leagues long. The headwaters of the St. Lawrence still awaited discovery.

Where the St. Lawrence River flowed over hard rock that resisted erosion it spilled over them in cascades of varying height, the first sault that of St. Louis at the island of Montreal. Five more were listed above on the St. Lawrence, the seventh (Niagara) between Lake Ontario and Lake Erie, the eighth between Huron and Superior (Sault Ste. Marie) resembling the one at Montreal. There were other difficult rapids.

Necessity had led these people to the invention of a suitable form of transport:

> These boats are made of the simple bark of birch over a frame of cedar wood that supports the bark, and they give the shape necessary to carry on water a rather large number of persons and baggage, however so fragile that if they hit a rock or are not carefully handled in taking them out of or putting into the water, they are easily damaged; so unstable that ten pounds more on one side than the other makes them overturn, which obliges one to kneel or sit flat; so light that one or two men at most carry them, and yet so made that some will hold six to eight persons with their belongings.

The manner of paddling, steering, and portage was also described.

Mainly the country was inhabited by Algonquian tribes, whom the French found in a state of war of long standing with the Iroquois. Indian warfare was by surprise attack,

---

17. Margry, I, 96-99.

18. The anonymous relation is in Margry, I, 167-192.

135

to capture or scalp enemies. The captives were condemned to death with horrible tortures or were adopted into the tribe. The Five Nations inhabited the south side of Lake Ontario and were able to assemble about two thousand warriors. Except in Mohawk territory beaver and moose had been hunted almost to their extermination. The Iroquois carried on their hunting mainly north of Lake Ontario on land formerly occupied by Hurons and others.

The great river to the west was called Ohio by Iroquois, Mississippi by Algonquians. By careful study of maps of Florida and Mexico it appeared not to have an embouchure like that of the St. Lawrence (that is, a drowned river mouth), which gave rise to the thought that it fell into a different sea (the delta extending into the Gulf of Mexico?).

XIV.

The Mississippi Valley Explored by Joliet and Marquette

GEOMORPHOLOGY AND THE BIRCHBARK CANOE

New France was a land unlike any the French had known, a highland massif north of the Great Lakes, south thereof plains and ridges of unconsolidated earth. Highland and lowland were shaped by the Pleistocene ice cap that covered them, abrading bedrock at the north, depositing detritus at the south. As the ice cap melted water spilled from one basin to a lower one, forming a greatly irregular network of lakes, streams, and marshes.

As for transportation the genial solution was the invention of the birchbark canoe, made and used by the northern Algonquian tribes from local materials, bark of paper birch (*Betula papyrifera*), ribs of white cedar (*Thuja occidentalis*), and pitch from balsam fir (*Abies balsamea*). Iroquoian Hurons used birchbark canoes, but not the Five Nations. This light-weight and light-draft vessel provided the common means for carriage of persons and goods, for fishing, for taking beaver, water fowl, and moose, and, especially west of Lake Michigan, to harvest wild rice.

The fur trade was based on transport by canoe, employing Indian canoemen. Ottawas in particular were thus engaged, trafficking and living with Algonquian tribes all about the western lakes. Common speech and customs were bonds of friendship that opened the way west for traders, Jesuits, and exploring parties. Jesuits now knew the extent of the St. Lawrence watershed and heard of a great river beyond called Ohio by the Iroquois; this river, Mississippi by the Algonquian name, was next to draw their attention.

JOLIET SENT TO DISCOVER THE MISSISSIPPI

Count Frontenac, appointed Governor of New France, arrived in September 1672 to continue the exploration Talon had directed. He wrote Colbert:

> M. Talon has also thought it expedient for the service to send the Sieur Joliet to the discovery of the South Sea by way of the country of the Maskoutens and the great river they call Mississippi, which is believed to discharge into the sea of California. He is a man well versed in such discoveries and who has been already quite near to this great river, the south of which he promises to discover. We shall have news this summer, as well as of the copper mine of Lake Superior, although I do not think that this will be of much utility when discovered because of the length of the route and the difficulty in transporting the material because of the falls and rapids that must be passed.[1]

1. Margry, I, 255.

Talon had sent Louis Joliet to find the copper along Lake Superior, who on his return made the first known passage from the Great Lakes to Montreal by way of the St. Lawrence. On Talon's recommendation Frontenac selected Joliet to undertake, in 1673, the discovery of the river known as Mississippi, an approach to be made through the country of the Mascoutens by way of Green Bay and the Fox River.

JOLIET JOINED BY FATHER MARQUETTE

Father Jacques Marquette had been visited by Illinois Indians at his first mission of St. Esprit on Lake Superior, was strongly drawn to them, and hoped to bring them into the Christian faith. The Illinois came to visit mission and traders at Green Bay and some settled there with their families. They were said to be a numerous nation, some living along the great river, others on rivers that flowed through prairies abounding in herds of buffalo.

When Joliet arrived at the mission of St. Ignace on the Straits of Mackinac to which Father Marquette had moved, the hoped-for opportunity was at hand. Joliet would carry on with his commission to explore the Mississippi to the sea, and Marquette would accompany him to open up a new mission field.

THE DISCOVERY VOYAGE

Joliet and Marquette wrote separate reports of the voyage of discovery, neither known in the original form. Joliet, returning to report to Frontenac, was wrecked in sight of Montreal, lost his canoe, his papers, was separated from a young Indian he had brought from distant lands, and almost lost his own life. Frontenac wrote Colbert in November 1673 that copies of Joliet's journals had been left with the fathers at Sault Ste. Marie and were expected to be sent the next year. Joliet gave a short account from memory of the map he had made, and a second one "while awaiting the relation of which father Marquette has a copy."[2]

Marquette's report was prepared for publication after his death by his Superior, Father Dablon. This was done at Quebec in 1678, and included a map.[3] It is not known whether Dablon made use of the map or relation that Joliet left with the Jesuits. Dablon's edited Marquette journal and the two short reports by Joliet agree as to sequence of time and place.

Joliet, Marquette, and five Frenchmen left St. Ignace May 17, 1673, Marquette having an Indian map of the course of the great river, its tributaries, and peoples and settlements. The route was to the head of Green Bay and up the Fox River, where the first people met were Menominees, the people of the wild oats whom Marquette had first known south of Chequamegon Bay. They came next to the Mascoutens or Fire Nation, then to Kickapoos, and farther up Fox River to Miamis, "of more civil habit and better appearance than the others who seemed peasants by comparison." (All were recent settlers, displaced from their eastern homes by Iroquois pressure.) On June 10 they left the known inhabited lands.

2. Margry, I, 259-262; and 262-270. The second account is an anonymous resumé with quotations from Joliet.

3. Text and map are reproduced in Thwaites, LIX, 86-163.

Miami guides took them up the Fox River by channels full of wild oats (wild rice) and helped carry the canoes across a protage of twenty-seven hundred paces to the Wisconsin River (now the city of Portage, an Ice Age spillway of the Great Lakes into the Mississippi River). Thereafter they were on their own, taking a week to drift and paddle down the Wisconsin to the Mississippi River.

Following the great river south for more than sixty leagues they came on June 25 to a path leading to villages, the first Indians they had seen since leaving the Miamis. These were three villages of Illinois Indians, half a league apart. Their language, much like the Algonquian known to the French, enabled an exchange of speeches along with the ritual passing of the calumet. The town of the great sachem was of three hundred large cabins, its name heard by Marquette as Peouarea (a western Illinois tribe, Peoria).

They left the Illinois tribe at the end of June, the pace of travel thereafter speeding up. While they were looking at monstrous figures painted on rocks high above the river (Piasa Bluffs above Alton), a mass of trees and debris flooded out of the mouth of a muddy river on the other side, the Pekitanoui (Missouri). (July was normal flood time of the Missouri bringing meltwaters from the Rocky Mountains.) It was hoped that this river might be a way to the sea of California.

As they hurried down the river they had a bad passage in a rocky narrows (Grand Tower) before coming to the mouth of the Ohio River (for which the Algonquian name Wabash was used, as it continued to be for some time, the Iroquois name Ohio unknown to the French in the west). This river was home of the Shawnees, who had been attacked by the Iroquois. (Joliet would have known of the former home of the Shawnees and of their displacement.) They had entered the wide lowlands of the lower Mississippi indicated by two remarks: the canebrakes began here, and this was also the homeland of mosquitoes. The Indians met thereafter slept on scaffolds over fires, the smoke driving the mosquitoes away.

Continuing down the river they came to a new people who had European trade goods, including muskets, and were told that the goods had been procured from Europeans who lived on the sea, not more than ten days' journey distant. (Spaniards did not supply guns to the Indians. The information may refer to English traders from Carolina.) A threatened attack by the next people (Chickasaws?) changed to welcome on the presentation of a calumet given the French by the Illinois. Ten leagues farther brought them to a village of the Arkansas, determined as at 33° 40'. (Joliet made observations of latitude, correct for the mouth of the Arkansas River.) A number of Arkansas villages were visited briefly. Hearing that the mouth of the Mississippi was only a few days distant but fearing to fall into the hands of Spaniards of Florida, they decided to turn back with news of their discovery.

The return began July 17, two months after they had set out from St. Ignace, a month after they had entered the Mississippi at the mouth of the Wisconsin River, and little more than two weeks after they left the Peoria villages. An extraordinary performance, supported by recorded observation.

The return was carried out at a rapid rate of travel. The canoes were paddled up river against the strong mid-summer current to the mouth of another river (Illinois), which gave an easier and more direct route north and a short portage to the southern end of Lake Michigan, a route that must have been known by prior information. A stop was made on the upper Illinois at the Illinois village Kaskaskia, of seventy-four houses (near

Ottawa, Ill.), Marquette promising that he would return soon and instruct them in the Christian faith. The portage (at Chicago) and voyage north along the west coast of the Lake of the Illinois (Michigan) was completed without incident, and they arrived at Green Bay in late September 1673, four months after the voyage began at St. Ignace.

OBSERVATIONS ON LAND AND LIFE

As they went south from Green Bay they noted the large amount of wild oats (wild rice) growing in shallow water along Fox River, and these oats emerged above water in June, were two feet high by August, and ready to harvest in September. The ripe grain was shaken into canoes, dried on wooden griddles over slow fire, put into bags of hide, trodden to separate grain from husk, and then winnowed. (Marquette summed up knowledge of the plant and its use by Indians.) From a village near the Fox River, inhabited by Indians of three nations and situated on an eminence, they had a beautiful view of prairies interspersed with groves as far as the eye could see.

The Wisconsin River was described as broad, shallow, and of many vine-clad islands. From there they saw prairies and ridges of woods of oak, walnut, basswood, and a tree armed with long thorns (Gleditsia, the honey locust, here at its northern limit). There were many deer and buffalo.

The Marquette account continued with note of the changed aspect of the country as they went down the Mississippi to a more open and less hilly land that abounded in deer and buffalo, also in bustards and swans, flightless at that season because they were in molt. Sturgeon were netted and a strange fish with a large bony snout as broad as a man's hand (Polyodon, the paddle-fish, also called shovel-bill). Buffalo shed their hair in summer, their skin becoming like velvet and used by the Indians to make into robes which they painted in various colors. Buffalo meat was found to be of superior quality (as in the Spanish accounts). As far as the end of the voyage on the Arkansas River buffalo, deer, and turkey were numerous. The Indians at the south knew nothing of beaver, their wealth being the hides of the wild cattle.

Joliet's oral report added particulars:

> The prairies and forests share this country equally, which furnishes good pasturage to the large number of animals that fill it. The wild cattle never flee. The Father has counted as many as 400 in a single herd. Cerfs, biches, chevreuils [American elk and Virginia white tailed deer] are almost everywhere. Cocs d'Inde [turkeys] promenade on all sides. Parakeets fly in bands of 10 to 12, and cailles [quail] rise in the prairies at every moment.[4]

The first people met on the Mississippi were Peorias of the Illinois nation, the town of the great chief consisting of three hundred large houses, Marquette and Joliet agreeing, the latter estimating it as having eight thousand souls. (As these were long houses, each occupied by a number of related families, Joliet's guess was reasonable.) The feast at the chief's house began with sagamité made of boiled cornmeal seasoned with fat and served in a great wooden dish. The second course was fish, the third a large dog, declined by the guests, and the fourth buffalo meat. The Peorias cultivated fields of corn, beans, and squash, some of the latter dried to be eaten in winter and spring. Also they grew excellent watermelons. (Earliest notice of the dissemination of this Old World melon north into the upper Mississippi Valley?) The Peorias had diverse Euro-

4. Margry, I, 265.

pean possessions, including muskets, which they said were procured from tribes that traded with the French. A peace calumet was given as a present to assure the French of a friendly reception by other nations, which it did.

Joliet included comment on dugout canoes:

> There are woods on both sides to the sea. The greatest trees one sees there are a kind of *cotonniers* [cottonwoods], of extraordinary thickness and height. The savages use them to make canoes of one piece, fifty feet long and three wide, in which thirty persons and their equipment can embark. They make them with greater skill than we use for ours. There are so many of them that in a single settlement we saw as many as 280.[5]

The people living below the mouth of the Ohio according to Marquette had muskets, axes, hoes, and knives of iron, and beads and bottles of glass, the latter used as flasks for gunpowder. The visitors were served buffalo meat, bear oil, and excellent white plums. (De Soto's party had commented in the same region on the excellent plums, grown in orchards.) The brief stay with the Arkansas revealed that the corn in this area was planted at different seasons, some ripe, some in the milk stage, and some lately sprouted. Cooking was done in large, well made earthen jars, the food served on pottery plates. Sagamité, roasting ears, and dog meat were served; and as a dessert, watermelon. Corn was stored in baskets woven of cane and in very large gourds (hollowed out pumpkins or true Lagenaria gourds?).[6]

This was a competent reconnaissance of the new country and its people, a people who had already begun to change by acquiring things from distant French, English, and Spanish sources. The river was free to all who came bearing the calumet of peace.

"THE UTILITY OF THIS DISCOVERY"

An anonymous abstract of Joliet's report concluded with proposals as to how the discovery should be put into effect, in the form of five 'remarks'.[7]

The first remark was that the discovery opened a great field for the conversion of docile and receptive native peoples, using the Illinois as the means.

Second, the course of the discovery indicated that the river would be found to discharge into the Gulf of Mexico, and not into the Gulf of Colorado (California).

Third, at Latitude 38° another river (Missouri) entered the Mississippi, by which there might be discovered another way by sea to Japan and China.

Fourth, a great advantage was that it would be possible to sail by bark to Florida (Gulf of Mexico), needing only a canal through half a league of prairie to enter from the head of the lake of the Illinois (Michigan) to the river St. Louis (Illinois). A ship should be built on Lake Erie (above Niagara Falls) from where it could sail through Lake Huron and so on to the Gulf of Mexico.

"The fifth remark concerns the great advantages by establishing new colonies in so beautiful a country and on such fertile soils." Such was the thought of Joliet, cited by quotation:

> At the beginning, when I was told of such land without trees, I imagined a burned over or barren country that would produce nothing, but found the contrary that none could be better, for wheat, vines, or whatever fruits.

5. Margry, I, 264.

6. Thwaites, LIX, 157.

7. Margry, I, 262-270.

The river that we have named St. Louis and which rises near the head of the lake of the Illinois [Lake Michigan] seems to me best and easiest to settle. Where we entered this lake there is an ample harbor [Chicago] for ships with shelter from wind; the river [Illinois] is wide and deep, filled with catfish and sturgeons. There is game in abundance, buffalo, deer, and turkey more than elsewhere; in a distance of eighty leagues I was not a quarter of an hour without seeing some.

There are prairies, three, six, ten, and twenty leagues long and three wide, bordered by forest of like extent, beyond which the prairies recommence, in such manner that there is as much of one as of the other . . .

An habitant there would not spend ten years cutting and burning trees. From the day he came he could start plowing the ground and if he lacked French cattle he would use those of the country . . . from the hides of the cattle he could make shoes and from their wool better cloth than much of that we bring from France; and thus he would find easily in that land wherewith to nourish and clothe himself. Nothing was wanting there, except salt.

Illinois was the promised land for French settlement and an open door to missions.

COLBERT AGAINST COLONIZING THE MISSISSIPPI VALLEY

The enthusiasm for a colony in the interior was not shared by Colbert, who wrote Frontenac (May 17, 1674) not to undertake large voyages up the St. Lawrence nor continue farther extension of French settlers. The settlers should be kept together building towns and villages, applying themselves to clearing and peopling the best lands nearest the coast, and staying in close communication with France, "not pushing discovery far into lands so remote that they can never be inhabited or possessed by Frenchmen." An exception might be made if their control was necessary for French commerce or there was danger of possession by another nation, but, this not being the case, the natives should be left in freedom to bring their peltry to trade. Another exception might be the discovery of a more southern sea than the St. Lawrence, which was closed to navigation for six months of the year.[8]

MARQUETTE'S LAST VOYAGE (1675)

Marquette started south on Lake Michigan in November 1674 to begin the mission he had promised the Illinois. Becoming ill on the way he camped for the winter at the river of portage (Chicago River), where there was adequate provision of buffalo, deer, turkeys, and partridges (prairie chickens, the cocks noted as ruffed). At the end of March flights of geese and ducks passed daily and pigeons (passenger pigeons) were taken also. French traders, camping elsewhere, brought supplies.

With the spring thaw the land became flooded, Marquette's party barely having time to stow their belongings in trees and to move to higher ground. The waters continued to rise, flooding the portage, over which they then paddled their canoes to the Illinois River, Marquette's journal ending March 29, 1675.[9]

8. Margry, I, 256-257.
9. Thwaites, LIX, 164-183.

Marquette made it to Kaskaskia, the village of five to six hundred fires on the upper Illinois River, where he preached to fifteen hundred men, not counting the women and children. His illness becoming worse, he started back along the east side of Lake Michigan and died on the way (at Ludington, Michigan), having been six years a missionary among Algonquian tribes of the west.

XV.

La Salle's Louisiana Project

FORT FRONTENAC

Governor Frontenac was briefed in 1672 by his predecessors on the state of affairs and the projects underway to enlarge New France. Governor Courcelles had gone in 1671 up the St. Lawrence River to Lake Ontario to exchange pledges of friendship with the Five Nations, and with their consent to look for a site for a fort on the lake. The prior regime had succeeded in winning the Iroquois to peace. Frontenac would make it a lasting peace and open another route to the interior:

> So that the Iroquois, who are rather susceptible to alarms, should not be disturbed by all the preparations, he thought to send them someone to tell them his plan to go to Quinté, visit the mission and French establishment there, and ask them to send there deputies of each nation. To this end he chose the Sieur de la Salle, as a person capable for such employment by the diverse voyages he had made thereabouts and by the relations he had established with the Savages.[1]

Thus incidentally La Salle was reintroduced in 1673 after several years of silence, largely spent among Iroquois. Quinté, on the northeast shore of Lake Ontario, had a lately established Sulpician mission to the Iroquois.

La Salle was ordered to leave Montreal, go to Onondaga, where the Five Nations held their councils, and have them send deputies to Quinté. Thus began the long and close association of Frontenac and La Salle.[2] The place of meeting was changed to Katarakoui (Kingston) at the outlet of Lake Ontario, where Frontenac was awaited (July 13, 1673) by three score of the elder and principal men of all Five Nations. Presents and speeches were exchanged for a week and the building of a post was begun there, to be named Fort Frontenac.

The advantage of a post at the outlet of Lake Ontario, as Frontenac saw it, was its access by water to the land of the Iroquois. Three of the Five Nations lived nearby to the south of the lake: the Oneidas, the Onondagas who were guardians of the council fire, and the Cayugas. To the southwest were the Senecas at the far end of Lake Ontario, to the southeast the Mohawks in the valley that still bears their name.

A year later Frontenac wrote Colbert (November 12, 1674) that the post he had built kept the Iroquois from being persuaded by the Dutch to renew hostilities against the French. The Iroquois kept their pledges, and "came this summer to Montreal in solemn embassy bringing eight children of their first families . . . Never has one seen so many savages come down to Montreal as this summer. The Iroquois who usually came only in

---

1. Margry, I, 198.

2. The voyage and ceremonial addresses are recorded in Margry, I, 195-238.

spring and toward summer have remained all winter," mingling in peace at Montreal with their former enemies, the Ottawas. The success had exceeded all expectations and promised to be lasting.[3]

Another letter (November 14) to Colbert recommended La Salle, then starting for France, as "a man of spirit and intelligence, and the most capable one I know here for all enterprises and discoveries one might confide to him, having a very perfect knowledge of the state of this land."[4] Thereby began the next advance of La Salle in the affairs of New France.

The proposal La Salle presented to Colbert in 1675 began: "The proponent, who knows the advantage to the colony of Canada of the establishment of Fort Frontenac, where he has been in command for some time, desiring to employ his means and his life in the service of His Majesty and the increase of the country, offers . . ." The six proposals made concerned his seigneury of the fort and the adjacent land.

La Salle was given everything he requested and more. On May 13, 1675, Louis XIV signed three elaborate documents, an *arrest* accepting the offers made by La Salle, letters conceding patent of concession for Fort Frontenac and adjacent lands, and letters of hereditary nobility. The seigneury and command of Fort Frontenac gave La Salle title to four leagues of land about the fort, the fishing and hunting rights on Lake Ontario and its rivers, and permission to settle the French and Indians at the fort. The patent of nobility stated that he had "risked the greatest perils to extend our name and empire to the end of the New World."[5]

La Salle was engaged through November 1677 in the business of establishing fort and settlement. He had cleared a thousand arpents of good ground to plant to grain, having found by trial that grain could be sown there in fall, which was not possible 'in Canada'. Horned cattle, swine, and hogs had been introduced. He built two villages, one of a dozen French families who were provided with houses and cleared land, the other of a hundred Indian families (Iroquois) whom he attracted by friendship. Under the care of two Recollect fathers it was hoped "that the two different villages would soon merge into one of good Christians and good Frenchmen."[6]

LA SALLE AUTHORIZED TO MAKE NEW DISCOVERIES

La Salle went again to France at the end of 1677 to present a project for the discovery in the west. The project stated that he had made various voyages south of the Great Lakes by which he discovered the Ohio River, which "he followed to where it falls from on high into vast marshes at Lat. 37°, after having been increased by another very large river from the north."[7]

The land to the south of the Great Lakes, in contrast to the forests, poor soils, and harsh climate of Canada, would produce everything grown in France. Cattle could

3. Margry, I, 273-277.

4. Margry, I, 277.

5. Margry, I, 278-288.

6. Margry, I, 333-335.

7. Margry, I, 330. The latitude of the Falls of the Ohio at Louisville is 38°, the distance thence to the marshy lowland (of the Mississippi) is several hundred miles. La Salle claimed to have gone to the Falls of the Ohio, but the statement is equivocal as to reaching the Mississippi.

pasture there throughout the winter. The wild cattle would yield superior wool and hides. The Savages of the west, who were in great number and for the most part of sweet and sociable nature, would accept French ways and in a few years add a large number of subjects to the Church and the King. The first step had been taken (at Fort Frontenac) and would be followed by advancing into these better lands.

La Salle therefore asked the King for permission to build two establishments, one at the outlet of Lake Erie, the other at the far end of Lake Illinois (Michigan). He asked also for the seigneurie of lands he would discover and people, the ownership of all lands cleared and abandoned by the savages of their own will, as they did at times, and his appointment as governor. He promised not to engage in commerce with the Ottawas, nor on lakes Nipissing, Huron, Superior and Bay of the Puans.[8]

The letters patent, signed May 12, 1678, gave La Salle the right to discover the western part of New France, "than which there is nothing closer to our heart than the discovery of that country, where it appears a way may be found to penetrate as far as Mexico." He was authorized to build forts wherever deemed necessary, was told not to trade with Ottawas or other Indians who brought furs to Montreal, and was given the monopoly of the trade in buffalo hides.[9]

BACKGROUND OF PARTISAN ANTAGONISM

La Salle was given the rights to western colonization that Joliet had been denied by Colbert the year before.[10] Joliet was a friend of the Jesuits, who were backed by Laval. La Salle had become the right arm of Frontenac, who had opposed Laval and the Jesuits.

Shortly after coming to Quebec Frontenac wrote Colbert (November 2, 1672) of his astonishment that none of the Indians under the charge of the Jesuits spoke French. He told the fathers that "while making the savages subjects of Jesus Christ they should also make them subjects of the King," teaching them French as the English taught English in their colonies. Until their missions, for the most part pure mockeries, had been reformed, he said the Jesuits should not be permitted to extend into farther parts, adding the invidious charge, "to speak frankly, they think as much of the conversion of beaver as of that of souls."[11]

Frontenac at first based his antagonism to the Jesuits on their failure to make Frenchmen of the Indians. Frontenac's antipathy to the Jesuits became an obsession. In 1677 he wrote Colbert a long series of accusations:

> Almost all the disorders of New France have their origin in the ambition of the ecclesiastics who, wishing to join to spiritual authority an absolute power over temporal affairs, cause suffering and complaint to all who are not wholly submissive . . . They have employed to this end the gratuities of the King, the alms they have from France, the concessions of the best and most important parts of Canada, which they have demanded and obtained, and finally the commerce in which they engage despite the prohibition by the King.[12]

8. Margry, I, 329-336.

9. Margry, I, 337-338.

10. Margry, I, 329.

11. Margry, I, 247-248.

12. Margry, I, 301-325.

Frontenac's accusations ended with the charge that, knowing that La Salle planned to ask for the concession of Illinois, the Jesuits were resolved to ask that Illinois be granted to Joliet and Lebert (a trader),

> persons entirely under their control, the former being one they had been backing, although he did not voyage until after the Sieur de la Salle, who will tell you himself that the relation of Sieur Joiliet is false in many particulars.

On his return from the Mississippi Joliet reported to Frontenac who accepted and transmitted the news of the discovery, in fact an acute and truthful account. That Frontenac later dismissed it as false and said that Joliet had been preceded by La Salle was a libel.

Laval, Bishop of Quebec, banned trading liquor to Indians under penalty of excommunication. The Council of State referred the matter to Colbert, who asked Frontenac to consult a group of principal citizens.[13] The assembly met in Quebec on October 10, 1678, La Salle, who had just returned from France, participating. Fifteen argued in favor of the trade, five against it. Joliet gave a moderate judgment against it, La Salle a strong and lengthy statement in its favor.[14]

The trade in liquor, La Salle said, was necessary to preserve the peace and commerce, leaving to the civil justice the punishment of disorders. Only laymen should decide what was good or bad in commerce. Canada had an annual trade of at most eighty thousand beaver pelts, of which about twenty thousand were paid for with brandy, usually a pint of brandy for a pelt, a rate of consumption that rarely led to drunkenness. Two thousand Iroquois and Hurons who lived in and about the French settlements maintained better order than did many of the French. A number of Indians had moved to Canada from New England and Manhattan in order to get away from debauchery by liquor provided by the English and Dutch. Twenty thousand natives living in Canada committed fewer disorders than were likely to occur at two or three fairs in any small town in Brittany. Also there were many natives who took neither wine or brandy. (This was confirmed by others, especially as true of the Ottawas.)

La Salle got along well with the Jesuit missionaries whom he met while working among the Iroquois. Later he turned against them. In 1679 at the beginning of his voyage, he suspected that they were traitors:

> I shall need some protection to carry it out. It traverses the commerce of certain people who will not suffer it readily. They profess to make of these parts another Paraguay, and the road that I am barring them from would facilitate an advantageous intercourse with Mexico. This barrier infallibly would mortify them, and you know how they react against those who resist them.[15]

La Salle, dedicated royalist, had become as bitter an enemy of the Jesuits as was Governor Frontenac.

13. Margry, I, 405-420.
14. Margry, I, 414-417.
15. Margry, I, 393.

La Salle left France in July 1678 with thirty men, including artisans, Recollect friars, and Henri de Tonty of the iron hand, who was to be his faithful lieutenant to the end. They got to Quebec in September and were at Fort Frontenac in mid-December.[16]

A party of fifteen was sent ahead by canoe with a valuable cargo of merchandise to await the others in the Illinois country. La Salle sent another party to locate a place above Niagara Falls at the outlet of Lake Erie, where a ship was to be built to sail the Great Lakes, Tonty describing the falls of Niagara River: "It forms vapors one can see from a distance of sixteen leagues and it can be heard from afar when the air is calm. Once swans and bustards are in its current, they are unable to rise and are dead before they are at the foot of the falls." For the next six months La Salle was engaged on Lake Erie at building a bark of forty tons, which he named the *Griffon*.

The *Griffon* sailed August 7, 1679, and in three days came to the *detroit* by which the lake of the Hurons discharged into Lake Erie, then passed a round lake named Lake St. Clair by the Recollects. A dozen men were required to tow the bark (through the St. Clair River) to Lake Huron. Saginaw Bay was named as it was crossed and Michilimackinac (St. Ignace) was reached August 27.

Here the plans went awry. La Salle found a number of men thought to be in Illinois, living in desperation on the remains of the ship's cargo. A half dozen more had deserted, taking a good deal of the merchandise with them. Tonty was immediately sent to Sault Ste. Marie in search of these defectors, while La Salle continued in the *Griffon* to an island at the entry to the Baye des Puans, inhabited by Potawatomies (Washington Island in Green Bay). "Here he found some of the men he had sent in previous years [!] to the Illinois, whence they brought him peltry to the value of twelve thousand livres."[17] La Salle then decided to send the *Griffon* back with the cargo of furs, and to go south by canoe. The separation took place September 17, the last that was seen of the *Griffon*, which by later word was lost in a storm.

The diminished party of fourteen in four canoes carried a forge and other equipment to be used in ship building intended for the descent of the Mississippi River. Six weeks were spent on Lake Michigan in repeated hazard of storms and alarm of Indians, who turned out however to be friendly. On November 1 they came to the place appointed to meet Tonty, the mouth of the river of the Miamis (St. Joseph River). Awaiting Tonty they then built a rude fort at the mouth of the river.

The reunited party of thirty men and eight canoes started up the river December 3, following it to a good trail leading south, over which they carried canoes and baggage for a distance of a league and a half to the river of the Illinois. (The portage was from Niles, Michigan, on the St. Joseph River to South Bend, Indiana, on the Kankakee River, the larger headwater of the Illinois River.)[18]

> The river of the Illinois . . . flows through vast marshes, making so many turns, although of good current, that at the end of a day's travel, one may find that one gained only two leagues

16. The so-called official relation is in Margry, I, 435-544; the relation by Tonty, 573-616.

17. Margry, I, 450. La Salle was enjoined from taking part in the northern fur trade. A valuable lot of furs could be procured by trade at Green Bay but hardly in the Illinois country. The statement appears to be an invention to cover illicit trade.

18. Margry, I, 463-464.

in a straight line; as far as the eye could see one saw only marsh, reeds and alders, and in forty leagues the only places to camp were patches of frozen ground on which to bed and make fire.

During the fall Miamis, engaged in buffalo drives, had set fire to the champaigns, buffalo bones and skulls being all about. The French party killed two of the wild cattle, and many turkeys as they went downstream to the Illinois village (Kaskaskia), which was reached January 1, 1680.

The route through lakes Erie, Huron, and Michigan to the Illinois River was by then common knowledge. What La Salle added was the demonstration that a ship could be sailed from above Niagara to the end of Lake Michigan. His plan was that ships and sails were to take the place of canoes in navigating the interior.

SELECTING THE BASE TO TAKE POSSESSION OF LOUISIANA (1680)

La Salle named his new concession Louisiana before he started from Fort Frontenac.[19] He was properly informed of the geography of the interior, including the Joliet relations, which he criticized severely and unjustly.[20]

The Illinois River was La Salle's planned entry to Louisiana. The first Illinois village (Kaskaskia, near Ottawa, Illinois) was deserted at the time, its people gone on winter hunt in the prairies. The so-called official relation reported:

> It has 460 cabins, made in the shape of long cradles and covered with double mats of rushes, so well made that they are impenetrable to wind, snow, and rain. Each cabin has 4 to 5 fireplaces, each fire one or two families who live together in good understanding.[21]

The cabins were multifamily long houses, their number perhaps an exaggeration or a misprint. The French were out of food, yet found Indian corn stored in pits, helped themselves, and continued down river.

On the fifth day they came to an inhabited village, Pimiteoui, of eighty long houses, a great many *pirogues* (dugouts) drawn up on the river bank (Peoria, Illinois). Ceremonial exchanges of gifts and speeches followed and this gave La Salle an opportunity to ask about the great river he had come to find. He was told that its navigation was free and easy throughout, that there were no Europeans at its mouth, and he was given the names of four nations which he thought he recognized as having been described in the De Soto relations. Also the natives knew of ships sighted at sea, firing shots with a noise like thunder.[22]

The river widened at Peoria into a lake with sufficient water to float a ship. La Salle began building a bark and a fort he named Crevecoeur. Word of the French brought visitors from afar, including Osages, Chickasaws, and Arkansas from the south, who confirmed that the great river was navigable to the sea. As he had built barks on Lake Ontario and Lake Erie, so would he do here to sail to the Gulf of Mexico.

19. The grant by him on June 10, 1679, of a seigneurie to La Forest, his lieutenant at Fort Frontenac, stated that he was about to go on the voyage of discovery of Louisiana (Margry, II, 21).

20. Margry, II, 1-180, a collection of documents by and concerning La Salle, to the start of his voyage down the Mississippi River.

21. Margry, I, 466.

22. Margry, I, 470.

La Salle was a romantic who made great plans, disregarded contrary facts, and continued to repeat his mistakes. He had sailed the Great Lakes and would sail the great river. To that purpose he had brought a forge, carpenters' and sawyers' tools, but "neither iron, nor cordage, nor sails."[23] Having come to navigable waters at Lake Peoria trees were felled and sawed into planks, the green timbers framed into a hull forty feet long. In early March 1680, leaving Tonty in charge, La Salle started out from Fort Crevecoeur to return to Fort Frontenac for the supplies needed for the bark. The fantastic journey included crossing on foot from St. Joseph River to Lake Erie, going on to Montreal, getting back to Fort Frontenac at the end of July, and reaching Mackinac in September by way of Lake Toronto (Lake Simcoe) and Georgian Bay. La Salle and Tonty spent a year wandering about the lakes and the Illinois valley, searching for each other, not to meet until the summer of 1681. The long and tedious details of La Salle's account tell of misadventures, desertions, anxieties, false rumors, and little else.

Tonty had been ordered by La Salle to return up the Illinois River and examine a defensive site beside the Indian village of Kaskaskia as a likely place to build a fort. (This was Starved Rock, a natural bastion rising above the river, noted by La Salle.) While Tonty was on this errand the men left at Crevecoeur deserted, plundered the merchandise and munitions, and demolished the fort, leaving Tonty, two Recollect priests, and two lads, in Tonty's words, "to subsist on the warmth of the natives."[24]

HENNEPIN'S VOYAGE UP THE MISSISSIPPI RIVER

La Salle brought Recollect friars from France to take part in the establishment of Louisiana, thereby adding Father Louis Hennepin to the historians of New France. Indians from the headwaters of the Mississippi visited the French at Crevecoeur and invited them to come to their country, promising good trade in beaver and other pelts. La Salle was interested in the prospect of fur trade in territory not reserved to the traders of the Great Lakes. Hennepin saw the opportunity to find a new missionary field and to discover unknown territory.

A party of three, Hennepin, Michel Accault (Acco), a seasoned voyageur, and another French canoeman, started out from Crevecoeur at the end of February 1680 to the headwaters of the Mississippi, La Salle providing Accault with a stock of trade goods. A week of paddling brought them to the mouth of the Illinois River, about which the Tamaroa, an Illinois tribe, had villages. They turned up the Mississippi, down which Joliet and Marquette had come seven years before, and entered unrecorded waters above the mouth of the Wisconsin River.

The party passed the mouth of Rivière Noir (still called Black River), then that of the Boeuf, thus named because of the number of wild cattle (now Chippewa River), and so came to the falls of the Mississippi River, named the Falls of St. Anthony by Hennepin. Five weeks after they entered the Mississippi they were captured by a party of Sioux who seized their merchandise and took them north to Sioux encampments. They were held in light captivity until fall when the Sieur Duluth, trading inland from Lake

23. Margry, I, 483.

24. Margry, I, 489-503.

Superior, secured their release. La Salle did not know what happened to the northern expedition until a year later, when it had no bearing on his plans.

Hennepin spent the winter of 1680-1681 at Mackinac and then returned to France to write his first version of his History of Louisiana, published in 1683. The Recollects having been excluded from New France for half a century, Hennepin wrote celebrating their return with La Salle, magnifying his own role, as will be considered later.

EXPLORATION OF THE MISSISSIPPI RIVER TO ITS MOUTH (1682)

La Salle assembled his men in mid-December 1681 at the mouth of the St. Joseph River.[25] The onset of winter was unusually severe. Finding that river frozen Tonty went ahead

around the lake [Michigan] to enter by a certain small river called Chicago. From this river there is a portage of a league and a half, which leads to another river [Desplaines] that falls into the Illinois, and as I found everything frozen, I had sleds made to carry our effects.

Mambré adds:

We continued our route over the ice, pulling our canoes and equipment not only to the village of the Illinois, where we found no one, all having gone to winter elsewhere, but for thirty leagues farther down, to the end of Lake Pimetoui [Lake Peoria], where, finding the navigation open, we descended to the Mississippi River.

Tonty named the male members of the party as consisting of La Salle, Father Membré, Tonty, twenty other Frenchmen, and eighteen Indians, Mahicans and Abnakis. There were ten squaws, five Abnaki, the others Nipissing, Huron, and Ojibway, also three infants. All were of Algonquian tribes, except one Huron woman, and most were from the New England-Quebec border.

The party camped at the ruins of Fort Crevecoeur while Indians made canoes of elm bark. Fishing by line for *barbue* (catfish), one of extraordinary size was caught that provided supper for all.

Six leagues below the mouth of the Illinois the river Emissourita (Missouri) was entered, reported as well peopled with villages to the west (Pawnee) where horses were used for war and for carrying the meat of the buffalos. Another six leagues took them to a village of a hundred eighty cabins (Tamaroa), east of the river, all the people again being away on a hunt. The location of the Tamaroa village suggests Cahokia in the American Bottoms east of St. Louis.

Nicolas de la Salle confirmed the account: the waters of the river of the Missouris were as muddy as those of the Mississippi. By native report this river was well peopled, a tribe living far up the river called Panis. Two leagues below the empty Tamaroa village camp was made on the right bank to rest for two days.

Here seven buffalo, four deer, turkeys, swans and bustards were killed. The country is beautiful. Along the river are nut trees, plum trees, oaks, and maples on low ridges here and there, also tall grass as fine as in our meadows. It was somewhat cold but there was neither snow nor ice. [Apparently the earliest description of the site of St. Louis.]

25. There are three accounts, all in general agreement: "Relation de Henri de Tonty," Margry, I, 573-616; "Récit de Nicolas de La Salle," Margry, I, 547-570; and "Lettre du Père Zénobe Membré," Margry, II, 206-212.

The next camp was at ten leagues in a very flat land subject to flooding (river bottoms at Ste. Genevieve). The next day they camped where the river was very narrow, trenched between two mountains, in its middle a great rock, forming an island (Grand Tower). In the following day's travel of fourteen leagues the river continued to be bordered to right and left by mountains, but there also began to be canebrakes along the river. (The account is like that of Joliet, the passage of the bluff-bordered stretch between Fountain Bluff and Cape Girardeau, in which the Missippi River cuts its course through limestone beds of the eastern Ozarks. Seen from the river the cliffs rising hundreds of feet give the impression of mountain country.) Another day brought them at sundown opposite the mouth of the river that flows from the land of the Iroquois. The camp opposite the Ohio River (thus named in Tonty's relation) was in a flat country filled with great woods of elms and other trees.

They had come to the great alluvial plain of the Lower Mississippi Valley. Shortly they began to "see to the left ridges rising at a distance from the river. The land there is red, as shown by the ravines in the ridges." Thus Nicolas de la Salle noted the high ground on the east, the river undercutting beds of Tertiary sediments as far as the Chickasaw Bluffs at Memphis. Overnight camps were made on the east bank, giving opportunity to hunt on the upland and to become acquainted with Chickasaw Indians.

Taking a Chickasaw guide they set out (from the vicinity of Memphis) on March 5, taking a week to follow the river's winding course for fifty leagues. There was little chance to hunt "because the borders of the river are so thickly grown with canes that it is almost impossible to enter the woods." In morning fog on the river they heard cries and the beating of drums and soon natives appeared in a pirogue. Asked in the Illinois language who they were, they answered "Akansa."

The Arkansas, living along the Mississippi about the mouth of the Arkansas River, gave the visitors a cordial welcome, and La Salle took occasion during the course of the ceremonies to claim this new land for the King of France.

> One can say that these are the best formed savages of all that we have seen. They cover themselves with buffalo skins. Their cabins are covered with the bark of trees that resemble cedars with trunks more than a hundred feet tall without a branch [*Taxodium*, bald cypress] and of which they make their pirogues that go as well as bark canoes do. There are peach trees there in abundance, cocks and hens [*des coqs et des poules*], and several kinds of fruits unknown to us.

Nicolas de la Salle told how the Arkansas danced to the calumet peace pipe, the tobacco pipes of red stone, the stems covered with feathers; the drums were pots covered with rawhide; the rattles were gourds filled with pebbles that sounded like a carillon as they chanted. During the ceremony La Salle was presented with sixty buffalo skins. The French were given presents of maize, beans, and a lot of dried fruit, such as *nèfles* (the French name for medlars, here meaning persimmons), prunes, and raisins, the latter crushed in water and given them to drink.

> The land is good, a bit high [a natural levee], full of large trees, such as elms, peaches, plums, and mulberries and others of unknown names. It was in the month of March that this happened. The peach trees were in bloom.

Father Membré was impressed by the good qualities of the Arkansas:

I do not know how to express the honesty and good treatment we had from these barbarians, who, seeing that we did not wish to lodge separately in their cabins, let us do as we wished, swept the place where we wanted to be, brought poles to make our cabins, provided firewood for the three days of our stay, and gave us one feast after another . . . What I am saying is nothing as regards the good qualities of the nature of these savages, who are happy, honest, and liberal.

The Arkansas were the first nation encountered on the Mississippi living in large villages located on natural levees that gave protection from flood, had good drainage, and very fertile land. Tonty and Nicolas noted peach trees and Tonty the presence of poultry, apparently chickens. Later there would be confirmation of such introductions from the south.

Arkansas guides took them five days down river to the allied Taensa (Tensa). An alligator killed on the second day was cooked and found good. The Tensa town was reached by going west up a small channel that led to a crescent-shaped lake. (This ox-bow lake is at St. Joseph, Louisiana, midway between Vicksburg and Natchez.)

The Tensa were an elaborately formal culture under a chief who had absolute authority, as Tonty reported:

I was never so surprised as on entering the cabin of the chief, those of the other savages not being built in the same manner. One recognizes in this nation some of the qualities of a civilized people. We entered a cabin of 40 foot frontage; its walls of mud, two feet thick and twelve high. The cover is in the form of a dome, of mats of cane, so well made that no rain passes through. Entering, we saw the chief on a couch, more than sixty elders facing him, covered with white sheets resembling the hammocks made by the people of the isles of America [West Indies]. A torch of dry canes was in the center of the cabin, about it a number of shields of yellow copper . . . a number of paintings, an alcove where the chief reposed and a number of cots for the chiefs of the eight villages about the lake. The elders about him had their hands on their heads and, howling like wolves, cried with one voice "Ho, ho, ho, ho." [The feast began.] The chief was served by slaves, no one else eating from his dishes, which are of clay, very well coated and made in the shape of cups. Their knives and hatchets are of flint . . .

The Taensas have a divinity. We saw a temple across from the house of the chief, in which there is a kind of altar and above it three eagles looking to the rising sun. The temple is enclosed by a kind of redoubt, above which they put the heads of enemies slain in war. It is guarded day and night. [There were lots of pearls; a hen could be had in trade for a needle.]

Father Membré thought the Tensas of fine appearance and customs:

From here to the sea all the savages are different from the others [to the north] in their clothes, in the form of their heads which are flattened, and in their houses and public places. They have temples where they keep the bones of defunct chiefs, and, it is to be noted, the chiefs have much more power and authority than among our Savages. They command and they are obeyed. [Examples are cited, including attendants who swept the way before the chief, attendants who went ahead of him with fans of white plumes, and carrying a sheet and round plaque of copper.]

As they neared the sea the pace of travel increased and the accounts were more brief. The Natchez and then the Coroas were visited briefly, both recognized as like the Tensa in culture. Both tribes lived on the east side of the river in hilly land (the loess upland from Natchez to Baton Rouge). Good land, good prairies, little ridges (Nicolas de la Salle also noted that "The cabins are in the form of domes, of large canes that sustain them from ground to top, fifteen feet high and without windows.")

In the delta a party was sent by each of three branches of the river to the Gulf. La Salle took possession on April 9, 1682, of Louisiana, specifying it as including the Mississippi to its head and all of its drainage basin, and naming the principal Indian nations.

RETURN UP THE MISSISSIPPI RIVER

Nicolas de la Salle's journal gives additional information for the return voyage. Starting back they had a brush with a tribe called Quinipissa (probably Choctaw). Preparing for the fray "these drank a beverage that is a sort of tea," which suggests that the hot 'black drink' made from a native holly (*Ilex vomitoria*) was used this far west. The French party ran out of food in the delta and reached the Coroas famished. "At the foot of their hills [the loess upland] was a large well beaten road." They were met by the chief and taken to an open square, as large as the one in front of the royal palace in Paris. Here they were seated on mats and served food. "All the Coroas have their heads flat; their mothers flatten them as soon as they are born."

The lake of the Tensa was reached on the night of June 1, 1682, the party met by elders with flaming torches and taken to the house of the chief, fed, and lodged.

> This village is a league long along the lake. Its temple, the chief's cabin, and seven or eight cabins of elders are surrounded by palisades, making a sort of fort; on the pales are placed human heads; the temple is in the form of a dome, its door painted red, and guarded day and night by two men . . . The temple is oval, thirty *pieds* [feet or paces] long and twelve wide inside, ornamented with works made of canes and all painted red. The dome is covered with very fine matting, its floor of earth . . . At night there are two flaming torches within. We saw that the women held up their infants to the sun and rubbed their bodies with their hands that they held also to the sun.

The chief came to see them off, his path again swept ahead of him.

They were given more food than the canoes could carry. (The three reporters were impressed by the difference in culture on the lower Mississippi, especially the sun cult and a class society ruled by chiefs with absolute authority.)

At the first Arkansas village they were given a feast of dog meat, at the second, which was located on the east bank of the Mississippi, of bear and buffalo meat, and at the third a great feast of roast dog. La Salle made the voyage to the mouth of the Mississippi River and back without the loss of a man, found the land fertile and of genial climate in contrast to Canada, and its natives friendly, with one exception.

Back on the Illinois River, they found a lot of bustards, swans, and ducks in molt, killing what they wanted with cudgels. Also they shot buffalo, deer, and turkeys. Fort Crevecoeur was found wholly destroyed and the bark burned. The village of the Illinois (Kaskaskia), at the time abandoned because of Iroquois raiding, was reached July 15, 1682.

FORT ST. LOUIS OF THE ILLINOIS

During the winter of 1682-1683 Tonty wrote, "we built Fort Saint Louis on an inaccessible rock." This was the natural bastion that had appealed to La Salle when he first went down the Illinois River, the village of Kaskaskia and its cultivated fields nearby. It is the present Illinois State Park of Starved Rock.[26] Under the protection of the fort, Shawnees, followed by Miamis, and then by Illinois, returned to their valley homes, Tonty going a hundred leagues into the prairies to call them back. La Salle left in August 1683 for France, Tonty remaining in charge.

LA SALLE'S OBSERVATIONS OF NATURE AND PEOPLE OF LOUISIANA

A letter La Salle wrote after the return from the Gulf gives his estimate of the Illinois country.[27] It began with an adverse opinion of the portage at Chicago that Joliet had recommended for a canal. This portage, La Salle said, was reached from the great lake (Michigan) by a river (Chicago River), navigable for about two leagues to a small lake, divided into parts by a beaver dam. At the time of high water, at most for two to three weeks in a year, the small lake overflowed into the Illinois River. Except in spring the upper Illinois River (Desplaines River) did not carry enough water for boats. The harbor at Chicago also was subject to blocking by sand. Joliet's plan was not feasible.

The Illinois River, he continued, had its main source in the marshes of the Teatiki River (Kankakee). Joined by the Iroquois River (still so called) it entered the lovely Massane country (Mazon Creek at Morris), where there were many 'stones of mines' (the famous Mazon ironstone concretions), also slate (shale), and seams of coal (which is correct). Two leagues below the Pestegonki River (Fox River) was the ancient village of Kaskaskia, abandoned three years earlier because of Iroquois attack. The fort he had built on top of a cliffed rock called the fleeing Indians back and attracted numerous other nations to settle in the adjacent valley. The opposite valleyside was wooded, the upland prairie beyond pastured by countless buffalo.

The lake of the middle Illinois River, Pimiteoui (Peoria), was of three connecting lakes, the lowermost ditched by Indians in summer when the water was low, enabling them to take fish in quantity. At that season there was a prodigious number of molting waterfowl, more than a hundred swans being clubbed in one day.

South thereof, throughout Louisiana, they found the fruit called *piaquimina* (plaquemine, persimmon) resembling medlar, but larger and better. Other fruits were wild apples (crab apples), plums of several kinds, nuts including one larger and oilier than those of France and of much thicker shell (butternut), the papaw (*Asimina*, well described but not named), grapes, mulberries, a wild cherry (*Prunus serotina*) much liked by parakeets and turkeys. Throughout Louisiana there was much sassafras, a tree with bark like that of the ash, its wood scented like anise and growing by preference on ridges, in places of gravel and sand and on red (sub) soils. The *mistquil* (mezquite) was a large tree that grew on rich land. Its description has having long, strong, and branched spines indicates that he mistook the honey locust (*Gleditsia*) for mezquite.

Of more than a half dozen edible roots the most important was the *macopin*, a staple Indian food that was baked in pits heated with stones and filled with alternate layers of roots and of leaves, baked for several days and then boiled. These were ready to eat when they turned red; if still white they burned the mouth, palate, and throat cruelly.

26. Starved Rock being made a state park in 1911, the Geographic Society of Chicago commissioned a volume on its geography, geology, and vegetation: Carl O. Sauer, G. H. Cady, and H. C. Cowles, *Starved Rock State Park and its Environs*, The Geographic Society of Chicago, Bulletin no. 6 (Chicago, 1918).

27. Margry, II, 164-180.

The plant grew in swamps, its roots as big as a man's arm. (This still undetermined plant has given name to a river and a county in Illinois, and will be referred to again.)

The letter ends with the discharge of the Missouri into the Mississippi. Above, the Mississippi was of very clear water, below it was scarcely drinkable because of the thick mud. This was true to its mouth, and could not be explained, La Salle thought, by the mud brought by the Missouri but was due to resupply of mud as the river churned its channel through the alluvial lowland.

Another letter added items on the Mississippi river system and its tribes.[28] The Illinois were a confederate of ten nations, the Kaskaskias being the 'true Illinois'. All were in process of joining and coming to settle at the fort. Also a party of Missouris and four other tribes had made fields at four leagues from the fort. He had hired a Pawnee youth from two hundred leagues to the west who told of horses the Pawnees had procured from tribes to the south,

> who sold them horses which they rob apparently from Spaniards of New Mexico. These horses I hope will be of great use to us. The Savages use them for war, for hunting, and for all kinds of transport. They do not have the custom of putting them up but let them stay outdoors, even in snow, and give them no other feed than to let them graze. Such horses must be very hardy and strong because they are said to carry the meat of two buffalos, weighing almost a thousand pounds.

LA SALLE'S ACCOUNT OF RESULTS
AND PROPOSAL OF FUTURE ACTION

In October 1682 La Salle wrote of what he had done and what he had hoped to achieve.[29] He had observed scrupulously the royal orders not to take part in the trade between the Great Lakes and Montreal. However his privilege of control of the trade in buffalo hides should include the right of commerce in general with the nations he had discovered.

Some belittled the glory of the late discovery by attributing it to good luck. On the contrary it had been made by taking great care in meeting strange nations, the chiefs of which were met with the ceremony of the peace calumet and provided food and services.

> The utility of this enterprise appears in first place by the commodity of the ports at the mouths of the river, in the vicinity of the Spaniards and near to the passage of their fleets. It would be easy to maintain there a strong colony, by reason of the fertility and quality of the land and its champaigns, ready to be cultivated and abounding in provisions found there. There is everything necessary to build entire fleets, lacking only iron which as yet has not been found. The embouchure of the river is easy to defend and in consequence the entry to the whole country . . . An army would find it very difficult to march by land because of the great stand of dense canes . . . Five tributaries come into it from New Biscay and New Mexico, where the Spaniards have found so many mines. From there it will be possible greatly to incommode and even to ruin wholly New Spain, merely by arming the Savages which can be easily controlled, having temples and chiefs whom they obey greatly and who have mortal hatred of the Spaniards because they are enslaved . . .

28. Margry, II, 196-203.

29. Margry, II, 288-301. The letter was addressed to the Abbé Bernou, his sponsor in the inner circle of political affairs in France.

I say nothing of the pearls we have found, of the wild cattle in prodigious numbers, of the aromatic gums, wood of all kinds, of the goodness and fertility of the land, of sugar, tobacco, silk, cochineal, and other things that could be produced there as readily as in the neighboring provinces of Mexico, nor of wine that would do well there; but I say that it is absolutely necessary for the conservation of New France . . .[30]

The prospect outlined by La Salle was continental in extent: 1) The Mississippi River would be the highway of commerce with France, the routes of the Great Lakes as well as its own drainage basin. 2) Upper Louisiana, land of buffalo prairies, of fertile soil and temperate climate, was greatly superior to Canada for French settlement. 3) Lower Louisiana, of subtropical climate and alluvial lands, could produce commodities of high price. 4) The Mississippi and its western tributaries would serve as bases from which to attack New Spain, seize it, and take possession of its mines.

LA SALLE'S ACTION BLOCKED

Frontenac was succeeded as Governor of New France by La Barre while La Salle was still on the Mississippi expedition, a strong patron replaced by an enemy. Late that year La Barre wrote Minister Colbert that he had received no report from La Salle, that he did not think much of the discovery, and that La Salle's imprudent conduct raised strong suspicion that La Salle was planning some disservice to the nation. In 1683 La Barre wrote again, that La Salle's head was turned, that he had told the Minister of a false discovery, and that he was trying to procure for himself an imaginary kingdom.[31]

La Salle, knowing that La Barre was taking action against him, left Fort St. Louis in August 1683 and sailed from Quebec in November, to arrive in France in January 1684. La Barre took possession of Fort Frontenac during the winter and in May 1684 ordered Tonty to surrender Fort St. Louis and come to Quebec, where the latter employed his enforced idleness to write his *Relation*.

30. Margry, II, 292-294.

31. Margry, II, 302-304, and 335-336.

XVI.

To Louisiana by Way of
the Gulf of Mexico

THE MISSISSIPPI RIVER: PART OF A GREATER PLAN

On the voyage to the mouth of the Mississippi La Salle drew up a procès-verbal at the Arkansas village (March 1682), taking possession of all lands, waters, and peoples as far as the River of the Palms. The act was repeated a month later at the mouth of the Mississippi, specifying that Louisiana comprised the river system from its head to its discharge into the Gulf of Mexico and land beyond as far as the embouchure "of the Palms."[1] The Río de las Palmas north of Tampico was the old boundary between Cortes' New Spain and Narváez' Florida, still more or less the northern limit of New Spain on the Gulf of Mexico in the seventeenth century.

In France, La Salle moved in the circle of the *Gazette de France*, the political journal, edited by the Abbés Renaudot and Bernou. The group, strongly royalist, was engaged in planning action against Spain.[2] The letter La Salle wrote the Abbé Bernou after his return from the mouth of the Mississippi (October 1682, cited above) told how he proposed a grand attack on New Spain from the Mississippi River. When La Salle again went to France at the beginning of 1684 it was to take part in organizing the invasion of New Spain from the Gulf of Mexico.

PLANS OF ATTACK ON NEW SPAIN

The time was opportune to strike at Spain at its most vulnerable front, the silver mines of northern New Spain, largest source of revenue to the Spanish Crown. The Abbé Bernou claimed the credit of having proposed the plan, using a Spanish refugee, the Count of Peñalosa: "It was I who gave him the thought of the grand design, of which he had not thought."[3] According to Bernou the count had a long and distinguished career in Peru and New Spain, including a term as Governor of New Mexico from 1661 to 1664, had been arrested by the Inquisition, imprisoned, and lost his property. Peñalosa was well acquainted with the mines of New Vizcaya, in particular with those of Parral, the most northern mining district. The injuries he had suffered prepared him to turn against his country.[4]

1. Margry, II, 181-193.

2. Margry, II, xxi-xxii, 343-435.

3. Bernou to Renaudot, Margry, III, 84.

4. Margry, III, 49-44.

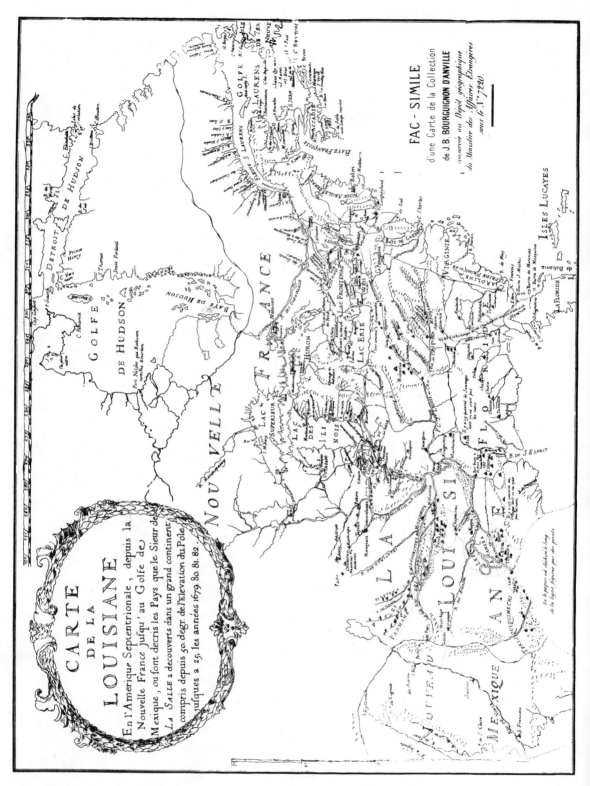

Fig. 12. Map of Louisiana "describing the lands discovered by the Sieur de la Salle," 1679-1682. *Découvertes et Établissements des Francais dans l'oest et dans le sud de L'Amerique Septentrionale, III*, edited by Pierre Margry, Paris, 1876.

The first memoir of Bernou proposed that French filibusters of Saint Domingue (Haiti) be taken to settle at the mouth of the Río Bravo (Río Grande), where they would trade with the natives, raise cattle as they were then doing in Haiti, and prospect for mines in the interior. When it pleased the King to begin war against Spain these Frenchmen would engage in the conquest of New Vizcaya and its rich mines. Two hundred freebooters would be more than adequate to take the province, which had only four to five hundred poorly armed and trained Spaniards, who moreover were far removed from help from Mexico.

A revised project, dated January 1684, substituted Pánuco for the Río Grande, as more convenient to the mines, the filibusters to be commanded by one of their leaders named Grammont, Count Peñalosa to be in overall charge.[5]

A third proposal was to conquer Nueva Vizcaya by an expedition going up the river the Spanish called Río Bravo, which "in fact was the Mississippi River that La Salle had discovered to its mouth" and had reported on in Paris. La Salle had the quality for great enterprise and a particular talent to govern natives. The main motive of his discovery had been to find a port on the Gulf of Mexico from which to go on conquest of Spanish lands. The river passed very close to New Vizcaya, some of the Savages along it being at war with the Spanish, as were the Pawnees, whom La Salle had seen mounted on horses. He would lead two hundred Frenchmen, starting from his Fort St. Louis with as many as fifteen thousand warriors, needing only very modest support from France of soldiers, supplies, and a ship.[6]

A month later (February 1684) Peñalosa was reported ready to carry out the proposed invasion. The more the enterprise was examined the easier, more useful, and glorious did it appear. Pánuco having been taken Peñalosa would march on Durango, capital of New Vizcaya, and seize Culiacán on the Pacific coast, to build ships there with which to capture the Spanish vessels on that ocean. By letters to his friends in New Mexico he would secure recognition of French rule there. Three forts would assure the conquest, one at Pánuco, one at Durango or at Parral, and one at Culiacán on the Pacific coast. Peñalosa would set up the expedition in Saint Domingue, recruit filibusters and buccaneers, store supplies, and get ships ready. Meanwhile La Salle, entering by way of the Gulf of Mexico, would go up his river (Mississippi), assemble his army of Savages into three corps, and attack New Vizcaya from three different points. "Thus the undertaking of the Count of Peñalosa and that of Sieur de la Salle would serve to support each other."[7] Some time after this curious plan, Peñalosa faded out of the action.

A memoir to Minister Seignelay, successor to Colbert, by La Salle (1684) outlined how he would conduct the campaign.[8] The principal fruit of his great perils and labors had been to satisfy the desire of the deceased Minister Colbert to have a post "by which to fatigue the Spaniards in the places from which they drew all their riches." The locality he proposed to fortify was sixty leagues above the mouth of the Mississippi

5. Margry, III, 48-55.

6. Margry, III, 55-63. A map of Louisiana "describing the lands discovered by the Sieur de la Salle" has the Mississippi turn from a southerly course, as far as the Chickasaws, to a southwesterly course, by way of the Arkansas and Tensas, to reach the Chichimecas of northern Mexico (Fig. 12).

7. Margry, III, 63-70.

8. Margry, II, 359-369.

River, which would give control of the whole continent. Its natives (the Tensas?) were friendly to the French and hated the Spanish for their tyranny, and offered to accompany him. More than eighteen thousand souls of diverse nations from two hundred leagues had gathered at one village ready to throw themselves into his arms and forget their old quarrels. He would be able to form an army of more than fifteen thousand savages, supported by the French and Abnakis in his suite, to invade New Vizcaya. This province, of more than thirty mines, lay some forty to fifty leagues from the River Seignelay (Red River). Its mines were nearer to French territory than to Mexico and could be exploited by river transport, whereas the Spanish had to take the silver by carts over the long road to Mexico. (The wish had distorted the geography.)

La Salle would start from France with two hundred men, add a contingent of filibusters in Saint Domingue, and order two troops of French to come from Fort St. Louis, accompanied by four thousand warriors. He asked for no troops from France, who would only be novices in the kind of warfare practiced by Indians and filibusters, which did not use the discipline of military order. He had the respect of the natives, knew their ways, and soon would make all of them good Frenchmen, making a strong colony without the necessity of bringing any large number of men from Europe. "Never has an enterprise of such great consequence been of such small risk and cost."[9]

PREPARATION IN FRANCE OF THE EXPEDITION

Action developed with remarkable speed. On March 4, 1684, De Cussy was ordered to govern Saint Domingue (the official beginning of the French colony in Haiti) and to assemble filibusters for an undertaking against New Vizcaya, to be ready by October.

On March 23 the King approved a budget of twenty-five items requested by La Salle, including a ship armed for attack, officers and men for a voyage of six months, arms and munitions, cannon and munition to equip two forts, and food and supplies for six months.[10] On April 14 La Salle was commissioned by the King

> to command in the lands that will be newly subjected to our domination in North America, from Fort St. Louis on the river of the Illinois to New Vizcaya, as well as the French and Savages whom he will employ in these enterprises.[11]

At the same time the Sieur de Beaujeu, a veteran naval officer, was commanded to take charge of the assigned warship, *le Joly*,

> and since the secret of the enterprise has been confided to the Sieur de la Salle as to its destination and he is charged to give account thereof to His Majesty, in all things he [Beaujeu] shall follow punctually his [La Salle's] advice and follow the route marked out.[12]

Thus began the troubles that beset the expedition and were in part responsible for its failure. Its destination was a secret that La Salle kept from Beaujeu, the public being led to think that the ships were destined for Canada. Beaujeu was in effect reduced to the function of navigator under orders of La Salle. The friction increased while the sailing

9. Margry, II, 377.

10. Margry, II, 378-380.

11. Margry, II, 382-383.

12. Margry, II, 384.

was being prepared, Beaujeu protesting bitterly of the indignity of his position, of the arrogance of La Salle in ruling on matters ranging from stowage of cargo to seatings at table, and of his ignorance and incompetence. Antagonism and suspicion continued to grow.[13]

FIRST OBJECTIVE: HAITI

The fortunes of the expedition are recorded by Henri Joutel in a journal of a hundred and thirty thousand words.[14] Joutel was a participant observer, remarkably attentive to events, where they took place, the nature of the country, and the ways of the inhabitants. He prepared the memoir some years after the events at the request of Iberville, when the latter was engaged in the establishment of Louisiana on the Gulf coast. The journal came into the hands of the Delisles, father and son, and was used in their maps.[15] Joutel's journal is the principal and most trustworthy account of La Salle's last enterprise and is thus utilized here.

The expedition made its final departure from La Rochelle August 1, 1684, in four vessels: the warship *le Joly* under command of Beaujeu, the frigate *la Belle* of sixty tons, given to La Salle by the King, the cargo ship *l'Aimable* of three hundred tons carrying most of the things intended for the settlement, and a ketch of thirty tons. In all there were about two hundred and eighty men, including a hundred soldiers.

Cape Finisterre was doubled August 8 without having encountered any privateers, of whom they had been warned. At Madeira on the 20th Beaujeu wanted to land for water and supplies. La Salle denied the request, the resulting arguments adding to the tension.

This was Joutel's first voyage in tropical waters. He told of the flying fish, of entering the trade winds, of crossing the Tropic of Cancer and the baptism of those who had not done so before.

On September 16 they passed the West Indian island of Sombrero (in the Anegada Passage). Short of water and with fifty men ill, including La Salle, it was decided to push on to Port de Paix (Cap Haitien), first port of Saint Domingue. Cape Samana was sighted on the 22nd, and on the 25th Beaujeu, for reasons unknown, passed Port de Paix, the residence of the French governor and port of most abundant supplies. Beaujeu continued on, doubling Cape St. Nicolas, entered the Gulf of Gonâve, and arrived at Petit Goâve on the evening of September 27. The voyage of the *Joly* had taken fifty-eight days, during which only two men died. The cargo ship *l'Aimable* and the barque *la Belle* joined them October 2, the ketch, it was learned later, having been captured by the Spanish.

At Petit Goâve, about twenty-five miles west of Port-au-Prince, La Salle moved soldiers and the sick, including himself, to a cooler place on an island, where there was a graveyard set aside for Protestants. Word having been sent to Port de Paix, the newly established governor of Ste. Domingue, De Cussy, and St. Laurent, Lieutenant General of the French Islands of America, came to visit La Salle, who was still ill. La

13. Letters of complaint in Margry, II, 395-458.

14. "Relation de Henri Joutel," Margry, III, 91-534.

15. Margry thus traced its history, III, 648-649.

Salle reproached Beaujeu for having bypassed Port de Paix and having landed at this remote settlement. The visiting crown officials tried to calm the quarrel, but when the expedition went on from Petit Goâve, La Salle transferred himself and the men he trusted to the cargo ship *l'Aimable*.[16]

Joutel thought the stay of four weeks at Petit Goâve excessive. "I believe it would have been better to have remained at this place only two or three days for the sake of our sick and to secure some refreshments. Its air is bad, and so are the fruits, and there were women here in number who are worse than the air and the fruits." It was at the far end of French settlement, provided supplies including maize and biscuit (cassava bread), and included natives who knew the waters and land ahead. Some said that the land to which they were going was not as La Salle had drawn it, but deserted and arid, lacking even in game, and patrolled by Spanish warships. One guide who said that he had navigated the length of that coast several times, advised taking the direct route west to Cabo San Antonio at the far end of Cuba, which island would shelter them from the north winds. Arrived at the cape they should await favorable wind to cross the gulf, at that season subject to violent northers.

CROSSING THE GULF OF MEXICO

The three ships left Petit Goâve November 25, keeping close company. They sighted the Cayman Islands and made a landing at Isle of Pines, giving Joutel occasion to describe it as uninhabited, but having wild pigs, stocked there by Spanish as they had done on the island of Haiti. The island was wooded, of strange vegetation. There were many parrots, larger than those seen at Petit Goâve. A caiman was killed, also two kinds of animals that resembled large rust-colored rats. Crocodiles and rodents were cooked and enjoyed. At the extremity of Cuba they encountered the winds of which they had been warned, which delayed their departure to December 19.

Forewarned of currents that might carry them east into the Bahama Channel the ships held as best they could to a northerly course across the gulf, La Salle leading in the *Aimable*. Determination of position showed that they had drifted several degrees East of North by the time they got into shallow waters at the north of the gulf. La Salle had a Spanish chart on which he relied and was convinced that they had come to Appalachee Bay. They took a course west along the shore (January 1), seeing a flat land of grass and marshes, with large trees stranded along the shore, apparently brought there by the current of rivers. (The first week of January 1685 was spent in making the circuit of the Mississippi delta, La Salle still thinking that they had reached land in Appalachee Bay. Depending on his Spanish chart, he failed to recognize the several arms of the Mississippi discharging into the gulf.)

16. The French islands of the Lesser Antilles were its most profitable colony, with plantations of sugar, tobacco, and indigo. Spain had withdrawn from the western part of Santo Domingo, which was occupied by filibusters, largely French. These were in process of being made respectable French citizens by appointment of De Cussy to govern. The memoir to Seignelay of January 18, 1682, gave the population of Saint Domingue as five to six thousand Frenchmen and seven hundred women, not including Negroes of both sexes. "It began with only fifty men, called *boucaniers*, who settled there and maintained themselves despite the Spaniards. Since then, having multiplied, a part turned to cultivation and commerce, especially of tobacco. The others, known as *filibustiers*, are occupied at coursing the seas." These filibusters numbered about eighteen hundred, all very good soldiers and sailors (Margry, III, 45).

They continued to follow the coast west and on January 13 saw the first natives, who were watching the Frenchmen from the shore. Longboats sent from the ships were unable to land because of the waves and so they signalled to the Indians to come to them. The natives then launched a tree trunk through the waves, holding to it with one arm, swimming with the other, and thus came aboard. La Salle found his knowledge of Indian languages useless. When the natives saw sheep, pigs, chickens, and turkeys on the ship they indicated that there were many such in their land. The next day the French saw from afar herds of what they judged to be deer running in the champaigns (the coast of southwest Louisiana where the Calcasieu prairies extend to the gulf) and a score of buffalos at the seashore, the first buffalo Joutel had ever seen. On the 15th they came to the first small sand dunes, saw natives following them along the shore and also what were thought to be more buffalos.

IN SEARCH OF THEIR DESTINATION

In mid-January they found the coast turning to southwest, the land higher, "not too good," flat and sandy and covered with herbs. (They were sailing southwest along the Texas coast.) The coast trending more and more to the south, La Salle became concerned that they might have gone too far. On the 19th Beaujeu and the *Joly* which had gone ahead rejoined them, having determined by instrument that he had reached Lat. 27° 50′ (that of Corpus Christi).

> After some arguments between them [La Salle and Beaujeu], as was common, the question was of the route one should take and of the place where one might enter. M. de la Salle thought that the banks at which we had anchored on the 6th of the month, could be one of the branches of the river we were seeking.[17]

Concerned that they had overshot their mark La Salle proposed returning east. Beaujeu blamed La Salle for having gone farther west than he should have done and said that to turn back the *Joly* would need supplies from the *Aimable*, which La Salle refused, and thus nothing was settled.

While the three ships remained at sea (somewhere off Matagorda Bay), boats were sent to land for water and wood, and hunting parties brought welcome supply of waterfowl and deer. La Salle meanwhile decided to unload cargo, Joutel helping to roll barrels of wine and brandy on land.

On February 4 La Salle sent a hundred men on land to explore eastward along the coast, the *Belle* to follow them at sea, Joutel put in charge of one land party. The leader of the other landing party reported that the river they thought they had come to was a large lake oriented East-West. (Apparently they were at the great sand bar of Matagorda Island. On the 14th they were joined at the entry to the bay by the *Joly* and the *Belle*, La Salle shortly coming up with the *Aimable*. The sea outside was breaking in great waves, the channel calm, porpoises in number going and coming through it. Soundings showed a depth of ten to twelve feet in its shallowest part. (Ships and men were assembled outside of Matagorda Bay.)

La Salle found the entry to the river or bay practicable and still hoped that it was an arm of the river he was seeking (Mississippi). Nothing more is heard thereafter of the grand plan to take New Vizcaya and its silver mines.

17. Margry, III, 135.

DISASTER

The channel into the bay having been carefully sounded, La Salle had markers placed in it and along shore. The *Belle*, smallest of the three ships, was ordered to enter the bay and passed the channel handily. The *Aimable* unloaded part of its cargo on February 19 and was told to enter the next day at high water.

The first mishap was by chance. La Salle sent men to fell a tree from which to make a dugout canoe. They came running back to camp crying that savages were upon them. La Salle went out to repel the expected enemies and found instead a friendly band that took him to their cabins for entertainment.

Meanwhile the *Aimable* started into the channel, disregarded the markers, and ran hard aground. When La Salle returned the cargo ship was a wreck that broke up over night. According to Joutel, later depositions proved that it was wrecked by design. The salvage of the next days rescued casks of powder, then those of farina and of wine and brandy, the masts, and some timbers.

A party sent to the Indian camp to trade for canoes found things at it that had been taken from the wreck. In retaliation the French plundered the place and made off with canoes. The angry Indians attacked the party, killed two and wounded two badly. Friendship with the Indians had ended.

Beaujeu had carried out his instructions, which were to go wherever La Salle decided, to disembark, and then to return to France. The *Joly* departed in mid-March. La Salle was left with the small *Belle*, what was saved from the *Aimable*, including nine cannon, powder, provisions, and trade goods, and with a motley lot of men, without useful skills or experience of this strange new world.

XVII.

French Settlement on the Texas Coast

SETTLEMENT BY NECESSITY

The cargo ship *Aimable* wrecked in the inlet, the warship *Joly* departed for France, there remained only the bark *Belle*. The immediate need was to salvage what could be saved from the wreck. A camp was set up at the side of the inlet, called Grand Camp, which served into mid-summer to store the recovered goods and to explore adjacent waters and land.

The camp at the inlet was well provided. A good part of the cargo of the *Aimable* had been taken ashore before the wreck, including cannon, arms, ammunition, and clothes. Casks of gunpowder, meat, meal, and wine were fished out of the water. Ship timbers and rigging were salvaged.

The Texas coast plain is an ancient sea floor, low and sandy in its outer part, a series of lagoons along its shores. The numerous rivers flowing into the Gulf of Mexico were embayed in their lower courses as sea level rose with the end of the Ice Age. Later, long and great sand bars formed an arcuate outer coast enclosing the submerged land by a series of lagoons. La Salle's party landed at the inlet to one of the major lagoons, Matagorda Bay, its Spanish name unknown to the French.

La Salle took five dugout canoes to look for a place to settle. On his return "he told us that he had found a good country, suitable for sowing and planting all kinds of grain, abounding in cattle and game; that he would build a fort farther inland."[1] The desired location was at the nearest drowned river mouth, Lavaca Bay, known to the French as Baie St. Louis (Fig. 13). The relocation began in June 1685, the bark *Belle*, dugouts, and rafts all used to transport the supplies. Seventy men went to prepare the new settlement, Joutel remaining with the rest at the camp on the inlet, an estimated total of a hundred persons.

KARANKAWAS

From Galveston to Corpus Christi Bay the Gulf coast was the home of a primitive people, later known as Karankawa.[2] Survivors of the Spanish Narváez expedition lived with them from 1528 to 1534, a good part of the time about Matagorda Bay. The next record is of the landing of La Salle's party in 1685, related by Joutel.[3]

1. Margry, III, 165.

2. Newcomb, Chapter 3.

3. Margry, III, 149-151.

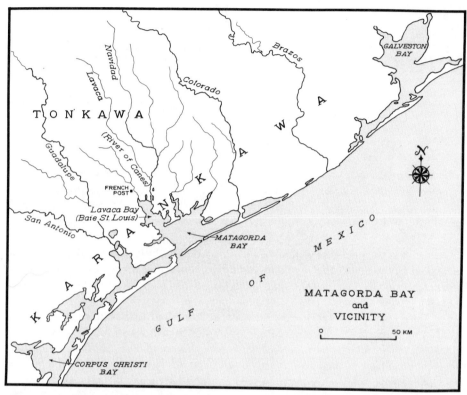

Fig. 13. Matagorda Bay and Vicinity.

The first meeting was friendly. The French laid down their arms, the natives did likewise and welcomed the visitors by rubbing their own breasts and then the chests and arms of the French. At the waterside village, of huts made of poles covered with mats and buffalo hides, the guests were served meat of porpoises, of which there were many in the bay. About forty dugout canoes of several sizes were beached there, supporting La Salle's notion that he was not far from the Mississippi, where craft of that kind were used.

The Karankawas were good archers, using long and powerful bows to hunt buffalo and deer (*boeufs* and *chevreuils*) for meat and hides. They went in parties to hunt in champaigns and prairies, at times setting fire to the herbage. (The French, like the Spanish, may have used the same name both for deer and pronghorn antelope, the latter grazing in herds as did buffalo. Recent excavation of the site of the French post above Matagorda Bay has yielded pronghorn bones.)[4]

The French found the Karankawas in goodly numbers living at ease, and well provided, mainly by hunting buffalo. In contrast the Spanish story a century and a half earlier had told of bare existence in a meagre land, the hardship of Spanish cast away among a primitive people. The contrast between the two accounts will have later attention.

4. Newcomb, 61n.

168

THE FRENCH HABITATION

La Salle chose a site for the settlement two leagues inland from Baie St. Louis (Lavaca), on a small eminence above a small river called Rivière aux Boeufs:

> from which one can see afar, to the west and southwest, champaigns that reach beyond the horizon, well joined, on which fine and good herbs grow that serve as pasture for an infinite number of cattle . . . To the north and northeast are some woods, mostly along the borders of rivers. There are as well some ravines. To east and southeast, towards the bay and the sea, the land also is very fine with groves at intervals agreeable to the sight, like a peopled land such as one sees for example in the land of Caux.[5]

The location was determined by Herbert Bolton, then a young professor at the University of Texas,[6] and confirmed by later excavation by the Texas Memorial Museum.[7] The grassy plains and groves described by Joutel are the present La Salle Oil and Gas Field.

La Salle planned and supervised the construction of a large habitation, comprising living quarters and storeroom, a log building in "the Canadian manner," the "logs laid horizontally in a queue joined at the corner, well fastened . . . La Salle marking their mortises and tenons."[8] Planks and beams were brought from the wrecked ship and buffalo hides served to cover the roof. Gardens were dug and planted. Buffalo hunting in the vicinity provided fresh meat, surplus made into boucan. Except for sickness and a few deaths, life at the settlement began in comfort and with good expectations.

JOUTEL'S FAVORABLE DESCRIPTION OF THE COUNTRY

Joutel, in charge of habitation at times when La Salle was absent, thought the country well suited for French living. In the bay doradoes, catfish, mullet, and other fish were easily taken by nets. In small salt ponds of the bay the French speared excellent flatfish resembling turbot and collected crusts of salt, white and of good quality.

Groves of trees scattered about the champaigns mainly were oaks of several kinds, recognizable as live, red, and white oaks. One kind was evergreen, with small leaves and sweet acorns. Some of the deciduous oaks were like those of France, others had a different kind of leaf. One kind that lost its leaves in winter bore nutgalls, small and in great number. Another kind with leaves like the oaks of Europe had a thick scaly bark and wood that when dry required sharp axes to cut.

A tree bearing small fruits, red and rather sweet when ripe, suggests the southern hackberry (*Celtis*). Another with fruit somewhat like that of the medlar but of different taste was the persimmon. Mulberry trees grew along the rivers, the fruits a little smaller than in France, but sweeter; their leaves would be of great use in raising silk worms in this almost winterless land.

5. Margry, III, 209-210. Joutel compared the landscape with that of his native Normandy.

6. Herbert E. Bolton, "The Location of La Salle's Colony on the Gulf of Mexico," *Mississippi Valley Historical Review*, II (1915), 165-182.

7. Newcomb, 61-62.

8. Margry, III, 179.

There were many grapevines, some rampant, others climbing up the trees, bearing grapes in quantity, fleshy and tart, unlike those in France and probably not suited for making wine, but used to make verjuice sauce for soups and stews. The ripe grapes did not last long, the animals knowing well how to find them.

Joutel described prickly pear cactus (*Opuntia*):

certain plants like those I have seen in France [where they had been introduced] and the Islands [Haiti], have the appearance of raquettes, because they have leaves [joints] of the shape of rackets, with flowers around them that produce fruit almost like figs; but the leaves are full of spines, including the fruits, which must be removed before eating them. [One of the soldiers died, having failed to do so. The fruits were not very tasty and were of several shapes, sizes, and colors.][9]

Also there were 'trees' with leaves three to four feet long, some with sharp points or margins that pierced clothing and skin. Some of these sent up a tall stalk of sixty to eighty cream colored flowers that formed thumb-length fruits, with a thin sweet exterior (Yuccas and the like).

In the champaigns there grew a small sorrel with leaves like clover, as tart and good as that in France. There were also onions of good flavor.

When the champaigns have been burned these are the first flowers to appear and the first green plants. Later they are smothered by other plants of several sorts and colors, which make a very agreeable blend of color when blooming. I noted some in flower and odor like tuberoses, their leaves however are different, like borage, woolly and with small prickles . . . The greater part of the flowers in autumn are yellow, the champaign at that time having that color.[10]

A description of the country about the settlement follows, champaigns and groves to west and southwest, along the river a marsh mostly of rushes, at three leagues northeast the River of Canes so called because of its borders (Lavaca River). Here there were many ponds frequented by water fowl, where it would be easy to make duck ponds. And so,

to commence with the cattle, which are very numerous there and which one could say were the daily bread. After them come the deer, turkeys, bustards, goose, swans, cranes, ducks, teal, water hens, plovers, becassines [snipe], partridges of two kinds, one large [prairie chicken], the other small [quail], these being the better. The large ones are like pheasant and spread a fan as turkeys do and have a cloche at each side of the throat.[11]

There were strange birds (pelicans) that filled their bills with fish, eaten later on land. The *spatules* were thus called because of the shape of their bill, were of the size of a chicken, and had beautiful rose-red plumage (roseate spoonbill). There were small birds of different kinds and colors, one having part of its plumage red and part black (scarlet tanager). One called *mouche* (fly), of beautiful irridescent plumage, usually was seen about flowers (hummingbird).

Eagles were of several kinds, most common those they called raven eagles, black like ravens and with a head like a turkey. These gathered where the Frenchmen were

9. Margry, III, 211-212.

10. Margry, III, 213.

11. Margry, III, 214.

170

hunting to scavenge whatever of the kill was left (turkey vultures). Another kind were called nun eagles because of their white collars and head covering (caracara).

"As the land is rich in all kinds of animals, so are the lakes and rivers in fish." The most common were the *barbues*, differing from those of France in lacking scales, having two spines at the side of the gills, and barbels below the mouth. In addition to these catfish there were fish like salmon and trout, and some with a long snout, rough skin, and poor flesh (gar).

Occasionally a sea turtle was caught while fishing by line; these were not as large as those in Haiti. A small turtle that lived in burrows in the champaigns had a round shell that made a good container for gunpowder. A four footed animal with a throat like a toad and a mailed back (armadillo) was suspect of being poisonous. There were venomous serpents with rattles on their tails, as both men and dogs had experienced. Pigs were fond of their flesh as were the French when they happened to be short of food.

Crocodiles or caimans were common in the rivers and came as far as the dwellings, Joutel killing several, an extremely large one being twenty feet long. Because of the short legs their bellies dragged on the ground, leaving a plain trail. They were not as dangerous as those of the Nile are said to be.

A variety of seeds brought from France were planted. The attempts to grow broad beans and wheat failed, none even sprouting. Chicory, beets, celery, asparagus, French melons, watermelons, and squash came up well and grew rapidly. Unfortunately the plants attracted animals. Rabbits in great numbers and also rats ate the tender shoots and fruits. A few squashes grew to maturity with hard rinds, to be eaten by a caiman (alligator). Beetles resembling cantharides ate the leaves of the beets, their roots finished off by rats. Rats were a great nuisance, carrying off whatever they found, even knives, to their places of storage (native pack rats).

The only plant that survived was cotton, seed of which Joutel had brought from Petit Goâve and planted at several sites.

The pigs thrived and multiplied greatly, and there was like hope of the rooster and hen.

LA SALLE'S FIRST SEARCH FOR THE MISSISSIPPI

The building completed, La Salle left at the end of October 1685 to go in search of the River Colbert (Mississippi). Joutel was left in charge at the settlement, which, he said, was in no sense a fort. The settlement did have eight cannons, it was true, but it lacked any cannon balls. The inventory listed about two hundred muskets, a like number of sabers and spears, a hundred barrels of gunpowder, several thousand pounds of lead in balls and sheets, and a diverse lot of plates and other iron, useless things intended for the invasion of the Spanish silver districts. Thirty-four persons remained at the settlement, including three Recollect priests and several French women and girls. There were twenty barrels of flour, several of wine and brandy, and breeding stock of pigs and chickens. Life at the habitation was quiet. Hunting buffalos, called *buffles* or *boeufs*, kept them in good supply. Occasionally some one was lost following a buffalo trail but found his way back. Joutel described the experience of mirage.

La Salle's party started out in two groups, one led by himself in dugout canoes, the other aboard the *Belle* sailing on the same course to the eastern end of the bay. Late in

March 1686, La Salle's band returned, in rags, diminished in number, and concerned as to what had become of the ship.

Outward bound along the north shore of the bay La Salle attacked an Indian band, capturing two women and a girl, "a victory that cost us dearly."[12] Arriving at the east end of the bay where a stream entered, La Salle sent the pilot of the *Belle* and five men to take soundings in order to find out where the river would lead,

> hoping to find there the right arm of the river Colbert, that is the branch he had passed on the right when he descended the river on his discovery . . . Never in the need to take counsel from any one and following only his own judgment, he always imagined that he would find there an arm of the river discharging into that bay.[13]

The survey party spent the night ashore, was surprised by Indians, all were killed, and their canoe smashed, which was in Joutel's opinion a reprisal for the prior French attack. La Salle put a number of his party on the *Belle* with a supply of buccaned meat, and gave orders to remain there until he sent further word.

La Salle's party continued east and north on foot:

> M. de la Salle told us of the fine lands they had discovered, rivers in number with beautiful woods on their banks and beyond them very fine champaigns, full of cattle and other game; he told that they had met a number of nations of Savages with whom they had made good contacts, meeting with them in peace; but he had not found his river.[14]

Nor did they find the *Belle* awaiting their return or any trace of it. The loss of the *Belle* became known after La Salle left on his second search for the Mississippi. Six survivors of the ship reached the settlement in May 1686 with the story of a disaster. The longboat had been lost, and the crew scattered searching for fresh water. Thereby ended the last possibility of escape or of succor by sea.

La Salle, it is inferred, had a broad triangle in mind. The latitude of the farthest point of the sea voyage (Corpus Christi Bay) was determined by instrument and found to be about a degree and a half less than that of the Mississippi river mouth, seen in January 1685. The base of the triangle was the east-west stretch between the Mississippi River delta and Matagorda Bay, its apex the point sixty leagues above the mouth of the Mississippi where La Salle imagined that he had seen a distributary leading southwest. The third side therefore was the leg north of east across the coast plain to the Mississippi. There is no record how those five months were spent by La Salle, during which he must have strayed far from the proper course.

THE EXPEDITION OF 1686

La Salle stayed a month at the settlement, starting out again at the end of April 1686 with twenty men, replacing the less robust with fresh personnel, well supplied with ammunition for hunting and with trade goods.

Joutel, again left in charge at the post, told of domestic affairs, of success at hunting, improved marksmanship, a short encounter with Indians, and of the nuisance of

12. Margry, III, 198.

13. Margry, III, 204 and 221.

14. Margry, III, 220.

mosquitoes in hot weather from which they sought relief by clearing a space about the buildings.

La Salle returned in the fall. "Before he told us anything I understood that he had not gotten to the Illinois; in consequence he had accomplished nothing."[15] There were eight men left of the twenty who had set out, one having been pulled under water by a crocodile while crossing a river. The good news was that La Salle brought five horses, laden with Indian corn, beans, squash seeds, and watermelons, all procured at a village near the river of the crocodile (the Colorado River of Texas?).

At the settlement fire was set to the champaign to provide grass for the horses. The cotton trees Joutel had planted were doing well except for frost damage by a norther during the past winter. (The cotton was a perennial woody kind.) Cotton, Joutel thought, was a promising commodity for that country.

LA SALLE'S LAST EXPEDITION (1687)

La Salle had found the way to Indians who farmed and had horses. He would take seventeen able bodied men and the five pack horses, return to these friendly people, get more horses, and go on to Fort St. Louis on the Illinois River, where Tonty had been left in charge.

The settlement had been left with adequate provisions. The buildings were in good condition. Fields and gardens had been planted. The pigs had increased to seventy-five, the chickens to a score. The prairies were full of buffalo and other game; the waters had plenty of fish. The local Karankawas were somewhat hostile but were readily driven off by French muskets. The settlement would take care of itself and prosper, an outpost of La Salle's Louisiana extending from the Great Lakes to the Gulf.[16]

La Salle took leave of the settlement on January 12, 1687, Joutel accompanying him and recording in attentive detail the progress of the journey. Joutel noted places at which La Salle had camped on his prior journey which they were backtracking in an unusually rainy winter. Travel was exceedingly slow. Streams were in flood and required detours to ford or to cross by aid of felled trees or by makeshift boats of buffalo hides. The horses became galled by their heavy packs, the men footsore in shoes made from buffalo hides. It rained day after day for weeks and at times they remained in a water-soaked camp for days. It took two months to get from the French settlement to the Brazos River near Navasota, about one hundred and fifty miles (Fig. 14).

There was no lack of game; herds of buffalos grazed in the prairies of the interfluves and flocks of turkeys lived in the valley woodlands. The route at first was north, across the sandy Outer Coast Plain, meeting small bands of Indians like those about the bay (Karankawas), engaged in hunting buffalo. On January 17 they came to a ridge on which they found the stripped frames of two hundred recently abandoned huts. (They were entering the higher Inner Coast Plain, crossing deep ravines that were running full of water from the rains.)

15. Margry, III, 249.

16. Word of the French 'fort' having come to Monclova, in 1689 a Spanish party was sent across the Rio Grande to destroy it. They came too late, Karankawas having wiped out the settlement and its inhabitants except for two boys who were taken back by the Spaniards.

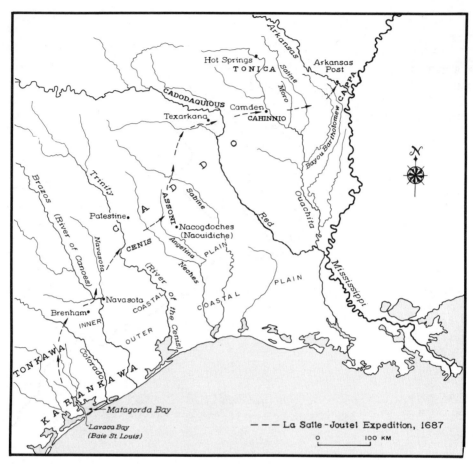

Fig. 14. La Salle—Joutel Expedition, 1687.

Turning somewhat west of north they were approached on the 21st by a band of different and friendly Indians, calling themselves Ebahamo, and were invited to visit their camp. A number carried round shields made of buffalo hide. It was told that at ten days' journey (in another direction) were men like the French, with only four large rivers to cross and good buffalo hunting most of the way. (These Indians are thought to have been one of the Tonkawa tribes, living south of the Colorado River. Their knowledge was of Spanish settlements south of the Río Grande.)

The rains continued, flooding streams and low grounds as they went north following the trail by which La Salle had returned the previous fall. A note of January 28 was of a good land with champaigns interspersed with groves as far as the eye could see.

On January 31 they came to a village, "on a height almost surrounded by the river" and stayed in that vicinity for a fortnight. The so-called village consisted of about twenty-four cabins in the form of outdoor ovens, covered with buffalo hides. Each held six men and numerous women and children. They used vessels of pottery to cook meat and roots and had small panniers made of cane or rushes. Dressed buffalo hides were

174

offered in trade for knives, the French acquiring a number of *colliers* of buffalo skins, which were very well made, and ornamented pack sacks, the tump lines providing long and supple straps used to replace the rude lashings of the packs on the horses. The villagers had two horses, which they declined to trade. The people kept dogs, prick-eared, with muzzles like foxes, which did not bark. Neither tribe nor settlement was named, but Joutel noticed that these people were not sedentary but wandered about hunting buffalo. Buffalos were the main dependence, their meat judged better than that of cattle of France, their wool superior, the hides of many uses, the jet black horns made into many things.

The French had reached the southeastern part of Plains Indian Culture, which was at the time already beginning to acquire horses. They were visited by Indians of various 'tribes', Joutel compiling a list of about fifty, half of them living north of the Maligne River, as La Salle named the stream in which a Frenchman had been drowned by 'a crocodile' on the prior journey. This river, Joutel understood, was a main boundary north and south between tribes.

Traveling north-northwest, always on the earlier route of La Salle, they came in mid-February to a land of deep black soil and of numerous rills of clear water, some of which issued from limestone rocks (the country about Brenham?), and thus to a well-beaten road running east, with many tracks of men, women, and horses. The black soil overlying the limestone formed an attractive landscape of groves of trees and prairies, recently burned, the land greening so as to look like the wheat fields of France in April.

The road led to a village on a hillside, forty cabins in a cluster, others scattered about. The settlement and people were like those they had left. Here it was learned that the people were "in relations with a nation called Choumans, whom they identified as friends of Europeans, who must be Spaniards." (Thus Jumanos of the middle Río Grande came to attention of the French in east central Texas.) The offer to purchase horses again was declined, the natives needing them to carry meat. La Salle succeeded in making a trade for a large roan, useless at the time because of a badly galled back.

Travel continued, still slowed by rains, the road taking them to the crest of a ridge (February 18), "from which one discovered a most agreeable girdle of hills, some covered with trees, some half covered, others open," above a large hollow. "It seemed that nature had taken pleasure in making this land and arranging its woods from place to place." The woods mainly were oaks and nut trees, the nuts harder than those of France. On February 19 and 20, three quarters of a league further, on the crest of a ridge, with cliffs of rock at the foot of the ridge, Indians called Palaquechauré took them a distance of a league and a half to their village, where the next day was passed in unsuccessful negotiation for horses, during which they learned that the Indian chief had been with the Jumanos visiting Spaniards, from whom the Jumanos had procured the horses which they traded to the local people.

On February 22, starting north-northeast through woods for a league and a half, the French made camp on a height of rock, at its base a small stream paved with flat stones, suitable for building and making lime. On the 23rd they made another try at horsetrading and set camp at "the border of a large brook that runs at the foot of one of the highest mountains in these parts." For four days they were halted by rain, then they continued

175

on the last day of February to a camp near this "mountain fortified by nature, having a scarp to one side, overlooking the land, a platform of about two arpents on top." Joutel thought this a good country for vineyards planted along the ridges. For the first four days of March, they were held up by more rain while they reconnoitered a great ravine "of very good stones, proper for building, being of different thickness." There were more delays by rain, mud, and streams. An attraction for settlement was seen in the mulberry trees as suitable for silk production, the bark used by the natives for roofing and for cordage. On March 13 they came to La Salle's River of Canoes (Brazos River above Navasota).

La Salle backtracked his route of the fall before, at first almost due north from their post by Matagorda Bay, later turning east into the Inner Coast plain of ridges and ravines which, Joutel wrote, seemed mountainous in comparison to the flat country in which they had been. There were outcrops of rock, scarps at the base of ridges and pavements of rock in the ravines. The rock was in beds of varying thickness, some suitable for building stone and burning lime. Their easterly route was along ridges of the Catahoula formation of Lower Miocene age, a long and narrow belt overlooking a lowland of weak Eocene beds to the north. Joutel recorded many details of relief, bedrock, soil, and vegetation.

Inland from the coastal Karankawas the people of the area next traversed may have been bands of Tonkawas, hunters and collectors.[17] The inhabitants of the villages in the hill country to the northeast, described by Joutel, are unidentified. They moved about, mainly to hunt buffalo; some planted patches of crops and had earthenware cooking pots. They owned a few horses procured from Jumanos. They were also in friendly communication with the Caddoan Cenis to the northeast as well as with Jumanos on the Río Grande. The hill people were a link in the cultural connection that extended from southwest to northeast Texas, between the Caddoan Cenis east of the Brazos River to Caddoan Jumanos of the middle Río Grande. The unnamed people of the inner coast plain about the Brazos River suggest that Caddoan peoples lived along the southeastern margin of the buffalo plains, from the Pawnees of Nebraska to the Jumanos of the Río Grande.

The journey was made in three winter months of unseasonably heavy and continuing rains and floods. Five days after the Brazos River was crossed La Salle, his nephew, the Shawnee who was his companion and bodyguard, a gentleman, and a valet, were assassinated by five conspirators who seized control and effects. The murder took place a short distance north of the town of Navasota, where a monument marks the event.

17. Newcomb, Chapter 6.

XVIII.

From the Brazos to the
Arkansas River (1687)

FROM THE BRAZOS TO THE TRINITY RIVER

The conspirators, having vented their grievances by the killings, took control of the party and decided that all should go on to the land of the Cenis, where La Salle had been the previous fall (Fig. 14).

> We continued the route and went straight north to pick up the road that leads to the village we were searching for, and by which all the Savages of those parts go and come . . . We found the land quite good, of fine champaigns and woods at intervals.[1]

They were joined by two Cenis, their wives, and horses, homeward bound. Rain held the party up for two days, while they prepared to cross a flooded river (Navasota River, more or less east of the campus of Texas A. & M. University). The land about was covered by a deposit of sand and mud; there was a good stand of trees, and a marsh on the far side.

On March 28, 1687, they came to the River of the Cenis (Trinity River), which was crossed by an improvised boat of buffalo hides, by log, and by swimming. Fine trees of several kinds grew along shore.

> One had been named Copal by M. de la Salle, which is a quite fine tree, with leaves resembling maple and linden. The tree gives out a very good odor as do its leaves. The tree grows very straight but its wood is not very hard. We saw here a tree on which M. de la Salle had marked the King's arms, and some others on which various persons had made crosses, all carved in the bark. [The tree is the sweet gum (*Liquidambar*), here near the western limit of its range in the United States.][2]

LAND OF THE CENIS

Beyond the river they entered a different land and another culture. Shortly (March 30) they were met by three Indians, two naked, one riding a fine gray horse. The third was dressed from flat-crowned hat to feet in the Spanish manner and at first was thought to be a Spaniard. He indicated that he had been where the blackbeards lived and showed a paper of papal indulgence printed in Spanish. The Indians brought a supply of cornmeal which was cooked and shared, providing a supper of welcome

1. Margry, III, 326.

2. Margry, III, 335.

change from the diet of buffalo meat on which the French had been living. Henceforth, they were among people who farmed, used horses, lived in permanent settlements, and had elaborate social organization.

Ahead was a land of ridges and hollows, largely covered with oak and nut trees (hickory). The pebbly terrain of the ridges in parts had great pineries, the trees bearing quite small cones. Land and pebbles were red and heavy and the waters tasted and looked like those in a country of iron mines. (They were travelling across ridges of ferruginous beds [Eocene], with stands of short-leaf pine, post oak, and mockernut hickory, south of Palestine, Texas.)

The vales between the ridges were cultivated, each cabin amid its own fields, clustered in hamlets of seven to fifteen houses. This being the season for planting, Joutel noted that men and women worked together in the fields, as many as a hundred planting the land, going from household to household:

> The day having been announced, all those so advised came to plant, using a kind of mattock made of the shoulder blade of a buffalo or a sliver of wood fastened with bark cords [to the handle]. While the workers are thus engaged the women of the cabin for whom the work is being done prepare a meal. Those who have been laboring rest at noon and are served the best food at hand. If some one returning from a hunt brings meat it is served for the feast. Lacking such, Indian corn is roasted in ashes or mixed with beans and boiled, wrapped in cornhusks . . . Having finished at one household they go to another on another day. Women have the duty of planting the corn, beans, and other things, men having no concern therewith [men dug, women planted].[3]

Cornmeal was made by pounding:

> They have large mortars made of tree trunks, hollowed to the desired depth by fire and scraped. As many as four women work together pounding the grain, each having a pestle five feet long, with which they pound in cadence like blacksmiths on anvils. After they have pounded for a time they remove the meal, which other women shake in sieves, well made of rushes. If they wish it very fine they use small baskets which they shake well, the finest remaining at the bottom, the coarse meal and broken coats of the grain above.[4]

The Frenchmen welcomed the change from a diet of buffalo, turkey, and deer meat. Indian corn was baked as bread and pones, boiled in husks (like Mexican tamales), cooked as mush, and the roasted meal stirred in water and drunk. Sunflower seeds and nut meats were worked into the corn bread. Dry beans were added to the corn porridge and green beans were cooked in the pod. Acorn meal was added to bouillon made from dried meat, for which a strong appetite was needed. Cooking was done in large earthen pots.

The manner of habitation was different from anything seen before:

> There are ordinarily eight to ten families in these cabins which are quite large, some as much as sixty feet in diameter. They are made in a different manner from those we have seen in the past. They are round, in the form of beehives, or rather like great haystacks and are like them except that they are higher; they are covered with straw from base to top. The fireplace is in the center, the smoke coming out through the straw at the top. These Savages build in a particular manner; they cut long trees as thick as one's leg, plant them in a circle and join them on high, after which they add cross strips and cover them from base to top. [Beds, well

3. Margry, III, 364.

4. Margry, III, 367.

made of branches, were raised three feet above the floor and the sleeping quarters were partitioned off by mats.][5]

In addition to the multifamily domed houses there were great round assembly halls, set apart from the domiciles.

This most southerly of the sedentary agricultural Caddo tribes had horses, known to them by the Spanish name *caballo*. Also they had bits of blue Spanish cloth, but no metal tools or arms. Some had been to Spanish settlements, presumably across the middle or lower Río Grande.

Joutel was impressed by their practice of tattooing, of which he gave a detailed description, beginning:

> These Savages have a singular method, which is to prick their bodies, on which they make all sorts of figures, which are permanent, in that after pricking they rub in finely ground charcoal, that makes marking last always. The men make them of birds and animals; others prick half of the body in zigzags; women prick their front in small compartments well designed and on their shoulders have large floral designs.[6]

Frenchmen who had remained there after La Salle's visit the previous fall were thus tattooed and had become habituated to the native mode of life. Two of them were naked from head to foot except for a mantle made of turkey feathers, worn about the shoulders in the native fashion.

Ten weeks were spent among the Cenis Caddos of the Trinity and Neches drainage.

WITH THE ASSONIS

The French divided into two groups at the end of May, the conspirators deciding to go no farther. Seven, including Joutel and La Salle's older brother, a priest referred to in the *Relation* as M. Cavelier, set out to find their way to the Illinois country and Fort St. Louis. They started out with six horses, loaded with their belongings and a fair supply of trade goods and crossed a river (Neches) into the land of the Assonis (Hasonai), another sedentary Caddoan tribe occupying the drainage of the Angelina River.

> The terrain seemed to me almost the same as before, namely ridges and dales covered with woods, one at a short distance from another; but the oak and nut trees of these woods were smaller than those we had seen previously. The ridges, which were gravelly, resembled in general iron mines. The bottoms between the ridges are quite good; those cultivated by the Savages yield very good Indian corn, beans, and other crops, and elsewhere very good herbage grows . . . Along the streams were elms, poplars, and other riverside trees.[7]

The Assoni hamlet of Naouidiche (Nacogdoches), meaning place of salt, was the source of the salt the Caddoan people used for seasoning their food. (There are salt domes in that part of the coast plain.)

The month of June was a busy time in the fields. On June 1 Joutel noted:

> On our road we found the men and women working at cultivating their fields, planting corn,

5. Margry, III, 345.

6. Margry, III, 349.

7. Margry, III, 387-388.

beans, and squash. Some corn was well advanced, being almost ready to eat, and a lot of beans were being eaten.[8]

At that season the food consisted largely of green beans, which were grown in quantity and did well there.

When corn was beginning to mature, a ceremony was observed:

Women gathered a large number of ears which they roasted and put into a basket, which they carried to the bench of ceremony, used only for that purpose and on which no one may sit . . . An elder, accompanied by the head of the cabin, then approached the seat where they mumbled to the ears of corn for more than an hour, after which these were given to the women who in turn passed them to the children and as well to us. [The men did not eat any until after the sun had risen and set eight times. After the ceremony the women gathered ears daily, which, not being ripe for grinding were roasted in the ears. At that time the dogs were muzzled to keep them from raiding the corn.][9]

Joutel understood that in each household the mother of its head man was mistress of the women, had charge of the food, and distributed it among the several families. One woman made the porridge for all, others provided corn or meal, the matron having care of serving the food. The elder woman saw to it that each of the visitors received his share, served in a dish of bark.

Cabins were like those of the Cenis, but less high. Above the door was a large deck (*plancher*) or perch on which corn ears were stored. On other porches they kept tuns or containers made of canes and bark, for shelled corn, beans, nuts, acorns, and other things, each family owning its particular tuns.

Supplied with guides, provisions, and horses the party set out on June 13, having been told that forty to fifty leagues in a northeasterly direction they would come to another kindred and friendly nation.

CADDO SETTLEMENTS OF THE RED RIVER

The ten days' journey was across rivers and swamps without mention of inhabitants. At its end they were greeted by the chief of the Cadodaquious, mounted on a fine grey horse, had a ceremonial smoke, and awaited the arrival of the elders who were to carry them to the village.

Our savages made signs that this was the custom of that country and that we should submit and let them do as they would. Although we were embarassed by the ceremony, seven of the principal men presented their backs or shoulders. M. Cavelier, as our chief, was first to mount and the others did the same. [Joutel, the tallest and heaviest and carrying musket, pistols, and a cooking pot, was carried by three porters, arriving in this 'ridiculous equipage' at the village. Next, they were told of the custom of bathing strangers on their arrival] but since we were clothed, they only washed our faces, which an elder did with clear water from a kind of tureen, washing only the face. [After this second ceremony they were seated on a sort of scaffold four feet high, to be harangued by four chiefs.] We listened in patience, understanding nothing of what they said, well wearied of its length and more so of the hot sun that beat down on us. [Another strange ritual observed was welcome and farewell by communal weeping.][10]

8. Margry, III, 392.

9. Margry, III, 400-401.

10. Margry, III, 405-406.

This nation of Cadodaquious (Kadohadachos, the main Caddo confederacy) they were told included four villages:

> The first called Assoni, of the same nation that we had left, the second Nastchez, the third Natschitos, and the fourth Cadodaquious, indicated as not being far distant from each other. All these villages gathered to greet us on the day of our arrival.[11]

The main Caddo villages occupied the wide and fertile flood plain of the Red River of northeast Texas. Joutel again compiled a list of several score tribes, those to the west having horses, those to the east not. That the horses had been procured from Spaniards was shown by the fact that some were branded on the thighs and two were geldings. "For the rest, the customs of this nation being much like those of the Cenis, I pass them over in silence."

Friendly nations to the east, they were told, included the Cahinnio (in the Ouachita Valley of south central Arkansas), the Tonica (farther up the Ouachita Valley), and the Cappa (Quapaw at the mouth of the Arkansas River). Tonica chiefs visiting the Caddos gave advice as to the route by mute conversation (sign language), their language quite different from that of the Caddo. (La Salle on his descent of the Mississippi River in 1682 had stopped to visit the Cappas.)

Thus assured that they were going in the right direction they started from the village where they spent a week, went to the (Red) river, crossed it in canoes, took leave of their good hosts, and followed the river "to the village of the Cadodaquis [sic], one of the four comprising the nation." They were at the end of the Caddo country (to northeast of Texarkana), leaving the Red River where it turns south.

The chief provided guides to take them east to the Cahinnios, midway on the route to the Cappas. Two Cahinnio men were at the village

> who had come to get bows from the Cadodaquious, for some came there for that purpose from a distance of fifty to sixty leagues for this wood, which was the best for making bows.[12]

This superior bow wood (*Maclura pomifera*, *bois d'arc* in French, Osage orange to the English) is thus recorded by Joutel as procured from the Caddos. Its range is from the bend of the Red River about Texarkana south to the Neches Valley, *Neches* its name in Caddoan. To my knowledge this is the earliest note of this tree, its habitat, and the value of its strongly resilient wood.

TO THE OUACHITA VALLEY

The men from Cahinnio gave the French to understand by sign language that they had been to the Cappa settlement and had seen there men like themselves, who used muskets to kill buffalo and sawed wood to build houses.

The uneventful march due east from the bend of the Red River to the Cahinnio town on the Ouachita River took five days.

> While we were stopped at a river bank to eat, we heard the sound of bells, and looking about we saw a Savage with a naked sword in hand, decorated with feathers of different colors and with two bells that made the sound we were hearing . . . The sword was Spanish and he took pleasure in jingling the bells.[13]

11. Margry, III, 408.

12. Margry, III, 412.

13. Margry, III, 415.

181

They were led to the cabin of the chief of the Cahinnios where they found bearskins spread out to sit on and were served a meal.

> The cabins of this village, to the number of about a hundred, are all assembled, whereas those of the Cenis Assonis and others we had seen earlier are in hamlets.[14]

(The Cahinnio also may have been a Caddoan people, John R. Swanton identifying the name of the chief given by Joutel as Caddoan.[15] The village was in the vicinity of Camden, Arkansas, where the Ouachita River leaves the hill country to enter the coast plain. De Soto's expedition spent the winter of 1541-1542 there.)

Five days and nights were spent in a round of entertainment. The visitors were presented with buffalo hides, otter pelts, and a finely dressed white buckskin. In an elaborate ceremony they were given a calumet in a buckskin case

> with the assurance that in going to any nations that were their allies, we would be well received everywhere, and this was the first time that we saw the calumet of peace, having had no prior knowledge of it.[16]

This was the last place at which horses were found, two fine grays noted by Joutel as a well matched team that would have served for a carriage. The guides who were to take them to the Cappas drew a map of the route on the ground and told of bark canoes on the great river. At the departure

> two other Savages of this nation came to join us, who said that they also were going to the Cappas. They were taking bows and arrows which they traffic and exchange for other things; they were also taking there salt in small loaves of two or three pounds. They gave us to understand that the salt came from the Tonicas.[17]

(The Tonicas lived in the Ouachita Mountains to the north and had been described by the De Soto expedition under the name Tanico as making salt in the region of Hot Springs. They were probably another Caddoan people, not to be confused with the Tunicas of the Lower Mississippi. A large extent of Caddoan territory is indicated in the Joutel *Relation*, from the Cahinnios of Arkansas to the Jumanos on the Río Grande.)

FROM THE OUACHITA VALLEY
TO THE MOUTH OF THE ARKANSAS RIVER

The departure from the Cahinnio village was on July 11. The going became slower, especially because the foot trails lacked clearance for the pack horses. On the 14th a buffalo was killed and camp made at a small river (Moro Bayou). On the 18th they forded a larger river (Saline) beyond which were groves and small prairies with more bands of buffalo, the quality of the land continuing to improve as they turned northeast into the alluvial lowland. On the 22nd they came to a deep river (Bayou Bartholomew):

14. Margry, III, 416.

15. John R. Swanton, *Indian Tribes of the Lower Mississippi Valley and Adjacent Coast of Mexico*, Smithsonian Institution, Bureau of American Ethnology, Bulletin 43 (Washington, D.C., 1911), 7n.

16. Margry, III, 418-419.

17. Margry, III, 424.

I noted that there were many caimans or crocodiles, which made us doubt that we were as far north as we had imagined, taking the report of the Savages who had told of seeing men like ourselves, from which we believed that we were nearing the river of the Missouris. M. de la Salle had said several times that there were no caimans above the Arkansas.[18]

They went on for five or six leagues northeast through "an intermingled land, some good, some poor" (the maze of minor alluvial landforms in the flood plain of the Mississippi). Two Indians who had been sent ahead came back bringing squashes and ears of corn to which they had helped themselves from fields. (They were moving northeast through the lowland between Bayou Bartholomew and the Arkansas River.) On the 24th they met the first local natives, at work cutting bark for roofs.

We continued to go through their clearings which extended for about a league along the banks of a sort of river which I took to be the one we had been told about. It had slight current, its waters were very clear and as I noted later it must have been the bed and course of the river at one time. We then passed a tract of woods where we saw very beautiful cedars, like those called of Lebanon, which are very good for building and to make whatever one wishes.[19]

The fields were along a natural levee of Bayou Bartholomew, formerly the course of a large river, as Joutel inferred correctly. Beyond was a stand of bald cypress trees, a new and impressive sight, and then they came to the river, not as yet recognized as the Arkansas.

It is very beautiful, as wide as the Seine before Rouen, but of more rapid current. We saw on the opposite shore, a large cross like those French missionaries plant. Near it was a house in the French manner, and a village of Savages below. When we saw the cross we judged that it was not English. In addition to the bands of savages going ahead of us, we saw others crossing the river in canoes. The men were made up in different colors, red, white, and black, on their heads the down of swans and bustards, dyed red. Others wore buffalo horns so that according to their caprice, they looked more like demons than men. But such is their way, however ridiculous.[20]

The date was July 24, 1687, when the refugees came to the end of their search, four months after the assassination of La Salle. They had lost one man, drowned while taking a swim in the Red River, and one horse that strayed. They were treated as friends everywhere and were furnished guides who took them by the most direct course from Navasota to the bend of the Red River at Texarkana and thence to the mouth of the Arkansas.

18. Margry, III, 432.

19. Margry, III, 435.

20. Margry, III, 436.

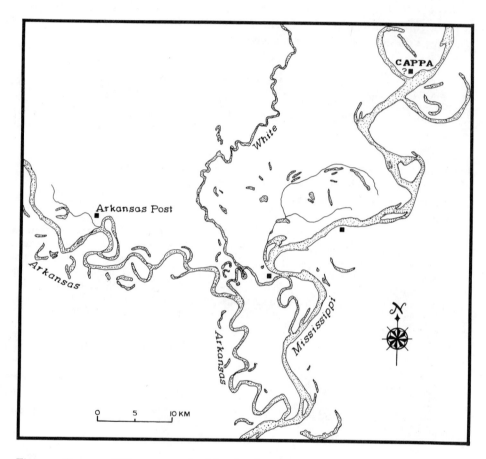

Fig. 15. Quapaw Villages near the Mouth of the Arkansas River.

XIX.

Louisiana Administered by Tonty

TONTY'S RETURN TO TAKE CHARGE OF FORT ST. LOUIS (1685)

La Salle left Tonty in charge at Fort St. Louis in the fall of 1683 when he left for France to prepare the expedition to the Gulf of Mexico. In the spring of 1684 Tonty was ordered by Governor La Barre to surrender command of the fort and to come to Quebec, which he did, using the enforced idleness to write the account of his services. La Barre's seizure of La Salle's concession was countermanded by order of the King, La Barre rebuked and recalled shortly, and Tonty appointed to govern at Fort St. Louis. Tonty left Quebec in the spring of 1685 for the Illinois country and was joined by La Forest, La Salle's lieutenant at Fort Frontenac, the two men forming a partnership to engage in Indian trade.[1] The immediate task was to quiet dissensions between the Illinois and the Miamis who had settled near the fort on Starved Rock.

TONTY'S SECOND VOYAGE
TO THE MOUTH OF THE MISSISSIPPI (1686)

While La Forest remained in charge of the fort Tonty set out in February 1686, hoping to find La Salle at the mouth of the Mississippi River. The canoe party made the voyage to the Gulf in less than two months, well received everywhere by the tribes who had first been visited four years earlier. Tonty followed the route of 1682 to the pass of the Mississippi delta at which La Salle had set up the King's arms, found them dislodged by flood, and reset them on higher ground. In search of La Salle, one canoe was sent thirty leagues east along the Gulf coast and another west.[2]

Finding no evidence that La Salle had been in the delta, Tonty started back up river. He met with the Quinipissas, a Choctaw tribe with whom there had been a brush on the discovery voyage, smoked the peace calumet with them, and exchanged pledges of friendship. Forty leagues farther upriver the Houmas, "the bravest tribe of savages on the river," pledged their alliance.[3] This Choctaw tribe at the time lived east of the river in the vicinity of Baton Rouge.

1. Edmund Robert Murphy, *Henry de Tonty* (Baltimore, 1941), 28-29. The book has the subtitle *Fur Trader of the Mississippi* and stresses those interests.

2. A letter to the King from Governor Denonville, who replaced La Barre in 1686, said that Tonty "on his return had learned from Savages that they had seen him [La Salle] at the mouth of the Mobile River, 40 leagues north of the mouth of the Mississippi River, from which he left to follow the coast south" (Theodore C. Pease and Raymond C. Werner, ed., *The French Foundations*, Collections of the Illinois State Historical Library, XXII (Springfield, Illinois, 1934), 89).

3. Kellogg, 307-308.

Tonty stopped at one of the Arkansas villages to choose a site for a post, left Frenchmen in charge, and went back to Fort St. Louis. The two posts, differing in land and life, foreshadowed the later development of Upper and Lower Louisiana.

JOUTEL'S RELATION OF THE ARKANSAS POST AND THE QUAPAW VILLAGES (1687)

The first village on the Arkansas River to which the survivors of the Texas settlement came was located six leagues above its mouth (now Arkansas Post State Park, that state's first white settlement and first territorial capital, a century and a half later than Tonty's post) (Fig. 15). Joutel described its location on the north bank of a meander loop of the Arkansas River:

The village where we were was on a small height which the river never floods. The [French] house is located at half a pistol shot from the village on somewhat high ground; it is built of large timbers fitted into each other, forming a queue in dovetail, the whole extending up to the roof, of good wood of cedar [bald cypress] and covered with bark that makes a satisfactory roof. The village of the Savages is built in a manner differing from those we had seen before, the cabins being elongated and built in the manner of a dome; they make them with long poles, set with the butt end planted in the ground and joined above like an arbor, but quite large. These are covered with bark. Each cabin holds a number of families, each of which has its own fireplace. These cabins are better than many we had seen but were inferior to those of the Cenis and Assonis [Caddos] in one respect: most of the Arkansas sleep on the ground like dogs, having only skins on which to lie.

These people are very well built and lively; the women there are more attractive than at the last place we passed. The Arkansas are skilled at making very good canoes, all of one piece, from a tree that they hollow out and finish very well. Of all such that I have seen in the past I have seen none better than these. They make also very good dishes [of wood] which they trade to other neighboring nations, these in turn bringing bows and arrows in exchange, knowing better how to make such. Others bring salt. Each trades with what it has.

They occupy a very good land and, according to report by the two Frenchmen, there were champaigns at no great distance, in which there was abundance of buffalo, deer, and elk, also woods with bear and other game. There are waterfowl of all kinds. There are river fish in abundance, which they know well how to catch by spearing and with nets they make. They enjoy good cheer beyond other people less well supplied with commodities. They traffic on the rivers with their canoes, which are well suited for the transport of whatever is needed. Moreover they produce a much greater amount of Indian corn, beans, and other legumes than others . . .

They have also several kinds of good fruits, among others very good peaches. Although these were not yet fully ripe, some were stewed to eat. They have also a good many plum trees and I have seen a lot of districts in France where the plums were not as good. They have good nuts of several kinds. One sort smaller than the others has a shape resembling acorns and a soft shell [pecan]. Others, also of good quality, have much harder shells. Another fruit is called *piaquiminia* [plaquemine, persimmon], resembling the medlars of France, but much better, of better color and more delicate flavor. They make a bread of it like spiced fruit cake, but of different taste. There are many mulberry trees, bearing good fruit in season, also grapes and other unfamiliar fruits in abundance.[4]

4. Margry, III, 442-444.

From the Arkansas post and its villages they went down the Arkansas River to a second village, about a musket shot above the discharge into the Mississippi, then to the third and smallest, located two leagues up the great river on its east bank. The final visit was to the largest of the Arkansas villages, Kappa (Cappa, Quapaw) eight leagues farther up the Mississippi on the west side, a good thirty feet above the river level. That it was built on a large natural levee is indicated by Joutel's statement that its cultivated fields extended a league and a half along the river and were a league in depth.

The clustered, long, multifamily houses that Joutel described as new to his experience were characteristic of the Indians of the Eastern Woodlands. Of the one at the mouth of the Arkansas he added:

> They make there a sort of scaffold fifteen to twenty feet high, on which they sleep to have more air and to be rid of mosquitoes, the most troublesome I have found in America, which, though small, prevent repose; but thanks to these scaffolds, these creatures are carried away whenever there is a little wind.[5]

The ten days spent with the Arkansas were passed in ceremonies of dancing, singing, speech-making, exchange of gifts, smoking the calumet, and feast after feast. While the guests were seated on buffalo and bear skins, the host, squatting on his haunches, directed the feast, without partaking of food. In contrast to the practice among the Caddos where each had his own plate, the service here was from large platters, beginning with the most notable persons. Spoons made of buffalo horn served to eat sagamité of boiled corn, the eating manners somewhat better than among the Cenis.

Food was abundant and varied. Indian corn of the previous harvest was pounded to make meal. New corn in the milk stage was roasted or boiled. At the time of the visit, in July, a second planting of corn was made. There were beans, squash, sunflowers in quantity and plum and peach trees in fruit at all the villages. Before they came to the trading post, Indian women working in fields south of the Arkansas River brought them watermelons, later also provided at all four villages.

> We had not seen them before, at least in fruit, for the Cenis and Assonis were engaged in planting them while we were among them. These fruits are well named watermelons, their flesh in fact is little else than water. There are several kinds. Those of red flesh and red seeds, grown there in quantity, have the sweetest and best taste. The flesh is good to refresh and to quench thirst, but of little nourishment.[6]

JOUTEL ON THE TRIP
FROM THE ARKANSAS TO THE ILLINOIS COUNTRY

August was spent getting from the village of Cappa to the mouth of the Illinois River:

> We took to the road to the number of nine, namely the four Savages who guided us and we five . . . We put foot on land whenever we found opportunity to walk, leaving only two in the canoe to manage it. The one who was doing the poling having hard work of it was relieved by the other each half league. We were obliged to cross the river repeatedly to avoid the strong currents found changing from one side to the other . . . The river serpentines greatly and forms many islands at the end of which much [drift]wood collects . . .

5. Margry, III, 454.

6. Margry, III, 434.

We continued thus, making five to six leagues a day, through much the same country along the river, covered with numerous kinds of trees, the most common being poplar, linden, willow, and cottonwood, so called because of the flying cotton that falls on water and land; these trees grow very thick and their branches extend quite wide; in certain localities there are very tall cedars, straight as poles [bald cypress].

When the large trees are sapped by the current of the Mississippi that mines the earth under them they fall into the river, their large branches catching on the bottom and holding them unless the waters are very great. Thereby [drift]wood piles up in mass and turns the course of the water from one shore to the other, causing the land to be eaten away first on one shore and then on the other. Islands are formed because the water of the river which is very muddy deposits mud in this driftwood and builds land, on which trees grow in time.[7]

On the fifth day a buffalo was killed. Before dressing the meat the Indians performed a ritual that included putting swan's down on its head and tobacco in its nostrils and between the toes, 'as a sacrifice'.

On the seventh day they came to bluffs on the east bank, eighty to a hundred feet high and consisting of beds of different colors, red, yellow, and white, which their Indian companions used to paint themselves. They were told that a trail led to the settlements of a nation called Chicacha (Chickasaw Bluffs at Memphis).

Nine days later they were at the mouth of the river Ouabache (Ohio), said to come from the land of the Iroquois, its waters very clear and of gentle current. The Indians halted there to make a sacrifice of tobacco and grilled meat and to observe a fast.

On August 25 the Indians took them to a salt spring, the ground about which was trodden by buffalo tracks. The ridges were of oak and nut trees. Plum trees bore red fruit of good quality and another fruit was described, recognizable as papaw (*Asimina*). (The indicated locality is Saline Creek in Ste. Genevieve County, Missouri.)

"On the first of September we passed the mouth of the river called Missouri, the water of which is always muddy, and at which our Savages did not neglect to make sacrifice." The next day they came to the bluff of the painted monster about which Father Marquette had written (Piasa Bluffs above Alton, Illinois), the natives again stopping to observe a ceremony. The quiet waters of the Illinois River were entered September 3rd and Fort St. Louis reached on the 14th. Before they came to the fort they were met by Indians who presented them with watermelons and cooked squashes.

WINTER OF 1687-1688 AT FORT ST. LOUIS

The Abbé Cavelier's party intended to hurry on to Michilimackinac and Quebec, hoping to take passage to France before winter closed the Gulf of St. Lawrence. They got as far as 'the place named Chicagou' on September 25 where they found the winds contrary and waves on the lake as great as on the sea. A brief trial at navigating Lake Michigan by birchbark canoe persuaded them to go back to Fort St. Louis, Joutel giving a good description of Chicago River and vicinity. They remained at the fort until late March, 1688.

We became acquainted with the chiefs who are established around the fort, two of the Illinois, one tribe called Casquasquias, the other Peorias; another was of Chaouanons

7. Margry, III, 464-467.

[Shawnees] who are settled there since the discovery of M. de la Salle. There was also another nation, called Miamis, at a most advantageous place for a strong town, being on a ridge cliffed all about, where the river passes at the foot of the rock just as it does at Fort St. Louis. [The Miami village was on Buffalo Rock, below Ottawa.][8]

Unlike the Illinois, the Shawnees could be relied on and did not steal, Joutel stated. The Shawnees, he thought, had moved from the English colonies, were attached to the French, and communicated less with other tribes than did the Illinois. The Illinois and Shawnees differed in the veneration of their dead. The Illinois disposed of principal persons on platforms mounted on four posts, death being an occasion of mourning, whereas for the Shawnees it was a time of rejoicing, feasting, and chanting.

The Illinois women bathed their children every morning, even when the river was frozen.

> I noted during the winter we passed there that they never missed a morning to go there, which served us as the clock that announced daybreak, like cockcrow, and as turkeys did when we were in the woods. During our stay the mothers thus bathed the small children and even the infants. I saw them at times yelling like ogres, red as boiled lobsters.[9]

The Illinois country had "everything necessary for life and its enjoyment, for to its beauty is joined fertility." On the valley floor were islands of differing size, some with trees of diverse kinds, others under Indian cultivation, planted to Indian corn and other crops, and yielding abundantly. On the valley sides rocks of sand or 'plaster' were exposed. Above the ridges the soil was dark, up to six feet deep, with stands of oak and nut trees. Behind these woods were large plains and champaigns of fine herbage, extending beyond the horizon. Pines (white pine) grew here and there along the valley sides, and seams of coal were exposed, now used by the blacksmith at the fort. French voyagers told of finding lead ore of high quality along the borders of another river (the Galena district of northwest Illinois). "To draw great wealth from this country only settlers were needed who could live there with greater ease than in other parts in which great expenditures had been made with little result."

From Haiti to Matagorda Bay, across Texas to the Red River, thence to the Arkansas River, up the Mississippi and Illinois rivers to Lake Michigan, Joutel provided the most attentive and detailed account of country and people.

COUNTEROFFENSIVE AGAINST THE IROQUOIS (1687)

French policy toward the Five Nations was to use them as a buffer between Canada and the English colonies. Stories reached Quebec that the Governor of New York had stirred up the Iroquois and was sending parties to seize the French posts at Mackinac and in Illinois.[10] In 1687 Governor Denonville called on aid from the west to stop the invasion. La Forest took a contingent to Detroit, where he joined Duluth. When Tonty got back from the Arkansas post he followed with sixteen Frenchmen, a hundred and fifty Illinois, and fifty Shawnee warriors. The punitive expedition laid the Seneca land

8. Margry, III, 481-482.

9. Margry, III, 503.

10. Pease and Werner, 85-87 and 132-135.

to waste, destroyed their cornfields, and feasted on the pigs the Senecas had learned to raise. On his return in late fall of 1687 to Fort St. Louis, Tonty told Joutel of the capture of Englishmen and their canoes laden with liquor, which he destroyed.[11]

The punitive campaign ended the Iroquois threat to Louisiana, the Illinois in turn raiding Iroquois country. Tonty wrote in March 1689 that in the war of 1687 the Illinois had made a good showing in contrast to the troops of Canada and were resolute and disciplined. "Since then our Illinois allies have brought us eighty slaves and scalps. We have made good broiling of the slaves. I am not counting those who were killed."[12]

TONTY'S VISIT TO THE CADDO COUNTRY (1689-1690)

Tonty remained ignorant of La Salle's death until the fall of 1689, whereupon he set out from the fort to investigate. The expedition took more than nine months and was reported by him briefly as to route and native people.[13]

A short stop made at the Arkansas post, he continued down the Mississippi to the mouth of the Red River. The canoes turned up this river, finding Caddo settlements along it to the Texarkana region, where they came to the overland route the Abbé Cavelier and Joutel had followed. All the settlements were of the same language, the houses set apart in the midst of fine fields. There was abundance of fish and game, but few buffalo. In the upriver settlements (of the Caddo proper), Tonty was met by a woman chief and her retinue, and taken to a ceremony in a great temple, the visitors welcomed by having their faces washed. The Caddos had horses in number which they used for warfare and hunting. They made saddles with horns and wooden stirrups and protected the chests of the horses with aprons of rawhide (Spanish type mount and stock saddle). Tonty procured four horses that had Spanish brands, two of which denoted that they were taken from a cavalry post.

Turning south to the land of the Cenis he was given to understand that the conspirators who had slain La Salle had killed each other. He continued on, perhaps as far as the Trinity River. Desertions and news of the approach of a Spanish party (from Monclova, led by Captain Alonso de León) led to a hasty return. Texas was of no further interest to the French.

FORT ST. LOUIS, TRADING POST

After the punitive expedition against the Senecas in 1687, in which Tonty and the Illinois Indians had a major part, the Illinois country was not again threatened by Iroquois or English. Bands of Illinois raided into northern New York, Tonty reporting that since 1687 the Illinois had killed or brought as captives 334 Iroquois men and boys and 111 women and children.[14] Fort St. Louis was managed as a trading post by Tonty and La Forest, and a Jesuit mission was established there. La Forest was at Montreal in

11. Margry, III, 495-496; and Murphy, 49.

12. Murphy, 105. A similar letter is in Margry, III, 564.

13. Tonty's Memoir of 1693, in Kellogg, 286-322.

14. Murphy, 70.

1688 and 1689, engaging voyageurs to take merchandise to the fort and bring back furs.[15]

After the death of La Salle became known and while Tonty was in Texas, La Forest went to France to petition that La Salle's concession be conferred on himself and Tonty, the two having maintained Fort St. Louis at their own expenses. The decree to that effect was issued July 14, 1690, with the statement:

> We wish particularly that the said de la Forest and Tonty, their heirs, and assigns, enjoy Fort St. Louis and the lands granted to the said de la Salle on the terms and conditions of the grant made to him, and the letters patent in confirmation.[16]

The partners took the grant to mean that they had the right to the fur trade of Louisiana, undefined as to extent. Count Frontenac returned for a second term as Governor of New France, supported the broad interpretation.

In the winter of 1691-1692 Tonty moved Fort St. Louis from Starved Rock down the Illinois Valley to the shore of Lake Peoria, where La Salle had built Fort Crevecoeur. There being no longer a menace of attack by Iroquois or other enemy the rock had the disadvantages of insufficient space, stages of low water when canoes could not be used, and the depletion of wood available for fuel and construction.

The Indians of the villages adjacent to Starved Rock agreed to relocate on the uncrowded shores of Lake Peoria, where there was abundance of fish and waterfowl and fertile land to cultivate. The Jesuit mission followed the Indian move. For Tonty the new location meant access to tribes south and west and the revival of La Salle's plan to navigate the Mississippi by bark to its mouth.[17]

Michel Accault became a third partner in 1693 by acquiring half of La Forest's interest. In 1682 La Salle had sent him with Hennepin to go to the headwaters of the Mississippi, from which he returned to Fort St. Louis, having prospered by trade, and having married a daughter of the Kaskaskia chief, the first French-Indian nuptials of record in Illinois.

The Tonty-La Forest-Accault partnership, favored by Governor Frontenac, was protested by merchants and traders of Canada. There was complaint of the poor quality of beaver pelts from Illinois, also that Frontenac licensed the partners to trade as far as the Assiniboins beyond Lake Superior, an unexploited source of furs to which Tonty went in 1695.[18]

The Illinois and Arkansas posts were indifferent locations for the fur trade. The prairie streams had only small colonies of beaver, inferior in quality to those of the lakes and marshes about the northern Great Lakes. The Arkansas post was said to be at the southern limit of beaver. La Salle's concession of Louisiana had excluded the Great Lakes and its beaver trade; Frontenac's tolerance allowed the partners to disregard the prescribed northern limits.

15. Pease and Werner, 145-192.

16. Pease and Werner, 228-234.

17. Pease and Werner, 276-282. Tonty's description of the Mississippi River from its source to the Gulf included the Yazoo and Red rivers by those names, the nations living on them, also the Missouri, Oto, and Osage nations on the prairies of the Missouri River.

18. Murphy, 74-76.

The French Crown, concerned about the dispersal of Frenchmen through the far interior, decreed in 1696 the abandonment of interior trading posts and the return of voyageurs and coureurs de bois to the eastern settlements. "Their privilege of going into the woods is forever abolished. The Indians can bring their peltries to Montreal as they formerly did."[19] An exception was made of Fort St. Louis, provided that it carried on no beaver trade. Supported by Frontenac the partners failed to comply. They built a warehouse at Chicago in 1697 to store furs obtained from the Miamis, another at Michilimackinac, and traded with the Sioux and beyond with Assiniboins. In 1698 Frontenac, in a last move to save the partnership, authorized the sending of two canoes yearly between Illinois and Montreal. In 1702 Tonty and La Forest abandoned their Illinois post and trade.[20]

19. Murphy, 76.

20. Murphy, 76-84.

XX.

Notices of Louisiana at the End of the Century

THE DE GANNES MEMOIR ON ILLINOIS

A manuscript memoir of Illinois, signed De Gannes, 1721, owned by the Newberry Library, was published by Pease and Werner in 1934.[1] De Gannes is unidentified, at least two officers of that name having served in Canada at that time. The editors determined that the real De Gannes was Pierre Deliette, a nephew whom Tonty brought to the Illinois country in 1687 and who lived on there to 1702. The memoir deals with fifteen years of life in Illinois, beginning at the fort on Starved Rock, then moving to Peoria, and ending at Chicago. The rambling discourse confirms and adds to earlier observations on the country and its inhabitants and also wanders into judgments of native ways but with little notice of the adverse effects of European acculturation.

ENTRY TO THE LAND OF THE ILLINOIS

The memoir begins:

The Illinois country undeniably is the most beautiful known from the mouth of the St. Lawrence River to that of the Mississippi, a thousand leagues distant. One begins to see its fertility at Chicago, at the head of Lake Michigan, a hundred forty leagues from Michilimackinac. This is a little river two leagues long, where there are prairies of similar size. This is the usual road into the country. In low water a portage of a fourth of a league is made from this river, in high water of only an arpent . . . The portage is known as the Oaks [Summit] and one has trouble enough to take the canoe into the small stream [Des Plaines] that discharges into the River of the Illinois . . . Ordinarily one arrives in summer or fall, when there are ten places where for half a league one must take out half or all of the baggage until good water is reached, and at times carry the canoe. In the vicinity of Mont Joliet there are four leagues of rapids [Lockport to Joliet] where portage almost always is necessary. [The Indian legend of the Deluge is again told, the mound at Joliet having been the ark that grounded there and in time changed to earth.] Here one usually began to see buffalo, lots of turkeys and a game bird, resembling the pheasant of France [prairie chicken], very good and formerly found about Chicago before Miamis settled there.

At four leagues farther one comes to the junction with the real river of the Illinois [Kankakee] . . . here one begins to see the beauty of the land, both as to the rich soil and the abundance of animals. On one side are prairies without trees, needing only to be plowed, on the other, valleys extending half a league to ridges wooded with nut and oak trees, and behind these more prairies. Going on by canoe one comes to open woods on both sides, nut trees, ash, *bois*

---

1. "Memoir of De Gannes Concerning the Illinois Country," Pease and Werner, 302-395.

193

Fig. 16. Map of New France (1703) *Delisle Atlas.*

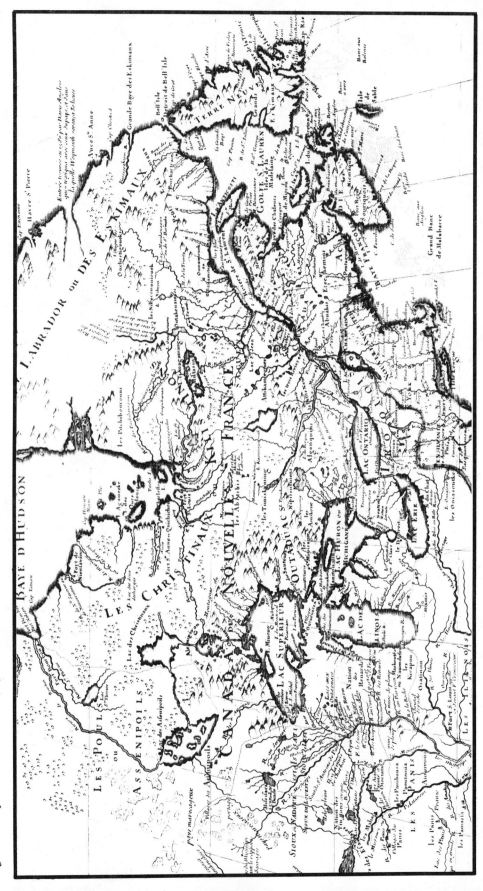

blanc [basswood], planes [sycamore], poplars, some maples, and herbs in places taller than a man. In fall and spring the marshes are full of bustards, swans, ducks, and cranes . . . About the Massane River [Mazon] one finds parakeets in flocks of fifty to sixty. These make a strange noise and are a little larger than turtle doves.

[Ten leagues farther the Fox River] enters from the northeast, near its mouth an abundant coal bed. There are nothing but prairies on either side of the river, with only a small strip of oak and nut trees all along its banks. It is two leagues thence to the old fort on a cliffed rock of very advantageous location.[2]

A BUFFALO HUNT

A buffalo hunt in the summer of 1688 gave occasion to describe life on the prairies. To learn the language of the Illinois young Deliette accompanied the people of the village adjacent to the old fort on a five weeks' hunt. The first camp was made at a distance of two leagues on the edge of the prairie, the women going into the woods to cut poles and peel bark for their summer hunting cabins while the young men went hunting. The first game brought to camp were two bucks that were cut up and stewed in metal kettles hung from wooden tripods.

The next day they found a large herd of buffalo in the prairie. After a lengthy harangue by two elders the young men divided into two bands, running to drive the animals by discharging their muskets. In summer, he remarked, buffalo had short hair, but from September to June were covered with very fine wool. A hundred twenty animals were killed. The party stayed at that camp for eight days drying the meat, using "a sort of cradle, eight feet long and three wide, at a height of four feet" over a small fire. Each carcass was divided into two sides and thus dried on the frame for a day, this being the task of the women. A detailed account was given of kindling fire by the fire drill.

The hunt went twenty leagues farther out on the prairie and took, he claimed, more than twelve hundred buffalo, as well as deer, bear, turkeys, and other game. Wide avenues extended across the prairies beyond the horizon, avenues created by the passage of countless buffalo going from marsh to marsh to water. Natives who had meat shared it with those who lacked it. Hospitality was also extended to strangers, such as frequent visits by Miamis, Ottawas, Potawatomis, Kickapoos, and others. Wood rats (opposum) were described and esteemed as food. Skunks provided black and white fur, and despite the odor, were eaten. Various tree fruits were tried in season and rated:

We found in the woods many trees laden with medlars [persimmons], others of nuts of delicate taste, shaped like olives, but twice as big, the shells very thin, of a taste that is very bitter, and dividing the kernel in two [pecans]. There were others, thick as a leg, bending under a yellowish fruit of the shape and size of a middling cucumber, which the savages call assemina [papaw, named *Asimina triloba* in 1763 by the French botanist Adanson] . . . Like the medlar it is not ripe until October. Grapes are there in such quantity that one does not go four arpents without finding trellises of them . . . but of all that I have tried, I have found none edible . . .

One finds there plums in quantity, as beautiful as those of France. I have found one no different from our *Imperiale* in form but of very different flavor. They never are freestone and have a very thick skin.

2. Pease and Werner, 302-306.

Fig. 17. Map of Mexico and Florida (1703) *Delisle Atlas.*

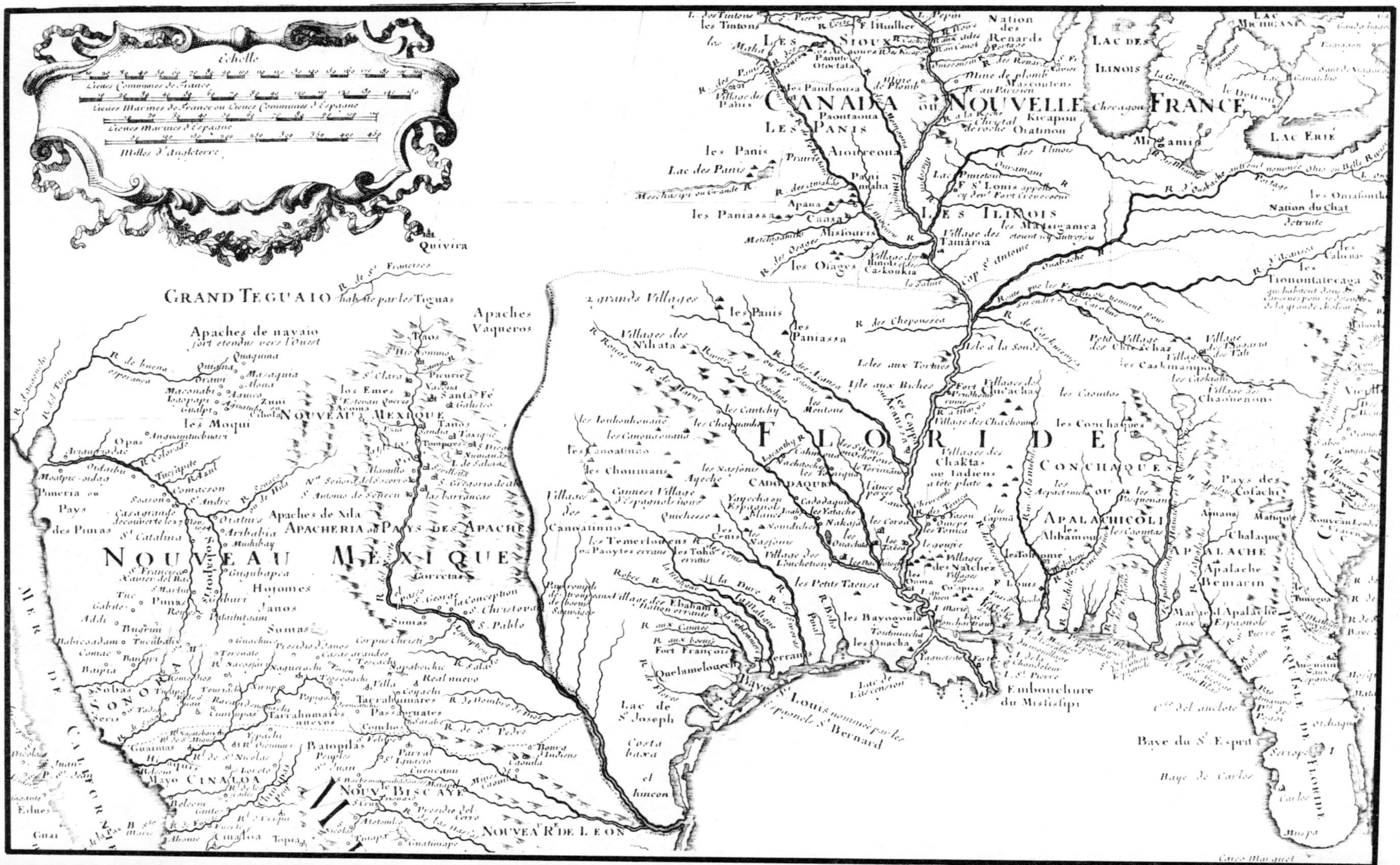

There are also numerous *vergers* [orchards] in the prairies, the trees of which are laden with apples the size of lady apples but very bad. I have never been able to eat them except boiled or after they had been frozen [prairie crab apple].[3]

ILLINOIS VILLAGE LIFE

Having told of hunting on the prairie and of the woodland borders the memoir continued with observations of village life. When Fort St. Louis was moved from Starved Rock to Lake Peoria, Indians followed to build a village at the end of the lake, which Deliette reported as having more than 260 cabins, with an average of two fires (households) and 800 warriors between the ages of twenty and forty.

The men were of medium height and slender build, legs as though drawn by an artist's pen, of light skin, and with regular and white teeth. Their bodies were tattooed from shoulder to heel.

> They are proud and vain . . . but are beggars, poltroons, licentious and entirely given to their senses . . . They are as jealous as Italians, thieves, gourmands, hypocrites, and perjurers. They would prostitute their daughters or sisters for a trifle [Deliette later admits that the Elders stated the corruption began with the arrival of the French.][4]

In a better mood, he continued with an account of marriage customs, childbirth, lamentation for the dead, and the practices of medicine men. The game of lacrosse was played before setting out on a hunt, at times between villages. A gambling game was played with straws, using as counters small beans that grew on thorny trees (honey locust, *Gleditsia*). Their addiction to this game was such that the player might lose whatever he had, including his women.

The women were industrious and rarely idle. They spun buffalo hair to make sacks, dressed and dyed skins, and decorated moccasins with porcupine quills provided from the north by Ottawas and Potawatomies. They began planting fields in May, working together at the digging. In June the corn was hilled up, after which most of the village set out on a buffalo hunt. Those women who remained went in dugouts on the river to cut rushes which they made into mats.

At the end of July the harvest of corn began, while the ears were still immature. Some was roasted on griddles and then shelled. More was boiled, the kernels cut from the cob, using clam shells as knives, and then spread on mats to dry. The harvest of mature corn began at the end of August, the ears husked and spread on mats, covered at night, exposed to sun during the day and thus treated for a week, after which it was threshed with big sticks in a place enclosed by mats.

Watermelons of excellent quality were grown, many as big as a water bucket, also squashes which they dried in a manner peculiar to this nation, to be used through the winter. This was done by removing the rind and cutting the flesh in rings an inch thick, stringing these together to dry in the sun. Cooked with meat and corn this made an excellent dish.

The Illinois River was a major source of provisions. In its shallow margins, especially about Lake Peoria, the women dug roots, wading out to their waists. The kind most

3. Pease and Werner, 320-321, 323.

4. Pease and Werner, 327-328, 330.

esteemed was the *macopine*, growing as long as a leg. These were cooked for three days in deep and large pits on a bed of burning wood, covered by stones, then a layer of water plants on which the roots were laid and covered with dry grass, and finally by a topping of earth. Several families joined in preparing the pit and in the steam cooking.

Another root in the same marshes was easy to prepare. It was cut into pieces that were strung and hung in the sun or in smoke to dry. The plant had large leaves that stood above the water and a fruit shaped like a drinking glass in which were edible seeds as large as hazelnuts (water chinquapin, *Nelumbo*).[5]

Fig. 18. Cartouche from the Map of New France (1703) *Delisle Atlas*.

5. Pease and Werner, 345-347. A third, found growing in the prairies, sweet and of good taste, resembled the topinambour, the French name of the tuberous sunflower, an American *Helianthus* by then well known in cultivation in France. Illinois is within its natural range.

In fall the Illinois River and Lake Peoria in particular were crowded with migrant waterfowl. The river had great fishing of *carp* (buffalo fish) two feet long, of which an Indian might spear sixty in a day. There were *barbues* (catfish) of monstrous size, one measuring sixteen inches between the eyes.

NEWS FROM FARTHER INLAND

Many nations lived along the banks of the Missouri River and more in the lands beyond. Indians from these parts came to trade with the Illinois and told that their river had its source in a great lake with an outlet on the far side, indicating its discharge into the sea of the West:

> The Pawnees and Paniassey [Wichitas] who live in those lands and the environs of this River have communication with the Spaniards, getting horses from them which they use to hunt buffalo. All those they have from the Spaniards are branded on the thigh with different letters [marks]. According to what I have heard they call them *Canalis* [misprint of *n* for *u*], having no proper name for them in their languages. Both nations have a good deal of turquoise, made like our small glass beads, and hung on nose and ears. . . .[6]

Other Indians who came to trade were Osages and Missouris, formerly at war with the Illinois, but then coming each year to procure hatchets, knives, awls, and the like, bring the Calumet, the symbol of peace among all southern nations. This pipe was made in the form of a hatchet, of red stone found in the land of the Sioux. It had a long stem, decorated with feathers, red, yellow, and black. The ritual was described in detail.

To the south (*au bas*), writing of the vicinity of Peoria, a number of lead deposits had been found. These were very rich, "French and Indians making use of no others and engaging in commerce with Indians who came to trade with them." (At the time the Mississippi River border of the Ozarks was under exploitation by Frenchmen, who collected lumps of galena in the soil, to be smelted by open fires.) According to the memoir this lead supplied the needs of both French and Indian muskets and was an important item of trade.

THE RESTLESS MIAMIS

Shawnees and Miamis, driven out of their eastern homes by the Iroquois, drifted west to Illinois. Shawnees followed La Salle and built a village under the protection of the old fort on Starved Rock. It was noted as having been of a hundred families. They did not take part in the removal to Lake Peoria and were not mentioned later.

The memoir ended with the years when Deliette was in charge of the warehouse at Chicago, where pelts obtained from the Miamis were stored.[7]

> In the four consecutive years that I stayed with the Weas at Chicago, the most considerable village of Miamis who have been settled there for ten or twelve years, I have found no difference in their customs and those of the Illinois, nor in their language, the only difference being that they stay settled in one place only for a very short time.

6. Pease and Werner, 387-388.

7. Murphy, 79, cites a Jesuit establishment there dated from about 1696.

Fig. 19. Enlargement of the Great Lakes area from the Delisle map of Map of New France (1703).

The first year that I came from France, they were settled on this side of the old fort [at Buffalo Rock]. A year later they separated, a part going to the upper Mississippi, others to the St. Joseph River and to the mouth of the river [Root River at Racine] that empties into Lake Michigan twenty leagues on this side of Chicago . . . where they remained only a very short time as was true also of those on the Mississippi. They went to form a village on the [Calumet] River that empties into the lake twelve leagues from Chicago . . . Three years later part of them left to go to the banks of the Wabash [the Algonquian name for the Ohio] where they still were when I went there . . . Those on the St. Joseph River stayed there until they were invited to Detroit [by the French commander. They rendered good service in the war against the Iroquois]. This nation, I believe, is as numerous as the Illinois and is made up of six villages [one of which was that of the Wea]. They are better hunters of beaver than the Illinois and make much more use of them. [The Miamis who went south settled at a short-lived trading post two leagues above the mouth of the Ohio. He had been there only in summer, but could speak of the year round attractions of that land of mild winters, knowledge he had from Illinois who went there each year to hunt, going afoot across sixty leagues of country].[8]

St. Cosme's Letter from the Arkansas

The Société des Missions Étrangères entered the mission field of New France at the end of the century, beginning with a seminary at Quebec. After La Salle's concession passed to Tonty and La Forest, Jesuit missions were established at Fort St. Louis and at Chicago. The new mission society looked to the trading post among the Arkansas to begin missions in farther Louisiana. Three seminarians left Quebec in the summer of 1698. One, Buisson de St. Cosme, wrote a letter to Bishop Laval at Quebec, giving the last outline of the century of conditions in the interior.[9]

ON LAKE MICHIGAN FROM MACKINAC TO CHICAGO

The usual canoe route was taken from Montreal to the Straits of Mackinac, where the visitors were guests of the Jesuit fathers at Mission St. Ignace. The adjacent Ottawa village then consisted of three hundred men, perhaps meaning that number of households. Tonty waited to take them south to the Arkansas. The party left the straits September 15, Tonty with one canoe, each of the three priests with one, and the Sieur de Vincennes with four canoes bound on military business to the Miamis of St. Joseph River.

On September 21 they "camped on an island called Isle du Detour because the lake begins there to trend south" (Summer Island, south of Pt. Detour of the Garden Peninsula). They were held there by strong winds for a week, spending the time netting excellent whitefish, and then crossed the entry to Puans Bay (Green Bay) from island to island. The bay was not entered, the letter telling at second hand of the Jesuit mission at its head and of the canoe route and portage thence to the Wisconsin River and on to the Mississippi. The Fox Nation at the time was at war with the Sioux to the west, barring the use of that route. Other nations reported as living about the bay were the Folles Avoines (Menominees), Potawatomies, and Sauks.

8. Pease and Werner, 392-394.

9. Kellogg, 342-361.

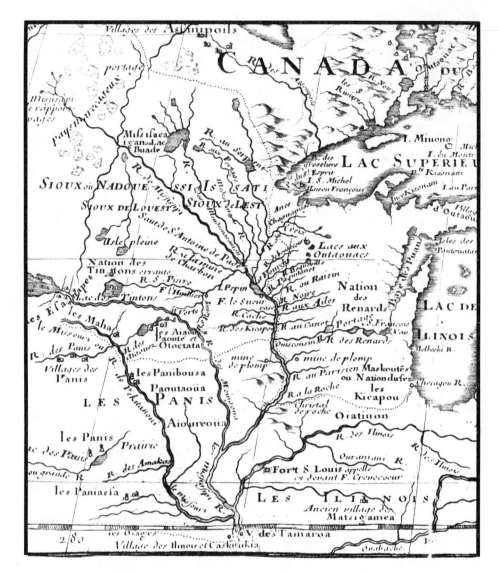

Fig. 20. Excerpt of the Upper Mississippi hydrography from the Delisle
Map of New France (1703).

Continuing south on Lake Michigan, stops were made at two Potawatomie villages
(one at the present site of Manitowoc). Milouakik (an early mention of Milwaukee) was
reached October 9, "a river where there is a village, which has been a large one,
consisting of Mascoutens, Foxes, and also of some Potawatomies." It took two days
from the trading post to Kipikaoui (site of Racine), where Vincennes and his canoes left
to cross Lake Michigan to the Miami settlements on St. Joseph River.

202

The four canoes of Tonty and the three priests went on for twenty leagues, to arrive at Chicago October 21, welcomed by the Jesuit fathers at their mission,

> built on the bank of a small river, with the lake on one side and a large prairie on the other. The village of the Savages contains more than a hundred and fifty cabins, and a league up the river is still another village, almost as large. They all are Miamis.

ACROSS ILLINOIS

The portage in late fall from the Chicago River to a headwater of the Illinois was at a time of low water. More portages were necessary as they went downstream (Des Plaines River) past Mont Joliet, where the story of the Deluge again was told. There was good hunting of waterfowl, turkeys, and deer. The junction with the Teatiki (Kankakee), "the true river of the Illinois," was reached November 11. Having passed

Fig. 21. Pueblo portion of the Delisle Map of Mexico and Florida (1703).

Fig. 22. The Lower Mississippi as known in 1703, by Delisle.

the last Miami village, its people away on a hunt, they saw their first buffalo at Massane (Mazon Creek) and killed four, these animals thereafter being seen almost daily.

> We arrived on the 15th of November at the place called the Old Fort. This is a rock on the bank of the river, about a hundred feet high, whereon Monsieur de la Salle had caused a fort to be built, which has been abandoned because the savages went to reside about twenty-five leagues farther down.

They came to the relocated Fort St. Louis on Lake Peoria November 19, St. Cosme impressed by the success of the Jesuits in planting the Christian faith. This lake being frozen when they left there November 22, dugout canoes were used to break the ice for their birchbark canoes until they came to open water. Several villages were passed on the lower Illinois River, one having a woman chief of high repute. The mouth of the Illinois was reached December 5, having had good provision of swans, bustards, ducks, and deer along the way.

DOWN THE MISSISSIPPI TO THE ARKANSAS

As earlier travellers had done, St. Cosme noted that the clear waters of the Mississippi were muddied by the discharge of the Missouri and that a place of painted rocks (Piasa Bluffs above Alton) was venerated by the Indians.

Having passed villages of Cahokias and Tamaroas of the Illinois nation they reached Cap St. Antoine December 12, a rocky bluff above the east bank. Two days were spent collecting gum needed for their birchbark canoes, this being the beginning of a land where there were pine trees. (At Fountain Bluff the Mississippi River leaves its broad valley and cuts across limestone beds of the eastern Ozarks, exposed in cliffs. The gum was procured from shortleaf pine.) Another day's travel brought them to a high rock island (Grand Tower), where there was a whirlpool in which occasionally a canoe was lost. In propitiation Indians offered sacrifice to that rock. The priests climbed it and planted a cross on top with due ceremony. Beyond, they began to see canebrakes and a kind of tree resembling the linden, which exuded a sweet gum. (The sweet gum, *Liquidambar*, here is at the northern limit of its range.) They made camp on the Mississippi above the mouth of the Wabash (Ohio), said to have its source near the country of the Senecas.

Having come to the great lowland of the lower Mississippi Valley, a land of woods and canebrakes without habitation along the river, there was little to report other than birds with beak and throat large enough to hold half a bushel of corn (pelicans). On the 22nd a small stream entered from the east and was said to lead to the villages of the Chickasaws (whom Tonty knew). On the 25th, while they were celebrating the holy day, a sharp short earthquake was felt at one o'clock.

IN THE LAND OF THE ARKANSAS

On the day after Christmas they passed the place where a large village of the Kappas formerly had been, and on the 27th they landed at an inhabited village of Arkansas, built on high ground. The visitors were carried on the shoulders of the natives to the cabin of the chief where the welcome continued through the night to the beating of drums and rattle of gourds. The formerly numerous nation had been ravaged by

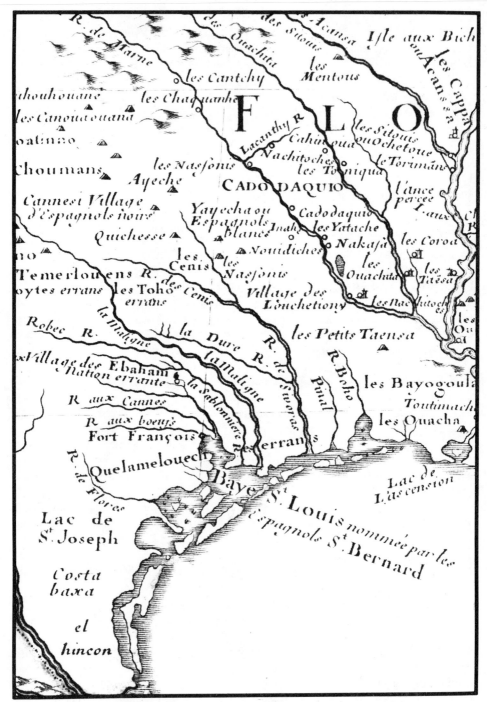

Fig. 23. Texas, as drawn by Delisle in 1703, based on Joutel.

smallpox. Not a hundred men were left in this village, the children all dead. St. Cosme reported the village largely a graveyard. On December 30th they left the Mississippi to go nine leagues up the Arkansas to the remaining village where there were more people, including children. (It is inferred that this was the village where Tonty had his trading post.)

St. Cosme was favorably impressed by the honesty and good behavior of the Arkansas. These people lived in houses like those of the Hurons (multifamily long house), had earthen pots instead of iron kettles, and very well made water jars. They had large store of corn, beans, and pumpkins but their population was greatly reduced by the smallpox. The letter was signed January 2, 1699, to be taken back by Tonty, the three priests going on down the Mississippi to seek sites for missions.

THE DELISLE MAPS

DELISLE, FATHER AND SON

The learning that flourished during the reign of Louis XIV gave new attention to geography, particularly as represented by maps. Claude Delisle (or de L'Isle, 1649-1720), a distinguished mathematician, undertook to collect, with a preciseness and on a scale previously unattempted, the coordinates of points on the earth's surface, the data of ships' logs, and accounts of voyages and journeys, contemporary and past. His objective was a factual description by maps of the world as it was at the time and as it had been in past times. Thus, while making his archive of sources he found the manuscript of Joutel's *Relation*, made a copy of it, and communicated with Joutel about particulars.[10]

Guillaume Delisle (1677-1726) continued the project of his father, publishing more than a hundred maps between 1701 and 1726, those dealing with classical antiquity indicated as made by Claude Delisle.[11]

MAP OF CANADA OR NEW FRANCE

The title of this map states that "it is drawn from numerous observations and a large number of printed and manuscript relations," which is borne out by the contents. The cartouche (Fig. 18) shows Indian warriors at the right, one holding a scalp. At the left are Indians at peace, the man with a calumet, the woman with an infant on a cradleboard. Above, a priest is preaching to natives, some of whom are being baptized, while below are a beaver, a fish perhaps representing the whitefish of the lakes, and a Canada goose. The design shows Canada as an Indian land.

A major contribution of the map is that it shows for the first time the distribution of different native peoples on a well outlined and located hydrography (Figs. 19 and 20).

Labrador, the land northwest of the Strait of Belle Isle, was the land of the Petits Eskimaux, the interior of Terre Neuve (Newfoundland) that of the Grands Eskimaux,

10. Margry, III, 648-649.

11. The Department of Geography at Berkeley has a folio *Atlas de De L'Isle* (Paris? c. 1700-1731) of 93 double-page maps. Parts of two maps, both dated 1703, are here reproduced as Figs. 16 and 17.

thus distinguishing between the small statured Eskimos and the taller Beothuks, who however were Indians, rarely seen and noticed.

West and southwest of the Gulf of St. Lawrence lived the Abnakis, Micmacs, Souriquois, and Etchemins (northeastern Algonquian tribes). North of the St. Lawrence River (the salt arm of the gulf) subtribes of the Montagnais were named and to their west and northwest (in the Laurentian Highland) the Abitibis at the north, to their south the Temiskamings, Nipissings, and Algonquins (all Algonquian tribes).

The depopulation of the interior and relocations of natives are recorded. The Sennentouans (Senecas), the only Iroquois nation that occupied territory beyond its former limits, are shown as extending about the eastern end of Lake Erie. To the west was the large empty land of *nations detruites*, the Chats (Eries) south of Lake Erie, to the north the Neutrals, Petuns, and Hurons. Beyond the present area of Ohio, Indiana, and the Lower Peninsula of Michigan no tribal names are entered except for the settlement of Miamis on St. Joseph River southeast of Lake Michigan. Algonquian tribes displaced from their eastern homes and relocated west of Lake Michigan were Potawatomies, Renards (Fox), Mascoutens or Fire Nation, and Kickapoos, and about the northern Great Lakes Ottawas. (The map shows tribal locations without affiliation of language.)

Western Algonquian tribes, in their traditional homes, were the Illinois, including the Tamaroas and Michigameas at the south. South of Lake Superior lived Mississagas and Saulteurs (both Ojibways). North of Lake Superior the Kilistineaux or Christineaux (Crees) extended as far as Hudson Bay. About the headwaters of the Mississippi were the Issatis or Sioux of the East and the Nadouessis or Sioux of the West. To their north were the Assiniboins (Siouan speaking), to the south Iowas, Otoes, and Omahas (also Siouan).

In the far interior Delisle entered the newly claimed discovery by Lahontan of strange peoples, adding: "The Long River or Dead River has been discovered lately by Baron Lahontan . . . unless Sr. de Lahontan has invented all these things, which it is difficult to resolve, since he alone has penetrated these vast countries." On a later map the fictitious discovery was omitted.

The eastern part of New France was divided as though the cartographer were drawing provinces of France. Canada was shown as the St. Lawrence lowland from Île d'Orléans to Montreal, Saguenay as the Laurentian Highland bordering on the St. Lawrence sound as far as Sept Îles, Gaspésie as the Gaspé Peninsula and the greater part of New Brunswick, Acadia was Nova Scotia and the opposite side of the Bay of Fundy, the Kennebec River taken as the boundary with New England. Newfoundland, with a French fort and settlement on Placentia Bay, was a part of New France.

MAP OF MEXICO AND FLORIDA

This, the earliest of several Delisle maps of the American South and Southwest, invented a boundary between New Mexico and Florida at the unnamed Pecos River. The pueblos were shown (Fig. 21) along the Río Grande, east of Santa Fe, and to the west the Zuñi and Hopi pueblos. Gila Apaches living to the south, Apaches Vaqueros to northeast, and Apaches Navajos to the northwest. The information was good, though somewhat outdated. For southern Arizona late Jesuit knowledge was used, in

208

particular the exploration by Father Kino. The Casa Grande ruin was properly located: "Casa Grande, decouverte le 27 Nov. 1694." South of the westward flowing Gila River, the Pima country extended from Aravaipa and the Sebaipuris to the Pimas (Papagos) on the Gulf of California.

The map assigns the land between the Appalachians and the Pecos and lower Rio Grande to France. An East-West dotted line, crossing the Mississippi River at Cap St. Antoine (Fountain Bluff), serves to demarcate Canada and Florida, a cartographer's fiction (Fig. 22). On later maps the Mississippi Valley appears as Louisiana.

Above Cap St. Antoine the Illinois are shown living east of the Mississippi, west of it also part of the Cahokia subtribe, with a village about at the site of St. Louis. South of the Missouri River were the Osages along the Osage River, next west the Missouris, and beyond, the Kansas and Pawnees. The source of the information is not stated but is correct.

The subtitle of the map, "Of the course and environs of the River of Mississippi," is in proper arrangement of drainage and location of Indian tribes and their villages. The *Relation* of Joutel which Claude Delisle had copied served as a major source. The course of the Mississippi below the mouth of the Arkansas and that of the Red River from its mouth to the Caddo country are in accord with Tonty's account.

The delineation of Texas is taken from Joutel and includes the French settlement on the river *aux boeufs* at the head of Baye St. Louis, the wandering tribes adjacent, "the land full of herds of wild cattle," river names, and the sedentary farming tribes to the northeast. Unexplained is the map entry in north Texas of two tribes, the Yayeches or white Spanish and the Cannesis or black Spanish, a myth not found in the matter-of-fact reports of Joutel and Tonty (Fig. 23).

XXI.

Apocryphal Accounts of Louisiana

HENNEPIN'S DESCRIPTION OF LOUISIANA

The Recollect friar Louis Hennepin was with La Salle from the time of Fort Frontenac to that of Fort Crevecoeur. At Fort Frontenac Hennepin served as chaplain and missionary to the Iroquois whom La Salle settled in an adjacent village. In 1679 Hennepin and the Recollect priests Membré and Ribourde accompanied La Salle on the voyage of the *Griffon* from Lake Erie to Green Bay and then by canoe to the Illinois River, where the construction of Fort Crevecoeur began in January 1680. Here Hennepin, eager to go exploring, was sent by La Salle with Accault, an experienced trader. They started out at the end of February, took a canoe and cargo of trade goods down the Illinois and up the Mississippi River, were taken prisoners by Sioux on the upper Mississippi in April, and were released by Duluth in the fall. Hennepin spent the winter of 1680-1681 at Mackinac, left there at Easter to go to Montreal, and sailed from Quebec to France that fall.

In France Hennepin was given privilege to print his *Description de la Louisiane*.[1] The book provided European readers with the first account of the interior of North America from the St. Lawrence to the Mississippi. Louisiana was a subordinate part in the narrative, which began with Hennepin's life at Fort Frontenac.

Hennepin published the first description of Niagara Falls, exaggerated as to height. The voyage on the *Griffon* was related in lively detail, with the arrival at Mackinac, its two Indian villages, one of Ottawas, the other of Hurons, their birchbark canoes at the time used in netting whitefish.

Continuing south by canoe on Lake Dauphin (Michigan), the French party visited Potawatomie villages, Hennepin describing the ceremonial of the peace calumet, the pipe made of finely polished red stone.

The canoes left the lake to ascend the river of the Miamis (St. Joseph) to the portage. The plains had been recently burned by Miamis hunting buffalo, with many remains of animals killed. Buffalo trails were as wide as roads in Europe, and wild purslane grew on their bed grounds.

The village of the Illinois (Kaskaskia) stood empty, its people gone on a winter hunt. Along the Illinois River seams of coal were seen on the valley sides, woods of good oaks, and flocks of parakeets. Continuing down river to a lake (Peoria) they came to an occupied village of eighty cabins, at which La Salle began to build the fort.

Hennepin told that he left La Salle at the end of February 1680, accompanied by

---

1. I have used the 1688 Paris edition. Bibliographical information is given by Victor H. Paltsits in *A New Discovery of a Vast Country in America, by Fr. Louis Hennepin*, ed. Reuben Gold Thwaites (Chicago, 1903), I, xlv-lxiv.

Accault and another Frenchman, to go down the Illinois and ascend the Mississippi, as related above (Chapter XV). There was no lack of game along the Mississippi; buffalo, turkeys, deer, beaver, and fish. At one place they took a big fish from an otter, this strange fish having a head ending in a sort of oar or beak a foot and a half long and five fingers wide (first notice after Joliet and Marquette of the paddlefish, *Polyodon*, a primitive species now in danger of extinction).

The book ended with a lengthy section on the customs of Indians, mostly what he had learned of Iroquois on Lake Ontario, as is evident by the context. Of material culture fishing practices had most detailed attention. Eels were speared at night by torchlight. Fish were snared by noose on a forked pole which caught them by their gills. Great hauls were made using large nets spread between canoes. Seines worked by two men were used in rivers to take sturgeon.

Hennepin represented himself as in charge of the exploration of the upper Mississippi, spoke disparagingly of Accault, and failed to give credit to Duluth. After he was released by the Sioux he reached Green Bay where he told of French traders there but said nothing of the Jesuit fathers who were his hosts. The winter spent at Mackinac again ignored the Jesuit establishment, other than noting that he met there a Jesuit father from his home town in Flanders.

HENNEPIN'S *NEW DISCOVERY* (1697) AND *NEW VOYAGE* (1698)

Hennepin got into serious difficulties after his return to France, and left to live in the Netherlands, where he wrote and published two more books, the *Nouvelle Decouverte* (1697) and the *Neuveau Voyage* (1698), both dedicated to William III, King of England and Prince of Orange-Nassau. An English translation of both was printed in London in 1698.[2] In the Preface to *A New Discovery* Hennepin presented it as a voyage

> in which I discover'd a Country, unknown before me, as large or larger than Europe. [He had said nothing of the kind in his earlier account of Louisiana.] I was then obliged to say nothing of the course of the River Meschasipi, for fear of disobliging M. la Salle, with whom I began my Discovery. This Gentleman wou'd alone have the glory of having discover'd the Course of that River; But when he heard that I had done it two Years before him, he could never forgive me, though, as I have said, I was so modest as to publish nothing of it. This is the true cause of his Malice against me, and of all the barbarous Usage I have met with in France.

The Preface continued with complaints of the persecutions he had suffered, including his fear of La Salle, who would have caused his death, La Salle having done away with one of Hennepin's companions on the discovery.

> God knows that I am sorry for his [La Salle's] unfortunate Death; but the judgments of the Almighty are always just.

Hennepin's earlier *Description of Louisiana* spoke at length of his good relations with La Salle. Fifteen years later, ten years after the death of La Salle, Hennepin made La Salle the villain for fear of whom he had kept secret his own prior discovery of the mouth of the Mississippi River.

2. Reuben Gold Thwaites, in his edition of *A New Discovery* cited above, republished the London translation of both works, prefaced by a review of the life of Hennepin and his claims of discovery. The bibliography by Paltsits lists editions in French (all printed in Holland, the last in 1737), and English, Dutch, and German translations. The citations following are from Thwaites' edition.

The alleged voyage started, as the actual one had, from Lake Peoria on February 29, 1680. Hennepin had intended to go up the Mississippi, as La Salle wanted him to do, but was forced by his two canoemen to go down the river.

> I was as good as sure that M. la Salle would slander me, and represent me to my Superiors, as a wilful and obstinate Man, if I presum'd to go down the Meschasipi instead of going up to the North, as I was desir'd, and as we had concerted together; and therefore I was very loath to undertake it; But on the other Hand, I was expos'd to starve, and threaten'd by my two Men, that if I oppos'd their Resolution of going down the River they would leave me a-shoar during the Night, and carry away the Canou wherever they pleased; so that I thought it was reasonable to prefer my own Preservation to the Ambition of La Salle.

The reluctant discoverer therefore claimed that he went down to the mouth of the Mississippi, returned north to its headwaters, was captured by the Sioux, and succeeded in getting to France.

The third book, *New Voyage*, was put together in a hurry as an answer to what Hennepin called the accusations and objections of his enemies. Those who thought the time too short to travel the length of the Mississippi did not know that a bark canoe could make twenty, even thirty leagues a day against the current. Enemies had tried to block the printing of the *New Discovery* without other objection claiming only that it had nothing extraordinary to relate; what then of his account of inland seas, of the Falls of Niagara about seven hundred feet high, of the two hundred nations unknown before?

Hennepin turned to attack those who had written that La Salle discovered the course of the Mississippi to its mouth. Father Chrétien LeClercq, who did not know those lands, had used the memoirs of Father Membré and a copy of Hennepin's journal. (Le Clercq's volume, published in 1691, included Membré's account of 1682, accompanying La Salle to the Gulf. There was no Hennepin journal. The voyage had not been made. Instead Hennepin fabricated his fictitious discovery from the accounts of Membré and other participants.) By Hennepin's own account written in 1682, he had been captured by the Sioux five weeks after starting up the Mississippi. In 1697 he wrote that he had lied on that occasion out of fear of La Salle. In 1698 he invented an impossible rate of canoe travel and claimed that others had used his journal. The big lie was elaborated anew. Hennepin claimed that La Salle had gone down the Mississippi two years after he had;

> which was the source and cause of his animosity against me; As I was the first European who discovered the course of the Meschasipi, and the delicious country about it; so all others have seen nothing but what I had seen before, and have related nothing material, but what they have abstracted out of the Copy of the Journal of my Voyage.

The Preface ends: "I should have a fair opportunity to avenge myself in this Preface of certain Persons of this very Town, who have aspersed me with the utmost Malice . . . but my Religion teaching me to forgive my Enemies, I follow that Precept, and do heartily forgive them."

The omissions of truth in the *Description* of 1682 became wild and libelous inventions in 1697 and 1698. Hennepin was last heard of in 1701 in Rome.

THE SPURIOUS TONTY RELATION

A crudely fraudulent account was published in Paris in 1697, *Relation de la Lesuisiane et du Mississippi*, written, it claimed, "by the Chevalier de Tonti." Tonty's disavowal notwithstanding, the account continued to be circulated and reprinted abroad. I have used an Amsterdam edition of 1720.[3]

The book contains much misinformation: The King gave La Salle proprietorship of all the Great Lakes and their dependent territory. The native fauna included wild asses and sheep. Canoes were made from the bark of elm, walnut, and alder. On his journeys La Salle carried provender of *cassamite* or *sagavite* (sagamité, corn meal), in some passages said to have been made from turnips or *toque* (bramble?) or cassava. Indian names were garbled or invented. Fort Crevecoeur was thus named by La Salle in sorrow for the loss of the ship (the *Griffon*) that he had sent back from Mackinac. (This story was current into the past century until John Gilmary Shea showed that La Salle so named the fort to commemorate the French capture of a fort of that name in the Low Countries in 1672.)

LAHONTAN'S *NOUVEAUX VOYAGES*

Baron Lahontan came to New France in 1683, a teen-age officer in the marines, and saw service in Governor La Barre's Iroquois campaign in 1684. For several years he was on garrison duty at various places, including Fort St. Joseph in 1687 (Port Huron, Michigan). At Mackinac he met the survivors of La Salle's Texas venture in the spring of 1688 and remained there until June 1689. From this, his farthest interior location, he returned to service in Canada, at sea, and finally to the lately built French fort at Placentia Bay in Newfoundland in 1693, where he got into grave trouble. Fearing arrest he escaped in 1694 in a fishing ship that took him to Portugal.[4]

Nouveaux Voyages was published first at The Hague in 1703, Professor Lanctôt listing thirteen editions and translations in the fourteen years following.[5]

Lahontan used the literary device of a series of letters, twenty-five in number, ostensibly written to a relative in France between 1683 and 1694. The volume was dedicated to King Frederick IV of Denmark. The Preface explains that other relations previously given to the public

> all have an essential fault, lack of objectivity and sincerity. The Authors are Missionaries, that is persons engaged by their profession to persuade people that their pains, which deserve praise, are not without fruit. Thus their narrations in fact are nothing but a detail of Masses, of Miracles, of conversions, and of other fraudulent minutiae.

The author, having despaired of vindicating his honor under the regime of France of the time, reluctantly agreed to the publication of the letters,

> his only concern to present things as they are; he disguises nothing, and he writes without regard to [*comme s'il n'avoit*] Nation or Religion.

3. "Relation de la Louisiane et du Mississippi," in Jean Frédéric Bernard, ed., *Recueil de Voyages au Nord* . . (Amsterdam, 1716-1729), V, 35-198.

4. The career of Lahontan is outlined by Gustave Lanctôt in his edition of *Collection Oakes. Nouveaux Documents de Lahontan sur le Canada et Terre-Neuve* (Ottawa, 1940).

5. I have used the 1707-1708 edition, published at The Hague. See also *New Voyages to North America, by the Baron de Lahontan*, ed. Reuben Gold Thwaites (Chicago, 1905).

The first four letters tell of sailing to Canada, the appearance of the town of Quebec, its nearby villages of Christian Indians, the river lined along both *côtes* (banks) as far as Montreal by habitations so that one might call them two villages sixty leagues in length (the term côte applied to the seigneuries into which the river frontage was divided).

The following letters describe how birchbark canoes were made and used and the life of the Iroquois nations. Governor La Barre, accompanied by Lahontan, marched against the Iroquois. In the ensuing parley between the governor and the Iroquois chief, which Lahontan represented as recorded verbatim, the chief was the better orator in the better cause. The charge that Iroquois had robbed Frenchmen was answered by stating that this happened only when the French were taking arms to the Miamis and Illinois. These enemies of the Iroquois raided Iroquois territory, cut down the trees that marked the limits of their land, and engaged in destructive hunting of beaver, "taking all, male and female, against all native custom."

The relation of people, events, and country continued through Letter XV to which he assigned the date September 28, 1688, at Mackinac. (He was there at that time and this was the farthest point he reached.)

Letter XVI, to which he gave the date May 28, 1689, at Mackinac, is an elaborate invention of a journey into a non-existent land. Lahontan claimed to have taken a detachment of soldiers and five Ottawa hunters from Mackinac by canoe to Green Bay, the Wisconsin River, and down the Mississippi River to the mouth of "Long River," where the discovery of unknown country began. He told, day by day, how they paddled up this river to the land of the "Eoskoros," a civil people who lived in long houses made of interwoven withes and rushes and plastered with clay. These worshipped the sun, moon, and stars and were said to be twenty thousand warriors, living in twelve fortified villages. Having passed the last of the villages the French stopped from time to time to set fire to the dense woods in order to drive out the hares that served them as meat.

After fifteen days of travel upriver from the land of the Eoskoros they came to that of the "Essenapes," going fifty leagues from their first village to the principal one of their great chief, who received them well and supplied them with abundant provision of peas, beans, and game. The chief was carried by six slaves, the path before him strewn with leaves. His cabin was in a separate quarter, surrounded by fifty houses of his relatives. The houses here were built in the form of large and tall ovens.

Having exchanged their bark canoes for pirogues, which they reduced in weight by half, reducing the thick sides by hatchets, they left, going through a lake covered with rushes, passed through a land of prairies and marshes and after fifteen days came to the land of the "Gnaesitares" December 19. They were well received by their great chief after he had been assured that they were not Spanish. Lahontan had natives draw a map on buckskin depicting the country beyond, a great salt lake, three hundred leagues in circuit, about and beyond which were other peoples, some living in flat roofed houses at a hundred large and small places, as numerous as the leaves of trees. These people wove cloth and made hatchets and other things of copper.

Having affixed the arms of France, graven on a lead plate, Lahontan started back on January 26, 1689, returning down the Long River, navigable for barks of fifty tons, entered the Mississippi River, met some Arkansas who showed them a crocodile they had taken, and continued to the river Ouabache (Ohio), taking good precaution against crocodiles. Thence he went up the Illinois River, stopping for three days with Tonty at Fort Crevecoeur, and by way of Chicago and the river of the Miamis (St. Joseph) got back to Mackinac on the 22nd of May, 1689.

Lahontan is remembered mainly for the impudent fraud of this letter.[6] This hoax damaged the credibility of the author, Delisle expressing his doubts almost immediately on the map of 1703.

The nature of the offense at Placentia Bay with which he was charged must have been most serious. For the rest of his life he was a refugee, first in Holland and later in Germany. Professor Lanctôt found two memoirs by Lahontan, written in Holland in 1698 for the information of the British government, one on the *Affairs of Canada*, the other *A Project to Capture Quebec and Placentia*. The refugee had become a renegade and traitor. There was not an Indian nation, he wrote, that did not hate the French, and at least half the Canadians wished for an English conquest. Except for the time when Frontenac was governor, the Jesuits were the actual rulers, caring less for the salvation of souls than for the large profit of beaver pelts. Officials in Canada were interested in getting rich and then getting out, neglecting the defenses of the country. He presented a plan to take Placentia and use it as base from which to capture Quebec. English possession of Placentia would also eliminate France from the dry cod fishery. Nothing came of the proposal.

Five years later Lahontan published the *Nouveaux Voyages* in Holland, spiced with tart comments about priests and officials. A companion volume, *Dialogues Curieux*, printed at The Hague in the same year, was an imaginary discussion between a Frenchman and an Indian chief, giving contrasting views of life, natural man against corrupt civilization. Reprinted again and again, its thesis of the noble savage had large influence on eighteenth century philosophy.[7]

Lahontan lived out his last untroubled years at Hanover as a friend of Leibnitz, drawn to the idealistic doctrine of the philosopher. He died in 1715.

6. The U. S. Geological Survey gave his name to the Pleistocene lake of Nevada of which Carson Sink is a remnant, and later it was given by the Bureau of Reclamation to the dam and reservoir on Carson River.

7. Louis Armand de Lom d'Arce, Baron de Lahontan, *Dialogues Curieux* . . . (The Hague, 1703). I have also used Gilbert Chinard's edition (Baltimore, 1931).

XXII.

Review of Land and Biota

NORTHERN LIMITS OF SPANISH INTERESTS

CALIFORNIA AND FLORIDA

The Viceroyalty of New Spain included Florida and the Philippine Islands. In 1602 Viceroy Monterrey sent Sebastian Vizcaíno to chart the coast of California and find a port at which the Manila galleons might take refreshment and refuge. The survey was competently carried out, giving names to capes and bays that are still in use. Sailing north from Acapulco, Vizcaíno found the bay he named San Diego suited to serve as port and settlement. Continuing north he came to an even more attractive bay that he named in honor of the Viceroy, providing shelter, fresh water, game, wood, and tall pine trees suitable for masts (Monterey pine, *Pinus radiata*). The Manila galleons continued to make their annual voyages south along the length of the coast of California without benefit of an established way station. California remained unoccupied by Spain.

New Spain was charged with the maintenance of Florida as guarding the sailing route to Spain. The peninsula yielded no income, its lone garrison and settlement of St. Augustine at the far end of the peninsula on a small inlet in the sandy coast plain. The meagre annals of the century report very little of land or sea.

Spain had thought to protect its life line, the *Carrera de las Indias*, by the naval base at Havana. The previous security of the Gulf of Mexico was threatened by French actions in the sixteen eighties, at the south buccaneers taking over western Haiti, La Salle at the north taking possession of the Mississippi to its discharge into the Gulf and planting in 1685 a colony on Matagorda Bay. The Council of the Indies, belatedly alerted to the French menace, instructed the Viceroy of New Spain to take precautionary steps.

Sigüenza y Góngora was sent in 1693 to locate a site for a fort and settlement on Pensacola Bay. The report of two weeks' observations is admirable as to content and vivid in description. Along the shores of the bay were magnolias, laurels, and water oaks, in the sounds dark and silent forests of bald cypress, on higher ground nut trees, mulberry trees, grape vines, palmettos, and stands of grass. The bay had variety of fish and shellfish, turtles and alligators, the land diversity of game, including buffalo, these described from remains found in abandoned cabins. (There were no buffalo when the Luna colony made its short lived settlement on Pensacola Bay in 1559 and moved north to the Coosa country in search of food.)

Viceroy Mendoza sent Coronado in 1540 to explore New Mexico by taking the western route through Sonora and Arizona to the Zuñi pueblos. Entries of the late sixteenth century were from the south (Chihuahua) and southeast (Nuevo León) and were undertaken at the initiative and expenses of individuals.

In 1581 the Franciscan Rodríguez and Captain Chamuscado set out from Santa Bárbara, the northernmost mining district, came to the Río Grande at the mouth of the Río Conchos and followed the Río Grande north to the Pueblo country, the course of the expedition recorded in detail by Hernán Gallegos (Fig. 5). As they went up the valley, fields alternating with stands of mesquite and cactus, they came to an abandoned rancheria they named Carneros because of the many horns of rams, greater than those of cattle. (Bighorn sheep indicated as numerous in the mountains of west Texas and Chihuahua.) A fortnight later they passed a stretch of eight leagues of swamps (below El Paso). From the pueblos of the middle Río Grande they crossed mountains of pine and juniper (from the Galisteo to the Pecos River) to make the excursion of three weeks into the buffalo plains that I have cited.

The Espejo expedition of the following year is recorded as to terrain and biota in the journal of Luxán. It started over the same route up the turbid Río Grande with numerous islands, sandy soil, and thickets of mesquite and came to the large *cienega* in winter, when its pools teemed with flocks of ducks, geese, and cranes. From the Río Grande pueblos Espejo turned west (across the Colorado Plateau), passing the *estanque del peñol* (the pond at Inscription Rock, El Morro National Monument), the Zuñi pueblos, and on to the Hopi Pueblo of Walpi, 'on a high rock'. In search of mines Espejo went southwest through forests of pine (*Pinus ponderosa*) and aspen (across the rim of the Colorado Plateau) into a warm land where there were grapevines and parrots (upper Verde drainage). Back at the Río Grande, Espejo went east into the buffalo plains, farther than the previous expedition had gone, giving another account of the herds of wild cattle.

Espejo returned to Santa Bárbara by a new route, down the Pecos River, which was followed for a month of midsummer, Indians gathering mesquite pods and taking catfish and *mojarras* (drumfish?). They left the river near where the town of Pecos now stands, led by Indians over the direct trail across the Davis Mountains to the Río Grande above the mouth of the Conchos. In these highlands of west Texas they saw *encinales* (groves of live oak), grapevines, and cherry trees with ripe fruit, like the ones in central Mexico (capulín, *Prunus serotina*).

The remarkable journey of Castaño de Sosa was made from Nuevo León to the Pueblo country accompanied by oxcarts. The route of more than eight hundred miles went up the Río Grande, left it below the mouth of the Pecos River in order to get around the steep and narrow canyon cut by the Pecos River across the Edwards Plateau. It took most of the month of October, using an Indian trail, to reach the Pecos, known as Río Salado, above the head of the canyon. On October 30 they came to a very great and white saline. Travel through November was at good pace, the valley less arid as they went north, mesquite woods and sand dunes giving way to savannas and gallery forests of cottonwoods and willows along the river. The largest catfish taken on the journey was recorded on November 24, on November 26 the first spring of fresh water since they had left the Río Grande. Late in December, in bitter winter cold, they came to the first pueblos on the upper Río Salado, thus called "although the salt water was left behind many leagues below." Leaving the carts "at the place of the Urraca" (magpie) the party rode west across snow covered mountains and through great pine woods to spend a month visiting pueblos in the valley of the Río Grande. There is no record of later use of Castaño's route between Nuevo León and the Pueblo country.

NEW MEXICO UNDER SPANISH OCCUPANCY

Juan de Oñate solicited and secured the appointment to govern and colonize New Mexico. The previous expeditions from Santa Bárbara had gone by way of the Conchos to its junction with the Río Grande. He had information, perhaps current at Santa Bárbara, that a shortcut north over plains led to a crossing of the Río Grande (El Paso) and provided a route for traffic by wheeled vehicles. Oñate thus moved his train, persons, animals, and baggage to the base in the upper Río Grande Valley. From here parties were sent east and west, mainly following routes Espejo had taken. In March 1599 Oñate wrote Viceroy Monterrey of his activities, of the great number of wild cattle on eastern plains and their fine wool, of the great riches of mines, and of the best salines in the world. (The mines were the copper ores Espejo had found on the Río Verde, the salines the salt beds about the dry lakes of the Estancia Basin.) As if he were unsure of the importance of these claims, he added that New Mexico was near the South Sea and therefore would have commerce with Peru and China and also engage in pearl fishery.

Oñate promised the King that he would give him a greater realm than Cortés had brought, but unlike Cortés he had no perception of what lay before his eyes and as a miner he was an incompetent prospector.

In the summer of 1601 Oñate made the long journey, accompanied by carts, across the buffalo plains to central Kansas, the Quivira where Coronado had thought to find great treasure. He took along a Franciscan friar, Francisco Velasco, who wrote a journal, telling how they followed a river (the Canadian) flowing east across the plains, the many fish in the stream, groves all along it, some with plum trees and grapevines, and on the grasslands great herds of the *cíbola* cattle and bands of deer of the size of horses (American elk). Turning northeast at the sand hills (Antelope Hills) they crossed several rivers, the prairies in full summer bloom and pastured by innumerable cattle, many deer and turkeys in and about the groves. As they neared the river of their destination (Arkansas) they rode through horse high grass (big bluestem, *Andropogon*) and found ripe fruit in the woods, mulberries and probably papaws. And so too they found the land of the Wichitas just about as Coronado had first seen it.

Oñate's only visit to an unknown country was the crossing of the Arizona Desert from the Verde to the Colorado River in 1605. The journal of Fray Francisco Escobar describes how they followed a river (Bill Williams) from pool to pool to its mouth into the Colorado (at Parker Dam), and then descended to the Yuma villages of the Colorado Delta. When Oñate asked to be governor of New Mexico, he proposed to open its commerce with Peru and China. This was his solution; he found no mines and there was no commerce.

The century added little to Spanish knowledge of the northern interior. The Benavides *Memorial* of 1630 made occasional reference to biota. The piñons differed from those of Spain, the trees small, the cones small, the nuts soft shelled and borne in great quantity. There were deer of several kinds, some like large mules, with tails like mules, also mountain sheep with very heavy horns on which they landed when forced to jump. The river had various kinds of fish, in particular catfish.

The friars told little and the officials even less of the nature of the country. It had hotter summers and colder winters than Old Mexico. Winter was bitterly cold in the high country. There were years when the summer rains failed and there was great suffering. At times drought lasted for several years. The pueblos of the salines (Estancia Basin) were in shortest supply of water. New Mexico impressed the Spaniards mainly as a semi-arid land.

The seventeenth century was a time of continuing decline of Spain, at home and overseas. At its beginning Herrera y Tordesillas published the last general review of the Spanish Indies, not including the late events of the northern frontiers of New Spain.[1] These and later records for the most part were filed in official archives, to remain unpublished and largely unknown until the latter part of the nineteenth century.

FRENCH OBSERVATIONS OF PHYSICAL GEOGRAPHY AND PLANT AND ANIMAL LIFE

The seventeenth was the great century of French exploration. It began on the coast of the Gulf of St. Lawrence and New England and before its end made known the course of the Mississippi River from source to mouth and the land west of it from the Arkansas River to Matagorda Bay. Beyond the routes traversed the French took information from Indians of farther lands, recorded on maps that gave new precision and content to the configuration of the continent. Travelling and living with Indians they acquired the native knowledge of topography, including place names, and of the biota. The French observations are remarkable for their sustained attention to the physical geography, flora and fauna, and native ways, continued from the time of discovery through later years.

As was the case in the Spanish Indies there were offiicial reports that gave information about land and life and missionaries also commented on their mundane surroundings. The largest and best descriptions are in accounts that participants wrote to inform the literate public. Beginning with Champlain's *Des Sauvages*, of 1603, volume after volume was written to meet the popular interest in the northern lands across the sea. Books on the nature and natives of New France had a large appeal in France and through western Europe as a natural world in contrast to that of western civilization. They were read for entertainment, as natural history, and as moral philosophy, and were imitated by a falsified literature.

---

1. Antonio de Herrara y Tordesillas, *Historia general de los hechos de los castellanos en las islas i tierra firme del mar oceano* (Madrid, 1601-1615).

ACADIA AND ADJACENT COASTS

Champlain began the search for a place at which to begin the settlement of New France in 1603 at Tadoussac on the salt St. Lawrence, continued up the St. Lawrence Valley, and heard at Gaspé of a mountain of copper south of the Gulf of St. Lawrence. The return in 1604 was to the Atlantic coast of Nova Scotia, in search of the copper mine and soil and climate suitable for planting. The result was the charting of the shores of the Bay of Fundy, the finding and naming of Port Royal (noting that the good growth of hardwoods indicated fertile land), and the continuation of exploration to Mount Desert Island, which Champlain named because of its bald top. The trial settlement at the mouth of the St. Croix River was abandoned after the hard winter and search resumed in the spring of 1605 for a milder country to the south, resulting in Champlain's description of Saco, Cape Ann, and Cape Cod. The last inspection south was made in 1606 and got beyond the dunes of Cape Cod into Nantucket Sound. No copper mine was found. The length of the east coast of New England was well charted and described, but obviously this was not the proper direction to get to the interior.

The memoir that Champlain presented to the French Chamber of Commerce in 1616 began with the great profit to be realized from the cod fishery along the shores of the Gulf of St. Lawrence. Almost as much would be gained from train oil, whalebone, walrus tusks, and seals. The inference is that walrus and right whales, important in the sixteenth century, still were present in goodly numbers.

Nicolas Denys' Geographical Description records his forty years of experience of Acadia, from Nova Scotia to Gaspé Bay. He knew its coast intimately, strand, marsh, and cliff, taking first notice of the coal beds exposed on Cape Breton Island and inferring by visits inland that most of the ponds and lakes were the result of dams built by beavers. The vegetation ranged from woods of conifers to diverse hardwoods and numerous upland prairies. Denys observed the order of plant succession in woodland clearings, an early recognition of ecologic stages. The fauna of salt and fresh waters was described as to kind of fish, fowl, and flesh. Land animals ranged in size from moose to rabbits, the avifauna from eagles to hummingbirds, a primitive taxonomy that identified kind as to habit and habitat.

ST. LAWRENCE VALLEY, HURONIA, AND SOUTHERN ONTARIO

Champlain went up the St. Lawrence River to Montreal in 1603, the fertility and vegetation of the lowland described in *Des Sauvages*. After founding Quebec, the site chosen because the narrows guarded access to the valley, he explored the route west going up the Ottawa River, portaging around its numerous rapids, the land "covered with great rocks," and continued by way of Lake Nipissing to Georgian Bay. The Indian canoe route followed was across the southern part of the Laurentian Highland. The land of the Hurons was entered on Georgian Bay, a land of lake plains, outwash plains, and moraines deposited in the Ice Age. A better country to the south extended beyond Huronia. Champlain knew southeastern Ontario, especially the then uninhabited land north of Lake Ontario, as a mixed and in part open woodland, in which there was good hunting of deer, turkeys, and many kinds of waterfowl, including cranes "as white as swans" (whooping cranes). In his memoir to the Chamber of Commerce items awaiting exploitation, unspecified as to location, were wild hemp (*Laportea canadensis*) and a root yielding a dye resembling cochineal (bloodroot, *Sanguinaria canadensis*).

In 1632 Father Gabriel Sagard published his account of Huronia, the second part treating of the fauna. It told of immense flocks of pigeons feeding on acorns, of cranes, geese, and crows that raided the corn fields, and of buffalo hides. (Champlain also mentioned *buffles*. They may have been taken beyond Huronia.) Sagard included a letter by Aillon, missionary to the Neutrals, telling of their fertile land and winters so mild that geese, cranes, and turkeys stayed there year-round.

The Abbé Gallinée passed the winter 1669-1670 on the north shore of Lake Erie, perhaps on Long Point Bay, the camp chosen because of the abundance of game. The woods were open, intermingled with prairies, the streams abounding in fish and beaver. There was good provision of nuts, chestnuts, and dry red grapes. Above all there was much land game, *cerfs*, *biches*, and *chevreuils*, which probably referred to elk as well as deer, some being 'large beasts'. This was the 'terrestrial Paradise of Canada', in which the settlers lived in greater comfort than they would have had in Montreal.

THE GREAT LAKES

Champlain got inland only as far as Georgian Bay. The map of New France that he published in 1632 showed the Great Lakes in good orientation and topographic detail. As one of his last acts he sent Nicollet in 1634 to the Baye des Puans (Green Bay), reputed to be a passage to the Orient.

By 1660 the upper Great Lakes were well known to the fur traders. Groseilliers and Radisson made trading voyages to Lake Superior, beginning in 1654. At its outlet, already known as Sault Ste. Marie, they took provision of *poisson blanc*, the famous whitefish of the Great Lakes. They recorded the voyage along the south shore of the great lake, passing the Pictured Rocks, Huron Islands, portaging across Keweenaw Peninsula (the names are modern), and landing in Chequamegon Bay, the home of the Indian canoemen. The winter was spent with Indians on a lake to the south (Court Oreille) where there was large supply of wild rice, here first described.

Jesuits followed the route of the fur trade to the upper Great Lakes, the first mission built in 1665 on Chequamegon Bay, the second at Sault Ste. Marie in 1668, the third in 1669 on Green Bay, and the one on the Straits of Mackinac in 1670. The mission at Sault Ste. Marie was at a place to which Indians of various tribes came to take store of whitefish. The Green Bay mission was located at the rapids of Fox River, five miles above its mouth, where Indians had a great weir for taking sturgeon and other fish. Above its rapids wild rice growing in the shallow river attracted great numbers of waterfowl that supplied the Indians with meat. The land north of Green Bay was described as forested and mountainous, to the south as prairies interspersed with groves. The prairies were said to extend south for a great distance, pastured by herds of *buffles*.

From 1669 to 1672 the Intendant Talon sent expeditions to the far end of the Great Lakes and beyond to explore and take possession for France. Joliet went to Lake Superior to look for the source of native copper and returned by way of Lake Erie and Lake Ontario. Saint-Lusson was sent on a similar mission and to look into the alleged passage to the Orient. Saint-Simon was to go to Hudson Bay and take possession for

France. La Salle began his explorations, taken by Seneca guides from Montreal to Lake Erie and thence to the river the Iroquois called the Ohio, which they said flowed through a country full of buffalo and discharged into the sea.

THE MISSISSIPPI VALLEY

Joliet was sent in 1673 to discover the river the Indians called Mississippi, the name meaning Great River. Accompanied by Father Marquette the route was from Green Bay up the Fox River to portage to the Wisconsin River, thus named, and down it to the Mississippi. They were following a spillway by which Lake Michigan discharged into the Mississippi during the Ice Age when the ice cap overlay the St. Lawrence Valley. The river was of gentle current until they came to the mouth of another large river entering from the west (the Missouri, in July at flood from the snow melt of the Rocky Mountains). On the return they took the more direct course up the river of the Illinois and portaged to a harbor (Chicago) at the south end of the great lake (another glacial spillway). Marquette, on his return from a second voyage to the Illinois, used a third spillway, the portage at South Bend from the Kankakee to the St. Joseph River. In later years the Chicago route was most commonly used between Canada and the Mississippi.

Louisiana at the time of La Salle and Tonty was well portrayed as to physical geography from the head of Lake Michigan to the delta of the Mississippi: of the Kankakee River winding through marshes, the different rock strata of the Upper Illinois Valley, Lake Peoria, the mouth of the Illinois River above that of the muddy Missouri, the Piasa bluffs above Alton, the limestone cliffs from Fountain Bluff (Cap St. Antoine), Grand Tower, the entry to the Lower Mississippi Valley above the mouth of the Ohio, the red and yellow clays of the Chickasaw Bluffs above Memphis, the loess uplands from Natchez to Baton Rouge. Joutel observed that the Mississippi River undercut its banks at the meander loops, built islands, and, changing its course, formed bayous.

The waters provided good supply of large catfish, sturgeon, and 'carp' (buffalo fish). Marquette and Hennepin recorded paddlefish (*Polyodon*) on the upper Mississippi. Swans and bustards (the large Canada goose) nested in river marshes of Upper Louisiana.

The upland plains of Illinois were great prairies, the valleys that trenched into them were woodland of hardwoods familiar in Canada, also with new kinds, honey locust, persimmon, sassafras, crab apple, plum, and papaw, at the border of woodland and prairie. Flocks of quail were all about the openings. Wild turkeys abounded in the woods and parakeets, these to the head of the Illinois drainage. Herds of buffalo, Virginia deer, and American elk ranged prairies and woodland at all seasons.

At the entry to the Lower Mississippi Valley above the mouth of the Ohio the vegetation changed to canebrakes (*Arundinaria*), sweet gum (*Liquidambar*), cottonwood, thus called from the drift of catkins on the water. To the south bayous and backwater swamps had stands of bald cypress (*Taxodium*). Buffalo occasionally pastured canebrakes. Below the mouth of the Arkansas alligators were encountered.

223

TEXAS

The coast plain of Texas was described in intimate detail by Joutel, from Matagorda Bay to the Red River at Texarkana. Joutel lived for two years on the coast at the habitation La Salle built on the river of the *boeufs* north of Matagorda Bay. The river was thus named for the abundance of buffalo that came within a league of the settlement. The French were well supplied at all times with buffalo meat, supplemented by deer, pronghorn, and turkeys. Waterfowl included bustards and other geese, swans, cranes, and ducks. Bay and streams provided porpoises, alligators, turtles, catfish, and oysters. Joutel compared the nature of the land with his native Normandy, open tracts interspersed with groves, predominantly oaks, some deciduous as in France, others evergreen. Mulberry trees and grapevines grew along the streams. The champaigns were of tall herbage, criss-crossed by buffalo trails. The description is in great contrast to that by the Narváez party a century and a half earlier as a meagre land in which man lived in constant struggle to survive.

Joutel's journal gives a day by day account of the exodus of La Salle's party northeast across Texas in January 1687. The winter was most extraordinarily rainy, even the smallest streams in flood, delaying the travel and obscuring its route. Joutel's journal took such notice of soil, relief, and outcrop of bedrock as to outline the diagonal crossing of the Coast Plain from Matagorda Bay to Texarkana, from the Recent sands of the outer Coast Plain across the earlier sea floors of Pleistocene and Tertiary age to Eocene beds at the north. The route was north by east beyond the Brazos River and then northeasterly across the hill country of the Piney Woods, the ferruginous beds weathered to a red subsoil.

South of the Trinity River they used buffalo trails across the prairie plains of the interfluves, having good hunting of buffalo except where the prairies had been lately burned by Indians. The woods fringing the streams provided amply supply of turkeys. Joutel made the earliest mention of *bois d'arc* (Osage orange, *Maclura*), native to Northeast Texas.

North of the Trinity River they travelled mainly through woodlands and agricultural clearings, finding occasional buffalo across southern Arkansas as far as the Mississippi River.

Prairie Plains in Review

LANDSCAPE NAMES

The Spaniards adopted the name *savanna* from the Arawaks of the Greater Antilles. They were described by Peter Martyr, Las Casas, and Oviedo, the latter writing "land without trees, but of much herbage, high or low." When the Spaniards came to the mainland, in Venezuela, Colombia, Panama, Costa Rica, and Florida, the Spanish called treeless, vegetated, and uncultivated plains savannas. Such plains mostly were low, a few at intermediate elevations thus named in Colombia. To the south, the plains of the Orinoco basin were called *llanos*; those of Andean lands below the cold altitudes of the Altiplano were known by the Quechua name *pampa*, which usage the Spaniards extended to the grassy plains of Argentina.

In New Spain the term savanna was rarely used, perhaps because there were few such tracts of land. The scrub covered plains in the northwest and north were known as *montes*, here a designation of vegetation, not of relief. When Coronado's party crossed the grassy plains of southeast Arizona these were noted merely as *despoblado*, uninhabited, but not as to their vegetation. The llanos of the Spanish North east of the Pecos were the plains of the wild cattle, later to be known as Llano Estacado. Plain and llano are of the same Latin root and have the same meaning of low relief. In Spanish American geography the term connotes also herbaceous plant association with trees along the streams.

Open plains at first were called *champaignes* in French, as in Verrazzano's description of the country inland from Narragansett Bay. The term *prairie*, meaning an extensive meadow land, was applied to open land in the interior of Acadia (Denys). In the St. Lawrence Valley a seigneury south of Montreal was granted in 1647, with the name La Prairie de la Magdeleine. The French found prairies south of Lake Ontario in the land of the Five Nations and were told that these were greater to the west. Green Bay marked a change in relief and vegetation: mountains and forests to the north, plains and prairies to the south with groves of trees on morainic ridges. The country of the Illinois was a land of great prairies, interlaced by wooded valleys. Indians from beyond the Mississippi visited the French and told of prairie plains extending far to the west. Called prairies, champaigns, or llanos, plains country from Canada to the Gulf of Mexico was covered with herbage, lacked trees and shrubs, had fertile soils, and the same climate as adjacent woodland. Early accounts took note that valleys within the plains had well wooded floors and sides. Also that in the fall Indians set fires that spread widely across the upland plains for the purpose, it was thought, of stimulating growth of herbage and good hunting.

GAME ANIMALS OF THE PLAINS

The plains buffalo was first seen by the French in southern Ontario, in greater numbers at the margins of the woodlands of the upper Mississippi, and in large herds on the Illinois prairies. The Spanish found them on the plains east of the Pecos and thence east into the prairies and woodlands of central Kansas. The French called them *boeufs sauvages*, or *buffles*, wild cattle, the Spanish *vacas*, *vacas de Cíbola*, and occasionally *cíbolas*. There are numerous and ample descriptions of how these animals resembled and differed from domestic cattle, how they grazed in herds, at certain seasons the bulls apart from the cows and calves, of the trails they made to watering places, of their bed grounds and wallows, and of their countless numbers.

In contrast to the large attention to buffalo, little was said of deer. In Oñate's expedition east across the buffalo plains there was mention of several kinds of *venados*, some of extraordinary size and living in herds. These, it may be inferred, were the American elk, of grazing and herd habit, found throughout the range of the plains buffalo. The French made the distinction between *cerf* (stag, red deer) and *chevreuil* (roe deer), the former probably the American elk, the latter the white-tailed or Virginia deer (*Odocoileus virginianus*). Neither French or Spanish identified the pronghorn (*Antilocapra*), companion of buffalo and elk on the western plains, probably considered another kind of deer. Their remains have been determined at the ruins of the French settlement on Matagorda Bay.

Prairie chickens were known to the French in Illinois.

EXPANSION OF THE BUFFALO RANGE

During the sixteenth century Spanish knowledge of the American Southeast extended north as far as Tennessee, the accounts especially attentive of food supply and of terrain. There was no mention of buffalo and little of any open country other than Indian farms. The De Soto expedition roamed north and south for four years, from Florida to the Carolina Piedmont, into East Tennessee, south through the length of Alabama, and north again to the Mississippi River below Memphis. Its first and perhaps only notice of buffalo was at an Indian village in northeastern Arkansas, at the entry of which were "many skulls of bulls, very fierce."

The Luna colony lasted from 1559 to 1561, survived on the charity of Indians of the Alabama and Coosa valleys, at times suffered famine, and made no mention of buffalo.

The survivors of the Narváez expedition, remembered mainly through Cabeza de Vaca, who lived on the Texas coast from 1529 to 1535, told of the bare survival on scant food, occasionally a successful Indian deer (*venado*) drive that probably was of pronghorn, but made no mention of seeing buffalo or open plains.

When the record is resumed with La Salle's settlement on Matagorda Bay in 1685 it presents a largely changed environment. Where the Narváez party and their Indian hosts had lived in hunger the French found herds of buffalo grazing in prairies near their establishment and were never in want of meat. Joutel's *Relation* is admirably clear in describing the country about the French settlement and the year-round provision of buffalos. The exodus, begun in January 1687, followed buffalo trails northeast from prairie to prairie between the woods that bordered the streams, was in continuous supply of buffalo meat, and met Indian buffalo hunting parties. From the bend of the Red River in northeast Texas the party turned east to the Ouachita Valley of southern Arkansas, still finding small numbers of buffalo. De Soto's party had spent the winter there getting its meat by snaring rabbits in their runways in the grass, a prairie without buffalo. The French party kept on east through woods and champaigns in which they took a few buffalo, and came to the Indian villages at the mouth of the Arkansas River, where they were told that nearby champaigns had buffalo, elk, and deer in number.

Sigüenza's report on Pensacola Bay in 1693 found the Indians cooking buffalo meat and making things of buffalo hide, wool, and horn.

In the sixteenth century the Spanish knew buffalo ranging in the plains of the interior from east of the Pecos River to central Kansas but not as present in the southeastern United States, the coast plain of Texas, or in Arkansas, except for the skulls mounted at the entry to one village in northeast Arkansas which apparently were trophies brought from elsewhere. By the late seventeenth century the buffalo range had expanded to the gulf coast of Texas, across Arkansas, and east of the Mississippi to West Florida. Joutel described them as in good-sized herds in prairies of the Texas Coast Plain from the Gulf to the Red River, the plains between the rivers apparently converted to prairies during the interval of a century and a half as the result of Indian burning, a practice that the French saw in common use. The extension of the buffalo range to Florida is inferred as from the north rather than across the Mississippi River.

226

XXIII.

Native Peoples and Cultures

INDIANS OF THE NORTHERN WOODS AND WATERS

Throughout the seventeenth century, the French were attentive and appreciative observers of native ways. Champlain became acquainted in 1603 with three tribes during the ceremonial *tabagie* at Tadoussac: local Montagnais of the Laurentian Highland, Etchemins (Abnakis) from south of the salt St. Lawrence, and Algonquins bringing their women from distant homes on the Ottawa River. The ceremony continued for days with feasts, dances, chants, speeches, and smoking the calumet, an assembly from afar of kindred nations, as the French called them.

Over a vast part of the north the French discovered that the natives were related in customs and language and united in friendship.[1] The French made use of the affinity between Algonquian speaking tribes to go from the Gulf of St. Lawrence to the Mississippi Valley. By the second half of the century Frenchmen were familiar with Algonquian Crees living north of Lake Superior and with Menominees to the south.

The most northerly Algonquian tribes inhabited the Laurentian Highland beyond the polar limits of agriculture. To their south the morainic lands about the Great Lakes and in Acadia were occupied by tribes that did some planting, Micmacs and Abnakis in Acadia, Algonquins on the Ottawa River, Ojibways and Menominees at the west, all living at the side of lakes and streams, the waters providing food, covering, and transport.

Fish, differing by season, were staple food, fresh and dried. Fish were speared and netted, the use of dip nets noted and spearing at night with torchlight. In Acadia and Canada the spring runs of salmon, sturgeon, alewives, and smelt provided large and long harvest, as did eels in their fall return to the sea. Landlocked sturgeon were speared in streams discharging into the upper Great Lakes. The prized salmonid whitefish were netted for winter store, Sault Ste. Marie being a gathering place of tribes for that purpose.

Moose pastured the marshes and in winter were hunted in the woods on snowshoes. Beaver gave excellent meat, their pelts warm clothing, as did otter and muskrat. Waterfowl were taken nesting in marshes and as they passed in great flocks in fall and spring migration on flyways that followed the Mississippi River. South and west of Lake Superior shallow margins of lakes and streams were harvested for wild rice (*Zizania*), waterfowl netted and hunted as they fed in fall on its ripe grain. The harvest of wild rice was by canoe, an important and assured supply of a superior cereal.

The native economy was competent and conserving in its use of resources. The long and severe winters were provided against by storage of food, supplemented by hunting

---

1. In 1885 Major J. W. Powell set up Algonquian as a major linguistic family, taking its name from a lesser tribe.

227

and collecting. Winter might become a time of hunger but not of malnutrition or scurvy. Habitations were moved with the seasons. The French did not use the Algonquian name wigwam, but called the housing *cabanes*, described as a framework of poles covered with bark or mats taken down and moved at will.

From the Gulf of St. Lawrence south to Maine and west beyond Lake Superior Algonquian tribes organized their life about the birchbark canoe, a genial invention made of a frame of the northern white cedar (*Thuja occidentalis*), covered with bark of the paper birch (*Betula papyrifera*), and made waterproof by the oleoresin of the balsam fir (*Abies balsamea*). White cedar also served for the strong, light paddles. The range of the three trees delimits roughly the distribution of the birchbark canoe, an adaptation to the complicated hydrography that was formed by the melting of the Pleistocene ice cap. The birchbark canoe made feasible portaging around rapids and falls and going from one waterway to another, a means of easy, rapid, and distant carriage of persons, goods, and information. Algonquians in Lower Canada instructed Champlain in the geography of the Great Lakes. From the Ottawas on Georgian Bay, the farthest locality west that he reached, he learned of far waterways by maps they drew for him.

Birchbark canoes of the same shape and construction were made and used by all northern Algonquian tribes. They were adopted by the French as means of transport in Canada and about the Great Lakes and were used by them to explore the Mississippi Valley. In winter Algonquian tribes of the north made use of snowshoes and toboggans, perhaps also their inventions.

Plant and animal resources in common, similar methods of provision, the same facilities of travel and transport, and related speech linked two thousand miles of the north, from the Gulf of St. Lawrence to the beginning of the Red River prairie plains.

FARMERS OF EASTERN WOODLANDS AND PRAIRIES

The earliest French experience with sedentary farmers north of Florida was in 1605. After their bad winter at St. Croix on the Bay of Fundy, they went south in June to look for a better land and a less rigorous climate. This voyage and the one of the following year were reported by Champlain, who gave the first account of Indian life on the coast of New England, prior to the plague that desolated it before the coming of the Pilgrims. Saco (in southern Maine) was the beginning of a better country and a different people, Champlain wrote. He described the gardens of Indian corn, squashes, beans, and tobacco and their living in permanent cabins, some protected by palisades. The canoes were of birchbark as far south as Cape Ann, beyond which dugouts were used. As they rounded Cape Cod Bay, he noted that tobacco was grown and that roots having the taste of artichoke were cultivated (the tuberous sunflower we call Jerusalem artichoke), also that before planting the fields were set afire and then dug with wooden spades. Of the voyage beyond Cape Cod in the fall of 1601, Champlain told that land was cleared by cutting down trees and burning the branches and that at a settlement north of Nantucket Sound, 'much given to agriculture', the houses were dispersed through the fields, the harvested corn stored in pits.

Lescarbot gave a similar account of Acadia with the added information that the plantings were manured (later Squantum told the Pilgrims of this practice), that the green corn was watched against predation by bird and beast, and that pottery was made in the shape of a nightcap. These early and valid observations of Algonquin farmers apply widely to the culture of the eastern woodlands.

All Iroquois nations were good farmers, their villages, usually palisaded, located amid well cultivated fields. The French were best informed about the Hurons, Huronia being twenty to thirty leagues of well cleared country, palisaded villages of large lodges, fields of corn, squashes, and sunflowers. Land was cleared by stripping trees of bark, piling the waste at their base and setting it afire (the practice of planting by 'deadening' which the American pioneer settlers later adopted). The lodges described were the communal long houses common to all the Iroquois, each with several fire-places and households. Father Sagard's *Long Journey* related that the Hurons planted more land than was needed for the year, the surplus being stored or traded, also that after ten to thirty years when the soil was depleted and the supply of firewood used up, the village was moved to a new location. (The sandy glacial drift was easy to dig, but low in mineral fertility.)

The adjacent Petun Nation was so named by the French because it grew tobacco (*Nicotiana rustica*) for trade. To the south the Neutral Nation had the best land (on the plain north of Lake Erie) and grew the largest crops of corn, beans, squash, and sunflowers. Of the Erie Nation there was little mention other than that, like the Neutrals, they were populous and prosperous and lived on the fertile land south of Lake Erie. The Five Nation Iroquois grew ample crops of corn, beans, and squash, and also sunflowers, from the seeds of which they made oil. Elm bark was peeled in spring to make casks to store grain and for heavy canoes used for fishing. Hennepin gave a detailed account of Iroquois fishing on Lake Ontario, spearing eels by torchlight and netting sturgeon.

The nine Iroquois nations occupied the land from the Mohawk Valley west to northern Ohio and north to Georgian Bay. All were well supported by the harvest of their fields, by fish and fowl of the waters, and by game in woodland and prairies.

WESTWARD DISPLACEMENT OF TRIBES

At mid-century the Five Nations destroyed their western kindred, whose land thereafter reverted to wilderness, occasionally used for hunting. The Five Nations then drove Algonquian tribes out of their homes south and west of Lake Erie, the Shawnees from the upper part of the Ohio drainage, Miamis from the middle Ohio basin, Potawatomies, Sacs, and Foxes from western Lake Erie and about Lake St. Clair. In less than thirty years the great and attractive country between Lake Erie and the Ohio River was depopulated and remained largely so during the eighteenth century. The Five Nations, mainly Senecas, continued to raid farther and farther west, thereby training their young men to be warriors. The raiding parties went on foot, moved fast and far, lived on the country, made surprise attacks, proved their success by taking scalps, and returned home. An exercise in physical fitness, tactics of ambush, and discipline of march. There was no economic motive, either to occupy territory or to acquire booty.

When the French came to Green Bay in 1669 and shortly thereafter to the head of Lake Michigan and the Illinois Valley they found that Foxes, Sacs, and Potawatomies had taken refuge west of Lake Michigan and Miamis to the south. Some Shawnees moved south across the Ohio River, others to the Illinois Valley. French acquaintance with these refugee Algonquian tribes began after they were relocated in the west, farming, hunting, and fishing, somewhat less sedentary than in their eastern homeland.

THE ILLINOIS

The Illinois nations, southwesternmost Algonquians, occupied approximately the present State of Illinois. Villages of the Peoria sub-tribe extended to the Iowa side of the Mississippi River; Tamaroas were established also on the Missouri side below the mouth of the Illinois River. The Illinois lived in villages of long houses each of several families, some villages reported as having several thousand inhabitants. The villages were in wooded river valleys adjacent to cultivated fields and convenient to good fishing and to hunting of waterfowl. Herds of buffalo on adjacent upland prairies provided meat and hides. During the great winter hunt all or most of the people of a village moved to live in camps on the prairie, in some cases not to return until spring, when preparation for planting fields began. Unlike their northern kinsmen the Illinois traveled afoot. They came on foot to visit the Jesuit missions on Lake Superior and Green Bay and went on foot to counterattack Iroquois in New York. Their dugout canoes were used mainly for local fishing and supplies.

The bounty of prairies and valleys of the Illinois country was not strained by the new and numerous immigrants from the east. These displaced kinsmen found ample space to live alongside the native Illinois.

NATIONS OF THE LOWER MISSISSIPPI VALLEY

Going down the Mississippi River the French entered the great lowland of the Lower Mississippi Valley above the mouth of the Ohio River. The southern tribes were of other languages and customs but with one minor exception the French, using the calumet, were welcomed everywhere. East of the river the people mostly were Muskhogean in language and affiliation, from the Chickasaws (Memphis) to the Coroas (Baton Rouge). The Quapaws at the mouth of the Arkansas River were a southern Siouan people, farming in the manner of their neighbors; the Tensas (of Tonikan language) who lived on a great bayou (Lake St. Joseph), were the first natives seen by the French "with the manners of civilized people."

Joutel reported that the Quapaws lived in large villages of long, bark-covered houses of several families, each with its own fireplace, made excellent dugout canoes (of bald cypress) accommodating twenty persons or more, grew large crops on the fertile soil of the natural levees, and had good hunting of buffalo, deer, and elk in nearby champaigns. Also they had good fruit trees, including plums of better quality than in some parts of France, as well as peach trees (of which more later) and nut trees with very good nuts shaped like acorns (pecans).

The Tensa chiefs had status and authority unknown in the northern nations, were treated with great pomp and deference, and officiated at a mysterious sun cult held in great and ornate temples, as was also noted for the Natchez. (Similar observations of an aristocratic and theocratic society had been made by the De Soto party. Its parallels existed in Mesoamerica, whence it may have been brought by the prehistoric 'Mound

Builders' to the Mississippi Valley.) In the southeast roast dog was a main dish at formal feasts, as had been noted also at the time of De Soto. Large plazas served for the observances of formal occasions. A culture in strange contrast to what the French had known among nations of the north.

THE CADDO PEOPLES AND THEIR ASSOCIATES

A large territory west of the Mississippi River was inhabited by peoples of Caddoan speech and ways. Quivira of Coronado was land of the Wichitas and Pawnees, farmers of valleys in Kansas and Nebraska, hunters of buffalo to the west, dwellers in villages of grass-thatched, dome-shaped huts. Oñate repeated Coronado's journey in 1601 with similar observations. French in Illinois learned about nations of the Missouri Valley, the Pawnees in particular.

De Soto's party spent the winter of 1541-1542 in the Ouachita Valley of southern Arkansas, Caddoan in culture. Arkansas was not revisited until the French came late in the seventeenth century and recorded Caddoan peoples and customs from Arkansas across Texas to the Río Grande.

French accounts, Joutel at length and Tonty concisely, described the Caddos on the Red River and the Cenis (Hasinai) of east Texas. Men and women were elaborately tattooed as to head and body. The houses had vestibules, were round, dome-shaped, and thatched, the frame of poles bent to converge at the top. Each family lived in its house on the land that it cultivated, forming hamlets, dispersed settlements. Men and women worked together in the fields. At planting and harvest time families of a hamlet joined in work, going from one property to another. The temples were great circular structures in which a perpetual fire was kept. Visitors were received with a ceremony of weeping and face washing, and were carried on the backs of their hosts.

At Naodiche (Nacogdoches, meaning place of salt) salt was made and traded. The Caddo settlements of the Red River specialized in making superior bows from the wood of a tree (*Maclura pomifera*, bois d'arc, Osage orange), limited to a small area about Texarkana and to the south. Bows were a major item of trade with nations to the north (such as the Siouan Osages), east to the Mississippi River, and to the southwest. Joutel related that people came from a distance of fifty to sixty leagues to trade at the Caddo villages along the Red River Valley. At one village the French were visited by Tonica chiefs and their families, who sang and wept and in customs were like the Cenis. (The Tonicas of Joutel were a Caddoan people of the Ouachita Mountains of southwest Arkansas, not related to the Tensa/Tonika of the lower Mississippi River.)

At another Caddo village, they met Cahinnios (from the Ouachita Valley about Camden), who had come to acquire bows. Continuing east to the Cahinnios (still a Caddoan people?), Joutel noted a change in culture, the houses were assembled in a village, the bread was baked in loaves, and the ceremony of the peace calumet was in use. They were joined here by traders on their way to the Cappas (Siouan/Quapaws) with bows, arrows (flint from the Ouachita Mountains?), and loaves of salt procured from the Tonicas. Joutel's journey from the Red River to the mouth of the Arkansas was over an active Indian trade route.[2]

2. The De Soto party made winter camp in the Camden vicinity. Coming from the north they crossed the Ouachita Mountains in which the Indians (Tonicas?) made salt from salt springs. During the years when Cabeza de Vaca was with Karankawas on Galveston Bay he made trading trips north to a distance of fifty leagues, exchanging shells and other things from the coast for red ochre, wood shafts, flints, and skins, indicating that he went to the Caddoan land.

A good case can be made for the extension of Caddoan peoples and culture southwest to the Río Grande. In 1582, Gallegos described in fair detail a striped (*rayado*) and merry people living along the Río Grande above the mouth of the Río Conchos, Espejo introducing the name Jumano in 1583. Their designation *rayado* indicates that they were tattooed, a distinguishing mark of Caddoan peoples. They lived in permanent villages, were ruled by chiefs, raised good crops of maize, beans, and squash, used powerful bows, had shields of buffalo hide, and went thirty leagues north on buffalo hunts. They were noted as traders in salt that they made and in many things brought from other parts, including fine colored cotton fabrics which they got from a nation to the west (the Opatas of Sonora?). Espejo, returning from the Pueblo country, was met by Jumanos on the Pecos River who took his party by a short trail across the Davis Mountains to the junction of Conchos and Río Grande.

Jumanos appear separately in the annals of New Mexico, living in one of the pueblos of the Salinas (Estancia Basin) until it was abandoned after 1670 and they retreated south. They were out of New Mexico before the Pueblo Revolt broke and took no part in it. Well into the eighteenth century Jumanos were known to the Spanish as farmers living along the Río Grande about and above the mouth of the Río Conchos, as collectors and hunters in Southwest Texas, and as traders ranging east across Texas. Their contact with the French will be considered in the next chapter.

PUEBLO CULTURE

The Spanish parties that went on northern exploration after Coronado's time gave more information about the life of the Pueblo peoples than was recorded later, when New Mexico was governed by Spanish officials and the Pueblos were assigned to mission stations. The earlier accounts described the Pueblos, although differing in language, as having a common culture, and living in similar, large yet compact villages. Spanish usage in the New World restricted the name *pueblo* to Indian communities which were aggregated (*formado*) in massed and permanent buildings, as in central Mexico. The people in the north of similar manner of habitation were therefore called the Pueblos.

The Pueblo houses were noted as multifamily, built of stone in some parts, in others of adobe, the latter whitewashed on the outside as well as within, and ranging from two to six and more stories. The houses were flat roofed, built wall to wall, the ground floor used for storage, the higher floors entered by removable ladders. The flat roofs served for additional storage. Each pueblo had one or more plazas with kivas, called *estufas*, "houses made underground and very secret" (Espejo), or *mezquitas* (mosque, Castaño de Sosa adding, "in the center of the plaza a large round house, half underground"). Estimates were given by pueblo of the number of houses and population. Ácoma, built on a high rock, supplied itself with water from cisterns (Espejo), the Hopi pueblos from deep wells (Luxán).

All work in the fields was done by men. Men also did all carrying of burdens, including water jars borne on the head, using pads as women did in Castile (Gallegos). Men were busy in the fields from morning to dark, women bringing their food (Espejo). Women did the work in the houses, to some extent the building and plastering. Women ground corn on metates (milling stones), which unlike Mexico were permanently fixed

232

on stands. Women cooked the meals, made the pottery, and did spinning and weaving (Gallegos).

Comparison was made with Mexican Indian ways, to the disadvantage of the latter, the observers failing to note that Pueblo life was unchanged by alien domination. Men and women were fully and well dressed, wearing garments woven of cotton or of the fine fibre of a wild plant, mantles of turkey feathers, wraps, jackets, and shoes of buckskin and buffalo hide (Gallegos, Espejo). Pottery was of many forms and fine decoration, "better than in New Spain" (Gallegos), "more beautiful than in Portugal" (Gallegos). Castaño de Sosa noted pottery of fine quality, red, black, and polychrome, some glazed; also that they made jewelry of turquoise (Gallegos also noted turquoise).

Crops were grown in *temporales*, fields dependent on summer rainfall, and also irrigation with a diversion of running water into channels, built with a skill that had to be seen to be believed (Castaño de Sosa). Good years provided a surplus that was stored against years of crop failure. Castaño de Sosa estimated that a pueblo on the upper Pecos had more than thirty thousand fanegas of maize stored, some of it several years old, the best he had seen, and, like their beans, of several kinds. He added grain amaranth, not mentioned by others, but a major Pueblo crop. Cotton was another important crop in warmer parts of the Río Grande Valley and also at the Hopi pueblos. (Hopi cotton is a variety, peculiar to the Hopi, selected for the shortest growing season of any New World cotton.) Turkeys were kept in number at many pueblos, prized for their feathers rather than as food. These observations have significant details that are not found in later or earlier accounts and which have in part escaped attention.

THE APACHES

New Mexico was the land of the Pueblos, extending from the headwaters of the Pecos River and the middle and upper Río Grande to the Hopi buttes in the west. It also included the bordering plains and mountains, the land of the Apaches, known at first as the Querechos.

Coronado met Querechos on the buffalo plains east of the Pecos. Gallegos described them in 1582 as moving about the eastern plains, hunting buffalo, living in tents of hide that resembled army tents, using dogs of medium size harnessed in long trains, and driving these to Pueblo villages, where they traded hides and meat of buffalo and *venados* (deer, elk, pronghorn?) for maize and cotton blankets. In 1583 Espejo found Querechos at Ácoma Pueblo trading salt, deer, rabbits, hares, and buckskins for cotton mantas and the like, the western location and the game indicating that these were Navajos.

By the time Governor Oñate rode into the buffalo plains the name Apache had replaced Querecho. Benavides in his *Memorial* of 1630 described the great Apache nation as surrounding the Pueblos on all sides, those of the eastern plains coming to the Pueblos, bringing their families and trains of dogs loaded with packs to trade hides for goods of the Pueblos. The Gila Apaches, living in mountains to the south, visited southern Pueblo missions. At the north Apaches de Navajó, *navajó* meaning cultivated fields, were beginning to be converted, Benavides conferring with their chiefs in a ceremonial peace pipe.

At the time these Athabaskan tribes, immigrants some centuries earlier from the north, were living in good relations with the Pueblos. The Plains Apaches retained

233

their northern ways, as mobile hunters, living in skin tepees and using dog trains to carry packs and pull travois loaded with tepees and their contents. The Gila Apaches planted small fields. The Navajos farmed on a larger scale and were held to be most advanced in their ways and to be most numerous.

In the last quarter of the century Apaches turned to raiding Pueblo missions and Spanish stock ranches. When the Pueblo revolt broke out they joined in, thereafter the enemies of New Spain's north.

SOUTHERN ORIGINS OF AGRICULTURE OF THE SOUTHWEST

The three parties that explored New Mexico after Coronado's time found the Pueblo communities living in the manner of Mexicans, by which they meant the natives of central Mexico, mainly Nahuas. By current terms of anthropology the Spanish visitors recognized other Pueblos of Mesoamerican Culture.

Pueblo agriculture practiced tillage by *temporal* and by irrigation as was done in central Mexico, growing maize, beans, squash, grain amaranth, and cotton, plants domesticated in Mesoamerica at an unknown remote time.

How and when the cultivated plants were taken north is not known. An interior route is indicated, a corridor extending north along the western margin of the Mesa Central, of temperate climate, adequate rainfall, and fertile soils. Archeology has found remains of high Mesoamerican culture in Zacatecas and probably extending into Durango; south of the Pueblo country are the Pueblo-related ruins of Casas Grandes in northwestern Chihuahua. Temperate climate forms of maize, beans, squash (*Cucurbita moschata*), and Mexican upland cotton (including Hopi cotton) link the Pueblo country with Central Mexico. Mesoamerican culture moved north by diffusion, not in so far as we know by migration of people.

The head of the Gulf of California was known as inhabited by Yuman tribes and Papagos, living in clusters of huts and growing crops on valley floor and alluvial fans watered by summer flooding. This is a desert of very hot summers, its cultivated plants tolerant of high temperatures and adapted to low need of water. The varieties grown differed from those of the Pueblos: the white Papago corn that flowers and sets ears at very high temperatures, the tepary bean (*Phaseolus acutifolius. var. latifolius*), popularly said to make a crop by three showers, the *tierra caliente* squash (*Cucurbita mixta*), and Pima cotton.

The plants of Indian cultivation in the Lower Colorado Valley and southwestern Arizona were introduced from tropical lowlands to the south. Mesoamerican high culture occupied the Pacific coast as far north as Sinaloa and is known to have flourished in the first millenium B.C. and earlier. At the beginning of the Christian Era an advanced culture, called Hohokam, appeared about the head of the Gulf of California. The Hohokam built an elaborate system of irrigation canals and reservoirs in the Gila and Salt River valleys. Their fine pottery, unlike any other of the Southwest, cremation of the dead with urn burial, and other traits link them to the distant south. After a thousand years Hohokam culture was replaced by simple farmers, Pimas at the east who continued to use irrigation works of the Hohokam, Papagos and Yumans to the west, all growing crops of remote southern origin.

234

INDIAN FARMERS OF THE HUMID EAST

From eastern Texas to the Gulf of St. Lawrence all Indian peoples engaged to some extent in farming. In the north, of short and uncertain growing season, planting on a small scale was done by Abnakis and Micmacs in Acadia, Menominees in northern Wisconsin, and Sioux at the headwaters of the Mississippi.

Throughout the East cultivated fields were in woodlands, usually hardwoods, commonly were made by 'deadenings', the trees killed by girdling, and the deadenings cleared by repeated burning. Such fields were called *deserts* by the French, as in the Lower Mississippi Valley, a term that has led to mistranslation.

Indian tillage was by planting stick or hoe, suited to work forest soil but not to break prairie sod. In prairie country Indian fields were confined to wooded valleys, as is recorded in detail for the Illinois. In the Lower Mississippi Valley natural levees provided well drained, fertile, and easily worked soil as did wooded, loess mantled uplands. To the west, Caddoan peoples, from the Wichitas of Kansas to the Cenis (Hasinais) of east Texas, farmed wooded valleys large and small. About the Great Lakes deposit of the last ice sheet formed a sandy terrain, as in southern Ontario, New England, and Wisconsin, occupied by part-time farmers. Of Huronia it was recorded that villages moved to a new site when the supply of wood was exhausted, by which time the sandy soils also had lost fertility. Whether on alluvium, loess, or glacial drift, Indians of the humid East farmed in woods clearings, as did the American pioneer settlers to follow.

As in the Southwest, the staple crops of the East were maize, beans, and squash, commonly planted together. In contrast to the Pueblos, however, labor in the fields was done by women; among the Caddoans men and women joined together at working in the fields. In southern New England Champlain noted huts built in the fields, watchers stationed against predation by birds and beasts. Joutel witnessed an elaborate green corn ceremony among the Cenis and described also how they roasted green ears of maize and boiled green beans, cooked corn meal and beans wrapped in corn husks (like Mexican tamales), and baked loaves of bread of corn meal. Throughout the East corn was pounded to meal in log mortars, not ground on stones (metates) as in Mexico and New Mexico. Corn meal was cooked as mush (sagamité); mixed with dried meat (pemmican) it was stored and served in travels. The long growing season of the Lower Mississippi Valley permitted successive plantings.

Later information tells of flint and sweet corn in the Northeast and probably flour corn varieties in the South. There is no notice of diverse kinds of beans such as were described among the Pueblos. In contrast to the Southwest the squashes in general cultivation were the common field pumpkin (*Cucurbita pepo*), a Mesoamerican species grown there in *tierra templada*, at elevations higher than the zone of *C. moschata*.

Indigenous plants taken into cultivation are few, minor, and in part uncertain. The common sunflower (*Helianthus annuus*) was planted for its oil, especially in the Northeast, but it was also grown by the Pueblos and in central Mexico. The tuberous sunflower or Jerusalem artichoke was common in fields of the Eastern Woodlands and its tubers were harvested, but it thrives in disturbed soil and may have been commensal with the complex of Indian fields rather than planted in them. Native plums, however, were reported as growing in orchards in the South, as cared for and of superior quality.

2 35

A tobacco (*Nicotiana rustica*), a hybrid cultigen of the northern Andes, was grown throughout the humid east. More potent than the tobacco of commerce (*N. tabacum*), which was unknown in North America, it was smoked in the ceremonies of tribal peace and trade.

Muskhogean nations inhabited our Southeast from the Lower Mississippi Valley to Florida. The straits of Florida were freely crossed in both directions by Florida Indians and Arawaks of the West Indies. There was no introduction of cultivated plants from the islands to the mainland. The island root crops that inclues *yuca* (manioc), and *batatas* (sweet potato), cotton, and *N. tabacum* (the tobacco of commerce) were not taken into the crop complex of the mainland.

At the west the buffalo plains lay between the Caddoan farmers and the Pueblos. The Apaches and other hunting tribes did not make use of the valley floors to grow crops nor is there archaeologic evidence of prior presence of sedentary population. The Pueblos cultivated cotton, grain amaranth, the *C. moschata* squash, and varieties of maize and beans unknown in the East. They ground corn on mealing stones; in the East it was pounded in mortars of hollowed tree trunks. The evidence of agricultural diffusion from Pueblo country to the east is negative.

The Gran Chichimeca, the land of mobile bands of hunters and gatherers, extended from the northern border of the Aztec state across the Río Grande, by Spanish usage, into the Texas coast plain. As the most direct land route from Mesoamerica to the Mississippi Valley it has been well examined by archaeologists, with the discovery of early primitive human presence but nothing that would indicate it might have served as a passageway for a more advanced culture. It has valleys and basins attractive for settlement but despite the nearness to old settled lands in northeast Mexico, and also to the coast plain of Texas, it remained a primitive wilderness.

Which raises the question, if not by land, could the plants domesticated by man in Mesoamerica have been taken by sea north of the Gulf of Mexico, around it or across it? The Hohokam may have come thus up the northern Gulf of California two thousand years ago. The Mississippi Valley north to Wisconsin and east to the upper Ohio River has many earthworks of various designs, mass, and age which the early American settlers ascribed to prehistoric Mound Builders. The first volume published by the Smithsonian Institution, by Squier and Davis in 1848, was on these remains.[3] This earliest classic of American archaeology noted the location of the structures in relation to navigable waters and tracts of fertile and readily worked soils, also that they were found east of the Mississippi drainage along rivers flowing into the Gulf of Mexico.

It is now known that large and elaborate earthworks, in particular in the Deep South, are ancient. Poverty Point in northeast Louisiana, excavated and described by James Ford, flourished at the time when Homer sang of the Trojan War.[4]

People and culture came from Mesoamerica to the Deep South a thousand years before the Hohokam were known in the Arizona desert. The notable absence of cotton in what became our Cotton Belt may suggest that cotton was not yet cultivated in Mesoamerica, a speculation that has some support from the fact that bark cloth, a felting

3. Ephraim G. Squier and E. A. Davis, *Ancient Monuments of the Mississippi Valley*, Smithsonian Institution, Contributions to Knowledge, I (Washington, D.C., 1848).

4. James A. Ford and Clarence H. Webb, *Poverty Point, a Late Archaic Site in Louisiana*, American Museum of Natural History, Anthropological Papers, XLVI, pt. 1 (New York, 1956).

process, was made in historic times by Indians of Central America and in our Southeast. The relation of historic Indians to these Mesoamericans is still unknown.

COMMON AND WIDESPREAD INDIAN TRAITS

Exploring parties depended on Indian knowledge of geography. Indian guides led them on land and on water by the most direct routes. Espejo on his return from the Pueblo country was taken back by a short cut from the Pecos to the Conchos River; Castaño de Sosa followed an Indian trail to get to the Pueblos by way of the Pecos. The survivors of La Salle's party were led from northeast Texas across Arkansas to the Mississippi River by the easiest route. Indians showed Frenchmen the way from the St. Lawrence to the Ohio River, from the Great Lakes to the Mississippi River and beyond.

Indians communicated a toponymy, properly arranged by drawing maps of location, direction, and distance, a primordial learning perhaps common to mankind. While exploring the coast of New England, Champlain found that Indians knew how to draw correct maps. He continued to make use of this skill to the end of his time, terminating with his map of New France that extended to the farther Great Lakes. La Salle had an Illinois Indian draw a map of the Mississippi River to its mouth. Oñate followed a map by a Yavapai across the Arizona desert to the Colorado River.

Trade was carried on between neighboring peoples of differing culture, Apaches with Pueblos for example. From Caddoan country bow wood, flint, and salt were traded to the Lower Mississippi Valley and in other directions. The Tobacco Nation of Ontario was thus named because it provided tobacco to other tribes. Strings and belts of wampum, made of shells of the Atlantic coast, were pledges of peace widely used in the Northeast, and served as medium of exchange. Turquoise of New Mexico, native copper of Lake Superior, porcupine quills of the north woods, and pipestone from Minnesota passed from tribe to tribe to great distances. The Ottawas were known all about the Great Lakes as a nation of traders, the Jumanos likewise from the lower Mississippi to the Río Grande.

Except in arid lands that lacked suitable vegetation, fires were set, to aid in collecting, to improve pasture of game, to drive game, and among farming people to prepare land for planting. Dugout canoes were made from New England to the Texas coast by the same process of charring and scraping.

The ceremony of smoking the peace pipe was solemnly observed from the Gulf of St. Lawrence to the length of the Mississippi. By presenting the ritual calumet, the pipe of the red stone, the stem decorated with the proper feathers, the French found welcome everywhere as they went into the interior. Benavides arranged for a mission among the Navajo by meeting with their chiefs, passing the calumet.

There were dances to suit the occasion, by tribes of disparate habits, to chanting, the beat of drums, and the rattle of gourds. Champlain saw the first scalp dance at Tadoussac in 1603 and was given a scalp to take as a present to his king. Taking scalps was recorded as far west as Illinois, suggesting that the practice at the time may not have reached the plains west of the Mississippi or Missouri.

The sweat bath was described by Lescarbot in Acadia. In California the Spaniards called it by its Mexican name *temescal*, a ceremonial institution of major significance in Mesoamerica.

237

Widely disjunct distributions of culture traits such as bark cloth, green corn festivals, dogs as festival food, motifs of decoration in pottery, burial customs, modes of dress and adornment are intimations of connections with Mesoamerica.

XXIV.

The European Impress on Native Ways

OFFICIALDOM IN NEW MEXICO AND NEW FRANCE

New Mexico, a remote and unprofitable appendage of New Spain, had small attention and support from the Viceroyalty and the Council of the Indies. Its governors were poorly paid; the soldiers were supported by being assigned pueblos which were in turn obligated to pay the beneficiary a prescribed tribute, payable yearly by each household. The tribute, mainly maize, beans, and cotton mantas, exacted in the same amount whether the season was good or poor, increasingly reduced the pueblos to a state of want. Officials added to their income by stocking cattle ranches that intruded on Pueblo lands, the livestock damaging Indian fields. Indians were forced to work in salines, the salt sold to mines in the south. The Spanish prospered little; the Pueblos suffered more loss of food and freedom. The distant authorities regretted the state of affairs but took little action.

New France began by a succession of patents to individuals and partners, was granted to the Company of New France in 1627, and was made a crown colony in 1663. New France was not established by military force, nor were its people deprived of their freedom or dispossessed of their land. Champlain blundered into a tribal feud that required most of the century to end the enmity of the Five Nation Iroquois. The French settlements in Canada (St. Lawrence Valley) and Acadia (Nova Scotia) were made and maintained in friendship with the natives. Using the elaborate ceremonial of the calumet, French officials pledged peace with the nations about the Great Lakes, La Salle thus continuing to the mouth of the Mississippi. The French observed the courtesies of polite intercourse, they engaged in the exchange of speeches and gifts, they enjoyed the strange foods served at the feasts, and they found welcome because they dealt with the natives as their equals.

MISSIONARIES

A main reason for appointing a Governor of New Mexico was that the Franciscans had begun instruction of the Pueblos. Juan de Oñate started their troubles as he brought the first group of friars, committing outrages as he allotted pueblos among the friars. The excesses of the first governor were reduced by his successors, but the levy of tribute by soldiers continued, as did forced labor and encroachment on Indian lands. The missionaries protested strongly and often, with little effect. Within the pueblo their authority was unlimited in temporal and spiritual affairs. They managed the economy, employed their charges in building and serving churches and convents, and suppressed any observance of former cults. As the result the native priests officiated in secret, the friars remaining ignorant of an organized resistance until 1675 when forty-seven shamans were arrested and punished. The rigorous action was ineffective; five years later the Pueblo Revolt prepared by shamans broke out suddenly. After eighty years of secular oppression and religious submission the Pueblos, most pacific of American peoples, rose in the longest rebellion against Spanish rule.

In New France the Jesuits, stoutly backed for half a century by Bishop Laval at Quebec, served as gentle missioners of the Christian life while protecting native ways. They were criticized for not making Frenchmen of the Indians, who were not compelled to speak the French language. Jesuit missions were founded at crossroads of the Great Lakes convenient to Indians of different tribes, some of whom settled about the missions. French traders came to visit these centers and were put on their good behavior, the dispensing of alcohol forbidden. The French missions were supported by French funds, not by Indian tribute or required labor. The Indians at the missions were there by their own free choice to stay or leave.

TRADERS

New Mexico was a very poor land that did not pay its costs. Once a year or less often the missions received supplies from the south, mainly gifts for the needs of churches and convents. Santa Fe lived on tribute from mission Indians, meagre official salaries, stock raising, salt from salines, occasionally slaves bought from Apaches. New Mexico therefore lacked a commercial economy.

The historical geography of New France is outlined by the fur trade, beginning with codfishers meeting Algonquian tribes on northeastern shores, the time and place unknown. Verrazzano, sailing north along the Atlantic coast in 1524, met Indians of the coast of Maine prepared to trade, asking for knives, fishhooks, and edged metal, a demand which must have been learned by prior contact with ships. Ten years later Cartier entering Chaleur Bay in the Gulf of St. Lawrence was awaited by Indians bringing furs to trade for hardware and other European goods. Thus early Indians living from Chaleur to Penobscot Bay had learned that men who came by ship in summer offered desirable new things for furs.

The best quality and largest quantity of furs were taken in and about the northern waters as the fur trade spread from the St. Lawrence River to the watershed of the Great Lakes and beyond into the upper basin of the Mississippi and somewhat into that of Hudson Bay. For the most part the natives were Algonquian tribes, their shared sense of kinship opening the way to the French.

Indians took the pelts and dressed them, an occupation of the cold season rarely seen and reported. In spring when the waters were open they loaded their cargo of pelts on canoes and took them to sell in Montreal, Quebec, or Trois Rivières, returning to their homes in fall. Such return voyages gave the occasion for Frenchmen to become acquainted with the new land and people. Thus Champlain in 1615 got to know a people on Georgian Bay, later called Ottawas, who traded west to a distance of hundreds of leagues. Thus Groseilliers in 1654 joined a returning fleet, was gone for two years, and came back with fifty canoes richly laden. In a second voyage in

1659-1660, accompanied by Radisson, he reached western Lake Superior, an un-exploited frontier, bringing back a hundred canoes and peltry to the value of a hundred thousand livres. The first Jesuits on the upper Great Lakes repeated Groseilliers' route in a homeward bound canoe party.

The fur trade as carried on in Acadia, Nicolas Denys charged, changed the native ways for the worse. The indictment was directed against the uncontrolled trade of the cod fishers. The natives were plied with liquor and had become drunkards. Their old customs and beliefs had broken down, their skills were being lost. Metal kettles replaced their vessels of wood and gave greater freedom to move about. They paid less attention to planting crops, some having ceased to do so. Muskets had taken the place of bow and arrow in hunting, exterminated big game in certain parts, and therefore increased idleness.

The native condition in the unsettled interior was by comparison good. Brandy was an important item in the fur trade, but in contrast to the traffic in firewater by the Dutch and English it was restricted, Bishop Laval and the Jesuits in unceasing opposition. Some nations, such as the Ottawas and Iroquois, were noted as more temperate than the French. Prior to the fur trade Indian harvest of animals had been in ecologic balance. The market for furs first reduced the numbers of otter, marten, fisher, mink, black and silver fox, carnivores present in limited numbers. The Paris fashion of top hats, made of the felted fur of beaver, made beaver the staple of the fur trade. La Salle testified in 1678 that sixty to eighty thousand beaver pelts were being shipped each year from Quebec. By that time the French fur trade had extended west beyond the Great Lakes and the Hudson's Bay Company was procuring furs from tribes about the bay.

NOTES ON THE INTRODUCTION OF WATERMELONS, PEACHES, AND HORSES

Governor Oñate, writing the Viceroy of his first impressions of New Mexico, told that the Pueblos grew watermelons (*Sandías*). Spaniards brought this favorite summer melon to the New World, where it was quickly adopted into Indian gardens. This Old World cucurbit did well wherever the native squashes and pumpkins were grown, was cultivated in the same manner, and provided a thirst-quenching fruit, kept cool in summer heat by its hard rind. It was taken from one farming people to another ahead of the Spanish advance, from Mesoamerica perhaps by way of the Jumanos of the middle Río Grande to the Pueblos.

Joutel recounted that La Salle's party on its way north first saw watermelon vines in the fields of the Cenis. (This Caddoan people of east Texas were the first farmers encountered.) The refugees reached the Quapaw at the mouth of the Arkansas River in July, where they were treated to ripe *melons d'eau*, the red-seeded ones having the best flavor. Approaching Fort St. Louis in the fall they were served watermelons by Illinois. Joutel found watermelons not very nourishing but agreeably refreshing.

At the time of the visit to the Quapaw villages (July 1687) "the peaches were very good. Although not quite ripe they were boiled to eat."[1] The first French notice of peach trees was five years earlier during La Salle's descent of the Mississippi River, and was at the same Quapaw villages. The stop was made in March when the peach trees

1. Margry, III, 443.

241

were in bloom and was reported in the accounts of Tonty and Nicolas de La Salle. (In my youth an 'Indian Peach' was found growing wild in creek bottoms of eastern Missouri, the fruit rather small, red fleshed, free stone, and of fuzzy gray skin. A similar peach, reproduced by seed, is still grown in Mexico.)

Tonty added to the Quapaw account that they also had cocks and hens. (Another European tradition by way of Mexico? Chickens and eggs were common items in the tributes collected by encomenderos in Central Mexico.)

Horses were known to La Salle in 1682 as kept by Indians. La Salle had the information at Fort St. Louis, naming six western tribes, beginning with the Pane (Pawnee), as having many horses, and thought that he could use them for transport during low water between Chicago and Fort St. Louis.[2] In another letter La Salle told of having spoken with a Pawnee youth from two hundred leagues to the west:

> These are neighbors and allies of the Gattacka [Caddodaqui Caddo of the Texarkana region] and Manrhoat [?], who are to the south of their [Pawnee] villages and sell these horses which they apparently steal from the Spaniards of New Mexico. These horses, I hope, will be of great use to us. These Savages employ them in war, in hunting, and in all manner of transport. They do not enclose them but leave them in the open even in snow, and give them no other feed than pasture. Such horses must be of great endurance and very strong and are said to be able to carry the meat of two buffalos, weighing almost a thousand pounds.[3]

La Salle understood correctly that the Pawnees had horses from the Caddo and that the animals were Spanish but erred in thinking that they came from New Mexico.

The next notices of horses are in Joutel's *Relation*. On his second attempt to find a way from Matagorda Bay to the Mississippi River La Salle returned (October 1686) from the north with five horses laden with maize, beans, squash, and watermelons, procured from the Cenis Caddo of east Texas. In the final exodus, begun in January 1687, they found horses at an Indian hunting camp between the Colorado and Brazos rivers. Joutel was informed that these people were in relations with a nation called Chouman (Jumano), "friends of Europeans who must be Spaniards."[4] Continuing northeast over the route previously taken by La Salle they came to the Palaquechauré (unidentified) whose chief "had been to the Spanish with Jumanos, a nation having some commerce with the Spanish, who gave them horses."[5] La Salle, it seems, had taken an Indian trade route, by which the party continued after his assassination, crossing the Trinity River into the land of the Cenis, the Caddo people from whom La Salle had first acquired horses. Joutel recorded their name for horse as *cahouaille*, also that he was addressed as *capita*. As far as the Caddodaqui of the Texarkana area the French found horses in common use.

When Tonty came to the Caddo settlements on the Red River he found horses with Spanish cavalry brands and saddles made after the Spanish manner. Three years earlier Joutel had seen them used only as pack animals. La Salle had heard in 1682 that the Pawnees west of the Missouri River (in eastern Nebraska) were well supplied with horses used in transport and that they got them from Caddos to the south. The French

2. Margry, II, 168.

3. Margry, II, 201-202.

4. Margry, III, 298-299.

5. Margry, III, 305.

information about Indians who kept horses was of Caddoan tribes, from the Pawnees in the north to Cenis in the south. Joutel supplied the evidence that Jumanos, living to the south and neighbors and friends of the Spanish, were the source of the horses and other Spanish items. The Jumanos, considered also a Caddoan people, thus extended the Caddoan linkage south to the Río Grande.

The Jumanos became known to the Spanish in the late sixteenth century; living along the Río Grande above the mouth of the Conchos, they were first known as good farmers and far ranging traders. The French found them a century later trading to the Red River, bringing horses and sundry Spanish things that indicated they came from a cavalry station and Spanish settlement south of the Río Grande. They were known into the eighteenth century as traders east across Texas, dealing peaceably with Indians and Spanish and keeping the Spanish informed of the condition of that frontier.

Stray horses of Coronado's party no longer are thought to have been the foundation of the horse herds of the Plains Indians. Nor was New Mexico later a likely source. It was in a continuing state of decline in the seventeenth century, accelerated by Apache raids on stock ranches. These are reported as beginning about 1670, too late to account for the horse herds of the Pawnees. The Apaches are unlikely agents of supply to the Plains tribes. Their raids on livestock were for meat and hides, not to breed animals nor to acquire riding animals. The Apaches were one of the last of the Plains tribes to become horsemen. When they became the scourge of northern Mexico in the eighteenth century they still raided afoot and drove off cattle, horses, and mules for their flesh and hides. They were hunters to whom domestic animals remained a foreign kind of game.

There has been little attention given to the priority of Caddoan tribes in raising horses or to the Jumanos as a trading people who traveled from the Río Grande to the Red River. They provided the Caddos with horses, which these sedentary farming peoples, living adjacent to and within the buffalo plains, used on buffalo hunts. It is also indicated that in like manner watermelons and peaches were taken north from Spanish settlements, peaches to Arkansas and watermelons to Illinois.

XXV.

Decline of Indian Population

NEW SPAIN KEYSTONE OF THE SPANISH EMPIRE

In the course of the sixteenth century Spain gained a greater empire than the world had yet known, its keystone the land that Cortés took and presented as New Spain to the King. This was the land of high native cultures (Mesoamerica), from Pánuco at the north to Honduras at the south: central and southern Mexico and Guatemala. By midcentury the discovery of great silver mines was under way in the interior north. Florida was attached to the Viceroyalty of New Spain in 1557 to guard treasure-laden ships sailing to Spain. Cortés sent the first ships across the Pacific from the Mexican west coast, foreseeing that this would provide the shortest route between Europe and the Far East. In 1564 the Orient trade became regular sailing, to be known by the Manila galleon. By 1590 the Philippine Islands were made a dependency of New Spain. New Spain supported an empire and did so at a heavy cost of native life.

DECLINE OF NATIVE POPULATION IN MESOAMERICA

Old World contagious diseases came with the Spanish as terrible epidemics. Smallpox spread ahead of the Spanish. Tarascans visiting Cortés in 1521 at Mexico, devastated at the time by smallpox, took the infection back to Michoacán, where it killed a multitude, including the Tarascan king and many of his household. Pedro de Alvarado, marching to the conquest of Guatemala, found it desolated by smallpox. Tropical lowlands of Vera Cruz and of the Pacific Coast were depopulated, malaria being thought largely responsible. Subsequent to the mass mortality of the first years, outbreaks of lethal epidemics took place from time to time throughout the century.

The subjugation of Mesoamerica by force and disease raised the concern of the Council of the Indies, which enacted the New Laws of the Indies (1543-1546) for the protection of the Indians. The abuses were gradually abated, the decline of the native population slowed. The monumental demographic studies of Sherburne Cook and Woodrow Borah, document the decimation of native numbers in central and southern Mexico during the century, as to manner, rate, and place.[1]

---

1. Sherburne F. Cook and Woodrow W. Borah, *The Population of Central Mexico in 1548*, Ibero-Americana 43 (Berkeley, 1960); *The Indian Population of Central Mexico, 1531-1610*, Ibero-Americana 44 (Berkeley, 1960); *The Aboriginal Population of Central Mexico on the Eve of the Spanish Conquest*, Ibero-Americana 45 (Berkeley, 1963); *The Population of the Mixteca Alta, 1520-1960*, Ibero-Americana 50 (Berkeley, 1968); *Essays in Population History: Mexico and the Caribbean* (Berkeley, 1971-1974).

POPULATION OF THE PUEBLOS

The Rodríguez-Chamuscado party set out in 1581 on northern exploration, three Franciscan friars and a small guard of soldiers, the friars to look for a new mission field of which they had heard, the soldiers hoping to find mines. The result was the first record of location, number and size of the Pueblo towns, the *Relación* of Hernán Gallegos.

The *Relación* recorded sixty-one pueblos in the order visited, counting or estimating the houses in each and their size. The first, entered as they went up the Río Grande, had forty-five houses of two to three stories. As they continued up river the number and height of houses increased, Nuevo Tlaxcala (Taos) being the greatest, with five hundred houses ranging to seven stories. Snow and cold prevented exploration further north, where they heard that there were more pueblos. East of the Río Grande Valley they visited five pueblos of the Salinas (Estancia Basin), and at the west they got to the five Zuñi pueblos, these totalling 386 houses of two to five stories. The pueblos visited in the Río Grande Valley added up to about five thousand multi-family houses, those entered farther east and west added another thousand. Gallegos gave an objective account of size of pueblos in terms of houses, without estimate of the number of inhabitants.

Soldiers who had taken part in the expedition were called to testify in Mexico. They agreed that the sixty-one pueblos visited contained more than a hundred thirty thousand souls. In terms of the house numbers of Gallegos this would assign a score or so of inhabitants to a house, a reasonable number for the multi-family, multi-story Pueblo dwellings. The estimate is moderate, I think, for a people of high skills, industry, and thrift, living in ecologic balance and undisturbed by external pressures. Parts of the Pueblo country to the north, east, and west were not included. Reexamination of the Pueblo condition before the Spanish occupation is indicated.

The ruin of the Pueblos began with the first governor. Oñate threw the people of one town out to make it his seat. Going to the pueblos of the Salinas he punished one for 'insolence', destroyed a part, and took away captives. The Pueblo of Ácoma, he informed the Viceroy, was of three thousand *indios*, who killed his lieutenant, and were therefore punished. Ácoma was a large town, the term *indio* perhaps meaning adult males, an exaggeration that underscored the danger he claimed to have overcome. His report to the Viceroy of the first year told of having visited all the provinces, with seventy thousand *indios* living in pueblos, whatever he may have meant by that word. Grave charges against Oñate were made in Mexico, of terror, flight of inhabitants of pueblos, hunger by seizure of their food, decrease in population. Inquiries as to their number gave estimates of fifty thousand or more, one being twenty-two to twenty-four thousand men and women, another of twelve thousand men not counting women and children, a third of fifty to sixty thousand inhabitants of a hundred and thirty pueblos. The continuing abuses led to Oñate's recall and exile in 1608.

Franciscan review of Pueblo provinces began with the Benavides *Memorial* of 1630, numbers of souls baptized given in round thousands adding up to about fifty thousand and not distinguishing between the living and the dead. The Zuñi and Hopi pueblos were not included. The revised *Memorial* was given to the King in 1634, indicating 34,380 Indians then living. The Prada report in 1638 was of eight thousand households paying tribute to soldiers, a Pueblo population of forty thousand or less after two recent epidemics. The friars' interest in numbers was mainly in baptisms. The pueblos east of the Río Grande Valley were in marked decline by the sixties. The Governor monopolizing the trade of the Apaches who had taken to rustling livestock from pueblos and ranches, the connection unexplained. The Pueblos of the Salinas had been directed by officials to furnish salt, were taken south to the mines, and therefore became unable to give needed attention to their crops. A great drought began in 1666 and continued for three years, four hundred fifty persons dying of hunger in one Salinas pueblo. There was great pestilence among people and cattle in 1671. The last of the Salinas pueblos was abandoned in 1679. The fixed yearly tribute required having eliminated the practice of storing the surplus of good years against the recurring years of drought, poor years brought starvation.

The complaints of the friars were against officials, against forced labor, injury to pueblo lands by livestock, and above all the payment of soldiers by fixed tribute imposed on pueblos. The abuses were known and deplored, both in Mexico and Spain. New Mexico was a liability with no prospect of mineral wealth and with a declining and impoverished native population. The suggestion was made that it should be abandoned. Little was done to ameliorate its condition.

Florida was the other remote and indigent appendage of New Spain. Its natives were Muskhogean tribes, served by Franciscan missions of obscure record. Mexico knew and did little about the Indians of Florida. Gangs were put to work at St. Augustine. There were occasional notices of revolt and of famine. Late in the century the Yamassees, a Creek tribe, got out and settled in Carolina.

INDIAN CONDITION ON THE EAST COAST

Nicolas Denys, describing the declining condition of the Indians, placed the blame on alcohol provided by codfishers. The fishermen camped on land to dry their cod, plied Indians with drink, and got pelts in return. Denys came to Acadia in 1632 and spent most of forty years on its coasts, trading from the Bay of Fundy north to Chaleur Bay.

Father Pierre Biard, Jesuit missionary at Port Royal and Mt. Desert Island from 1611 to 1613, reported that at most nine to ten thousand Indians lived from Newfoundland to Saco (Maine), their numbers greatly reduced since they had intercourse with the French. Biard observed that they had become addicted to drink and were afflicted by dysentery in summer.

Champlain made his surveys of coast and natives from 1603 to 1606. Lescarbot came to Port Royal in 1605 to remain a year. Neither mentioned disease, drunkenness, or decline, both found the Indians in good circumstances.

Champlain made two voyages along the coast of New England, getting as far as Nantucket Sound. From Saco south the Indians lived in villages, cultivated fields and were in goodly number. Fifteen years later the Pilgrims found the fields and villages abandoned and attributed the empty land to plague sent by Providence. At the time the bubonic plague carried by rats was ravaging parts of western Europe. Norway rats infested houses and crossed the Atlantic on ships. Lescarbot told how their ship brought rats to Port Royal and that these spread promptly from the French settlement to the Micmac village, a nuisance previously there unknown.

French and English ships occasionally visited the Massachusetts coast. One ship, carrying infected rats, would suffice to introduce the contagion to natives that lived congregated as they did in agricultural villages of southern New England. Ships also carried house flies and other vectors of pathogens, suggested by Biard's reference to summer dysentery.

THE EMPTY VALLEY OF THE ST. LAWRENCE

Cartier found the St. Lawrence Valley well inhabited by natives living in palisaded villages of long houses and cultivating ample fields. The lower valley was called Canada; at the upper end of the valley was the island that he named Montreal, and the major Indian town of Hochelaga. His description of the Indian society included a vocabulary of their speech that certifies them as Iroquois. Cartier found them prosperous, numerous, and living at peace. Sixty years later Champlain found a greatly different condition of the country, no settled people or cultivated fields, the valley a great woodland with some prairies near Montreal.

Champlain's description of well grown trees of hardwoods and hemlock, and of many great grape vines indicates a vegetation of ecologic balance, the small prairies perhaps being former cultivated fields. Champlain's description suggests also that the change came shortly after the time of Cartier.

Explanations have been offered that the attractive valley, occupied by a people superior in numbers, organization, and skill, was abandoned because of attack by enemies such as Algonquins and Montagnais, lesser hunting tribes. Instead, the introduction of Old World disease was sufficient to cause the disaster. In 1535 Cartier and a company of a hundred ten French went up the St. Lawrence River to Montreal and returned to winter quarters adjacent to the Canada village of Stadacona (near Quebec). The Indians confined to the close quarters of their crowded long houses experienced a great sickness (a new respiratory contagion?), the cause of which neither they nor the French understood. Mass mortality followed Spanish, French, and English in the New World, the more so the more the natives lived congregated in clustered houses of several families. Mexicans, Pueblos, and Iroquois were prone to grave contagion by mode of habitation.

NATIONS DESTROYED

The tabagie in 1603 at Tadoussac celebrated a victory of Montagnais, Algonquins, and Abnakis over Iroquois. Montagnais were hosts; the two allied and kindred nations came from afar for the scalp dance. This was the first notice the French had of Indian warring and alliance.

The French became involved in 1609 when Champlain, ignorant of the cause of the enmity, joined a raiding party of Montagnais, Algonquins, and Hurons going to the land of the Mohawks. This is the first record of alliance of Algonquian tribes and Iroquoian Hurons against Five Nation Iroquois, the Hurons thereafter known as 'the good Iroquois'.

Champlain in 1610 took part in another savage raid on the Mohawks. He came to Huronia in 1615, was awaited there by a large Huron war party, and went with it across

248

Lake Ontario to attack an Oneida town. The attack was repulsed and the attackers returned home. Champlain took no further part in these raids thereafter.

Missionaries in Huronia recorded recurrent Huron raids across Lake Ontario and the bringing back of Iroquois captives, the men usually tortured to death, the women and children adopted into Huron society. The initiative was Huron; Algonquian bands were minor participants. Occasionally Iroquois made a counterattack. The last Huron invasion of the Five Nations was in 1638.

Informed missionaries estimated the Huron population in the sixteen-twenties as thirty to forty thousand. Later they were ravaged by a series of epidemics. In 1634 a sickness, thought to be measles or smallpox, broke out among Montagnais at the trading post of Trois Rivières, spread to Huronia and continued there for two years with high mortality. Another great sickness, probably smallpox, came to Huronia in 1639 by way of Algonquins of the Ottawa River, who had brought it from Quebec. By missionary report the Huron nation in 1640 had been reduced to a third of its former numbers. Disease had cost them the initiative in the long and deadly feud.

The Senecas, westernmost and largest of the Five Nations, took the lead in the events that were to change the course of history. In 1648 a Huron party, hunting in the no man's land north of Lake Ontario, was ambushed by a Seneca war party. In 1649 Senecas led the offensive that laid waste Huronia, killed its people, took them captive, or drove the remnant to distant refuges.

Having disposed of the Hurons and the affiliated Tobacco Nation the invaders continued north to devastate the land of the Nipissings, an Algonquian tribe that apparently had no part in the conflict. The Iroquoian Neutral Nation was next to be destroyed, reputedly because it had given refuge to Hurons. The Erie Nation, last of the non-aligned Iroquois, was eliminated in 1658. Eries and Neutrals, occupying lands on opposite sides of Lake Ontario, were the most populous nations of the Northeast, each perhaps greater than the combined Five Nations. Neither had sides in the intertribal and intra-Iroquois feud. The records do not report what became of the survivors.

In the course of ten years the Five Nations eliminated their four kindred nations to the west, leaving an empty land, still thus known at the end of the century on Delisle's map as *nations détruites*.

Algonquian tribes living to the west between the Great Lakes and Ohio River were next to be dispossessed. Shawnees, Miamis, Potawatomies, Kickapoos, Foxes, and Sacs, drifted west beyond Lake Michigan and the Illinois River to find respite from Iroquois raids. They had not taken part in the feuding and appear not to have suffered great damage. When the French came to know them in their new homes they were numerous, in good condition, and apparently in normal proportion of sex and age.

The French relations of the Mississippi Valley and the western Great Lakes, elaborate and diverse in detail, lack mention of mass sickness and unusual mortality, an exception being St. Cosme's finding the Quapaw villages at the mouth of the Arkansas (1698) newly decimated by smallpox and in part abandoned.

XXVI.

The End of the Century

NORTHERN BORDERS OF NEW SPAIN

The thousand miles of California coast were sailed yearly by Manila galleons untroubled by enemy or storm. There was no need of the ports Vizcaino had surveyed. California remained unoccupied and unknown inland.

Santa Fe was retaken in 1693, the last Pueblos brought to submission in 1697. The Hopi pueblos, distant from the rest, were not put under mission management. A number, such as those of the Estancia Basin, were not reoccupied. Colonists were brought from the south to stock lands with cattle and sheep and take over former Pueblo fields and irrigation works. Where Coronado had made his base on the Río Grande the New Mexican town Bernalillo was settled in 1698 and then farther up river a colony was located at Santa Cruz. Spanish creoles, mestizos, and some Mexican Indians thus began to envelop the Pueblo missions.

The Council of the Indies became concerned with Louisiana as a French design against New Spain. The ship sent from Vera Cruz in 1685 to search the north coast of the Gulf of Mexico found no French activity. For reasons undisclosed the selection of Pensacola Bay was deferred to 1693, years after La Salle already had failed. The bay had long been known to Spanish; the professor of mathematics at the University of Mexico was sent to make its survey; Sigüenza y Góngora sounded the channel, found a good site to build, and composed a competent and vivid appraisal of west Florida. Pensacola was built in 1693 on a sheltered harbor, convenient to watch the mouths of the Mississippi and whatever the French might be doing. It was well located with regard to Vera Cruz and Havana. The land inland was judged by its vegetation to be proper for cultivation and livestock, correctly rated by Sigüenza. The new town was the base of Spanish West Florida, St. Augustine to the east continuing to have indifferent attention.

NEW FRANCE

When New France was made a crown colony in 1663 the French population was little more than two thousand, mainly male, impermanent, and engaged in fur trade, civil and military duties, and in the service of the church. The French lived mostly in Quebec, Montreal, and Trois Rivières, with some two hundred about Port Royal.

Colbert, as Minister of the Marine in charge of French affairs overseas, held that a viable colony needed to be based on small farmers, habitants, who would raise crops, livestock, and many children, thereby making a new France of the Valley of the St. Lawrence. The habitants of Canada, as the valley was known, would feed the colony and give defense against the growing numbers of English and Dutch neighbors. Colbert's aim was to populate Canada and keep the French from dispersing into distant parts.

The enduring organization of New France was put into effect in the first decade of the crown colony, the Intendant Talon its administrator. At the end of Talon's tenure the French population had increased to seven thousand, from Quebec to Montreal, was mainly rural, and provided ample supply of crops and livestock.

In the same decade Jesuit missions were built at the crossroads of the Upper Great Lakes, Indian settlements growing up about them. Talon sent parties to explore and take possession of the extremities of Canada. La Salle went on his exploration, Seneca guides taking him to the falls of the Ohio River. Talon heard also of portages by which to get to Florida and to Mexico. As one of his last acts Talon engaged Joliet to start on the discovery of the great river, known as the Mississippi. The hydrography of North America was becoming outlined from Hudson Bay to the Gulf of Mexico.

The simple colonial plan continued to work. At the end of the century there were fifteen thousand French, living mainly along the St. Lawrence from Île d'Orleans to Montreal, the slow doubling of population in thirty years mostly by natural increase. The townspeople were in Quebec, Montreal, and Trois Rivières, the habitants in côtes, strings of farmsteads along the waterside.

The interior remained in Indian possession. After the death of La Salle Jesuit missions were added among the Miamis at Chicago and Illinois on Lake Peoria. At the end of the century the Crown ordered *voyageurs* and *coureurs de bois* out of the interior, holding that Indians were capable to take the furs to market, thus reaffirming the policy of restricting French settlement to the east.

The economy of the fur trade was a free partnership of French and Indians. Indians took the pelts and dressed them; theirs were the skills of purveyor and processor, of which there was rarely mention. Indians made, manned, and owned the canoes that carried the furs to market, Ottawas in particular middlemen of trade and transport. Jesuit missions were hosts to French and Indians, maintained order and sobriety. Indians were not subjected to any of the servitudes imposed by the Spanish. Unlike the English colonies there was no advancing frontier from which Indians were being driven.

The extractive nature of the fur trade brought early depletion of the resource of aquatic mammals. Otter, marten and other carnivores were soon much reduced in number. The growing demand for beaver was met by finding new beaver dams. By the end of the century the fur business was exploiting the headwaters of the Mississippi and the drainage of the Assiniboine. The extension west was arrested at the prairies. At the north, the Hudson Bay Company was moving onto the Laurentian Highland. With declining yields, Montreal and Quebec sought more and more remote sources.

The friendly and equal relations between French and Indian did not have their like in other European colonies. Champlain did blunder into enmity with the Iroquois which continued beyond his lifetime but ended in a peace of consent, not of force. French officials met Indian dignitaries in ceremonies of elaborate ritual, or oratory, dance, feast, and smoking the calumet of peace, and the pledges were kept. Missionary priests ministered to natives without duress or support of soldiers. Traders engaged Indians by

252

mutual agreements. There was peace throughout after the Iroquois were conciliated, a peace of respect and good will.

The Indian way of life was admirable, it was agreed, before it was changed by European influence. Verrazzano thought these Indians to be living in the Golden Age. Lescarbot came to Acadia to escape from corrupt civilization. Denys deplored the loss of morals and customs he witnessed in Acadia during his lifetime. Lahontan portrayed Iroquois as exemplars of a good society. Rousseau adopted Lahontan, and created the 'Noble Savage'. At the end of the seventeenth century New France was still Indian country beyond Montreal.

Bibliography

Barcia Carballido y Zuñiga, Andrés González de. *Chronological History of the Continent of Florida*. Tr. Anthony Kerrigan. Gainesville, 1951.

————. *Ensayo cronológico para la historia general de la Florida*. Madrid, 1723.

Benavides, Alonso de. *The Memorial of Fray Alonso de Benavides, 1630*. Tr. Mrs. Edward E. Ayers. Annotated by Frederick W. Hodge and Charles F. Lummis. With facsimile of original. Chicago, 1916.

Bernard, Jean Frédéric, ed. *Recueil de Voyages au Nord, contenant divers mémoires trés utiles au commerce at à navigation* . . . 8 v. Amsterdam, 1716-1729.

Bloom, Lansing B. "A Glimpse of New Mexico in 1620." *New Mexico Historical Review*, III (1928), 357-389.

Bolton, Herbert E. "The Location of La Salle's Colony on the Gulf of Mexico." *Mississippi Valley Historical Review*, II (1915), 165-182.

————, ed. *Spanish Exploration in the Southwest, 1542-1706*. New York, 1916.

Champlain, Samuel de. *Des Sauvages* . . . Paris, 1603.

————. *Les Voyages* . . . Paris, 1613.

————. *Voyages et descouvertes* . . . Paris, 1619.

————. *Les Voyages de la Nouvelle France* . . . Paris, 1632.

————. *The Works of Samuel de Champlain*. Ed. H. P. Biggar. (Champlain Society. Publications.) 6 v. Toronto, 1922-1936.

Chapin, Thomas. *Jean Talon, Intendant*. Quebec, 1904.

Clark, Andrew H. *Acadia. The Geography of Nova Scotia to 1760*. Madison, 1968.

Colección de documentos inéditos relativos al descubrimiento, conquista, y organización de las antiguas posesiones españolas de América y Oceania . . . (*CDI*). 42 v. Madrid, 1864-1884.

Cook, Sherburne F., and Woodrow W. Borah. *The Aboriginal Population of Central Mexico on the Eve of the Spanish Conquest*. (Ibero-Americana 45.) Berkeley, 1963.

————. *Essays in Population History: Mexico and the Caribbean*. 2 v. Berkeley, 1971-1974.

————. *The Indian Population of Central Mexico, 1531-1610*. (Ibero-Americana 44.) Berkeley, 1960.

————. *The Population of Central Mexico in 1548*. (Ibero-Americana 43.) Berkeley, 1960.

————. *The Population of the Mixteca Alta, 1520-1960*. (Ibero-Americana 50.) Berkeley, 1968.

Delisle, Claude and Guillaume. [*Atlas de De L'Isle.*] [Paris? c. 1700-1731.]

Denys, Nicolas. *The Description and Natural History of the Coasts of North America* (*Acadia*). Ed. and tr. William F. Ganong. With reprint of original. (Champlain Society. Publications, II.) Toronto, 1908.

————. *Description Géographique et historique des costes de l'Amérique septentrionale, avec l'histoire naturelle du pais*. 2 v. Paris, 1672.

Documentos para servir a la historia del Nuevo México. Madrid, 1962.

Du Creux, François. *The History of Canada or New France 1625-1658.* Tr. Percy J. Robinson. Ed. James B. Conacher. (Champlain Society. Publications, XXX, XXXI.) Toronto, 1951-1952.

Dunkle, John R. "Population Change as an Element in the Historical Geography of St. Augustine." *Florida Historical Quarterly*, XXXVII (1958), 3-32.

Espinosa, J. Manuel, ed. and tr. *First Expedition of Vargas into New Mexico, 1692.* Albuquerque, 1940.

Ford, James A., and Clarence H. Webb. *Poverty Point, a Late Archaic Site in Louisiana.* (American Museum of Natural History. Anthropological Papers, XLVI, pt. 1.) New York, 1956.

Friederici, Georg. *Amerikanistisches Wörterbuch.* Hamburg, 1947.

Hackett, Charles W., ed. *Historical Documents Relating to New Mexico, Nueva Vizcaya, and Approaches Thereto, to 1773, Collected by Adolph F. A. Bandelier and Fanny R. Bandelier.* (Carnegie Institution of Washington. Publication 330.) 3 v. Washington, D. C., 1923-1937.

—————, ed. *Revolt of the Pueblo Indians of New Mexico and Otermin's Attempted Reconquest, 1680-1682.* 2 v. Albuquerque, 1942.

Hakluyt, Richard. *The Principal Navigations.* 10 v. London, 1927-1928.

Hammond, George, and Agapito Rey, ed. and tr. *Don Juan de Oñate, Colonizer of New Mexico, 1595-1628.* 2 v. Albuquerque, 1953.

—————. "The Rodríguez Expedition to New Mexico, 1581-1582." *New Mexico Historical Review*, II (1927), 239-268; 334-362.

Harris, Richard C. *The Seigneurial System in Early Canada.* Madison, 1966.

Hennepin, Louis. *Description de la Louisiane, nouvellement decouverte au Sud'Oüest de la Nouvelle France, par ordre du Roy . . .* Paris, 1688.

—————. *A New Discovery of a Vast Country in America . . .* Ed. Reuben Gold Thwaites. 2 v. Chicago, 1903.

—————. *Nouveau Voyage d'un Païs plus grand que l'Europe . . .* Utrecht, 1698.

—————. *Nouvelle Decouverte d'un trés grand pays, situé dans l'Amérique . . .* Utrecht, 1697.

Herrera y Tordesillas, Antonio de. *Historia general de los hechos de los castellanos en las islas i tierra firme del mar oceano.* 4 v. Madrid, 1601-1615.

Hodge, Frederick W. *Handbook of American Indians North of Mexico.* (Smithsonian Institution. Bureau of American Ethnology. Bulletin 30.) 2 v. Washington, D. C., 1907-1910.

Kellogg, Louise Phelps, ed. *Early Narratives of the Northwest, 1634-1699.* New York, 1917.

Kelley, J. Charles. "Historical Materials Relating to the West Texas Route of Antonio de Espejo." *Sul Ross State Teachers College Bulletin*, XVIII (1937), 7-25. (West Texas Historical and Scientific Society. Publication no. 7.)

—————. "Juan Sabeata and Diffusion in Aboriginal Texas." *American Anthropologist*, LVII (1955): 981-996.

Lahontan, Louis Armand de Lom d'Arce, Baron de. *Collection Oakes. Nouveaux Documents de Lahontan sur le Canada et Terre-Neuve*. Ed. Gustave Lanctôt. Ottawa, 1940.

_____. *Dialogues Curieux . . .* The Hague, 1703.

_____. *Dialogues Curieux . . . et Mémoires de l'Amérique Septentrionale*. Ed. Gilbert Chinard. Baltimore, 1931.

_____ *New Voyages to North America, by the Baron de Lahontan*. Ed. Reuben Gold Thwaites. 2 v. Chicago, 1905.

_____ *Nouveaux Voyages de M. le Baron de Lahontan . . .* 3 v. The Hague, 1707-1708.

Le Clercq, Chrétien. *New Relation of Gaspesia, with the Customs and Religion of the Gaspesian Indians . . .* Ed. and tr. William F. Ganong. With reprint of original. (Champlain Society. Publications, V.) Toronto, 1910.

_____ *Nouvelle Relation de la Gaspesie . . .* Paris, 1691.

Leighly, John. *California as an Island*. San Francisco, 1972.

Lescarbot, Marc. *Histoire de la Nouvelle France*. Paris, 1609.

_____ *History of New France*. Tr. W. L. Grant. With reprint of 3d ed., Paris, 1618. (Champlain Society. Publications, I, VII, XI.) 3 v. Toronto, 1907-1914.

Margry, Pierre, ed. *Découvertes et Établissements des Français dans l'ouest et dans le sud de l'Amérique Septentrionale (1614-1754)*. 6 v. Paris, 1879-1888.

Mathes, W. Michael, ed. and tr. *The Capture of the Santa Ana, Cabo San Lucas, November, 1587*. Los Angeles, 1969.

_____ *Vizcaíno and Spanish Exploration into the Pacific Ocean 1580-1630*. San Francisco, 1968.

Mecham, J. Lloyd. "The Second Spanish Expedition to New Mexico." *New Mexico Historical Review*, I (1926), 265-291.

Murphy, Edmund Robert. *Henri de Tonty. Fur Trader of the Mississippi*. Baltimore, 1941.

Newcomb, W. W., Jr. *The Indians of Texas*. Austin, 1961.

Nute, Grace Lee. *Caesars of the Wilderness. Médard Chouart, Sieur de Groseilliers, and Pierre Esprit Radisson, 1618-1710*. New York, 1943.

Pease, Theodore C., and Raymond C. Werner, ed. *The French Foundations (1680-1693)*. (Illinois State Historical Library. Collections, XXIII.) Springfield, Illinois, 1934.

Pérez de Luxán, Diego. *Expedition into New Mexico Made by Antonio de Espejo, as Revealed in the Journal of Diego Pérez de Luxán, a Member of the Party*. Tr. George Hammond and Agapito Rey. Los Angeles, 1929.

Radisson, Pierre Esprit. *Voyages of Pierre Esprit Radisson*. Ed. Gideon D. Scull. (Prince Society. Publications.) Boston, 1885.

Rostlund, Erhard. "The Geographical Range of the Historic Bison in the Southeast." Association of American Geographers. *Annals*, L (1960), 395-407.

Sagard, Gabriel. *Le Grand Voyage du Pays des Hurons . . .* Paris, 1632.

_____. *Histoire du Canada . . .* Paris, 1636.

_____ *The Long Journey to the Country of the Hurons*. Ed. George W. Wrong. Tr. H. H. Langton. With reprint of the original. (Champlain Society. Publications, XXV.) Toronto, 1939.

Sauer, Carl O. *The Distribution of the Aboriginal Tribes and Languages of Northwestern Mexico.* (Ibero-Americana 5.) Berkeley, 1934.

——— *The Early Spanish Main.* Berkeley, 1966.

——— *The Geography of the Ozark Highland of Missouri.* (Geographical Society of Chicago. Bulletin no. 7.) Chicago, 1920.

——— *Geography of the Pennyroyal.* (Kentucky Geological Survey. Ser. 6. Geologic Reports, XXV.) Frankfort, Kentucky, 1927.

——— *Geography of the Upper Illinois Valley and History of Development.* (Illinois State Geological Survey. Bulletin no. 27.) Urbana, 1916.

——— *Northern Mists.* Berkeley, 1968.

——— *The Road to Cíbola.* (Ibero-Americana 3.) Berkeley, 1932.

——— *Sixteenth Century North America. The Land and People as Seen by the Europeans.* Berkeley, 1971.

———, G. H. Cady, and H. C. Cowles. *Starved Rock State Park and its Environs.* (Geographical Society of Chicago. Bulletin no. 6.) Chicago, 1918.

Scholes, France V. "Church and State in New Mexico, 1610-1650." *New Mexico Historical Review*, XI (1936), 9-76; 145-178; 283-294; 297-349; XI (1937), 78-106.

——— "The Supply Service of the New Mexico Missions in the Seventeenth Century." *New Mexico Historical Review*, V (1930), 93-115; 186-210; 386-404.

——— "Troublous Times in New Mexico, 1659-1670." *New Mexico Historical Review*, XII (1937), 134-174; 380-452; XIII (1938), 63-84; XV (1940), 249-268; 369-417; XVI (1941), 15-40; 184-205; 313-327.

———, and H. P. Mera. "Some Aspects of the Jumano Problem." *Contributions to American Anthropology and History*, VI, no. 34. (Carnegie Institution of Washington. Publication 523, 265-299.) Washington, D. C., 1940.

Sigüenza y Góngora, Carlos de. *Documentos inéditos de Don Carlos de Sigüenza y Góngora.* Ed. Irving A. Leonard. México, 1963.

——— *Mercurio volante con la noticia de la recuperación de las provincias del Nuevo México* . . . Antwerp, 1693.

——— *The Mercurio Volante of Don Carlos de Sigüenza y Góngora. An Account of the First Expedition of Don Diego de Vargas into New Mexico in 1692.* Ed. and tr. Irving A. Leonard. With facsimile of original. Los Angeles, 1932.

Squier, Ephraim G., and E. A. Davis. *Ancient Monuments of the Mississippi Valley.* (Smithsonian Institution. Contributions to Knowledge, I.) Washington, D. C., 1848.

Swanton, John R. *Indian Tribes of the Lower Mississippi Valley and Adjacent Coast of the Gulf of Mexico.* (Smithsonian Institution. Bureau of American Ethnology. Bulletin 43.) Washington, D. C., 1911.

Thwaites, Reuben Gold, ed. *The Jesuit Relations and Allied Documents.* 73 v. Cleveland, 1896-1901.

Torquemada, Juan de. . . . *Monarchía indiana* . . . Ed. Antonio González de Barcia Carballido y Zuñiga. 2nd ed. 3 v. Madrid, 1723.

Trudel, Marcel. *Histoire de la Nouvelle France.* 3 v. Montreal, 1963-1966.

Vázquez de Espinosa, Antonio. *Compendio y descripción de las Indias Occidentales.* Ed. Charles Upson Clark. (Smithsonian Institution. Miscellaneous Collections, CVII.) Washington, D. C., 1948.

———— *Compendium and Description of the West Indies.* Tr. Charles Upson Clark. (Smithsonian Institution. Miscellaneous Collections, CII.) Washington, D. C., 1942.

West, Robert C. *The Mining Community in Northern New Spain: The Parral Mining District.* (Ibero-Americana 30.) Berkeley, 1949.

INDEX

Ambergris, 22

American Bottoms, east of St. Louis, 152

Amotomanco Indians, *see* Jumano Indians

Amsterdam (Netherlands), 24, 214

Andes Mountains, 64, 224, 236

Andropogon, see Big bluestem grass

Anegada Passage, 163

Angelica, 85

Angelina River (Texas), 179

Anghiera, Pietro Martire d', Peter Martyr, 224

Anian, Strait of, imaginary passage to Orient, 28-29, 30, 34, 42, 64

Annapolis Royal, Nova Scotia, 78. *See also* Port Royal

Antelope (*Antilocapra*), meat, 46; pronghorn, 168, 225-226, 233; as *chevreuil* 168; as *venado*, 225-226, 233

Antelope Hills (Oklahoma), 52, 219

Anticosti Island, as Isle of Assumption, 73, 97

Antilia, imaginary island, 69

Antilocapra, see Antelope

Apache Indians, 39, 43, 47, 52, 53, 66, 67, 68; as Querecho Indians, 46, 50, 64, 233; as Vaquero Indians, 51, 54, 55, 63, 64, 208; as Perillo Indians, 61, 63; Gila, Xila Apaches, 63, 64, 208, 233, 234; Benavides on, 63-64; summary of Spanish reports, 233-234, 236; and introduction of horses, 243

Apalachee Bay (Florida), 23, 24, 26, 164

Apalachee Indians, 23, 24

Apalachicola River (Florida), 23

Apios tuberosa, see Groundnut

Appalachian Mountains, 19, 209

Apple, 29; crab apple, 156, 197, 223

Apricot, 62

Aravaipa, Arizona, 209

Arawak Indians, 12; source of term *savanna*, 224

Arcadia, Arcadie, 77, 78

Archive of the Indies, 53

Arctic Circle, 28

Arctic waters, 71, 72

Argall, Samuel, 89

Argentina, 224

Arizona, 12, 37, 49, 218, 225; Melchior Diaz across, 35; Oñate to, 35, 48 (Fig. 6), 56-57, 219, 237; Espejo to, 41, 45, 46, 218,219; Farfan de los Godos to, 50, 51-52; on

Delisle map, 208-209; native agriculture, 234, 236

Arkansas, 11, 13, 17, 231, 237, 243; De Soto expedition reports buffalo, 26, 226; Joutel on French traversal, 181, 183, 186-187, 224, 226

Arkansas Indians, 150, 161n, 215; Joliet and Marquette visit, 139, 141; described by Nicolas de La Salle and Membré, 153-154, 155; as Akansa Indians, 153; Joutel on land and life, 186-187; visited by St. Cosme, 201, 205, 207

Arkansas Post, French establishment on Arkansas River, 183, 184 (Fig. 15), 186-187, 189, 190, 191, 201, 205

Arkansas River, 53, 139, 140, 153, 181, 183, 186, 187, 189, 207, 209, 219, 220, 223, 226, 230, 241, 249

Armadillo, 171

Arriola, Andrés de, 26

Arundinaria, see Cane

Ascención, Fr. Antonio de, 34&n

Ash, 83, 93, 156, 193

Asimina triloba, see Papaw

Asparagus, 171

Aspen, 41, 218

Ass, wild, 214

Assiniboine River, 252

Assiniboin Indians, 129, 134, 191-192, 208

Assoni, Caddo Indian village in northeast Texas, 181

Assoni Indians, Joutel on land and life, 179-180, 182, 186, 187; as Hasonai Indians, 179

Assumption, Isle of, *see* Anticosti Island

Asturias (Spain), 73

Athapascan tribes, 46, 233

Atlantic coast, 13, 19, 221; early voyages, 69-75 *passim;* early French exploration and settlement, 77-87 *passim,* 89-96 *passim;* summary of New England, 220, 221, 247-248

Atlantic Ocean, 18, 28, 29, 42, 75, 247

Atole, 44

Audencia of Mexico, 55

Azores Islands, 13, 71

Aztec Indians, 37, 236

Baccus, Isle of, *see* Richmond Island

Baffin Island (Northwest Territories), 19

Bahama Channel, 21, 23, 164

Bahama Islands, 17

Baie St. Louis, *see* Lavaca Bay

Bailey, Alfred G., 100

Baleen, 72, 73, 74

Balinger, whaling ship, 72

Baratillo, El, "the junk store," Indian settlement in Florida, 25

Barbue, see catfish

Barcia Carballido y Zúñiga, Andrés Gonzáles de, 22&n-24, 25n, 34

Bark cloth, 236-237, 238

Basque fishers and whalers, 71-75, 78, 85, 86n, 92, 99, 110; as Sibiburo, 73

Basswood, 140; as *bois blanc*, 193, 195

Batata, see Sweet potato

Baton Rouge, Louisiana, 154, 185, 223, 230

Baye des Molues, *see* Mal Baie

Bayou Bartholomew (Arkansas), 182-183

Bay, *see* Laurel

Bean (*Phaseolus*), 40, 42, 92, 106, 153, 173, 178, 186, 233, 239; maize-bean-squash complex, 13, 24, 38, 44, 45, 54, 57, 80, 81, 83, 103, 110, 140, 179-180, 187, 207, 228, 229, 232, 234, 235, 236, 242; *P. vulgaris*, 80; "of Brazil," 80, 81, 83; broad, introduced by French, 171; tepary (*P. acutifolius*), 234

Bear, 31, 86, 90, 93, 94, 105, 122, 133, 186, 195; kept for food, 106, 108; oil, 132, 141; meat, 155; skin, 187

Beaubassin, at head of Chignecto Bay, 95

Beaujeu, commander of *Joly* in La Salle's Gulf expedition, 162-166

Beauport, *see* Gloucester

Beaupré, Quebec, 113, 127

Beaver, 26, 74, 85, 90, 94, 99, 101, 107, 122, 123, 133, 137, 140, 191, 201, 207, 212, 215, 221, 227; pelts, 25, 86, 87, 148, 151, 191, 241; dams, 93, 252; threatened extermination, 108, 136, 215; as food, 121; southern limit, 191

Becassine, see Snipe

Bedbug, Spanish introduction?, 55

Bee, 50n

Beech, 79, 81, 83, 92, 93, 107

Beef, Nation of, *see* Sioux Indians

Beet, 171

Belle, ship in La Salle's Gulf expedition, 163-167, 171-172

bbelle Isle, Strait of, 207

Benavides, Fr. Alonso de, *Memorial* on New Mexico and Indians after Oñate, 61-65, 219-220, 233, 237, 246

Beothuk Indians, as Grands Eskimaux, 207-208

Bermuda, 22

Bernalillo, New Mexico, 251

Bernard, Jean Frédéric, 214n

Bernou, Abbé, 157n, 159&n, 161

Betula papyrifera, see Birch

Biard, Fr. Pierre, on life at Ste. Croix, 79n; account of land and life in Acadia, 89&n-90, 94, 247, 248; on alcohol effects, 90, 247

Biches, see Deer; Elk

Big bluestem grass (*Andropogon*), 53, 219

Biggar, H. P., 77n

Bill Williams River (Arizona), 57, 219

Birch (*Betula*), 92, 93, 104, 107; paper (*B. papyrifera*), in birchbark canoe, 135, 137, 228

Bird Rocks (Quebec), 92; as Island of Penguin, 73

Biscay, Bay of (Spain-France), 71, 72

Biscaynes, Castilian fishers of Asturias, 73

Blackbird, redwing, 81

"Black drink," from *Ilex vomitoria*, 155

Black River (Wisconsin), as Rivière Noir, 151

"Black Spanish," Cannesis Indians, on Delisle map, 209

Blanc Sablon Bay (Quebec), 71

Bloodroot (*Sanguinaria canadensis*), 107, 222

Bloom, Lansing B., 60n

Blueberry, 104, 110

Boeuf, River of the, *see* Chippewa River

Boeuf, see Buffalo

Boeufs, Nation of, *see* Sioux Indians

Beoufs, Rivière aux (present-day Texas), La Salle's settlement on, 169&n-173 *passim*, 209, 223

Bois blanc, see Basswood

Bois d'arc, see Osage orange

Bolton, Herbert E., 34n, 51&n, 52n, 53, 169&n

Bonin Islands, 27

Borage, 170

Borah, Woodrow W., 245&n

Boston, Massachusetts, 134

Boucan, of buffalo meat, 169

Boucaniers, see Buccaneers

Bow and arrow, 25, 53, 82, 94, 95, 104, 168; Jumano compound bow, 46; replaced by firearms, 95, 241; Osage orange for bows, 181, 231; in trade, 182, 186, 231

Bramble, as *toque?*, 214

Brant, 92, 93

Bras d'Or Strait (Nova Scotia), formerly Labrador Strait, 92

Brasil, imaginary island, 69

Brazil, beans of, *see* Beans

Brazil, French in, 18, 19, 75, 105; source of term *petun*, 80, 105; of term *topinambour*, 85n

Brazos River (Texas), 173, 224, 242; as River of Canoes, 176

Brebeuf, Fr. Jean de, 114&n, 115

Brenham, Texas, 175

Bretons, sailors, 18, 97; fishers and whalers, 71-75 *passim*

Brion Island, as Brians Island, 73

Bristol (England), 72, 73

Bristol Channel, 71

Brittany (France), 71, 75, 97, 148

Bromelia pinguin, 31

Bromus sp., grass, domesticated for seeds, 57

Bruce Peninsula (Ontario), 105

Brûlé, Etienne, 121

Buccaneers, 217; as *boucaniers*, 164n

Buff, *buffe, buffle*, buffler, *see* Buffalo

Buffalo, 13, 38-47 *passim*, 51, 52-53, 138, 142, 150, 152, 155, 156, 165, 168, 169, 173, 174, 175, 176, 182, 186, 188, 190, 193, 195, 197, 205, 211, 212, 222, 223, 224, 225, 230, 233; as *cíbola*, cattle of Cíbola, *vaca de Cíbola*, 24, 26, 50, 52, 63, 219, 225; as *boeuf*, 26, 168, 171, 225; as buff, 26; as buffler, 26; as wild cattle, 44, 50, 53, 129, 132, 140, 151, 158, 218, 219, 225; as *buffe*, 72; as *buffle*, 104, 105, 130, 171, 222, 225; hides, 25, 26, 39, 40, 41, 43, 46, 50, 51, 63, 64, 65, 72, 104, 107, 108, 123, 124, 140, 147, 153, 157, 168, 169, 173, 174-175, 182, 187, 197, 222, 226, 230, 233; horns, 25, 26, 123, 175, 182, 187, 226;

meat, 25, 26, 39, 43, 46, 51, 52, 63, 64, 140, 141, 152, 153, 169, 175, 179, 226, 230, 233; wool, 26, 50, 63, 64, 175, 197, 219, 226; tallow, 51, 63; chips, 124; extension of range, 26&n, 217, 226; summary of terms, 225

Buffalo fish, as *carp*, 199, 223

Buffalo plains, 39, 40, 44, 46, 49, 51, 52, 53, 158, 176, 218, 233, 236

Buffalo Rock (below Ottawa, Illinois), 189, 201

Bullfrog, 108

Burial customs, Indian, 95, 103, 189, 234; Mesoarmerican connections, 238. *See also* Rites and ceremonies

Bustard, *see* Canada goose

Butternut, white walnut, 156; northern limit, 101

Caballo, horse, term in use among Caddoan tribes, 179

Caban, see Wigwam

Cabbage, in Acadian gardens, 92

Cabeza de Vaca, Álvar Nuñez, and party, 37, 38, 40, 43, 226, 231n

Cabo San Antonio (Cuba), 164

Cabot, John, 71, 74

Cabot, Sebastian, 71

Cabot Strait, 71, 74n, 98

Cabri Indians, *see* Jumano Indians

Cabrillo, Juan Rodríguez, 17

Cacique, term introduced from Arawak Indians, 45, 46

Cacique Carlos, Calusa Indian chief, 23

Cactus, 51, 218; *Opuntia* sp., as *nopal*, 26; fruit as *tuna*, 26; described by Joutel, 170

Caddo Indians and country, 47n, 64, 237; Joutel on, 180-181, 186, 231; as Cadodaquious, Kadohadachos Indians, 180-181; as Assoni and Ceni Indians, 186; Tonty's expedition to, 190, 231; and horses, 181, 190, 242-243

Caddoan tribes, 47n, 53-54, 63n, 176, 179, 180-182, 241; and horses, 182, 242-243; summary of reports on culture, 231&n-232, 237; agriculture, 235, 236

Cadie, Coste de, on Levasseur map, 77

Cádiz (Spain), 28

Cadodaquious, Caddo Indian village in

northeast Texas, 181

Cadodaquious Indians, also Cadodaqui, as Kadohadachos, Caddo Indians, 180-181, as Gattacka Indians, 242

Cady, G. H., 156n

Cahiague, Huron Indian village, 104, 105

Cahinnio Indians, 181-182, 231

Cahokia, Indian settlement in American Bottoms east of St. Louis, 152, 205, 209

Cahouaille, see Horse

Cailles, *see* Quail

Caiman, *see* Alligator

Calabasa, *see* Squash

Calamus, sweet flag, 85

Calcasieu prairies (southwest Louisiana), 165

California, 12, 13, 59, 237; Spanish exploration of coast, 17, 19, 27-35 *passim;* as an island, 34-35; summary of reports on terrain and biota, 217; at end of century, 251

California, Gulf of, 34, 35, 57, 59, 209, 234, 236; as *Mar bermejo, Mer vermeille*, 132; as Gulf of Colorado, 141

California, Sea of, 64, 137, 139

California, University of, 12, 207n

Calumet, *see* Peace pipe

Calumet River (Illinois), 201

Calusa Indians, 23-24

Camden, Arkansas, 182, 231&n

Canada, 13, 14, 134, 146, 147, 148, 158, 162, 189, 190, 191, 193, 214, 215, 223, 225, 227, 228; as (lower) Saint Lawrence Valley, 18, 19, 73, 75, 77, 87, 97, 124, 125, 208, 239, 248, 251-252; French exploration from Cartier to English capture of Quebec, 97-111; French return, 113-114; Indian destruction by warfare and disease, 114-120, 248-249; Colbert's plans for peasantry, 127; "terrestial Paradise" of, 133, 222; Delisle map of Canada and New France, 194 (Fig. 16), 198 (Fig. 18), 207-208; Lahontan to English on, 216; summary of reports on terrain and biota, 221-222; decline in Indian population, 248-249

Canada, River of, *see* Saint Lawrence River

Canadian River (New Mexico-Texas-Oklahoma), 51, 219; as Río Magdalena, 52

Cane (*Arundinaria*), as *otate*, 25; baskets of, 25,

141; domed cabins of, 154, 155

Canebrake, 139, 153, 205, 223

Canes, River of, *see* Lavaca River

Cannesis Indians, "black Spanish," on Delisle map, 209

Canoe, dugout, 24, 25, 81, 123, 140, 150, 166, 167, 168, 186, 205, 228, 230, 237; tule rush, 30; plank, 31; bark, 83, 86, 182; birchbark-dugout boundary, 81, 228; birchbark, 81, 94, 102, 120, 121, 122, 132, 135, 137, 188, 205, 211, 213, 215, 228; routes, 99, 101, 128, 221; elm bark, 132, 152, 214, 229; pirogue, 150, 153, 215; La Salle's plan to replace with sailing ships, 150

Canoes, River of, *see* Brazos River

Canso, Nova Scotia, 71, 73, 78, 85, 86&n, 91

Canso, Strait of, 92

Cantharides beetle, 171

Cape Ann (Massachusetts), 82, 221, 228; as Cape of Islands, 81, 83

Cape Blanco (Oregon), 31

Cape Bonavista (Newfoundland), 71

Cape Breton (Nova Scotia), 72, 73, 74, 75, 77, 78

Cape Breton Island (Nova Scotia), 91, 92, 95, 221

Cape Canso (Nova Scotia), 91

Cape Cod (Massachusetts), 69, 83, 111, 221, 228; as White Cape, 81, 83

Cape Finisterre (France), 163

Cape Gaspé (Quebec), 91, 100

Cape Girardeau, Missouri, 153

Cape Hatteras (North Carolina), 19

Cape Mendocino (California), 30, 31

Cape North (Nova Scotia), 92

Cape of Islands, *see* Cape Ann

Cape Race (Newfoundland), also Cap Raz, 71, 73

Cape Sable (Nova Scotia), 78, 83, 90, 95

Cape St. Nicolas (Haiti), 163

Cape Samana (Haiti), 163

Cape San Lucas (Baja California Sur), 28, 30

Cape Tormentine (Nova Scotia), 92

Cap Haitien, Haiti, as Port de Paix, 163, 164

Capita, Joutel addressed as by Ceni Indians, 242

Cap La Have (Nova Scotia), 80, 85, 91

Cappa Indians, *see* Quapaw Indians

Cap Raz, *see* Cape Race

Cap St. Antoine, *see* Fountain Bluff

Capulín, see Cherry, wild black

Caracara, as nun eagle, 171

Carde, see Sunflower, tuberous

Cardinal, 24, 25

Caribbean Sea, 12

Carib Indians, 116

Caribou, 83, 90, 92

Carmelite fathers, 21, 34

Carmel River (California), 31

Carneros, abandoned Indian settlement, Chihuahua, 38, 218

Carolinas, 23, 24, 139, 226, 247

Carp, see Buffalo fish

Carrera de las Indias, 217

Carreta, cart, 43, 49

Carson River (Nevada), 216n

Carson Sink (Nevada), 216n

Cartagena, Columbia, 19

Cartier, Jacues, 13, 18, 74, 75, 86, 97, 98, 99, 100, 101, 116, 240, 248

Casa Grande ruins (Arizona), 209

Casas Grandes ruins (Chihuahua), 234

Casquasquia Indians, *see* Kaskaskia Indians

Cassamite, see Sagamité

Cassava, 164, 214

Castaño de Sosa, Gaspar, expedition to New Mexico, 36 (Fig. 5), 43-44, 45, 46, 218-219, 232, 233, 237

Catahoula formation (Texas), 176

Catfish, 42, 44, 51, 52, 142, 152, 169, 218, 220, 223, 224; as *barbue*, 171, 199

Cat Indian Nation, *see* Eire Indian Nation

Cattle, 29, 42, 55, 60, 66, 91, 107, 127, 146, 239, 251

Cattle, Nation of, *see* Sioux Indians

Cattle, wild, *see* Buffalo

Caux (France), 169

Cavelier, Jean, La Salle's older brother, 179, 180, 188, 190

Cavendish, Thomas, 28, 29, 30

Cayman Islands, 164

Cayuga Indians, 116, 119, 145. *See also* Five Nations

"Cedar," *see* Cypress, bald

Cedar, red (*Juniperus virginianus*), as *ciprés*, cypress, 25, 82, 103

Cedar, white (*Thuja occidentalis*), in birchbark canoe, 135, 137, 228

Cedros Island (Baja California Norte), 31

Celery, 171

Celtis, see Hackberry

Ceni Indians, 176, 235; Joutel on land and life, 177-179, 181, 182, 186, 187, 231; and horses, 177-179, 242-243; as Caddo Indians, 186; Tonty visits, 190, 231; as Hasinai Indians, 231, 235

Cenis, River of the, *see* Trinity River

Central America, 12, 237

Cerfs, see Deer; Elk

Cermeño, Sebastián Rodríguez, 30

Cervus, see Elk

Chalchibuite, see Turquoise

Chaleur Bay (Quebec-New Brunswick), 74, 91, 92, 240, 247

Chama River (New Mexico), 49

Chama Valley (New Mexico), pueblos, 39

Champaign, 168, 169&n-171, 173, 174, 177, 186, 224; summary of use of term, 225

Champlain, Lake, 102, 116; as first lake of the Iroquois, 99-100

Champlain, Samuel de, first voyage and account in *Des Sauvages*, 14, 77&n-78&n, 220, 237; exploration of Acadia and New England and account in *Les Voyages*, 78&n-84 (& 79n), 85, 87, 89, 91, 228, 247; maps by, 78&n, 81, 84, 86&n, 109 (Fig. 10), 110&n-111, 222, 237; explorations and accounts of Canada, 98&n-107 (& 102n-106n), 121, 240, 248; use of Indian maps, 99, 101, 103, 111, 121, 228, 237; involvement in Iroquois-Algonquian warfare, 102-103, 105, 116, 119, 239, 248-249, 252; proposals for development of Canada, 106-107; return to govern New France, 113-114, 117; summary of accounts of terrain and biota, 220-222

Chamuscado, Sánchez, expedition with Rodríguez to New Mexico, 36 (Fig. 5), 37-40, 44-47 *passim*, 65, 218, 246

Channel Islands (California), 31

Chaouanon Indians, *see* Shawnee Indians

Chapin, Thomas, 127n, 131n

Jesuit-Indian policy, 131, 147-148; against colonizing of interior, 142, 251-252

Colbert, River, *see* Mississippi River

Colombia, savannas in, 224

Colorado, Gulf of, *see* California, Gulf of

Colorado Plateau, 37, 46, 49, 50, 51, 57, 68, 218

Colorado River (Arizona-California), 34, 35, 56, 219, 237; as Río Buena Esperanza, 57

Colorado River (Texas), 173, 242; as Maligne River?, 175

Colorado Valley, Lower, 234

Columbus, Christopher, 12, 13, 17, 43, 69, 74, 75

Comale, 38

Company of New France, 91, 239; also known as Company of One Hundred Associates, 113; in control of Acadia and Canada, 113, 119; replaced by Crown Colony, 127

Company of One Hundred Associates, *see* Company of New France

Conacher, James B., 114n

Cook, Sherburne F., 245&n

Coosa River (Alabama), country, 217, 226

Copal, *see* Sweet gum

Copper, Río Verde, Arizona, 41, 51-52, 56-57, 218, 219; Acadia, 77-80, 82, 84, 86, 87, 221; Lake Superior, 99, 101, 123, 129, 132, 133, 134, 137, 138, 222, 237; Champlain's prospects for, 107; Green Bay, 111; Tensa Indian shields, 154; "Gnaesitares" hatchets, 215

Coq d'inde, see Turkey

Coquina, 22

Coral, 56

Cormorant, 78

Corn, Indian, *see* Maize

Cornwall (England), 72

Coroa Indians, 154, 230; flattening of heads, 155

Coronado, Francisco Vásquez de, and expedition, 17, 35, 37, 38, 41, 46, 50, 53, 64, 65, 218, 219, 225, 231, 232, 233, 234, 243, 251

Corpus Christi, Texas, 165

Corpus Christi Bay (Texas), 167, 172

Corte-Real, Gaspar and João Vaz, 74

Cortés, Hernán, 17, 27, 30, 50, 56, 59, 159,

219, 245

Cosa, Juan de la, 69

Costa Rica, savannas in, 224

Côte, in seigneurial system, 215, 252

Cotonnier, see Cottonwood

Cotton, Pueblo, 38, 45, 65, 233; Hopi, 41, 45, 233, 234; Colorado River, 57; Pima, 234; Mesoamerican connections, 234, 236; West Indies, 236. *See also* Cloth; Clothing

Cottonwood, 51, 188, 218, 223; as *cotonnier*, 141

Council of the Indies, 30, 34, 55, 56, 59, 217, 239, 245, 251

Courcelles, Daniel de Rémy, Sieur de, 135&n-136, 145

Courge, see Squash

Court Oreilles, Lake (Wisconsin), 123, 222

Cowles, H. C., 156n

Cows, River of the, *see* Pecos River

Crab, 29

Crab, horseshoe, 83; carapace as tool (*signoc*), 80; tail as arrow tip, 82

Crane, 13, 26, 49, 92, 108, 110, 170, 195, 218, 222, 224; whooping, 105, 221

Cree Indians, 134, 227; Radisson's supposed visit, 123-124&n; as Christino Indians, 123; as Christineaux, Kilistineaux Indians, on Delisle map, 208

Creek Indians, 24, 247

Crocodile, 164, 171, 183, 215-216

Cromwell, Oliver, 23

Crow, 108, 222; skin, 123

Cruzado Indians, *see* Yavapai Indians

Cuba, 12, 17, 22, 23, 164

Cucurbita, see Pumpkin; Squash

Culiacán, Sinaloa, 161

Currant, red, 81

Custard apple, 53

"Cypress," *see* Cedar, red

Cypress, bald (*Taxodium*), 153, 217, 223, 230; as *sabina*, 25, 43; as "cedar," 183, 186, 188

Dablon, Fr. Claude, 128, 138

Dauphin, Lake, *see* Michigan, Lake

Davis, E. A., 236&n

Davis, John, 13, 75

Davis Mountains (Texas), 42, 46, 218, 232

Davis Strait, 13, 19, 75

Deadening, *see* Fire

Dead River, fictitious discovery by Lahontan, 208

De Cussy, French official, 162, 163-164&n

Deer, 26, 53, 56, 105, 110, 129, 142, 152, 155, 165, 186, 195, 203, 205, 212, 219, 220, 221, 223, 224, 226, 230, 233; skins, 25, 41, 43, 46, 65, 104, 107, 182, 233; meat, 46, 179; probably meaning elk, 52, 219; as *cerfs, chevreuils, bitches*, 133, 140, 168, 222, 225; Virginia (*Odocoileus virginianus*), 140, 223, 225; summary of terms, 225; as *venado*, 226, 233

De Gannes, memoir on Illinois, actually by Pierre Deliette, 193&n-201

Delaware River, 118

Deliette, Pierre, on Illinois, as actual author of De Gannes memoir, 193&n-201

Delisle, Claude and Guillaume, map of Louisiana, 23; use of Joutel's account, 163, 207, 209; reproductions from maps, 194-206 *passim* (Figs. 16-23); map of Canada or New France, 207&n-208; map of Mexico and Florida, 208-209; use of Lahontan's account, 208, 216; and Tonty's account, 209

Del Rio, Texas, 43

Deluge, Indian legend of, 193, 203

De Monts, Pierre du Guast, Sieur, 77, 78-80 (&79n), 80-82, 82-83&n, 86-87

Denonville, Jacques René de Brésay, Marquis de, 185n, 189

Denys, Nicolas, *Geographical Description*, on land and life of Acadia, 91&n-95, 221, 225, 241, 247, 253; on changes in Indian ways, 94-95, 241; on firearms among Indians, 94-95, 120, 241; on effects of alcohol, 95, 241, 247

De Pere, Wisconsin, 130

Desert, as French term, 235

De Soto, Hernando, and expedition, 13, 17, 22, 25, 26, 141, 150, 226, 230, 231&n

Des Plaines River (Illinois), 152, 156, 193, 203

Detroit, Michigan, 111, 129, 133, 189, 201

Detroit River (Michigan-Ontario), 133

Devil's River (Texas), 43

Dewberry, as *zarzamora*, 26

Díaz, Melchior, 35

Disease, introduction by Europeans, 13, 90, 100, 103, 114-116, 245, 247, 248; scurvy, 18, 79-80, 83, 85, 86, 98, 101, 228; smallpox, 65, 66, 114, 115, 205, 207, 245, 249; *cocolixtli*, 65; around Massachusetts Bay, 82, 228, 247-248; dysentery, 90, 101, 247, 248; sweat bath against, 94; gout, rheumatism, 94; and Iroquois of St. Lawrence Valley, 100, 248; measles, 114, 249; plague, 228, 247-248; malaria, 245

Division of labor, Pueblo Indians, 38, 62, 232-233; Indians of Acadia, 94; Huron Indians, 106; Ceni Indians, 178; Caddoan tribes and Eastern Indians, 235

Dog, 25, 38, 92, 175; as pack animal, 39, 43, 51, 63, 64, 233, 234; as food, 94, 106, 108, 140, 141, 154, 230, 237

Dollier de Casson, Fr. François, 132-133

Dolphin, 97

Dominican Republic, 12

Dorado, 169

Dove, 195

Drake, Francis, 19, 28, 30, 34

Drakes Bay (California), 30

Drought, in Pueblo country, 66, 247

Drum, 153, 205, 237

Drumfish, as *mojarra?*, 218

Dry cod fishery, *see* Cod

Duck, 26, 40, 92, 94, 105, 142, 155, 170, 195, 205, 218, 224

Du Creux, Fr. François, on Huron Indians and Huronia, 114-120 (& 114n-120n)

Duluth, Daniel Graysolon, Sieur, 151-152, 189, 211, 212

Dunkle, John R., 21n

Durango (city), 161

Durango (state), 40, 43, 234

Dutch, 22, 34, 64, 108, 127, 145; fur trade and alcohol, 96, 148, 241; fur trade and French rivalry, 110, 119-120, 134, 135

Dwellings, European, 101, 169, 183, 186

Dwellings, Indian, Florida, 25, 26; California, 29, 30; Pueblo and Southwest, 37-38, 38-46 *passim*, 46, 57, 61, 232; Apache, 39, 51, 63, 64, 233, 234; Plains, 53, 54, 123, 124; Acadia, 73, 79, 81, 82, 84, 94; long house, 81, 105, 114, 116, 140, 150, 187, 205, 229, 230, 248; wigwam, 94, 124, 228; Canada, Huronia, 105, 114, 116, 228, 229, 248; tepee, 124, 234; Illinois, 140, 150, 230;

69-75 *passim;* cod fishery, 71-75 *passim,* 78, 91, 92, 93, 97, 99, 216, 247; fishing rights and colonial policy, 74-75, 77, 97; fishers and trade with Indians, 74, 75, 85, 95, 96, 97, 240, 241, 247; Champlain on economic prospects, 107, 221; at La Salle's Texas settlement, 169

Fishing, Indian, net, seine, 40, 86, 94, 106, 108, 129, 130-131, 140, 186, 211, 212, 227, 229; line, 81, 140; weir, 86, 104&n, 130-131, 222; spear, 86, 93, 94, 186, 212, 222, 229

Fishing grounds, North Atlantic, 69-75 *passim* (& 70, Fig. 8); Ice Age geomorphology, 69, 71

Five Nations Indians, 102, 103, 116, 117, 118, 119, 120, 128, 136, 137, 145, 189, 225, 229, 239, 248-249. *See also* Iroquois Indians; Cayuga, Mohawk, Oneida, Onondaga, Seneca Indians

Flattening of heads, 155

Flea, 84, 108

Flint, 231&n, 237

Florida, 77, 136, 141, 236, 252; Spanish in and reports on, 13, 14, 17, 18, 21-26, 59, 75, 134, 139, 159, 217, 224, 226, 245, 247, 251; French in, 13, 18, 19, 21, 75, 83, 85n; Delisle map, 196 (Fig. 17), 208-209; expansion of buffalo range to, 226

Florida, Straits of, 18, 21, 236

Florida Keys, 24

Flounder, 92

Fly, 248

Flying fish, 163

Folles Avoines Indians, *see* Menominee Indians

Food crops, *see* entries for individual crops, as, Bean; Grain amaranth; Maize; Squash; etc.

Ford, James A., 236&n

Fort Crevecoeur (near Peoria, Illinois), 150, 151, 152, 155, 191, 211, 214, 216

Fort Frontenac (at Kingston, Ontario), 145-146, 149, 150&n, 151, 158, 185, 211

Fort St. Joseph (at Port Huron, Michigan), 214

Fort St. Louis (Illinois), at Starved Rock, 155-156, 158, 161, 162, 173, 179, 185, 186, 188-189, 190-191, 193; Jesuit mission at, 190, 191, 201, 205; moved to Lake Peoria, 191-192, 193, 197, 205; and notices of watermelons and horses, 241-242

Fountain Bluff (Illinois), 153; as Cap St.

Antoine, 205, 209, 223

Fourche Indians, 130

Fox, 25, 93, 107; black, 108, 241; silver, 241

Fox Indians, 129, 130, 134, 201, 202, 229; westward displacement, 129-130, 229, 249; as Outagami Indians, 130; as Renard Indians, 208

Fox River (Illinois), 195; as Pestegonki River, 156

Fox River (Wisconsin), 130, 138, 139, 140, 222, 223

France and French, 13, 14, 23, 24, 47n, 64; in Florida, 13, 18, 19, 21, 75, 83, 85n; in Brazil, 18, 19, 75, 105; summary of 16th century activities in North America, 18-19; fishing interests in North Atlantic waters, 69-75 *passim;* early exploration and settlement in Acadia and New England, 77-87; resettlement in Acadia, 89-96; early exploration and settlement in Canada, 97-111; involvement in Iroquois-Algonquian warfare, 98, 99-100, 116-120; New France under Company of New France, 113-114; exploration of Great Lakes, 121-125, 126 (Fig. 11); exploration, missionary and colonizing efforts under Crown Colony, 126 (Fig. 11), 127-136; church-state conflict, Jesuit-Indian policy, 127-128, 131, 147-148, 239-240; Talon's proposal to extend limits of New France, 134-135; La Salle's Louisiana project, 145-158; La Salle's Gulf expedition, 159-166; French in Texas, to La Salle's death, 167-176; survivors' return to Illinois, 177-189; Five Nations policy and Iroquois offensive, 189-190; restriction of fur trade, 191-192, 252; summary of reports on terrain and biota, 220-226; summary of reports on peoples and cultures, 227-231, 235-238; summary of impact on native ways, 239-243 *passim;* New France and end of the century, 251-253. *See also* New France

Franciscan fathers, in Florida, 21, 22, 23; in New Mexico, 37-47 *passim,* 49-58 *passim,* 59-68 *passim,* 218, 219, 239-240, 246-247; in church-state conflict, 60, 66, 239-240, 247

Francis I, King of France, 75

Frederick IV, King of Denmark, 214

Free trade, fishing rights and states' claims, 74-75, 77, 97

French Bay, *see* Fundy, Bay of

French River (Ontario), 104

Frobisher, Martin, 13, 19, 75

Frontenac, Louis de Buade, Comte de, 128, 131, 137-138, 142, 145-146, 147-148, 158, 191, 216

Fruit, introduction by Europeans, citrus, 28n; summary on watermelons and peaches, 241-242, 243

Fruit, see entries for individual types, as, Apple; Grape; Mulberry; Plum; etc.

Fuca, Juan de, 29

Fundy, Bay of, 71, 74, 82, 84, 85, 87, 95, 221, 228, 247; as French Bay, 78

Fur trade, 14, 19, 86, 87, 97-98, 99, 104, 119, 127, 222; fishers in, 74, 75, 85, 95, 96, 97, 240, 241, 247; alcohol in, 74, 90, 95, 96, 116, 148, 241, 247; Champlain on prospects, 107; French-Dutch rivalry, 119-120, 134, 135; Great Lakes, 122-125, 135, 151, 157, 240-241; Hudson's Bay Company in, 123, 125, 134, 241, 252; Ottawa Indians in, 124, 125, 128, 137, 147, 237, 240, 252; summary of role of birchbark canoe in, 137; La Salle excluded from northern, given buffalo hide trade, 147, 149&n, 151, 157, 191, 201; Tonty and La Forest in partnership, 185, 190-192, 201; French restriction of interior trade, 191-192, 252; summary of impact on native ways, 240;241; summary on depletion of game animals by, 241, 252; at end of century, 251-253

Galena, Illinois, 189

Galisteo River (New Mexico), 59, 61, 62, 218

Galisteo Valley (New Mexico), 38, 44; pueblos of, 39, 41, 62, 67

Gallegos, Hernán, account of Chamuscado-Rodríquez expedition, 37&n-40, 44-47 passim, 218, 232, 233, 246

Gallican clergy faction, 127

Gallinas River (New Mexico), 51, 52

Gallinée, Fr. René Brehánt de, account of La Salle's and Joliet's first expeditions, 132-133; map of Great Lakes and route south, 133, 134; at Lake Eire, 222

Galve, Gaspar de la Cerda Sandoval Silva y Mendoza, Conde de, 24, 67

Galveston Bay (Texas), 37, 167, 231

Game animals, depletion by hunting and fur trade, 95, 108, 136, 215, 241, 252;

summary of French and Spanish notices of plains, 225-226; summary on extension of buffalo range, 226. See also entries for specific kinds, as, Beaver; Buffalo; Deer; Moose; etc.

Gannet, 78

Ganong, William F., 78n, 80, 91n, 92, 96n

Gar, 171

Garden Peninsula (Michigan), 201

Garnet, 56, 57, 62

Gasco de Velasco, Luis, 52n, 54, 55

Gaspé Bay (Quebec), 77, 99, 100, 221

Gaspé Peninsula (Quebec), 71, 91, 92; as part of Gaspésie, 208

Gaspésie, as including Gaspé Peninsula and greater part of New Brunswick, 208

Gaston, Rapids of, see Sault Ste. Marie

Gattacka Indians, see Cadodaquious Indians

Gazette de France, 159

Geological Survey, U.S., 216n

George's Banks (North Atlantic Ocean), 69

Georgian Bay (Ontario), 104, 105, 111, 116, 117, 118, 119, 122, 124, 128, 151, 221, 222, 228, 229, 240

Germany and Germans, 216; immigrants in Missouri, 11

Gila Apache Indians, see Apache Indians

Gila River (Arizona), 37, 57, 63, 209, 234

Gilbert, Humphrey, 19, 75

Ginger, 25

Gleditsia, see Honey locust

Gloucester, Massachusetts, as Beauport, 83

"Gnaesitares," fictitious people created by Lahontan, 215

Goat, 55

Gold, 17, 29, 34, 56, 64

Gonâve, Gulf of (Haiti), 163

Goose, 40, 86, 92, 94, 108, 110, 142, 170, 218, 222, 224

Goose, Canada, 80, 207; as bustard, 82, 86, 90, 93, 105, 140, 149, 152, 155, 170, 183, 195, 205, 223, 224

Gorreta Indians, see Manso Indians

Gourd (Lagenaria), vessels, 40, 141; rattles, 153, 205, 237

Gout, see Disease

Grace, English fishing ship, 73

Grain amaranth, 44, 45, 233, 236; as *quelites*, 44, 45; Mesoamerican origin, 234

Grammont, French filibuster, 161

Gran Chichimeca, 236

Grand Baie (Canada), 73; as salt sound of St. Lawrence River, 75; as Gulf of St. Lawrence, 97; as Great Bay, 98

Grand Banks (North Atlantic Ocean), 69, 71

Grand Camp, La Salle's settlement on Matagorda Bay, 167

Grand Canyon, 17

Grand Eskimaux, *see* Beothuk Indians

Grand Tower, Illinois, 139, 153, 205, 223

Gran Quivira National Monument (New Mexico), 66n

Grant, W. L., 84n

Grape, 13, 22, 24, 25, 83, 106, 107, 156, 170, 186, 195, 222

Grapefruit, *toronja*, 28n

Grapevine, 41, 42, 52, 79, 80, 92, 99, 102, 106, 170, 217, 218, 219, 224, 248

Grass, 53, 57, 219

Great Bay, *see* Grand Baie

Greater Antilles, 12, 17, 224

Great Ireland, in Norse sagas, 13

Great Khan, 29

Great Lakes, 13, 14, 99, 101, 103, 105, 118, 119, 138, 146, 158, 173, 214, 227, 228, 235, 237, 239, 249; early French exploration, 121-125, 126 (Fig. 11); fur trade, 122-125, 135, 151, 157, 240-241; Ice Age geomorphology, 122, 137, 139, 221, 223, 235; establishment of Jesuit missions on, 126 (Fig. 11), 128&n-131, 240; French exploration under Crown Colony, 132-136; La Salle sails, 149-150, 151; Delisle map, 200 (Fig. 19), 208; summary of French reports on terrain and biota, 222-223

Great Plains, also High Plains, 39, 41, 46, 51, 52-54; summary on terrain and biota and terminology, 224-226

Green Bay (Wisconsin), 111, 138, 140, 211, 212, 215, 223, 225, 229; Jean Nicollet reaches, 121-122; as Bay of Puans, 129, 130, 134, 147, 149&n, 201, 222; Jesuit mission at (St. Francis Xavier), 129-130, 130-131, 201, 212, 222, 230

Greens, 92

Griffon, La Salle's ship on the Great Lakes, 149, 211, 214

Groseilliers, Médard Chouart, Sieur de, explorations of Great Lakes with Radisson, 122-125, 128, 222, 240-241; serves Hudson's Bay Company, 125, 134

Groundnut (*Apios tuberosa*), 99

Grouse, Canada, as black partridge, 93

Guadalcázar, Diego Fernández de Córdoba, Marqués de, 60

Guadalupe del Paso, monastery below El Paso, 67

Guale, Spanish province of lower Savannah River, 23

Guam, 27, 30

Guatemala, 245

Gulf coast, 23; account by Sigüenza y Góngora, 24-26; La Salle's expedition along, 164-166

Gulf Stream, 69, 85

Gull, 26

Hackberry (*Celtis*), 169

Hackett, Charles W., 60n, 65n, 66n, 67

Hague, The (Netherlands), 214, 216

Haiti, 17, 170, 171, 189, 217; as St. Domingue, 161-164&n

Hakluyt, Richard, 29; reports on Gulf of St. Lawrence from *Principal Navigations*, 72&n-74&n, 75n, 90

Halibut, 93

Hamilton, Ontario, 133

Hammond, George, 37n, 40n, 49n, 52n, 53, 54n, 55n, 56n

Hanover (Germany), 216

Hare, 92, 215, 233

Harris, Richard C., 113n

Hasinai Indians, *see* Ceni Indians

Hasonai Indians, *see* Assoni Indians

Havana (Cuba), 21, 22, 24, 217, 251

Havre l'Anglais, *see* Louisburg, Nova Scotia

Hawaiian Islands, 27

Hawkins, John, 19

Hazel and hazelnut, 94, 97

Hébert, Louis, 107

Helianthus, see Sunflower; Sunflower, tuberous

Hemlock, 248

Hemp, wild (*Laportea canadensis*), Champlain on economic prospects, 107, 222

274

153, 155; at Fort St. Louis, 155-156, 185, 188-189, 190-192; La Salle on, 156-157; Joutel on, 188-189; in war against Iroquois, 189-190, 201, 230; De Gannes memoir on, 193&n-201; on Delisle map, 208, 209; summary of French accounts of terrain and biota, 223; summary of French accounts on native ways, 230, 235

Illinois River, 139, 143, 149-150, 151, 152, 155, 156, 162, 172, 187-188, 189, 193, 197, 199, 203, 205, 211, 212, 216, 223, 230; as St. Louis River, 141, 142

Illinois State Geological Survey, 11

Illinois Valley, 11, 13, 151, 191, 223, 229, 230

Indé, Durango, 40

Indiana, 208

Indians, summaries of French and Spanish reports on, northern woods and coasts, 227-228; eastern woods and prairies, 228-229; westward displacement, 229-230; Illinois, 230; Lower Mississippi Valley, 230-231; Caddoan tribes, 231-232; Pueblo, 232-233; Apache, 233-234; southwest agriculture, 234; eastern agriculture, 235-237; common and widespread traits, 237-238. *See also* entires for individual tribes, and for such subjects as Agriculture; Burial customs; Clothing; Rites and ceremonies; etc.

Indigo, 164n

Indio, as meaning adult male?, 246

Inner Coast Plain, *see* Texas

Inquisition, Spanish, 159

Inscription Rock, *see* El Morro National Monument

Iowa, 230

Iowa Indians, 208

Ireland and Irish, monks in New World, 13

Iron, reported in Nova Scotia, 78; Champlain's prospects of, 107; ferruginous beds in Texas, 178, 179, 224

Iroquois, first lake of the, *see* Champlain, Lake

Iroquois, Lake, *see* Ontario, Lake

Iroquois, river of the, *see* Richelieu River

Iroquois Indians, 122, 127, 133, 137, 153, 188, 191, 214, 215, 223, 253; warfare with Algonquian tribes and Hurons, 98, 99, 100, 102, 103, 105, 108-110; lost settlement in St. Lawrence Valley, 100, 248; Champlain in raids against, 102, 103, 105, 116, 119,

252; allied with English and Dutch, 110, 134, 145, 148, 189-190; destruction of enemy nations, 116-120 *passim*, 128, 135-136, 239, 248-249; peace with French, 117, 120, 122, 145-146; westward displacement of other tribes, 128, 129, 130, 138, 139, 155, 156, 199, 229-230, 249; use of elm bark canoes, 132, 229; settlement at Ft. Frontenac, 145-146, 211; and liquor, 148, 241; French war against, 189-190, 201, 230; on Delisle map, 208; Hennepin on fishing, 212, 229; summary of French accounts, 229-230. *See also* Five Nations Indians; Cayuga, Mohawk, Oneida, Onondaga, Seneca Indians

Iroquois River (Illinois), 156

Irrigation, *see* Agriculture, Indian

Isabella I, Queen of Spain, 42, 59

Isle du Detour, *see* Summer Island

Isleta pueblo, 67

Issati Indians, *see* Sioux Indians

Italy, 29

Jacksonville, Florida, 18

Jacques Cartier Passage, 97

Jalisco, 27, 28n

James, Thomas, 72

James Bay (Ontario-Quebec), 99

James I, King of England, 90

Japan, 29, 34; passage to, 124, 125, 141

Jémez Indians and pueblos, 39, 62, 64, 67

Jémez River and Valley (New Mexico), 62; as Valle de Santiago, 39

Jerusalem artichoke, *see* Sunflower, tuberous

Jesuit fathers, in Mexico, 12; on Great Lakes, 14, 122, 124, 125, 128, 134, 135, 137, 138, 203, 205, 212, 222, 240, 241; in Acadia, 89, 103, 247; expelled from New France, 110; readmitted replacing Recollect fathers, 113; return to Huronia, 114, 121; on disease in Huronia, 114-116; in Iroquois warfare, 116-118; antipathy to Dutch, 119-120; interest in passage to Orient, 124-125; church-state conflict, alcohol and Indian policy, 127-128, 131, 147-148, 240; accounts used by Delisle, 208-209; Lahontan on, 216; summary of role in New France, 240. *See also* Jesuit missions; Jesuit Relations

Jesuit missions, to Hurons (St. Joseph), 117; at

276

Livestock, introduced, in New Mexico, 42, 49, 55, 60, 63, 64, 65, 66, 67, 239, 240, 243, 247, 251; in New France, 91, 127, 146, 190, 251, 252; in Texas with La Salle, 165, 171; summary on introduction of chickens and horses, 242-243. *See also* entries for individual kinds of animals, as, Cattle; Horse; Sheep; Pig; etc.

Llano, summary of use of term, 224-225

Llano Estacado, *see* Staked Plains

Lobster, 73, 93

Lockport, Illinois, 193

Lomas Colmenares, Juan Batista de, 42-43

London (England), 34, 73, 212

London Company, 89

Long Island (New York), 77

Long Point Bay (Ontario), 222

Long River, fictitious discovery by Lahontan, 208, 215

López de Mendizábal, Bernardo, 66

Louisburg, Nova Scotia, as Havre l'Anglais, 92

Louisiana, 165, 236&n

Louisiana, French, 14, La Salle's project and exploration, 23, 24, 145-158 *passim;* named by La Salle, 150&n; division into Upper and Lower, 158, 186; La Salle defines geographical limits, 159; in La Salle's Gulf expedition against New Spain, 159-166 *passim;* map of, showing La Salle's discoveries, 160 (Fig. 12), 161n; administered by Tonty, 185-192 *passim;* De Gannes and St. Cosme accounts, 193-209; on Delisle map, 209; apocryphal accounts, 211-216; summary of reports on terrain and biota, 223; summary of accounts of native peoples and cultures, 230-232 *passim*, 235-238 *passim*

Louis XIV, King of France, 127, 131, 146, 207

Louisville, Kentucky, 132, 146&n

Lower Allumette Lake (Ontario-Quebec), 103

Lower California, 12, 28, 30

Lower Miocene age, 176

Ludlington, Michigan, 143

Luna y Arellano, Tristan de, 217, 226

Lutherans, 29

Luxán, Diego Pérez de, account of Espejo expedition, 40&n-42, 46, 218, 232

Lynx, 93, 107

Macao, 29

Mackerel, 71, 92

Mackinac, Straits of (Michigan), 121, 138, 151, 152, 189, 201, 211, 212, 214, 215, 216, 222; as Straits of Michilimackinac, 130, 149, 188, 192, 193; Jesuit mission (St. Ignace) at, 130, 138, 139, 140, 149, 201, 212, 222

Mackinac Island (Michigan), 121

Maclura pomifera, *see* Osage orange

Macopin, unidentified edible root, 156-157, 198

Macoupin County and River (Illinois), 157

Madeira Islands, 163

Madeleine Island (Wisconsin), 128

Madrid (Spain), 61n

Magdalen Islands (Quebec), 73, 92; as Ramea, 72, 73

Magellan, Ferdinand, 27

Magellan, Straits of, 28

Magnolia (*Magnolia grandiflora*), 25, 217

Maguey, 39; as agave, 51

Mahican Indians, 152

Maine, 69, 71, 74, 75, 79, 91, 228, 240, 247; first French exploration and accounts of coast, 80-82

Maize (Indian corn), 25, 37, 40, 41, 42, 51, 62, 111, 129, 132, 153, 164, 173, 183, 186, 189, 239; maize-bean-squash complex, 13, 24, 38, 44, 45, 54, 57, 80, 81, 83, 103, 110, 140, 179-180, 187, 207, 228, 229, 232, 234, 235, 236, 242; storage, 26, 38, 84, 85, 108, 150, 180, 233; ground, 38, 39, 44, 82, 86, 103, 104, 106, 108, 177-178, 180, 214, 235; cooked, 54, 106, 108, 140, 141, 177-178, 180, 187, 197, 214, 235; *mingan*, 106; *sagamité*, 108, 140, 141, 187, 214, 235; green corn ceremony, 180, 235, 238; pounded, 187, 235; white Papago variety, 234; flint, sweet, flour varieties, 235

Malaria, *see* Disease

Malay islands, 27

Mal Baie (Quebec), as Baye des Molues, 92, 99

Malebarre, *see* Nauset Harbor

Malecite Indians, *see* Etchemin Indians

Maligne River, *see* Colorado River (Texas)

Mangrove, 22

Manhattan Island (New York), 134, 148

Manila (Philippines), 28, 30, 31

Manila galleons, 27 (Fig. 2), 28-31, 34, 217, 245, 251

Manioc, as *yuca*, 236

Manito, 95

Manitowoc, Wisconsin, 202

Manso Indians, 67; also as Gorreta Indians, 61

Manzano Mountains (New Mexico), 39, 50

Maple, 93, 107, 152, 195

Maps, national claims on early 16th century, 74; Levasseur, 77; Champlain, 78&n, 81, 84, 86&n, 109 (Fig. 10), 110&n-111, 222, 237; Mercator, 97; Champlain's use of Indian, 99, 101, 103, 111, 121, 228, 237; Gallinée, 133, 134; Joliet and Marquette, 138&n; of Louisiana, showing La Salle's discoveries, 160 (Fig. 12), 161n; Cappa, for French, 182; Delisle, 194-206 *passim* (Figs. 16-23), 207&n-209; summary on Indian maps and European use, 237

Mar bermejo, see California, Gulf of

Marcos de Niza, Fray, 17

Mardi Gras, 106

Margry, Pierre, 14, 131n-135n, 137n, 138n, 140n-142n, 145-152n, 156n-159n, 161n-165n, 167n, 169n, 170n, 172n, 177n-183n, 186n-191n, 207n, 241n, 242n

Marigold, English ship, 72

Marquette, Fr. Jacques, on Illinois Indians, 129; founds mission St. Ignace, 130; at mission Ste. Marie du Sault, 133; exploration of Mississippi with Joliet, and accounts of land and life, 138&n-141, 151, 188, 212, 223; last expedition and death, 142-143

Marten, 25, 74, 93, 99, 107, 241, 252

Martín Palacios, Gerónimo, 30

Mascouten Indians, 134, 137, 202; as Fire Nation, 119, 130, 138, 208; westward displacement, 138

Masks, Huron, 106

Massachusetts, Champlain's reconnaissance of coast, 81-82, 83-84, 221, 228, 235; early devastation by disease, 228, 247-248

Massachusetts Bay, 82

Massane, *see* Mazon Creek

Matagorda Bay (Texas), and La Salle's settlement on, 64, 165-167, 168 (Fig. 13), 172, 176, 189, 217, 220, 224, 226, 242

Matagorda Island (Texas), 165

Matamoros, Juan Pedro, 25n

Mathes, W. Michael, 28n, 29n, 30n, 31n, 34&n

May apple (*Podophyllum*), 104

Mazatlán, Sinaloa, 31

Mazon Creek (Illinois), as Massane, 156, 195, 205

Mazon ironstone concretions, "stones of mines," 156

Measles, *see* Disease

Mecham, J. Lloyd, 37n

Medlar, French name for, *nèfle*, applied to persimmon, 153; persimmon compared to, 156, 169, 186, 195

Mekezen, shoes, 86

Melon, Spanish in Florida, 22; Pueblo, 50&n, 55; French in Florida, 171. *See also* Watermelon

Melon d'eau, see Watermelon

Membré, Fr. Zénobe, account of La Salle's Mississippi expedition, 152&n-154, 211, 213

Memphis, Tennessee, 153, 188, 223, 226, 230

Mendoza, Antonio de, 17, 18, 27, 218

Menéndez de Avilés, Pedro, 18, 21, 23

Menominee Indians, 124, 235; as Nation of Wild Oats, 123, 130, 138; as Folles Avoines Indians, 130, 201; as Algonquian tribe, 227

Mera, H. P., 46n

Mercator, Gerhardus, world map of 1569, 97

Merluche, see Cod

Merrimac River (Massachusetts), 81

Mer vermeille, see California, Gulf of

Meschasipi, River, *see* Mississippi River

Meseta Central (Mexico), 37, 234

Mesoamerica, 12, 17, 230; as agricultural source, 234, 236-237, 241; as cultural source, 237-238; decline in native population, 245&n

Mesquite, 44, 218; pods, 38, 42, 218; as *mistquil*, 156

Messi-sipi River, *see* Mississippi River

Metate, 232, 235

México, 12, 17, 23, 24, 27, 34, 37, 43, 44, 45, 54, 56, 57, 64, 82, 116, 134, 136, 147, 148, 161&n, 162, 218, 220, 225, 232, 234, 235, 236, 242, 243, 245, 246, 252; Delisle map, 196 (Fig. 17)

México, D. F., 28, 37n, 40, 49, 58

Mexico, Gulf of, 13, 17, 18, 64, 135, 136, 141,

150, 155, 167, 173, 191, 217, 225, 226, 236, 252; La Salle's expedition against New Spain via, 159-166, 185, 217, 251

Mexico, University of, 24, 251

Mezquita, see Kiva

Miami Indians, at Green Bay, 130, 134, 138, 139; as Oumami Indians, 130; westward displacement, 130, 138, 229-230, 249; buffalo drives by fire, 150, 211; at Ft. St. Louis, 156, 185; at Buffalo Rock, 189; at Chicago, 192, 193, 203, 252; De Gannes on, 193, 195, 199, 201; on St. Joseph River, 201, 202, 211; Lahontan on, 215

Miamis, River of the, *see* St. Joseph River

Michigamea Indians, tribe of Illinois Indians, 208

Michigan, 208; early French explorations, 121-125 *passim*, 222; Jesuit missions in (at Sault Ste. Marie and Straits of Mackinac) and accounts, 129, 130, 133, 134, 138, 139, 140, 149, 201, 212, 222; Marquette's death, 143; La Salle in, 149, 151, 152; St. Cosme in, 201

Michigan, Lake, 121, 122, 130, 139, 143, 149, 150, 152, 156, 188, 189, 193, 201, 208, 223, 229; as Lake of the Illinois, 140, 141, 142, 147; St. Cosme crosses, 201-203; as Lake Dauphin, 211

Michigan, University of, 12

Michilimackinac, Straits of, *see* Mackinac, Straits of

Michoacán, 17, 245

Micmac Indians, 72, 73, 208, 227, 235, 247; as Souriquois Indians, 74&n, 79, 85-86, 89, 90

Midland, Ontario, 117

Milouakik, *see* Milwaukee

Milpa, 24

Milwaukee, Wisconsin, as Milouakik, 202

Minas Basin (Nova Scotia), 84, 95

Mingan, 106

Mink, 74, 215

Minnesota, 124, 237

Mirage, Joutel on, 171

Miscou Island (New Brunswick), 91, 92

Misfortune Port, French landing in New England, 84

Missions and missionaries, Spanish in Orient, 28, 30; Oñate's prospects for, 50; system in

New Mexico, 60; Benavides on, 61-65; suppression of native ways and Pueblo Revolt, 66-68; Champlain's prospects for in New France, 106, 107; prospects for from Joliet's and Marquette's discoveries, 141, 142; Lahontan on, 214; summary of impact on native ways, 239-240; in New Mexico at end of century, 251. *See also* Carmelite, Franciscan, Jesuit, Recollect, Sulpician fathers; Société des Missions Etrangères

Mississaga Indians, tribe of Ojibway Indians, 208

Mississippi River, 25n, 123, 131, 132, 136, 146n, 168, 182, 187, 189, 190, 193, 199, 201, 217, 220, 225, 226, 227, 230, 231, 235, 237, 240, 251; in strategy of La Salle's Gulf expedition against New Spain, 24, 157-158, 159, 161&n, 162, 165, 185&n; as Messi-sipi River, 130; La Salle's false claim of discovery, 134, 148; Joliet sent to discover, 137-138, 252; exploration by Joliet and Marquette and accounts of land and life, 138&n-141, 151, 153, 188, 212, 223; proposals on utility of discovery, 141-142; La Salle prepares to descend, 149, 150&n; Hennepin's ascent, 151-152, 211&n-212; falls of as Falls of St. Anthony, 151; La Salle's exploration, 152-155, 181, 239, 252; La Salle's accounts of land and life, 156-157, 223, 241; proposals for future, 157-158; La Salle searches for from Texas, 171-176, 242; as River Colbert, 171, 172; land forms of flood plain, 183; Tonty's voyages, 185&n-186, 190, 191&n; Joutel on, 187-188; hydrography on Delisle map, 202 (Fig. 20), 207-209; St. Cosme's voyage, 205, 207; Hennepin's false claim of discovery of mouth, 212&n-213; as River Meschasipi, 212, 213; Lahontan's supposed descent, 215; summary of French accounts of terrain and biota, 223. *See also* Mississippi River Delta; Mississippi Valley

Mississippi River Delta, 136, 155, 164, 172, 185, 223; as Río de la Palizada, 26

Mississippi Valley, 13, 14, 22, 153, 205, 227, 228, 235, 236, 237, 249; Joliet and Marquette on land and life, 140-141, 153, 188, 212, 223; Colbert against colonizing, 142; La Salle on land and life, 156-157, 223, 241; summary on tribes of, 157; summary of French accounts of terrain and biota, 223; summary of French reports on native peoples and cultures, 230-231, 249. *See also*

Neches, *see* Osage orange
Neches River (Texas), 179
Nèfle, see Medlar; Persimmon
Nelumbo, see Chinquapin, water
Nepisiquit Bay and River (New Brunswick), 91, 92
Netherlands, 212
Neutral Indian Nation, 110, 116, 208, 222, 229; destruction by Iroquois, 118-119, 249
Nevada, 216n
Newberry Library, 37n, 193
New Biscay, *see* Nueva Vizcaya
New Brunswick, 79, 91, 92, 208. *See also* Acadia
Newcomb, W. W., Jr., 46n, 53, 167n-169n, 176n
New England, 13, 125, 148, 152, 208, 235, 237; as Norumbega, 75; French exploration of coast, 80-82, 83-84, 220, 221, 228; decline in Indian population, 247-248
New Englanders, in Missouri, 11
Newfoundland, 13, 19, 90, 208, 214; early explorations of coasts and waters, 69-75 *passim;* as Terre Neuve, 207; decline in Indian population, 247
New France, 18-19, 75, 77, 87, 121, 201, 214; Lescarbot's history, 84&n-86; shifting political control, 90, 111; Denys on climate, 92-93; Champlain's prospects for future, 106-107; Champlain map, 109 (Fig. 10), 110; French restoration under Company of New France, 113, 119, 127; as Crown Colony, 125, 127, 251, 252; church-state conflict and Indian policy, 127-128, 131, 147-148; Talon extends limits, 134-135, 252; summary of geography as known to 1672, 135-136; La Salle and extension west and south, 145, 146, 147; La Salle's prospects for future, 157-158; Delisle map of, 194 (Fig. 16), 198 (Fig. 18), 207-208; summary of accounts of terrain and biota, 220-224 *passim,* 224-226 *passim;* summary of accounts of native peoples and cultures, 227-232 *passim;* 235-238 *passim;* summary of European impact on native ways, 239-243 *passim;* decline in Indian population, 247-249; at end of century, 251-253. *See also* Acadia; Canada; France and French
New Lands, *see* Terres-neuves
New Mexico, 14, 19, 34, 35, 157, 159; late 16th century Spanish exploration and accounts,

37-47; Spanish rule under Oñate, 49&n-58; Spanish rule after Oñate, Pueblo Revolt and reconquest, 59-68; on Delisle map, 208; summary of reports on terrain and biota, 218-220; summary of reports on native peoples and cultures, 232-234, 235, 237; summary of Spanish impact on native ways, 239-243 *passim;* decline in Indian population, 246-247; at end of century, 251. *See also* New Spain
New Netherlands, 119
New Spain, 12, 21, 38, 42, 44, 45, 49, 52, 57, 68, 217, 220, 225, 233, 234; New Mexico as part of, 14, 59, 60, 65, 239, 251; Florida as part of, 14, 18, 26, 217, 245, 247, 251; 16th century limits, 17-18; Pacific coast of, California, and Oriental trade, 17, 27-35, 50, 59, 217, 219, 245; La Salle's plans for seizing mines of, 24, 157-159, 217, 251; Philippines as part of, 28, 217, 245; as keystone of Spanish empire, 245; at end of century, 251. *See also* Spain and Spanish
New Sweden, 118
New Vizcaya, *see* Nueva Vizcaya
New York, 100, 102, 189, 190, 230
Niagara Falls (Ontario-New York), 99, 111, 133, 135, 141, 149, 150, 211, 213
Nicollet, Jean, 121-122, 222
Nicollet Watch Tower, 121
Nicotiana, see Tobacco
Niles, Michigan, 149
Nipissing, Lake (Ontario), 104, 118, 122, 133, 147, 221
Nipissing Indians, 104, 121, 152, 208; destruction by Iroquois, 118, 128, 249
Nixtamal, soaking and wet grinding, 44
Noble savage, Lahontan and thesis of, 216, 253
Nombre de Dios, *see* Puerto de Bastimentos
Nopal, see Cactus
Normandy (France), 71, 169n, 224
Norse, settlements in Greenland, 13; Great Ireland in sagas, 13
North Channel (Ontario), 122
North Mexican Plateau, 43
North Sea, 42
Norumbega, 79; as New England, 75
Nova Scotia, 18, 221, 239; early fishing voyages and accounts, 71-75 *passim;* French exploration, settlement, and accounts, 77-87 *passim,* 89-96 *passim;* shifting political

control, 90-91, 113; on Delisle map, 208. *See also* Acadia

Nueva Galicia, 49

Nueva Tlaxcala, *see* Taos pueblo

Nueva Vizcaya, also New Biscay, New Vizcaya, 49, 157, 158, 159, 161-162, 165

Nuevo León, 43, 44, 218, 219

Nun eagle, *see* Caracara

Nute, Grace Lee, 122&n, 124n

Nut trees, 13, 25, 79, 80, 82, 83, 152, 175, 179, 188, 189, 193, 195, 217. *See also* specific kinds, as, Hazel; Pecan; Walnut; etc.

Oak (*Quercus*), 13, 31, 42, 53, 72, 79, 80, 81, 82, 83, 93, 104, 107, 133, 140, 152, 175, 179, 188, 189, 193, 211, 224; live, 24, 169, 218; swamp chestnut (*Q. prinus*), 25; red, white, 169; post, 178; water, 217

Oak openings, 130

Oaks portage (at Summit, Illinois), 193

Oats, Nation of Wild, *see* Menominee Indians

Oats, wild, *see* Rice, wild

Odocoileus virginianus, *see* Deer

Ohio, 208, 229

Ohio River, 26, 133, 141, 153, 201, 229, 230, 236, 237, 249; as Iroquois name, 132, 136, 137, 139, 223; falls, at Louisville, Kentucky, 132, 146&n, 252; as Wabash River, 139, 201, 205; as Ouabache River, 188, 216

Ojibway Indians, also Chippewa, 129, 134, 152, 208, 227. *See also* Saulteur Indians

Okeechobee, Lake (Florida), 23

Oklahoma, 52

Olla, 25, 38, 44

Omaha Indians, 208

Oñate, Juan de, 59, 61, 65; expedition to find South Sea, 35, 48 (Fig. 6), 56-57, 219, 237; takes charge of New Mexico, 48 (Fig. 6), 49-51 (& 50n), 219, 239; expedition to Quivira, 52-54 (& 53, Fig. 7), 55, 64, 219, 225, 231; abuses, charges, and recall, 54-56, 57-58, 246; summary of expeditions and accounts, 219; on watermelons, 241

Oneida Indians, 116, 117, 119, 145, 249. *See also* Five Nations

Oneida Lake (New York), 105

Onion, 170

Onondaga, New York, 145

Onondaga Indians, 116, 119, 145. *See also* Five Nations

Onondagas, Lake of the, *see* Ontario, Lake

Ontario, 110, 118, 119, 221, 225, 235, 237

Ontario, Lake, 99, 116, 117, 121, 132, 133, 134, 135, 136, 145, 146, 150, 212, 221, 222, 225, 229, 249; as Lake of the Onondagas, 105; as Lake Iroquois, 110; as Lake St. Louis, 111

Ontonagon River (Michigan), 129, 134

Opata Indians, 47, 232

Opossum, as wood rat, 195

Opuntia, *see* Cactus

Oraibi pueblo, 46, 68

Orange, 28n

Ordre de bon temps, 85

Oregon, 17, 30, 31

Orient, passage to, 13, 18, 28-30, 69, 222; Spanish trade with, 27-30, 245

Orinoco River (Venezuela), 224

Ornament, turquoise jewelry, 62, 233; body paint, 82, 104, 123; feathers, horns, etc., 123, 183, 197; Mesoamerican connections, 238. *See also* Tatooing

Osage Indians, 53, 150, 191n, 199, 209, 231

Osage orange (*Maclura pomifera*), bow wood, as neches, 181; as *bois d'arc*, 181, 224, 231

Osage River (Missouri), 209

Otate, *see* Cane

Oto Indians, 191n, 208

Otomi Indians, 41

Ottawa, Illinois, 140, 150, 189

Ottawa Indians, 133, 146, 195, 197, 211, 215, 228; as Cheveux Relevées Indians, 104, 105, 110, 128; as middlemen in Great Lakes fur trade, 124, 125, 128, 129, 137, 147, 237, 240, 252; westward displacement, 124, 128; as Outaouak Indians, Upper Algonquin Indians, 128; missions to, 128, 129, 130, 133, 201; non-use of alcohol, 148, 241; on Delisle map, 208

Ottawa River (Ontario-Quebec), 99, 103, 104, 115, 116, 122, 132, 133, 221, 227, 249

Otter, 26, 74, 90, 93, 182, 212, 227, 241, 252

Ouabache River, *see* Ohio River

Ouachita Mountains (Arkansas), 182, 231&n

Ouachita River (Arkansas), 181, 182

Ouachita Valley (Arkansas), 181-182, 226, 231

284

Persimmon, 223; as *nèfle*, 153; compared to medlar, 156, 169, 186, 195; as *piaquimina*, plaquemine, 156, 186

Peru, 19, 28, 42, 50, 56, 107, 159, 219

Pestegonki River, *see* Fox River

Peter Martyr, *see* Anghiera, Pietro Martire d'

Petit Goâve, Haiti, 163, 164, 171

Petits Eskimaux, *see* Eskimo

Petun, *petum*, *see* Tobacco

Petun Indian Nation, *see* Tobacco Indian Nation

Phaseolus, *see* Bean

Pheasant, *see* Prairie chicken

Philip II, King of Spain, 29, 30, 42

Philip IV, King of Spain, 61

Philippines, 27-29 (& 28n), 30, 42, 217, 245. *See also* New Spain

Piaquimina, *see* Persimmon

Piasa Bluffs (above Alton, Illinois), 139, 188, 205, 223

Piciete, *see* Tobacco

Picton, Quebec, 105

Pictou, Nova Scotia, 92

Pictured Rocks (near Munising, Michigan), 122, 222

Picurí, Picuríes Indians and pueblo, 51, 62, 67, 68

Pig, 133; wild, 29, 164; introduced by French, 127, 146, 165, 171, 173; introduced by Spanish in West Indies, 164; raised by Seneca Indians, 190

Pigeon, 81, 92, 129, 222; passenger, 108, 142

Pike, 108

Pilado pueblo, 61

Pilgrims, 228, 247

Pillage Bay (Quebec), 97

Pima cotton, *see* Cotton

Pima Indians, 57, 209, 234

Pimetoui, Pimiteoui, Lake, *see* Peoria, Lake

Pimiteoui, village of Illinois Indians at site of Peoria, Illinois, 150

Pine (*Pinus*), 24, 25, 29, 31, 41, 44, 56, 78, 93, 103, 104, 107, 133; ponderosa (*P. ponderosa*), 51, 218; piñon, 61, 62, 219-220; shortleaf, 178, 203; white, 189; Monterey (*P. radiata*), 217

Pines, Isle of (Cuba), 164

Piney Woods (Texas), 224

Pinus, *see* Pine

Pipestone, 123, 153, 199, 211, 237

Pirogue, *see* Canoe

Piro Indians and pueblos, 38, 39, 41, 52, 61, 66, 67; as Tompiro, Salinero Indians, 62, 63

Pizarro, Francisco, and family, 59

Placentia Bay (Newfoundland), 71, 73, 208, 214, 216

Plague, *see* Disease

Plains, summary of terms for, terrain, and biota, 224-226

Plancher, storage deck, 180

Plane, also sycamore, 107, 195

Plankton, 72

Plaquemine, *see* Persimmon

Pleistocene, *see* Ice Age

Plover, 26, 92, 93, 170

Plum, 13, 29, 52, 54, 141, 152, 153, 156, 186, 188, 195, 219, 223, 230, 235

Podophyllum, *see* May apple

Point Año Nuevo (California), 31

Point Detour (Michigan), 201

Poisson blanc, *see* Whitefish

Polyodon, *see* Paddlefish

Pomegranate, 22

Pomelo (*Citrus grandis*), also shaddock, as *toronja*, 28n

Ponce de León, Juan, 17

Pont-Gravé, François, 98, 99, 102

Poplar, 179, 188, 196

Population, European, St. Augustine, 21-22; Santa Fé, 65; Spanish in New Mexico, 66, 67; French in Acadia, 90-91, 95-96; French at Quebec, 108; French in Canada by 1663, 113; French in Canada in census of 1666, 127; French in St. Domingue, 164n; La Salle's Texas settlement, 171; French in New France at end of century, 251, 252

Population, Indian, decline in Caribbean under Spanish, 12-13; Pueblo Indians, 38-40 *passim*, 41, 45, 50, 54-55, 61-65 *passim*, 66, 68; Escanjaque Indians, 53; Colorado River tribes, 57; Christian Indians in New Mexico at time of Pueblo Revolt, 67; Acadia, 90, 94; Nipissing Indians, 104; Huron Indians and Huronia, 106, 114, 115; Five Nations, 119, 136; Radisson on Cree and Sioux, 124; at Green Bay, 129, 131; Illinois Indians and tribes, 140, 143, 197; Tensa? exaggerated estimate by La Salle, 162; Ottawa Indians at St. Ignace, 201; decline, on Delisle map, 208; decline, summary, 245&n-249

Porcupine, 93; quills, 123, 197, 237

Porpoise, 72, 165, 224; as food, 168

Portage, Wisconsin, 139

Port-au-Prince, Haiti, 163

Port de Paix, *see* Cap Haitien, Haiti

Port Huron, Michigan, 214

Port Royal (Nova Scotia), now Annapolis Royal, 76 (Fig. 9), 78, 90, 91, 95, 221, 247, 251; settlement, early life, and withdrawal, 82-87 *passim* (& 83n); resettlement, destruction, 89

Port Royal Sound (South Carolina), 18, 21. *See also* Santa Elena

Portugal and Portuguese, 13, 18, 30, 34, 38, 131, 214; fishing interests about Newfoundland, 69-75 *passim*

Potash, 107

Potawatomie Indians, 111, 133, 195, 197, 202, 208, 211; at Green Bay, 129, 130, 134, 149, 201, 229; westward displacement, 129, 130, 229, 249

Pottery, Indian, Florida, 25; Pueblo Indians, 38, 44, 46, 51, 233; Acadia, 86, 228-229; Arkansas Indians, 141, 207; Tensa Indians, 154; Texas, 174, 176; Hohokam, 234; Mesoamerican connections, 238

Poultry, Spanish, destroyed in Pueblo Revolt, 67. *See also* Chicken; Turkey

Pourpié, *see* Purslane

Poutrincourt et de Saint Just, Jean de Biencourt, Sieur de, 83&n-84, 85, 86, 89

Poverty Point, archaeological site in northeast Louisiana, 236&n

Powell, John Wesley, 227n

Pozo, 66

Prada, Juan de, report on New Mexico, 65, 66, 246-247

Prairie chicken, 226; as partridge, 142, 170; as pheasant, 193

Prairie de la Magdeleine, seigneury south of Montreal, 225

Prairie, Illinois, 11, 138, 141-142, 193, 195, 197, 223; Kansas, 17; north of Ohio River,

26; plains, 52-53, 124, 219; south of Green Bay, 130, 140, 223; south of Lake Ontario, 132-133; Calcasieu, southwest Louisiana, 165; Texas, 168, 224; summary of terms for, terrain, and biota, 224-226; Red River of the north, 228

Prescott, Arizona, 56, 57

Prévert, Jean Sarcel de, 77-78, 100

Prince Edward Island, 95; as Ile St. Jean, 92

Prune, 153

Prunus serotina, *see* Cherry, wild black

Puala pueblo, *see* Sandía pueblo

Puan Indians, *see* Winnebago Indians

Puans, Bay of, *see* Green Bay

Puans, River of the, 111

Puaray pueblo, *see* Sandía pueblo

Pueblo, Spanish use of term for Indian community, 45, 232

Pueblo Indians, pueblos, and Pueblo country, as known by Spanish in 16th century, 17, 37-47 *passim*, 218-219, 246; under Oñate's rule, 49-58 *passim*, 219-220, 239-240, 246; decline under Spanish and Pueblo Revolt, 59-68 *passim*, 232, 234, 240; reconquest by Vargas, 68, 251; on Delisle map, 203 (Fig. 21), 208; summary of accounts of terrain and biota, 218-220; summary of accounts of native ways and agriculture, 232-233, 234-238 *passim*, 241, 247; Mesoamerican connections, 236-237, 238; summary of European impact, 239-240; summary of population estimates and decline, 246-247, 248; at end of century, 251

Puerto de Bastimentos (Panamá), as Nombre de Dios, 19

Puerto Rico, 12

Pumpkin (*Cucurbita*), 83, 141, 207, 241; *C. pepo*, 80, 235. *See also* Squash

Purslane, 211, as *pourpié*, 81

Quail, 31, 223; as *caille*, 140; as partridge, 170

Quapaw Indians and villages, also Cappa, Kappa, 181-182, 184 (Fig. 15), 187, 205-206, 230, 231, 241-242, 249

Quebec (city), 18, 84, 103, 107, 114, 115, 122, 125, 134, 138, 147, 148, 149, 158, 185, 188, 189, 201, 211, 214, 216, 240, 241, 249, 251, 252; first colony, 75; meaning "river narrows," 99; at site of Stadacona, 100, 101, 248; founding, 101, 221; English

Santa Maria River (Arizona), 57

Santiago, Valle de, *see* Jémez River and Valley

Santo Domingo (city), 19

Santo Domingo (island), 164n

Santo Domingo pueblo, 59, 67

Sardine, 107; as alewife, 86

Sassafras, 83, 156

Sauer, Carl O., 17, 19, 47n, 69n, 74n, 97n, 156n; summary of own career and writings, 11-14 (& 11n-13n)

Sauk Indians, 201

Saulteur Indians, tribe of Ojibway, or Chippewa, Indians, 129, 133, 208

Sault Ste. Marie (Michigan-Ontario), 122, 124, 125, 135, 138, 149, 222, 227; as Rapids of Gaston, 111; Jesuit mission (Ste. Marie du Sault) at, 129, 133, 134, 222

Savalet (Nova Scotia), 86n

Savanna, 43-44, 218; summary on use of term, 224-225

Savannah River (Georgia-South Carolina), 23

Scalp, in Iroquois-Algonquian warfare, 102, 116, 136, 190, 229, 248; dance, 102, 237, 248; on Delisle map cartouche, 207; geographical limits, 237

Scholes, France V., 46n, 60n, 66&n

Scull, Gideon D., 122n

Scurvy, *see* Disease

Sea, Nation, People of the, *see* Winnebago Indians

Sea Islands (South Carolina), 18, 23

Seal, 72, 89, 92, 93, 97, 107, 221

Sea ox, *see* Walrus

Sebaipuri Indians, 209

Seignelay, French official, 161, 164n

Seignelay, River, *see* Red River (Texas)

Seigneury and seigneurial system, 83n, 113&n, 225; Talon's organizing of, 127; La Salle's at Ft. Frontenac and beyond, 146, 147; La Forest's at Ft. Frontenac, 150n; and term *côte*, 215, 252

Seine River (France), 183

Seneca Indians, 116, 117, 118, 119, 132, 145, 189-190, 205, 223, 229, 249, 252; as Sennentouan Indians on Delisle map, 208. *See also* Five Nations.

Senecú pueblo, 61, 65, 67

Sennentouan Indians, *see* Seneca Indians

Sept Iles, Quebec, 208

Seven Cities, 69. *See also* Cíbola

Sevilla (Spain), 28

Sevilleta pueblo, 39, 61

Shad, 90

Shaddock, *see* Pomelo

Shawnee Indians, 156, 176, 189; westward displacement, 129, 139, 199, 229-230, 249; as Chaouanon Indians, 188-189

Shea, John Gilmary, 214

Sheep, in New Mexico, 42, 55, 60, 66, 67, 251; in New France, 91, 127, 165; claimed as native in spurious Tonty relation, 214

Sheep, wild, bighorn, 38, 55, 56, 218, 220

Shellfish, for manure, 85, 190. *See also* Clam; Crab; Mussel; Oyster

Shield, 46, 104, 154, 174

Shovelbill, *see* Paddlefish

Sibiburo, *see* Basque

Sierra Azul, imaginary silver range of Colorado Plateau, 68

Sierra Madre Oriental (Mexico), 43

Signoc, *see* Crab, horseshoe

Sigüenza y Góngora, Carlos de, exploration of Pensacola Bay and Gulf Coast and account, 24&n-26 (& 25n), 217, 226, 251; *Mercurio volante* on Pueblo Revolt and reconquest, 67&n-68

Silk, 158

Silkworm, 169

Sillery, Quebec, 113, 118

Silver, 29; New Spain, 17, 18, 42, 49, 159, 162, 165, 171, 245; Mexico, 24, 28, 37; New Mexico, 40, 56, 59, 68; New France, 78, 107

Simcoe, Lake (Ontario), 104&n, 105; as Lake Toronto, 151

Sinaloa, 37, 234

Siouan tribes, 53, 123&n, 130, 208, 230, 231

Sioux Indians, 125, 192, 199, 201, 235; as Nadonseron Indians, 123&n; as Nation of Beef, Boeufs, Cattle, 124; as Nadouessis Indians, 129, 130, 208; capture of Hennepin, 151, 211, 212, 213; as Issati Indians, 208

Skunk, as food, 195

Slave trade, 19, 66, 240

Smallpox, *see* Disease

Smelt, 86, 92, 227

Smithsonian Institution, 236&n

Snipe, 92; as *becassine*, 170

Snowshoe, 80, 86, 94, 101, 123, 227, 228

Soap, castile, 72

Société des Missions Etrangeres, 201

Socorro, New Mexico, 38, 61

Sombrerete, Zacatecas, 34

Sombrero Island (West Indies), 163

Sonora, 12, 37, 46, 218, 232

Sorrel, 170

Souriquois Indians, as Micmac Indians, 74&n, 79, 85-86, 89, 90; on Delisle map, 208

South America, 12, 85n

South Bend, Indiana, 149, 223

South Carolina, 18

South China Sea, 28

South Sea, 50, 56, 106, 137, 219; as Pacific Ocean, 134

Spade, wooden, 80, 82, 228

Spain and Spanish, 14, 19, 131, 167, 168; in 16th century New Spain and Indies, 12-13, 17-18, 164n, 220&n, 224; in Florida, 13, 14, 17, 18, 21-26, 59, 75, 134, 139, 159, 217, 224, 226, 245, 247, 251; 16th century explorations and accounts of New Mexico, 14, 37-47, 218-219, 246; trade with Orient and exploration of California coast, 17, 27-35, 50, 59, 217, 219, 245; La Salle's expedition against in New Spain, 24, 157-158, 159-166 *passim*, 171; first decade of rule in New Mexico, under Oñate, 49-58, 219-220, 239, 246; in New Mexico after Oñate, Pueblo Revolt and reconquest, 59-68, 239-240, 246-247, 251; source of horses for plains tribes, 157, 175, 181, 190, 199, 242-243; evidences of contact with among Texas and Arkansas tribes, 174, 175, 177, 179, 190; summary of explorations and accounts of terrain and biota, 217-220; summary of plains landscape and game animal terms, 224-225; summary of notices of extension of buffalo range, 226; summary of accounts of native peoples and cultures, 231-238 *passim;* summary of impact on native ways, 239-243 *passim;* and introduction of watermelons and peaches, 241-242, 243; and decline of Indian population, 245-247; in New Spain at end of century, 251

Spatule, see Spoonbill

Spear, 82, 93, 94, 95, 171, 186, 212, 222, 229

Spice Islands, 27

Spoonbill, roseate, as *spatule*, 170

Spruce, 93

Squair, J., 78n

Squantum, Indian of Massachusetts, 228

Squash (*Cucurbita*), 25, 26, 40, 42, 104, 129, 132, 171, 173, 183, 188, 241; maize-bean-squash complex, 13, 24, 38, 44, 45, 54, 57, 80, 81, 83, 103, 110, 140, 179-180, 187, 228, 229, 232, 234, 235, 236, 242; as *calabasa*, 38; as *citrouille, courge*, 80; *C. pepo*, 80, 235; *tierra caliente* (*C. mixta*), 234; *C. moschata*, 234, 235, 236. *See also* Pumpkin

Squid, 93

Squier, Ephraim G., 236&n

Squirrel, 93

Stadacona, Indian village at site of Quebec, 100, 101, 248

Staked Plains (New Mexico-Texas), 17; as Llano Estacado, 225

Starved Rock (Illinois), 11, 151, 156&n; Ft. St. Louis at, 155-156, 185, 193, 199; Ft. St. Louis moved from, 191, 193, 197

Stefansson, Vilhjalmur, 13

"Stones of mines," *see* Mazon ironstone concretions

Sturgeon, 85, 86, 90, 92, 93, 107, 108, 129, 130, 133, 140, 142, 223, 227, 229

Sugar, 158, 164n

Sulphur, 50, 130

Sulpician fathers, admitted to counter Jesuit influence, 128; Indian school at Montreal, 131; with La Salle, 132-133; map of Great Lakes and route south, 133, 134; mission at Bay of Quinté, 145

Summer Island (Michigan), as Isle du Detour, 201

Summit, Illinois, 193

Sun cult, 154, 155, 230-231

Sunflower (*Helianthus*), 13, 110, 187; seed, 104, 132, 178, 229; oil, 104, 132, 229, 235; *H. annuus*, 235

Sunflower, tuberous (*Helianthus tuberosus*), as Jerusalem artichoke, 81, 83, 228, 235; as *carde*, 83; as *topinambour*, 85&n, 198n

Superior, Lake, 111, 122, 123, 124, 215, 128,

133, 134, 135, 147, 151-152, 191, 208, 222, 227, 228; copper of, 99, 101, 123, 129, 132, 133, 134, 137, 138, 222, 237; Jesuit mission (St. Esprit) on (Chequamegon Bay), 128-129, 131, 138, 222, 230

Swan, 80, 105, 140, 149, 152, 155, 156, 170, 183, 188, 195, 205, 223, 224

Swanton, John R., 182&n

Sweat bath, 86, 94, 106; as *temescal*, 38, 237

Sweden and Swedish, 118, 127

Sweet flag, *see* Calamus

Sweet gum (*Liquidambar*), 205; as copal, 177

Sweet potato, as *batata*, 236

Swordfish, 93

Sycamore, *see* Plane

Sydney, Nova Scotia, 92

Tabagie, ceremonial festival, 90, 98, 103, 227, 248

Tadoussac, Quebec, 77, 97, 98, 99, 100, 101, 102, 107, 116, 128, 221, 227, 237, 248

Taensa Indians, *see* Tensa Indians

Talauma, *see* Yolosuchitl

Talon, Jean, becomes Intendant of Crown Colony of New France, 127, 252; sends expeditions to extend limits of New France, 128, 132, 134-135, 137-138, 222, 252

Tamale, 44, 178, 235

Tamarind, 28n

Tamaroa Indians, tribe of Illinois Indians, 151, 152, 205, 208, 230

Tamemes, burden bearers, 60

Tampa Bay (Florida), 17

Tampico, Tamaulipas, 159

Tanager, scarlet, 170

Tanico Indians, *see* Tonica Indians

Tanos Indians and pueblos, 62, 67

Taos pueblo, 40, 45, 51, 65, 67, 68; as Nueva Tlaxcala, 39, 247

Tarahumar Indians, 37

Tarascan Indians, 37, 245

Tatooing, Jumano Indians, 46, 232; Ottawa Indians, 104; Caddoan tribes, 179, 231, 232

Taxodium, *see* Cypress, bald

Teal, 92, 93, 170

Teatiki River, *see* Kankakee River

Tehuantepec, Isthmus of (Oaxaca-Vera Cruz), 31

Temescal, *see* Sweat bath

Temiskaming Indians, 208

Temporales, fields dependent upon summer rains, 45, 233, 234

Tennessee, 11, 13, 19, 226

Tensa Indians, also Taensa, 154, 155, 161n, 162, 230-231

Teoa Indians, *see* Tewa Indians; Tigua Indians

Tepee, 124, 234

Tepehuán Indians, 43, 57

Terre Neuve, *see* Newfoundland

Terres-neuves, New Lands, about Gulf of St. Lawrence, 75

Tertiary beds, 153, 224

Tesuque pueblo, 59, 67

Tewa Indians and pueblos, 62, 63, 67; as Teoa, 62

Texarkana, Arkansas-Texas, 181, 183, 190, 224, 231, 242

Texas, 17, 47&n, 51, 52, 218, 226, 231, 232, 235, 241, 243; La Salle on coast and settlement, 64, 165-169, 217, 224, 226; Joutel on country, 169-171, 224, 226, 242; La Salle across, 171-176, 242; Inner and Outer Coast Plains, 173, 176, 224, 226, 236; French across after La Salle's death, 177-181, 186, 189, 214, 224, 226, 237, 242; Tonty's expedition to and end of French interest, 190, 191, 242; Delisle map, 206 (Fig. 23), 209; summary of French accounts of terrain and biota, 224, 226; Indian use of fire and prairie formation, 225, 226

Texas, University of, 169

Texas A & M University, 177

Texas Indians, also Teyas, 47n, 63n

Texas Memorial Museum, 169

Thwaites, Reuben Gold, 89n, 90n, 114n, 115n, 116n, 119n, 121n, 128n, 129n, 131n, 138n, 141n, 142n, 211n, 212n, 214n

Thuja occidentalis, *see* Cedar, white

Tigua Indians and pueblos, 39, 41, 61, 62, 67; as Teoa, Tiwa, 61

Tiguex, early Spanish name for valley north of Albuquerque, 41, 61

Timucua Indians, 24

Tinaja, 38

Tiwa, *see* Tigua

Tlaxcalan Indians, 18

Tobacco (*Nicotiana rustica*), 13, 63, 110, 158,

164n, 188, 228, 229, 237; as *piciete*, 45; as *petum*, petun, 80, 81, 105; of commerce (*N. tabacum*), 236

Tobacco Indian Nation, 237; as Petun Nation, 105, 110, 116, 208, 229; destruction by Iroquois, 117-118, 119, 229, 249

Toboggan, 105, 228

Tomato, 24, 52

Tomcod, as *panamo*, 90

Tompiro Indians, *see* Piro Indians

Tonica Indians, 181-182, 231&n; described by De Soto expedition as Tanico, 182

Tonikan tribes, 230, 231

Tonkawa Indians, 176; Ebahamo Indians probably a tribe of, 174

"Tonti, Chevalier de," spurious account of Louisiana, 214

Tonty, Henri de, with La Salle to Illinois, 149&n; at Ft. Crevecoeur, 151; exploration of Mississippi with La Salle and account, 152&n-154, 223; at Ft. St. Louis, 155-156, 173, 185; forced to return to Quebec, 158, 185; partnership with La Forest at Ft. St. Louis, 185, 190-192, 201; search for La Salle, 185&n-186, 190; offensive against Iroquois, 189-190; expedition to Caddo country, 190&n, 231; brings Deliette to Illinois, 193; with St. Cosme to Illinois and Arkansas, 201-203, 205, 207; and Delisle map, 209; disavows spurious relation of Louisiana, 214; Lahontan claims to visit, 216; on peaches, chickens, horses, 242

Topinambour, *see* Sunflower, tuberous

Toque, *see* Bramble

Toronja, applied to both pomelo and grapefruit, 28n

Toronto, Lake, *see* Simcoe, Lake

Torquemada, Juan de, 34&n

Torture, in Iroquois-Algonquian warfare, 102, 109, 116, 136, 190, 249

Trade, Indian, Calusa Indians with Havana, 24; Apache-Pueblo, 39, 46, 51, 54, 55, 63, 64, 65, 233, 237; Jumano, 47, 232, 237, 243; Wichita with English and Dutch, 64; Indians of Acadia as merchants of French goods, 85; Huron, in copper, 99; Lower Mississippi tribes with Europeans, 139; Peoria, 140-141; Caddoan tribes, 182, 186, 231&n; Illinois, 199; summary on, 237; and horses, summary, 242-243. *See also* Fur trade

Trade, European, summary of impact on native ways, 240-241. *See also* Free trade; Fur trade

Train oil, 72, 73, 74, 93, 99, 107, 221

Travois, dog, 51, 234

Tribute, enforced, from Pueblo Indians, 52, 54, 56, 66, 239, 240, 247; as *encomienda*, 60, 62, 64, 65

Trinity Islands, *see* Huron Islands

Trinity River (Texas), 179, 190, 224, 242; as River of the Cenis, 177

Trois Rivières, Quebec, 99, 102, 113, 114, 117, 119n, 122, 127, 135, 240, 249, 251, 252

Trojan war, 236

Tropic of Cancer, 163

Trout, 62, 92, 171; sea, 107

Trudel, Marcel, 75n, 77n, 83n, 84n, 89n, 90n, 98n, 100, 108n

Tuberose, 170

Tule rush, 30

Tuna, *see* Cactus

Tunica Indians, 182

Tupi Indians, 80

Turbot, 169

Turkey, 38, 39, 53, 105, 108, 110, 129, 140, 142, 150, 152, 155, 156, 173, 178, 193, 195, 203, 212, 219, 221, 222, 223, 224; feathers, 25, 41, 54, 82, 179, 233; domesticated, 45, 54, 82, 165, 233; as *coq d'inde*, 82, 140

Turkey vulture, as raven eagle, 170-171

Turnip, 214

Turquoise, 38, 51, 56, 57, 62, 199, 233, 237; as *chalchihuite*, 44

Turtle, 26, 171, 217, 224

Ultramontane clergy faction, 128

Unamuno, Pedro de, 29

Urdaneta, Andrés de, 27

"Urraca, place of the," 219

Ursuline sisters, 113

Uto-Aztecan language family, 47n

Van Noort, Olivier, 28, 30

Vaquero Indians, *see* Apache Indians

Vargas, Diego de, reconquest of New Mexico, 67-68

Vázquez de Espinosa, Antonia, on Florida, 21&n-22; on introduction of fruit from Far

East, 28n; on California as an island, 34

Velasco, Fr. Francisco de, account of Oñate's expedition to Quivira, 52-54, 219

Velasco, Luis de, the Elder, 18, 24

Velasco, Luis de, the Younger, 30, 34, 59

Venado, as elk, 225, 233; as antelope, 225-226, 233; as deer, 226, 233

Venezuela, 224

Venice (Italy), 29

Vera Cruz, Vera Cruz, 18, 19, 23, 26, 28, 245, 251

Verjuice sauce, 170

Verrazzano, Giovanni, 13, 18, 74, 75, 77, 225, 240, 253

Vicksburg, Mississippi, 154

Village, palisaded, 81, 104, 105, 107, 108, 110, 116, 132, 154, 155, 228, 248; geographical extent, 104n

Vincennes, Jean Baptiste Bissot, Sieur de, 201, 202

Vinland, 13

Virginia, 13, 19, 75, 89, 91, 115

Virgin of Socorro, convent, 61

Vizcaíno, Sebastián, survey of California coast, 30-31, 34-35, 217, 251

Wabash River, see Ohio River

Walnut, 53, 106, 107, 140, 214

Walnut, white, see Butternut

Walpi pueblo, 41, 218

Walrus, 69, 72, 74, 92, 97, 221; hides, 72; tusks, 72, 107, 221; as morse, morsse, 72, 73; as sea ox, 72, 73

Wampum, 86, 110, 117, 237

Washington Island (Wisconsin), 149

Waterfowl, 31, 73, 129, 131, 137, 199, 203. See also entries for specific kinds, as, Brant; Crane; Duck; Swan; etc.

Water hen, 170

Watermelon, 50&n, 55, 62, 140, 141, 171, 173, 187, 188, 197; as sandía, 241; as melon d'eau, 241; summary on introduction, 241, 243

Wea Indians, tribe of Miami Indians, 199, 201

Weapons, European, effects of introduction, 94, 95, 241

Webb, Clarence H., 236n

Wellfleet, Massachusetts, 83

Welsh fishers and whalers, 71

Werner, Raymond C., 185n, 189n, 191n, 195n, 198n, 199n, 201n

West, Robert C., 37n

West Indies, 12, 23, 74, 154, 236

Wet cod fishery, see Cod

Whale, 69, 73, 99; sperm, 22; right, 72, 74, 221; beluga, 72, 97; whalebone, 72, 107, 221

Whaling, 72, 73, 74, 75, 99, 107

Wheat, introduced by Spanish, 37, 55, 59, 60, 62-63; destroyed in Pueblo Revolt, 67; introduced by French, 79, 83, 91, 171

White Cape, see Cape Cod

Whitefish, 122, 133, 201, 207, 211, 222, 227; as poisson blanc, 129, 222

"White Spanish," Yayeches Indians, on Delisle map, 209

Wichita, Kansas, 53

Wichita Indians, 47n, 53, 63&n-64, 219, 231, 235; as Quivira Indians, 63-64; as Paniassey Indians, 199

Wigwam, 94, 124, 228; as caban, 228

William III, King of England, 212

Willow, 44, 188, 218

Winnebago, Lake (Wisconsin), 130

Winnegago Indians, as Puan Indians, 111, 121, 129, 130; as Nation, People of the Sea, 121, 122

Wisconsin, 134, 139, 235, 236; early French explorations, 121-125 passim, 222; Jesuit missions in (on Chequamegon Bay and Green Bay) and accounts, 128-131, 138, 201, 212, 222, 230; Joliet and Marquette in and accounts, 138-139, 140, 223; St. Cosme in, 201-202; Lahontan's supposed visit, 215; summary of accounts of terrain and biota, 222, 223, 225

Wisconsin River (Wisconsin), 139, 140, 151, 201, 215, 223

Wolf, 86, 108

Wolverine, 93

Woman chief, Caddo Indians, 190; on lower Illinois River, 205

Wood rat, see Opossum

Wrong, G. W., 108n

Xila Apache Indians, see Apache Indians

Yamasee Indians, 23, 24, 247